For Frank Sugeno
with gratitude, affection,
and esteem.
From
John Woolverton
December 2005

Robert H. Gardiner and the
Reunification of Worldwide Christianity
in the Progressive Era

# Robert H. Gardiner and the Reunification of Worldwide Christianity in the Progressive Era

John F. Woolverton

UNIVERSITY OF MISSOURI PRESS

COLUMBIA AND LONDON

Library of Congress Cataloging-in-Publication Data

Woolverton, John Frederick, 1926–
    Robert H. Gardiner and the reunification of worldwide
Christianity in the Progressive Era / John F. Woolverton.
        p.    cm.
    Summary: "Biography of Robert Hallowell Gardiner III,
Progressive Era leader of the Christian ecumenical movement,
the Young Manhood Movement, and the World Council of
Churches. Includes discussions of George Wharton Pepper,
Francis Stetson, John R. Mott, Newman Smyth, Cardinal James
Gibbons, Bishop Charles Henry Brent, Vida D. Scudder, and
others"—Provided by publisher.
    Includes bibliographical references and index.
    ISBN-13: 978-0-8262-1603-8 (alk. paper)
    ISBN-10: 0-8262-1603-X (alk. paper)
    1. Gardiner, Robert H. (Robert Hallowell), 1855–1924.
2. Ecumenists—United States—Biography.   I. Title.
    BX6.8.G37W66     2006
    280'.042'092—dc22                              2005021955

∞™  This paper meets the requirements of the
American National Standard for Permanence of Paper
for Printed Library Materials, Z39.48, 1984.

Designer: Kristie Lee
Typesetter: Phoenix Type, Inc.
Printer and Binder: Thomson-Shore, Inc.
Typefaces: Adobe Garamond and Peignot Display Light

For Robert T. Handy,
teacher and adviser,
with gratitude

# CONTENTS

❧✝❧

# Preface

꙳✠꙳

Reflecting on the end in 431 BC of the long peace and on the conduct thereafter of the Peloponnesian War that led to the downfall of Athens in 405, the historian Thucydides judged "the real cause" of the war to be the "growth of the power of Athens and the alarm which this inspired." Whatever his limitations as a historian, Thucydides may still be appreciated today for his brilliant literary and psychological analyses. He was at his best when describing the drastic internal changes that war inflicts on participants. As the struggle between Athens and Sparta came to invest all the cities of Hellas, even the words people used changed their ordinary meanings. "Reckless audacity," wrote Thucydides, "came to be considered the courage of a loyal ally; prudent hesitation, specious cowardice; moderation was held to be a cloak for unmanliness; ability to see all sides of a question, inaptness to act on any." Preemptive violence was a sign of macho policy, behind-the-scenes deception a justification of self-defense. "The advocate of extreme measures was always trustworthy; his opponent a man to be suspected."[1] Thucydides might just as well have been describing U.S. foreign policy in the watershed first decade of the twenty-first century AD.

This study reminds us of a different era from our own, one of international cooperation, community building, and goodwill. In doing so it harks back to a man and his associates who worked perseveringly toward these ends. While I analyze and interpret my subject, Robert Hallowell Gardiner III (1855–1924), as a winsome advocate of such qualities, I am aware that it is also possible to see him and the movement for Christian unity that he ardently espoused as a mask for Western, and American, elitist hegemony over the affairs of others. For that,

---

1. Thucydides, *History of the Peloponnesian War,* translated by Richard Crawley (London and Toronto: J. M. Dent, 1926), 16, 224.

I leave the reader to decide. One thing is sure: Gardiner considered himself, however reticently, to have a clear vision of what was true, good, and even beautiful. His faith, his nation, and the democratic political system he admired informed and shaped his actions. In this sense he was indeed elitist.

Recent scholarship in American religious studies has dealt with outsiders and dissenters from the so-called mainline Protestant churches. Concurrently, there has been a challenge to examine afresh aspects of that Protestant establishment. As William R. Hutchison has remarked, whereas "some transdenominational movements, such as revivalism, have been studied extensively[,] others, such as the ecumenical movement, have remained relatively neglected." This inquiry seeks to rectify that imbalance and at the same time introduce Gardiner to a wider audience. But it attempts more than these things. I shall argue that the failure on the part of the mainliners to recognize diversity and pluralism, to discover the rest of religious America, and to face up to their own limitations and be less bumptious may in Gardiner's case be seriously questioned. Certainly, he shook them up. As Hutchison puts it with respect to the "Seven Sisters" of the elite Protestant establishment (Congregational, Episcopal, Presbyterian, Methodist, Disciples of Christ, American Baptist, and Lutheran churches) between 1900 and 1960: "One can easily, and with justification, criticize [them] . . . for not recognizing such realities earlier [as pluralism and their own minority status], for having lingered between the times instead of seizing a new time—for having taken so long to discover America. Yet only the more facile or contemptuous of their critics would entirely dismiss what these churches attempted, or what they achieved during an era of bewildering transformations."[2] If by the recognition of diversity we mean awareness of the turmoil of denominational disagreements and differences, not always a bad thing in itself, then Robert Gardiner qualifies as one who knew these realities firsthand. If by diversity we mean a greater degree of inclusion of such outsiders to the establishment as Eastern Orthodox, Roman Catholic, Old Catholic, Dunkers, and so forth, then Gardiner cannot be seen as having lingered between the times. As will become apparent later, although neither Unitarians, Mormons, nor Christian Scientists qualified for admission, he sought out holiness groups, Pentecostals, and the

---

2. Hutchison, *Between the Times: The Travail of the Protestant Establishment in America, 1900–1960* (Cambridge: Cambridge University Press, 1989), ix, viii. Hutchison marks important exceptions to the charge: Catherine Albinese, Robert T. Handy, and Martin E. Marty.

smallest Christian communities as well as the churches of African Americans. In this effort he was not successful.

If we speak both of the discovery of America and of the rest of the Christian world, then Gardiner did indeed seize a moment of opportunity. If we mean by diversity awareness of many religions or of no religion at all, here again he qualified, but then achieving some sort of cooked-up, lowest-denominator commonality was not on his agenda. Still, at a time when, after 1906, "the United States experienced a surge in the diversity of its Christian communions," Gardiner represented the high point of a countervailing drive for the reunion of just those diverse bodies.[3] As he participated in that movement, his promptitude and sharpness of insight also illumine the alteration of an Old World religion—Anglicanism—in a New World setting.

To cast a critical eye: although it is desirable that historians should be aware of the animation and variety of religion in present-day America, we should also remember that pluralism was not and is not the only show in town. For those who wish to deal with diversity alone, the historical search is, of course, more for the threads than for the cable. However elusive, American national life has its own wiring to which each of those threads contributes. Indeed, to assert the very existence of such a unity is, or was until lately, to open oneself to the accusation of chauvinism. In recent memory denationalization was the order of the day. Almost but not quite.

Without evading or denying ethnic and cultural differences, John Higham for one has sought to redirect our attention to prevailing values and to ways in which Americans have historically found common ground. Among other things, this study finds suggestive Higham's three ways of explaining that ground: first, by primordial unity or a shared sense of place and kinship; second, by participation in ideological unity; and, third, by the achievement of "technical unity"— for example, inventing new organizations to connect people "by occupational function" for the "reordering of human relations by rational procedures designed to maximize efficiency" and to develop critical thinking, orderly systems, but also innovation. In his famous 1974 presidential address before the Organization of American Historians, Higham concentrated on "the sequential unfolding of [these] three forms of unity" in U.S. history. Later in the address, however, he

---

3. Mark A. Noll, *The Old Religions in a New World: The History of North American Christianity* (Grand Rapids, MI, and Cambridge, England: William B. Eerdmans, 2002), xi.

intimated that "the primordial, the ideological, and the technical dimensions of culture" can and now do exist simultaneously and that future historians might bring them "into some kind of workable counterpoise with one another."[4]

Robert Gardiner sought both to implement and greatly to expand the three forms described by Higham. He wanted nothing so much as to bring together, not only in the United States but also worldwide, Protestants, Roman Catholics, Eastern and Russian Orthodox, and Anglicans. Though primordial unity has its obvious limitations to particular kinships, the places where those kinships are maintained often include many different peoples. Thus, in the state of Maine where Gardiner resided Protestants and Roman Catholics, and to be sure Ortho-dox, lived side by side in a single commonwealth. There they rubbed elbows, and in so doing a larger common kind of kinship evolved. All equally became "down-easters," enjoyed the same jokes, and spoke with the same understate-ment. Similarly among the churches such common ground, Gardiner believed, could also be uncovered. He sought to unearth it through broader ideology and greatly improved methods of communication.

Then, too, Gardiner himself evinced a strong primordial sense of place, kin-ship, and ancestry. The place, Gardiner, Maine, was named after his own family. In that locale he embraced a communal loyalty that already cut across class divi-sions and hitched together down-easters in a dour perception of something called "life in general," notoriously expressed in terse and often humorous monosylla-bles. He enjoyed a sense of command that sprang from five generations of fam-ily prominence. Within that family, persistent loyalty to the Anglican church, whether in its colonial form as the Church of England or in its succeeding American vintage, was maintained. Whereas the latter helped define place and ancestry, he was aware that Anglicanism, however venerable, represented a mi-nority tradition in his state and elsewhere. That the generality of these factors should place him alongside those Americans who have found their primordial origins in an Eastern European *sobor,* in a Jewish shtetl, or in an African king-dom would have momentarily raised his eyebrows in amused disbelief. But not for long; indeed, a subtheme of this study will be his own discovery of just such Americans in their "otherness." Given the limitations of his day, he came not merely to tolerate certain religious groups, which by itself would have meant he basically did not give a damn about their traditions, but also actively to open

---

4. Higham, *Hanging Together: Unity and Diversity in American Culture* (New Haven, CT: Yale University Press, 2001), 3–4, 14, 16, 21.

up to what was positive in them. And he emboldened others to do likewise. He encouraged still others to listen to what was being said to them by those others.

Then, second, Gardiner participated in Higham's "ideological unity" based as it has been in the United States on individual values derived from Protestantism, from the Enlightenment, and in political thought from both the Enlightenment and the radical, antimagisterial wing of the Reformation. Once again, because he was a High Church Anglican and a conservative Whig, the very idea of participation in the Anabaptist heritage would have seemed strange to him. His eyebrows would have climbed even higher and probably remained there. But while there was some inherited nostalgia in his mind for the aristocratic attitudes of colonial times, he participated fully in those American social arrangements inherited from left-wing continental reformers even as the historical source eluded him. To drive home the point, Gardiner consistently, but privately, disparaged the establishment of the Church of England, not only in colonial America but in twentieth-century England as well. He believed wholeheartedly in the separation of church and state.

Third, Gardiner emerges as a participant in and an advocate of Higham's "technical unity" of bureaucratic organization and cooperation. He was forever talking to his colleagues about efficiency and critical thinking. He thus provides a good example of the Progressive Era's achievement in bringing together democratic and religious ideals with bureaucratic techniques. As Higham put it, there was in the period 1898 to 1918 an "extraordinary quickening of ideology... in the very midst of a dazzling elaboration of technical systems."[5] Gardiner participated in the momentary integration of the two. During the first two decades of the new century he was busy creating fresh means to solve old problems and constantly inventing ways of overcoming antagonism and disunity. He did so through participation in Social Gospel efforts, in new youth organizations, and in such new structures as the Federal Council of Churches (FCC) in the United States. He became one of that organization's chief promoters. In his championing of a world conference on faith and order and the means of achieving such a goal, he was for many years the key player. His unremitting labor for making the world conference a reality will be the major topic of this book.

What is most remarkable in this man's life is the intensity with which he pursued participation in each of Higham's suggested areas of expanded commonality. Given the clerical nature of church organizations, that Gardiner made

5. Ibid., 18.

his mark as a layman and on an international scale is even more noteworthy. In addition to searching for common ground, his role as a layman provides yet another theme to this study. He and other men and women in the first quarter of the twentieth century were the culmination of a long period of participation by the unordained in the leadership of America's churches. These laypeople busied themselves in social Christianity, in youth work, in missions, in evangelism, and in ecumenism. They went from one to another often sequentially, sharing common convictions and influencing each other across denominational lines. Their efforts were reformatory and restorative, not only of society but finally of the churches themselves. They sought humane, not violent, solutions to conflicts; they wanted to share their wealth, not hoard it. They knew the desperation caused by the squalor and poverty of the many, and they wanted to change it. They refused to demonize. Gardiner's life shows such progression from the Social Gospel to youth work, to church unity, and to world cooperation and peace. It was a trail followed by many.

Along the way in researching and writing this work, I should like to thank the following librarians and archivists: Laura E. Moore of the St. Mark's Library of the General Theological Seminary; Mitzi Jarrett Budde of the Bishop Payne Library of the Virginia Theological Seminary; Danny D. Smith, secretary of the Gardiner Library Association; Douglas Brown, archivist of Groton School; David A. Mittell, trustee of the Roxbury Latin School; and the staffs of the following: the Boston Athenaeum, the Cumberland County Historical Society, Library of Congress, Pusey Library at the Harvard University Archives, Archives of the Episcopal Church and of the Episcopal Diocese of Massachusetts, Boston Public Library, Lamson Library at Plymouth State University, Samuel Wentworth Library, and Lake Wales Public Library.

I am particularly indebted to my friend and classmate Charles W. Gardiner for his generosity with Gardiner family papers and for access to the records at "Oaklands," to Jane Gardiner for entertaining my wife and me so unstintingly in the spacious house on the Kennebec in which Robert Gardiner lived, to Mary Pillsbury Crowley whose sense of literary style is memorable, and to Annette Wenda for her superior editing of the manuscript.

Finally, I am grateful to three colleagues who read the manuscript in its first draft and offered penetrating criticisms as well as encouragement: Professors Frank E. Sugeno of the Episcopal Theological Seminary of the Southwest,

Joseph A. Conforti of the University of Southern Maine, and Alfred A. Moss Jr. of the University of Maryland. They are beloved friends. I am also in the debt of the late Floyd W. Tomkins whose correspondence and records were given to me by Frank Sugeno and proved to be of notable value in the early stages of research.

# Robert H. Gardiner and the Reunification of Worldwide Christianity in the Progressive Era

# Introduction

֍✝֍

In a time when minority, multicultural, and gender studies dominate the academic scene, writing about an elite, white, Anglo-Saxon, Protestant male takes nerve. Or just foolhardiness. This study nonetheless steps up to that plate. It is an account of an arresting, and distressingly neglected, figure in twentieth-century American church history: Robert Hallowell Gardiner III. Gardiner was an Episcopal layman, a high churchman, and in his day an acknowledged international church leader. From 1910 to his death in 1924, more than any other person, he kept the flame of worldwide Christian unity burning brightly. He did so by gaining the often grudging approval of his contemporaries to undertake a vast correspondence with prominent Christians both in his own country and around the world. Discarding letters of praise for himself as well as many of a routine nature, Gardiner kept *only* eleven thousand of the countless ones he sent and received. Long before the Internet he spun an effective web and created a global network of trusted allies and, in not a few cases, adversaries. He very nearly single-handedly brought about the first pan-Christian World Conference on Faith and Order (theology and church government, then as now, the two most sensitive subjects dividing churches). That conference took place in Lausanne, Switzerland, three years after his death. There, four hundred representatives from more than one hundred churches the world over, Protestant, Anglican, Eastern Orthodox, and Old Catholic, met to discuss Christian unity. In terms of its scope and subject matter, the Lausanne assembly was the first of its kind. As one historian has noted, the movement toward this conference "owes its origin and development to a great extent to an American layman, the indefatigable Robert Gardiner!"[1] No one has yet written on his life and work.

---

1. Hans-Reudi Weber, "The Rediscovery of the Laity in the Ecumenical Movement," in *The Layman in Christian History,* edited by Stephen Charles Neill and Hans-Reudi Weber (Philadelphia:

But of all the men and women mentioned in this study, none perhaps was more quickly forgotten than he. Why the amnesia? For the moment it is enough to say two things: first, he died relatively early, and, second, he did not push himself but kept his ego under strict control. Because he single-mindedly championed a cause rather than personal fame, he was often outshone by others seeking the spotlight. Nonetheless, to a remarkable degree he changed the character and attitudes of participating churches toward one another in what is called today the Ecumenical Movement. Because it appears unbiblical to Fundamentalist Christians, the very word *ecumenical* is anathema. Gardiner himself never used the term. It is not so much that Fundamentalists formally reject the principles he enunciated; rather, they increasingly speak out of a different theological culture, and not one given to discussions, for instance, of the Incarnation and not one seeking to overcome religious differences. But those same conservatives cannot avoid—but do—dealing with Christian disunity any more than liberal Christians can brush aside—but do—the theological witness of their conservative sisters and brothers.

Along with his friend Methodist John R. Mott (1865–1955), Gardiner looms large on the horizon of lay leadership in American religious history. The two friends were not alone. By the mid-nineteenth century many other Christians from the pews had become highly visible reformers: William Lloyd Garrison, the Grimke sisters, Harriet Beecher Stowe, Frederick Douglass, and Sojourner Truth, to name just a few. They helped tear down the wall that in colonial days had separated commoners from gentlemen, parishioners from clergy, the catechized from the catechizers. No longer would "habits of deference and subordination" characterize church life. One historian has noted that by 1820 New England ministers themselves associated order with self-control rather than with acceptance of institutional authority: "They no longer looked to an organic, hierarchical community as either an agency or locus of social order."[2]

But with self-control went self-assertion. The energy released in the earlier

---

Westminster Press, 1963), 385. Recently, Gardiner's significance has been recognized by David L. Holmes in "The Anglican Tradition and the Episcopal Church," in *Encyclopedia of the American Religious Experience,* edited by Charles H. Lippy and Peter W. Williams, 3 vols. (New York: Charles Scribner's Sons, 1988), 1:410b; see also Paul A. Crow Jr., "The Ecumenical Movement," in ibid., 2:986b.

2. Donald M. Scott, *From Office to Profession: The New England Ministry, 1750–1850* (Philadelphia: University of Pennsylvania Press, 1978), 36.

revivals continued into the Gilded Age. Dwight L. Moody, Frances E. C. Willard, Vida D. Scudder, Jane Addams, Lugenia Burns Hope, Richard T. Ely, and Mary Baker Eddy continued many of the traditions of their pre–Civil War mentors. Though there were no longer slaves to be freed, Bible reading, tract distribution, agitation for temperance, peace, and prison and mental asylum betterment continued. Added to the earlier agenda were woman suffrage, fair wages, decent working conditions, foreign missions, and finally church unity. All brought forth lay advocates who spoke their lines, rolled up their sleeves, and went to work. In a number of these areas Gardiner, Mott, and others I shall name later were among them. As has been observed, "Even the ecumenical movement, often perceived as the special preserve of top-level clerical bureaucrats only, turned out at voting time to involve far more than those ministers who had been elevated to 'headquarters.'"[3] This study bears out the wisdom of that generalization.

The American laity of the Progressive Era were hopeful. Across the board, as I have said, they sought to answer current problems with fresh insights and novel institutions. Rather than expressing nostalgia for a lost order of small-town life, they looked to the future and valued compassion for the fate and well-being of others. To borrow words from a current commentator, theirs was "the impulse toward altruistic giving and sharing, and the militant refusal of inequality, violence and oppression." Some, of course, were bitter. The black intellectual W. E. B. Du Bois, in his *The Souls of Black Folk: Essays and Sketches* (1903), prophesied that the greatest problem in the nation's future for the next hundred years would be that of the color line. Du Bois volunteered that his Episcopal Church's "record on the Negro problem has been simply shameful," and in the light of that shame his "religious faith shriveled in the hot breath of hypocrisy and intolerance." How could he have maintained, as his biographer claims, a "*serene* agnosticism"?[4] Du Bois did nothing of the sort and ultimately left both his church and his nation. Others, young people, also quit the premises

3. Edwin S. Gaustad, "The Pulpit and the Pews," in *Between the Times: The Travail of the Protestant Establishment in America, 1900–1960,* edited by William R. Hutchison (Cambridge: Cambridge University Press, 1989), 34.

4. Robert H. Wiebe, *The Search for Order, 1877–1920* (New York: Hill and Wang, 1968), 2–4; John Keane, "Who's in Charge Here? The Need for the Rule of Law to Regulate the Merging Global Society," *Times Literary Supplement,* May 18, 2001, 13; Du Bois, *Souls of Black Folk,* 14th ed. (Chicago: A. C. McClurg, 1924), 40; Eric Anderson and Alfred A. Moss Jr., *Dangerous Donations: Northern Philanthropy and Southern Black Education, 1902–1930* (Columbia: University of

but for a very different reason. Unlike their black brothers and sisters, white youths sailed from home in the interest of international Christian missions. Robert Gardiner was among the slightly older men and women who worked with and inspired American youth along just such lines of Christian service. He was the indirect but no less significant heir of Moody's stunningly successful organizations of young people with their denominational comprehensiveness.

It is well known that Moody's revivals were ecumenical; they took place outside sectarian confines and "were organized by business men but not for business men" in particular. Among Moody's imaginative structures was his creation and leadership of the Northfield Bible Study Conference (1886) that initiated for the next thirty years the extraordinary lay collegiate movement into foreign missions. That action was also spurred by the Young Men's Christian Association (YMCA) and the Young Women's Christian Association (YWCA). In 1888 many of these Christian impulses among young people coalesced in the Student Volunteer Movement for Foreign Missions (SVM). Under the leadership of John R. Mott, more than 40,000 students signed up.[5] At a time when there were only 379,000 college students in the country (a mere 2.9 percent of the total population of the United States), the students associated with SVM represented nearly 10.5 percent of all men and women enrolled in the nation's colleges.[6] SVM's motto, "Evangelization of the world in this generation," and the eager and heady atmosphere accompanying it converged with the professional interests of older missionaries and administrators at the World Missionary Conference in Edinburgh, Scotland, in 1910. "The conference featured such prominent laymen as William Jennings Bryan," notes one historian, "who participated actively rather than serving as ornaments at an opening ceremony."[7] In the general religious ferment few stood on the sidelines. But none of it could have happened without Moody.

---

Missouri Press, 1999), 119; David Levering Lewis, *W. E. B. Du Bois: Biography of a Race, 1868–1919* (New York: Henry Holt, 1993), 66, 65 (emphasis added).

5. Kathryn Teresa Long, *The Revival of 1857–58* (New York: Oxford University Press, 1998), 129; Kenton J. Clymer, *Protestant Missionaries in the Philippines, 1898–1916* (Champaign: University of Illinois Press, 1986), 12.

6. In 1910 there had been 25,208 students enrolled out of a college population of 350,000, or 7 percent, for an increase of 3.5 percent in only four years. See U.S. Department of Commerce, *Historical Statistics of the United States from Colonial Times to 1970,* 2 vols. (Washington, DC: Bureau of the Census, 1975), 1:383.

7. Valentin H. Rabe, *The Home Base of American China Missions, 1880–1920* (Cambridge: Council on East Asian Studies, Harvard University, 1978), 43.

Moody's influence on religion in the United States was both galvanizing and proliferating among conservatives and liberals equally. Beginning at the turn of the century and for more than forty years thereafter, Henry Parsons Crowell, president of the Quaker Oats Company, chaired the Moody Bible Institute. Similar offspring, such as the American Bible Institute movement, Lucy Peabody's Association of Baptists for World Evangelism, and Henrietta Mears's Gospel Light Publications, appeared. Moody's influence also stretched to young Methodists and to the Episcopalians' Brotherhood of St. Andrew (BSA) of which Robert Gardiner became director in 1904. As much as any other college-oriented organization, the Episcopal brotherhood was the result, even if indirectly, of Moody's ascendancy.[8] Although the BSA drew from Ivy League colleges, its membership was by no means limited, as shall be shown, to those schools. Nor could the Episcopalians alone glow with the nimbus of wealth and influence.

Though now forgotten, in his day Moody's most popular heir among youths was William W. Borden, known as "Borden of Yale." Stroke of the Yale crew, Borden was Presbyterian. He proved golden in wealth, personality, and renown. During a trip around the world at age sixteen, he was stirred by the romance of Christian missions. When he inherited a fortune at twenty-one, he was not content merely to give away large sums of money but determined to become a missionary to China himself. With the kind of adulation bestowed on another later hero, Charles A. Lindbergh, Borden set off to work and preach among the Muslims of northwestern China. In April 1913 in Cairo, where he was also learning Arabic, he suddenly died of cerebrospinal meningitis. All, of whatever religious stripe, mourned the loss of the young crusader. The modernist-conservative split might thereafter plague denominations, but the idea of Christendom, led by the likes of Borden, was still predicated on a consensus, and to it most adhered. As one historian has pointed out, "Many parties were aligned across a wide and changing spectrum of opinion."[9] People like Borden appealed to the majority in that alignment.

8. At the turn of the century—before the split between Fundmentalists and liberal Social Gospelers became a gulf—there were more conservative organizations than SVM and its subordinates; the Young People's Missionary Movement, which in 1911 became the Missionary Education Movement; the Laymen's Missionary Movement; and the latter's successor, the short-lived Interchurch World Movement. See ibid., 24, 26, and 30.

9. Mrs. H. Taylor, *Borden of Yale, '09: "The Life That Counts"* (London and Philadelphia: China Inland Mission, 1926); Robert T. Handy, "Changing Contexts of Church-State Relations

Other wealthy laymen, such as George Foster Peabody, Valentine E. Macy, George Jones of the *New York Times,* and Charles Schwab, "were related by a common interest in philanthropy and evangelism among [New York City's] poor and in many cases by personal friendships or close association in political, business or reform ventures."[10] Once again, as we shall see, Gardiner's involvement as a layman in Boston was significant to the Social Gospel in that city.

And then there was William Jennings Bryan. Because of his role in the *Scopes* trial of 1925, Bryan is remembered not as one of the celebrated lay participants in the Edinburgh Conference of 1910, but as a radical rightist, a Fundamentalist, even as something of a buffoon, but seldom as a latter-day Jeffersonian. Bryan in fact stood for progressive labor legislation; a graduated income tax; government aid to farmers and workers; public ownership of railroads, telegraphs, and telephones; federal development of water resources; and a government guarantee of bank deposits. In the Senate he "added his voice to the cries for stricter enforcement of laws regulating the trusts." Bryan was no reactionary, but he believed that the essential message of Christianity was not an individual one so much as a social one.[11] He discussed social and economic problems in Christian terms, and such discussion led him to support woman suffrage, to champion federal control of the Federal Reserve Board, and to oppose the anti-Catholic American Protective Association. Bryan has been, as one historian claims, diabolized in liberal circles, beginning with Clarence Darrow himself. In his famous exchange with Bryan, the Chicago attorney seemed "incapable of seeing that . . . [Bryan's] *moral* argument against *social* Darwinism . . . was not touched by ridicule of the Genesis account." Moreover, there was something to be said for the right of the people to control what was taught in their schools. Evolution was not, as Bryan himself stated, the real issue.[12]

---

in America, 1880–1920," in *Caring for the Commonweal: Education for Religious and Public Life,* edited by Parker J. Palmer, Barbara G. Wheller, and James W. Fowler (Atlanta: Mercer University Press, 1990), 28.

10. Clyde C. Griffen, "Rich Laymen and Early Social Christianity," *Church History* 36:1 (1967): 48. See also Garry Wills, *Under God: Religion and American Politics* (New York: Simon and Schuster, 1990), chaps. 9–11.

11. Louis W. Koenig, *Bryan: A Political Biography* (New York: G. P. Putnam's Sons, 1971), 92; Lawrence W. Levine, *Defender of the Faith: William Jennings Bryan, the Last Decade, 1915–1925* (New York: Oxford University Press, 1965), 358, 364.

12. Wills, *Under God,* 110; Levine, *Defender of the Faith,* 331. See also Ferenc M. Szasz, *The Divided Mind of Protestant America, 1880–1930* (Birmingham: University of Alabama Press, 1982), 123.

In the American religious scene the terms *modernist* and *fundamentalist* present more definitional problems than they solve. As one historian has pointed out, "The largest number of Americans who, on grounds of Christian beliefs, rejected various aspects of evolutionary theory were reasonably orthodox Christians, but not part of any fundamentalist crusade" (at least not until after 1910). Some were from European churches, such as Roman Catholic, Lutheran, and Wesleyan, and some were from Reformed denominations; others had more largely American roots, as in Seventh-Day Adventists, Mormons, and Pentecostals. The sharpest divisions were elsewhere and involved race—white versus black. Moody, Mott, Bryan, Gardiner, and their white college students with voices raised for the cause of missions, evangelization, and Christian reunion contrasted sharply with the cry of black youth, "Why did God make me an outcast and a stranger in mine own house?" Separated from fellow countrymen and women within the "Veil of Color," declared Du Bois, every black person lived a double life as citizen and as African American. But the animation and promptitude of white American youth in the 1910s also differed markedly from many sobersides Europeans. Germans such as the venerable missionary eminence Gustav Warneck growled that the Anglo-Saxons in fact commanded, "Go ye and teach English to all nations." Worse, evangelization of the world in one generation seemed to snatch the missionary movement "out of the hands of those who had understood it longest and most deeply."[13] Others, the Scandinavians for instance, were less restive.

Among those enthusiastic Americans of the Progressive Era who sought through travel, personal contact, and extensive correspondence to heal the divisions in Christendom, none was more important than Gardiner. In January 1916 the *New York Times* reported at length on the letters of "Gardiner of Gardiner." Their author, the *Times* suggested, was the "wielder of the largest religious correspondence that one man has ever conducted in America." He wrote letters "with the gift of tongues.... [He was] the centre of an epistolary Pentecost." If the fractures in Christendom were to be healed, "continued schism" set aside,

13. Paul K. Conkin, *When All the Gods Trembled: Darwinism, Scopes, and American Intellectuals* (Lanham, MD: Rowman and Littlefield, 1998), 50; see 53–76 for a definition of Fundamentalism, the emerging crusade, and the founding of the World Christian Fundamentals Association in 1919. See also George M. Marsden, *Fundamentalism and American Culture: The Shaping of Twentieth-Century Evangelicalism, 1875–1925* (New York: Oxford University Press, 1980); Lewis, *W. E. B. Du Bois*, 280; and William R. Hutchison, *Errand to the World: American Protestant Thought and Foreign Missions* (Chicago: University of Chicago Press, 1987), 134, 131.

and "members of all Christian creeds...come into one household of faith, 'Gardiner of Gardiner' will in ages to come be a figure in Church history." In towns of comparable size, the report continued, no other postmaster than the one in Gardiner, Maine, "has seen more strange kinds of stamps"; letters "from China, from Japan, from every country in the world [arrive] clad in outlandish wrappings and bearing strange writing." Not a few were directed, the *Times* revealed, to "Robert H. Gardiner, United States," for "the correspondents do not understand how the name and the post office can be alike." Gardiner of Gardiner was the key player in "the colossal task of bringing together again the widely separated flocks of Christianity into one fold."[14]

The line of march of highly significant laymen and -women did not, of course, end with the Progressive Era. Influenced by it but reaching their most important years after it were such laypeople as Roman Catholic Dorothy Day and two famous Episcopalians—the penologist Miriam Van Waters and Secretary of Labor Frances Perkins—among others. In the latter half of the twentieth century, in the "toxic political environment," as one historian graphically terms the desegregation era following the Supreme Court's decision in *Brown v. Board of Education,* we discover laymen and laywomen in Robert Hallowell Gardiner's own church whose faith was clearly the primary motivation for their actions. Justice Thurgood Marshall; South Carolina's federal district court judge J. Waties Waring; black psychologist and professor at City College of New York Kenneth B. Clark; author Sarah Patton Boyle; Mississippi editor and church historian Hodding Carter II and his wife, Betty Carter; and Carl and Anne Braden all took courage and spoke out of their Christian faith.[15] Though for the moment I wish to place Gardiner in the context of lay leadership in the United States, there were notable clergy from many churches who also inspired and maintained the Social Gospel and the cause of modern church reunion; they will be dealt with in this study. In such a larger company we must place Robert Gardiner. He would have understood them and they him. And nowhere else in the world at the time did such a lay movement arise.

At the turn of the century, in 1900, many of the major Christian communions were both proud and nationalistic. Outside America's borders before 1914

14. *New York Times Magazine,* January 30, 1916, 16.
15. Gardiner H. Shattuck Jr., *Episcopalians and Race: Civil War to Civil Rights* (Lexington: University Press of Kentucky, 2000), 74, 59–64, 70–71, 72–74.

the age was still monarchical, one of vast European empires stretching from the African continent to India, Asia, and the islands of the Pacific. Those empires in turn were ruled by either absolute or constitutional monarchs and their aristocracies. Churches were beholden to the states that supported them in England, Germany, Russia, and in the Roman Catholic and Greek Orthodox nations as well. In such a world scene the suggestion of Christian reunion, coming as it did from the American republic, was brash and was resented by many accustomed to initiating actions rather than responding to them. Within the United States, that an Episcopal layman and his denomination should become the central actors on this stage was considered by many fellow countrymen as insolent and was, as we shall see, resented. Among other denominations, Episcopalians had a reputation for being highfalutin, stuck on themselves, and committed to liturgical practices and niceties by which they self-consciously set themselves apart from the rest of the pack. As a result American Protestants suspected Episcopalian motives. That Robert Gardiner and his church, as I shall show, should then have been taken seriously and either accepted or rejected attests to the strength of this New England lawyer's personal currency.

Gardiner wanted a global civil society, a Christendom truer to its roots in the belief that a providential God was actively engaged in reconciling humankind with himself and with itself. That he thought in terms of "Christendom" at all may appear at best old-fashioned, at worst imperialistic and illusive. But insofar as Christendom was a challenge, something to be achieved in the future, not a subject of nostalgic contemplation, he may have had a point: the purpose of any Christian's life was not to contemplate the world and its past history, but, as Karl Marx himself recognized, to change it. Gardiner intended to restring the harps and break out the cymbals. He wanted churches to learn to listen and to respect each other, to place firmly the ideal type of global society ahead of their own parochial interests, and to come to see that the catholic faith of the church demanded a transnational attitude. Unity was not, in theory at least, a matter of like-minded individuals coming together and deciding to cooperate. It was mandated by both scripture and doctrine. He not only recognized all this but also pried open its possibilities and freed its latent energies. He had, as we shall see, a high theology of the church to match and underwrite the biblical mandate that all were to be one in heart and mind. But he was under no illusions about the difficulty of the task before him, of achieving a working confidence not only among differing denominations but often within churches themselves, not the least that of Episcopalians. It turned out to be his own fellow church people who at first provided some of his most tenacious critics and opponents.

But Gardiner was tough: born in the American West two decades before the frontier closed, he was also a gentleman, very much a member of the elite-Protestant-establishment, northeastern-boardroom variety. A pupil at America's second oldest school, Roxbury Latin, founded in 1645, he was as well a graduate of its oldest college, Harvard, founded nine years earlier. There "New England gentlemen taught other New England gentlemen."[16] After a stint at the Harvard Law School, he became a lawyer on stylish Pemberton Square, in Boston. He was as well a reformer: first, as a missionary to the wretched and the poor in Boston in a time of terrible depression (1893–1897); second, as a leader among his denomination's youth in the decade of high hopes and aspirations (1900s); and third, among the Episcopal Church's ecclesiastics, whether thick-ribbed or thoughtful, he led the way to the World Conference on Faith and Order of which I have already spoken (1910s and early '20s). Since few others were much aware of the complexity of what they had set out to accomplish in reuniting the churches, Gardiner was forced to devise methods of leadership both diplomatic and firm in order to take them to places they did not want to go. And he was organized to beat the band.

But his importance should not be overstated. In point of fact he built on what his predecessors had accomplished. He also followed the general tendency toward broader catholicity then evident in the American religious scene. Not the least in his own denomination were men who had raised the issue of Christian divisions and in varying ways had suggested solutions: Calvin Colton, Thomas Hubbard Vail, William H. Lewis, William Augustus Muhlenberg, and, most important of all, William Reed Huntington, who will be dealt with later in this study.[17] They suggested various solutions: the Episcopal Church should alone lead the new American empire (Colton). Other churches should come to us: we already have all that is needful for Christian unity (Vail and Lewis). Come to us: we have tailored our theology and ecclesiology to accommodate others

---

16. Lawrence Summers, "War of Words," *Harvard Magazine,* March–April 2002, 61. Since Boston Latin School was founded in 1635, it nosed out Roxbury Latin by ten years.

17. For Colton, see John F. Woolverton, "Whither Episcopalianism: A Century of Apologetic Interpretations of the Episcopal Church, 1835–1964," *Anglican Theological Review,* supp. ser., no. 1 (July 1973): 142–45; and Colton, *The Genius and Mission of the Protestant Episcopal Church in the United States* (New York: Stanford and Swords, 1853). On Vail, see Thomas Hubbard Vail,

(Muhlenberg and the early Huntington). Come to us and together we can create an "American catholicity" by equal contribution (Huntington).[18] And finally, the dramatic change that stated that without prior demands, we are seeking out other churches to achieve worldwide Christian unity (Gardiner).

There were, of course, broader influences and reasons for the rising interest in church unity. Among them were awareness of history and the development of the church historically, as evidenced in both the Oxford Movement and the Calvinist High Church Mercersburg theology in nineteenth-century America and in Samuel Simon Schmucker of the Lutheran General Synod whose writings gained national attention. Influential leaders like Schmucker and great scholars such as the high Calvinist theologian John Williamson Nevin and historian Philip Schaff, both from the Reformed side, contributed significantly to ecumenism. The founding by Alexander Campbell of the Disciples of Christ after 1809 sought to restore specifically the unity of the "primitive church." At the other end of the century bodies such as those of the Lutherans, Presbyterians, and Episcopalians began to draw together into world alliances, while cooperative efforts on the frontiers both of the West and of the burgeoning industrialism after the Civil War brought men and women together to face common problems. All this is well known and has been told before in many places and needs only to be mentioned here.[19]

---

*The Comprehensive Church; or, Christian Unity and Ecclesiastical Union in the Protestant Episcopal Church* (1841; reprint, New York: D. Appleton, 1879). On Lewis, see William H. Lewis, *Christian Union and the Protestant Episcopal Church in Its Relations to Church Unity* (New York, 1858). For Muhlenberg, see Alvin W. Skardon, *Church Leader in the Cities: William Augustus Muhlenberg* (Philadelphia: University of Pennsylvania Press, 1971), chap. 9. And for Huntington, see John F. Woolverton, "William Reed Huntington and Church Unity: The Historical and Theological Background of the Chicago-Lambeth Quadrilateral" (PhD diss., Columbia University, 1963).

18. See Huntington, *The Church-Idea: An Essay toward Church Unity* (New York: E. P. Dutton, 1870); and Huntington, *The Four Theories of Visible Church Unity* (New York: John H. Smith, 1909).

19. See, for instance, Don Herbert Yoder, "Christian Unity in Nineteenth-Century America," in *A History of the Ecumenical Movement, 1517–1948,* edited by Ruth Rouse and Stephen Neill (Philadelphia: Westminster Press, 1967), 221–59.

# ONE

❧✝❧

## The Legacy of Education

### *Fort Tejon, California, 1855–1916*

Throughout his life Robert Gardiner retained an interest in education. As a young man he proved to be an enlightened schoolteacher and later school trustee; in addition, he oversaw and directed the reform of religious education in the Episcopal Church. Gardiner derived his commitment to better education from his parents, particularly from his father, a well-read and intellectually alert military officer. The son's concern for education began in an unlikely place and time: at Fort Tejon amid the chaos of post–gold rush California.

His birth occurred on September 9, 1855, in a primitive two-room adobe house. The dwelling had a canvas roof and was located at the far southern end of California's San Joachin Valley. Though he spent only the first three years of his life in California, that frontier state would, through his parents, have a strong if indirect influence. The example of his mother and father's stability, maintained in primitive surroundings, and their frugality and determination to bring order—the values of family, religious observance, and education in legal procedures—in the midst of anarchy shaped their son's life then and later. Fort Tejon (Spanish for "raccoon") was a newly constructed, in 1854, policing station of the United States Army. The fort was a hot, unpromising camp set in a bowl of brown "parched up" mountains with little water and a "few trees [that] look starved."[1] It was also built on a dangerous geological fault line.

---

1. Anne Hays Gardiner to her stepmother, Eleanor Blaine Hays, July 17, 1855; John William Tudor Gardiner to Eleanor Harriet Gardiner, July 31, 1855, Fort Tejon Transcripts, Gardiner

Tejon guarded Grapevine Pass through the Tehachapi Mountains, which prospective gold hunters traveled on their way to Placerita Canyon, just north of
Los Angeles. Fifteen miles from the fort was the Tejon Reservation of the Emig-
diano Indians, an inland group of unconverted, nonmission Indians, the Chumash people of Santa Barbara. Many of these Native Americans were employed
as servants at the fort. Nearby were other tribes: Shoshone Gitanemuks and
Yokuts. California's superintendent of Indian affairs, Colonel Edward F. Beale,
was determined to protect these and other displaced native peoples from a
developing slave trade in Indian children. (The youngsters were often taken to
the southern part of the state and there sold by traveling gold hunters who
found the additional business in humans profitable.)[2] Robert Gardiner's father
was part of the attempt to protect both native peoples and the environment in
which they lived.

From 1848 to 1860 California was the scene of lawlessness and misrule
caused by a large migration of westward-bending frontiersmen. On the heels of
approximately four hundred American trappers and traders of the early 1840s
came a steadily increasing stream of adventurers and, after 1848, gold hunters
from around the world, many of them criminals. In the great bay of San Francisco gold was the sustaining force that changed an unimportant Spanish and
later Mexican settlement into an instant boomtown in which "there was nothing but gold and men." Women constituted a miserable 8 percent of the population in 1850. During 1849 alone, eighty thousand prospectors reached California either by sea or overland. They were contemptuous of Mexican traditions
and customs. Mexican law was ignored. "Vigilance committees" simply took
matters into their own hands, even to on-the-spot executions. Greed knew few

<hr />

Family Papers, Oaklands, Gardiner, Maine. By the treaty of Guadalupe Hidalgo, California was
ceded by Mexico to the United States in 1848; state government was established on December
20, 1849, and California was admitted to the Union as a free state on September 7, 1850.
    2. Anne Hays Gardiner to Emma Jane Tudor Gardiner, June 30, 1855, Gardiner Family Papers.
See also Joseph E. Engbeck Jr., *Fort Tejon: State Historic Park* (Sacramento: Department of Parks
and Recreation, 1991), 3; Campbell Grant, *The Rock Paintings of the Chumash: A Study in California Indian Culture* (Berkeley and Los Angeles: University of California Press, 1965), 54–55;
and Sherburne F. Cook, *The Conflict between the California Indian and White Civilization* (Berkeley and Los Angeles: University of California Press, 1976), 3, 311. See Sharon Malinowski and
Melissa Walsh Doig, eds., *Gale Encyclopedia of Native American Tribes,* 4 vols. (Detroit: Gale,
1998), vol. 4, for these tribes in southern California. Cook's assertion that "the officers entrusted
with the care of the Indians on the new reserves were a pretty bad lot" (4:57), at least in the case
of both Beale and John W. T. Gardiner, should be challenged.

constraints. Environmental pollution matched human depredations. In the Sierra Nevada hydraulic mining for gold made use of the mountain torrents by re-directing and forcing cascading streams to blast away the earthen overburden of California's great gravel beds, the natural products of ancient river channels. "With 300 feet of head and a six inch diameter nozzle, 1,600 cubic feet of water per minute could be discharged at a velocity of 140 feet per second." The results were disastrous: "As the scale of operations mounted and spread through-out a large part of the state, vast quantities of earth, sand, and gravel found their way increasingly into the streams and rivers of central California, especially the tributaries of the Sacramento River."[3] Riverbeds, now full of debris and unable to absorb the flow of swollen waters during the rainy season, overflowed their banks, ruined farmlands, and made river navigation impossible. Much-needed legislation in the 1880s brought a virtual end to the misuse of such technology.

Robert's father, Captain John William Tudor Gardiner, second in command of Fort Tejon, had intellectual, scientific, and environmental interests. In May 1856 he thanked his mother for sending him "Reed's lectures" and pronounced himself "very glad indeed to get Macauley, particularly as I did not expect to have the opportunity of reading him while out here." He had by his own admission "a preference for mathematical pursuits." He also wanted to know about his surroundings and to make them known to others. He captured small animals and reptiles at Fort Tejon. "Tudor is making a collection of things for the Smith-sonian Institute [*sic*]," wrote his wife, Anne Gardiner. "Down in the cellar [of their new quarters] there is a keg of alcohol, in which is all manner of things, snakes, lizards, horned frogs, toads, etc., and although I know they are dead, I cannot help watching the keg when I go down for fear I may see a snake put-ting his head out." Tudor showed himself to be a keen observer of nature, of the

3. Gunther Barth, *Instant Cities: Urbanization and the Rise of San Francisco and Denver* (New York: Oxford University Press, 1975), 121. The *Encyclopedia Britannica,* 11th ed., says the figure for women in the mining communities was 2 percent and that the percentage of population increase in the decade 1850 to 1860 was 310.3, the largest in the state's history (s.v. "population increase"). See also Neal Harlow, *California Conquered: War and Peace on the Pacific, 1846–1850* (Berkeley and Los Angeles: University of California Press, 1982), 49; William Tecumseh Sherman, *Memoirs of General W. T. Sherman* (New York: Library of America, 1990), in which Sherman refers to a "Lt. Gardner" who served in the army in California in 1852 (137–38); and Louis C. Hunter and Lynwood Bryant, *A History of Industrial Power in the United States, 1780–1930* (Cambridge: MIT Press, 1991), 405, which also states that 30 feet of head is the equivalent of 130 pounds per square inch (406–7).

countryside, and of the history of California.[4] Both he and Annie, as his wife was called, took time to learn the names of the flowers and trees around the fort. Later their son Robert showed an almost obsessive concern for his land and trees in Maine.

The parents cared as well for the less fortunate. California's Native Americans were hunter-gatherers, "splintered among a hundred tribelets, none of which required a war to be defeated." Toward them most Americans at the time displayed insensible brutality. That loose cannon John C. Frémont had "no room for prisoners" and cold-bloodedly shot unarmed men. In doing so he reversed a century of colonial paternalism. Beginning in the eighteenth century patriarchal Spanish landowners and their friars sought to make the Indians "civilized by example" on more or less "humanely run slave plantations." The American immigrants, on the other hand, recognized no human resources in native peoples and tapped only the material wealth of what became their new state. As a result, disease, starvation, and the destruction of homes, tools, and clothing accompanied outright homicide of native peoples. This was particularly grievous in inland areas never penetrated by either the Spanish or later the Mexicans.[5] Only the elder Gardiners and their allies sought the assimilation of Native Americans and Mexican Californians. In Gilded Age Boston their son would likewise espouse the cause of equal citizenship for Italian and Irish immigrants.

Both before and after independence from Spain in 1821, California needed farmworkers, lawyers, and educators; instead, they got musicians, printers, tailors, gamblers, and idlers from Mexico City. Mexican California remained without common law. Justice depended on the whim of local officials who believed in property and position. They were only "tentatively republican" and excluded Indians and blacks from the franchise. So, after 1849, did the Americans. Both

4. J. W. T. Gardiner to Emma Jane Gardiner, May 31, 1856, Gardiner Family Papers. He probably meant by the first reference Sampson Reed's *Observations on the Growth of the Mind* (1826), and assuredly he referred to Thomas Macauley's *History of England* (1848–1855), volumes 3–4 of which had just been published and were enjoying wide circulation in the United States as well as in England. J. W. T. Gardiner to Lewis Cass, January 18, 1836, Application of John William Tudor Gardiner to West Point, in Donny D. Smith, "Notes for Family History," Robert H. Gardiner Collection, Archives of the Episcopal Church, Austin, TX; Anne H. Gardiner to unknown, July 13, 1856, Gardiner Family Papers; J. W. T. Gardiner to Emma Jane Gardiner, June 30, 1855, Gardiner Family Papers.

5. Jared Diamond, *Guns, Germs, and Steel: The Fates of Human Societies* (New York: W. W. Norton, 1997), 374; Harlow, *California Conquered,* 110, 75; C. Alan Hutchinson, *Frontier Settlement in Mexican California: The Hijar-Padres Colony and Its Origins, 1769–1835* (New Haven, CT: Yale University Press, 1969), 52, 59, 221; Cook, *Conflict,* 3, 92 (for Indian reductions).

groups of white rulers displayed high passions and low scruples. With the quickening flow of gold, crime increased.[6]

Educated men such as Tudor Gardiner tried to bring a degree of fairness and discipline to the territory to which they were assigned. The elder Gardiner, determined to restrain white aggression, for those inclined to follow his inducements, provided law books and the opportunity to study them. He handpicked justices of the peace. Tudor wrote home of one unfortunate who fell under his pedagogy, saying the man "never has acted before in his official capacity. I have given him an intelligent soldier for a clerk, and he, the justice, is preparing himself by reading a thick volume of [the new] California laws." The prospective justice's appearance was hardly reassuring, exclaimed Gardiner: "He is in his shirtsleeves with a hat considerably the worse for wear, a huge pair of Mexican spurs with buckskin leggings, and, of course, what no Californian travels without, a revolver in his belt." However unpromising, it was a beginning. But Gardiner was remarkably successful, "a perfect gentleman," as Indian agent Edward A. Stevenson remarked of him.[7] The determination to overcome ignorance and license remained with the Gardiner family long after they had forsaken Fort Tejon. The father's civilizing influence was an example to his son. Through Tudor Gardiner, the family came to believe in system, fairness, propriety, and the rightness of things.

In addition to science and law, there was the church. In Gardiner, Maine, a long tradition had already spun its web. The Episcopal parish, Christ Church, and its antecedent, St. Ann's, provided a godly heritage to which Robert Hallowell Gardiner's generation was the fourth to uphold. His great-grandfather Dr. Silvester Gardiner had founded the parish, and it retained something of the atmosphere of a family chapel. Anglican religion did not die out with the old Tory doctor. There were Episcopal clergy: the sister of patriarch Silvester Gardiner had married the Reverend James MacSparran in 1722. The doctor's grand-

6. Hutchinson, *Frontier Settlement*, 344–45; Harlow, *California Conquered*, 342, 283; Patricia N. Limerick, *The Legacy of Conquest: The Unbroken Past of the American West* (New York: W. W. Norton, 1987), 102.

7. J. W. T. Gardiner to his family, July 13, 1856, Gardiner Family Papers; William F. Strobridge, unpublished study included in Danny D. Smith, "Notices of John William Tudor Gardiner," Gardiner Library. Other men of the same mind as Gardiner were Colonel Edward F. Beale; military governors Richard B. Mason, Persifor F. Smith, and Bennet Riley; as well as San Francisco banker William Tecumseh Sherman. See, for instance, John F. Marzalek, *Sherman: A Soldier's Passion for Order* (New York: Free Press, 1993), 107–15. For the beginnings of law in California, see Sherman, *Memoirs*, 65–66.

son, with the curiously redundant name of John Silvester John Gardiner, whose father had been disowned by the old curmudgeon for siding with the Patriots in the Revolution, had from 1805 to 1830 been the longtime influential rector of Trinity Church in Boston.[8]

Then there was Robert's uncle, the Reverend Frederic Gardiner, a rector first in Saco, Maine, then at Bath, and finally professor of biblical literature at the Berkeley Divinity School in Middletown, Connecticut. Professor Gardiner was quite an academic. He regularly contributed to the *Bibliotheca Sacra* and other weighty periodicals. He wrote articles on such books of the Bible as Genesis, Leviticus, 2 Samuel, Ezekiel, Acts, Galatians, Hebrews, and Jude. Not content with biblical studies and divinity, he branched out, contributing to the *American Journal of Science* an article titled "Ice on the Kennebec." Late in life he assayed "The Universality of the Laws of Heredity and Variability." His best-known work, however, was *Aids to Scripture Study.* On the whole he was not overly learned and, if his contemporaries are to be trusted, was a boring teacher. His son, the Reverend Frederic Gardiner Jr., was dean of the Episcopal cathedral in Sioux Falls, South Dakota, and later a well-known headmaster at Pomfret School. Following in his father's more or less scientific shoes, the younger Frederic later became an instructor in biology and geology at Trinity College in Hartford, Connecticut. The family's intellectual interest in Christianity extended as well to a younger brother of Robert, John Hays Gardiner, a professor at Harvard, who wrote *The Bible as English Literature.*[9]

Robert also had a younger sister, Eleanor Harriet Gardiner, also born in California, who in 1893 became an Anglican nun in the Order of St. Mary. She

8. Evelyn L. Gilmore, *Christ Church, Gardiner, Maine: Antecedents and History* (Gardiner, ME: Reporter Journal Press, 1893), 49–62; *American National Biography,* s.v. "MacSparran, James." See also Olivia E. Coolidge, *Colonial Entrepreneur: Dr. Silvester Gardiner and the Settlement of Maine's Kennebec Valley* (Gardiner, ME: Tilbury House Publishers and Gardiner Library Association, 1999), 9–13; and T. A. Milford, "J. S. J. Gardiner, Early National Letters and the Perseverance of British-American Culture," *Anglican and Episcopal History* 70:4 (December 2001): 407–37.

9. It may be that "The Universality of the Laws of Heredity and Variability" is by Frederic Gardiner Jr. but is not listed as such. See Danny D. Smith, "Draft Genealogy of Dr. Silvester Gardiner," item 41, Gardiner Collection; "Published Works of Rev. Frederic Gardiner, D.D.," Gardiner Library, n.d.; F. Gardiner, *Aids to Scripture Study* (Boston: Houghton Mifflin, 1890); Edward R. Hardy to Floyd Tomkins, January 27, 1966, Floyd Tomkins Papers, Archives of the Episcopal Church, Austin, TX; Joseph G. H. Barry, *Impressions and Opinions* (New York: E. S. Gorham, 1931), 105–6; Smith, "Draft Notes," item 64; *Who Was Who in America: A Companion to Who's Who in America* (Chicago: A. N. Marquis, 1942), 1:439; and J. H. Gardiner, *The Bible as English Literature* (1918; reprint, New York: Charles Scribner's Sons, 1927).

later was Sister Superior of Trinity Hospital in New York City. A woman of wit, "sometimes trenchant," she also showed to the world a "cordial, welcoming kindness."[10] To the family's Anglican heritage Robert Gardiner would make an even more noteworthy contribution than his clerical uncles, cousin, sister, and brother. It was a powerful religious heritage: locally Anglican, but then stretching beyond Christ Church, Gardiner into something more broadly biblical and after a fashion scientific.

An examination of the backgrounds of Robert's parents reveals startling changes of fortune. They and their respective families knew both wealth and poverty. Both had status, moved in high circles, and had deep roots in the soil and in America's history, colonial and national. By circumstance or choice, both moved away from familiar scenes and took risks, though not always without a backward glance. Robert's mother, Anne Elizabeth Hays Gardiner, was the daughter of a prominent Cumberland County, Pennsylvania, businessman, John Hays. She was brought up in one of the wealthiest households in Frankford Township. Her father owned and operated three mills, a farm, and a distillery. The Hayses lived well. In the larger Hays clan were physicians, attorneys, bank presidents, and manufacturers, mostly in the iron and railroad-equipment trades. They boasted army officers such as Texas Ranger captain Jack Hays, a Mexican War scout, and Major General William Hays, who rose to command the Second Corps of the Army of the Potomac in the Civil War. And they had their big-screen heroes. One cousin, John M. Hays, a lawyer, was killed at the Alamo in 1836. Hays women were educated in private schools. In religion many of them were Presbyterians. They were public-spirited, useful citizens.[11]

10. Laura E. Richards, *Stepping Westward* (New York: D. Appleton, 1931), 355.
11. Anne Elizabeth Hays Gardiner was not a Virginian, as one member of the family claimed; see ibid., 355–56. The information about her father's businesses comes from Carlisle Tax Record, Franklin Township, 1820, 1823, 1826, Cumberland County Historical Society, Carlisle, Pennsylvania. Besides twenty-four barrels of whiskey, the inventory of John Hays's estate at the time of his death in 1854 listed extensive—and expensive—furniture, carpets, wine decanters, china, wagons, buggies, horses, mules, and 113 "fat hogs" valued at $847.50. On the death of John M. Hays, see Danny D. Smith, "The Hays Family," draft transcribed from manuscripts, July 1996, Special Collections, Gardiner Library. On the women's education, see George P. Donehoo, ed., "Biographical Sketches," *History of the Cumberland Valley in Pennsylvania,* 2 vols. (Harrisburg, PA: Susquehanna Historical Association, 1930), 2:174. "Hays" variously from First Presbyterian Church, Parish Records; Big Spring Presbyterian Church; and Silver Spring Presbyterian Church, *Index of Church/Cemetary Records,* April 29, 1998, 9–15, Cumberland County Historical Society, Carlisle, Pennsylvania. See, for instance, Anna A. Hays to Mrs. James Burch, April 12, 1939, Hays Family Papers, Cumberland County Historical Society, Carlisle, Pennsylvania.

Like the rest, they sustained losses. Anne Hays's mother died two years after Anne was born. Her father was remarried to a woman named Eleanor Wheaton, a cousin of James G. Blaine. The Hayses were fortunate in her presence among them, and Anne was close to her stepmother. The young girl was lively. Possessed of a "bubbling sense of humor and a buoyant nature," she "radiated energy and gayety," was a good sport and adventurous, and on the trip from Los Angeles to Fort Tejon "enjoyed the camping out very much." When the Indians laughed at her attempt to bargain with them in Spanish, she joined in the merriment but then went on to study the language. She treated the Indians with courtesy, and they responded accordingly. Indian women "used to come in & stand in a circle to watch her bathe her babies."[12]

Anne was frank and open. She admired handsome men. Above all she brought a sense of order and homelikeness to her primitive surroundings. Despite adverse circumstances Anne Gardiner worked hard to make a life for herself, to entertain, however simply, the officers on the base, and to celebrate holidays for her growing family. She meant to look "civilized" and decorated her home even if only with "a piece of druggett [coarse felt] before the fire place." At first, though, she said, "Housekeeping is a great worry, particularly when you know nothing about it," and "My cooking book is my constant daily companion, a thing that I despise." Even when they had "beef and potatoes one day and mash and beans the next," Anne learned to keep house, cook, and get along without servants. She made her energy count for those around her. Occasionally, fear took hold. Pregnant at age thirty-four, she experienced depression. "I try to keep up a cheerful heart and when I am well, can succeed in doing so," she wrote. As the birth of the baby approached she confided, "I must only trust that all will turn out right," to which was added, "It looks rather dark at present." None of it was easy. She had in fact been married before and had buried her first child. Amid the barren Tehachapi Mountains of southern California her mettle was

12. Elizabeth Gardiner, *Golden Memories for My Family* (Augusta, ME: Kennebec Journal, 1960), 13. Elizabeth Gardiner was "recognised in the family as having many charming qualities but not always great accuracy of detail. This is shown in her book 'Golden Memories'" (Anna L. Shepley to Floyd Tomkins, March 1, 1965, Tomkins Papers, Gardiner Collection). See also Richards, *Stepping Westward,* 356; J. W. T. Gardiner to his mother, Emma Jane Tudor Gardiner, June 30, 1855, Gardiner Family Papers; Anne Hays Gardiner to Fenwick and Hallowell Gardiner, August 20, 1855, Gardiner Family Papers; and Anna L. Shepley to Floyd Tomkins, November 17, 1964, Tomkins Papers, General Theological Seminary, New York. In appreciation of her friendship, remarked a granddaughter, "the native women gave her the grass bowl used at my Father's baptism."

tested again in the perils of childbirth, this time in far more primitive surroundings. Time and again she thought of the comfort of the Gardiners' estate on the Kennebec River: "This morning when I was dressing, I was thinking how nice it would be, if I were dressing in my room at Oaklands, and could refresh myself by looking out at the beautiful Kennebec, and then go down stairs to that cool breakfast room and meet you all."[13] She was tired of wind, dust, and flaking bits of adobe.

Anne Hays's first marriage took place in 1841. She was nineteen, one month shy of her twentieth birthday. Her husband, Richard Henry West, was thirty-five. Like Tudor Gardiner, West was an officer in the First Dragoons; the two men knew each other, were friends, and served together briefly at the Carlisle Barracks. West's grandfather Edward Lloyd was "one of the principal leaders of the American Revolution in Maryland." West was also the nephew by marriage of Francis Scott Key and of Chief Justice Roger Brooke Taney. Despite his "good principles and most respectable family connections," West's father admitted ruefully in 1824 to his son's "lack of making a full confession" of certain "aberrations."[14] Whatever those irregularities were, in December of the following year West's resignation as a West Point cadet was accepted, and he was "discharged from the service of the United States." In 1837 he was again back in the army as an officer, this time in the First Dragoons. Less than a month after his marriage to Anne Hays, he was posted to Fort Leavenworth, Kansas Territory. In 1843 he became ill; a year later he died. Anne Hays knew tragedy in

13. Anne Hays Gardiner to Anne Richards, June 26, 1855, with regard to the Episcopal bishop of California, William Kip; to Fenwick and Hallowell Gardiner, August 20; to Eleanor Wheaton Hays, December 17, 1857; to Fenwick and Hallowell Gardiner, August 20, 1855; to Anne Richards, June 26, 1855; to Fenwick and Hallowell Gardiner, July 17, August 20, 1855, Gardiner Family Papers.

14. *Carlisle (PA) Herald and Expositor,* September 29, 1841; *American Volunteer,* September 30, 1841; Letta Brock West, *The West Family Register* (Washington, DC: W. F. Roberts, 1928), 231; Danny D. Smith to the author, December 11, 1995, Robert H. Gardiner Collection, Archives of the Episcopal Church, Austin, TX. Lloyd was an extremely wealthy legislator from Talbot County, Maryland, who kept a deer park, owned nearly four hundred slaves, raced horses at the Maryland Jockey Club, and had, besides his imposing plantation, "the Woodyard," a town house in Annapolis. The grandfather "lived a life of splendor and of lavish hospitality" (*Dictionary of American Biography,* s.v. "Lloyd, Edward"). In 1824 West applied to Secretary of War John C. Calhoun for admission to West Point; his application was signed by no fewer than ten Maryland congressmen. See "Delegation from Maryland to John Calhoun, January 22, 1824," in "Notes for Chapter 2: [Gardiner] Family History," by Danny D. Smith, Gardiner Collection; Richard W. West to James Barbour, February 11, 1824, in ibid.; and Military Academic Order, no. 33, in ibid.

the death of her child and then of her husband; she had also gone from riches to austerity. Later she would again cope with the death of another child and with the premature illness and death of her second husband.

Ten years after West's death in 1854, Anne Hays married Tudor Gardiner in St. Thomas Parish in Prince George, Maryland; he was thirty-seven, she thirty-three. As a youth Gardiner was well, if erratically, educated. After surviving a particularly mean and harsh family tutor in his childhood home in Maine, Tudor was sent for an undetermined number of years to "a school kept by a Mr. Putnam at Andover [Massachusetts]," and then for a short time to the famous Round Hill School in Northampton, where his elder brother Robert had preceded him. Adequate, even exceptional, education was a family emphasis. Round Hill had been founded in 1823 by George Bancroft and Joseph G. Cogswell. Its famous founders sought to constitute their school as a family. Boys came not only from New England and New York but also from Virginia and South Carolina. Education at Round Hill was very expensive. Its rolls were "a living register of John Adams's artificial aristocracy." After Round Hill, Tudor went first to Bowdoin College in 1832 for one year and then to Harvard College from 1833 to 1836.[15] Suddenly, in his senior year at Harvard, he decided to change yet again, this time to the Military Academy at West Point.

Was the switch voluntary? Probably not. More likely there was no longer money enough to continue expensive education in Cambridge. West Point would not have cost the family anything; in fact, as a cadet Gardiner would himself have been paid by the government. Later he settled in Massachusetts in the public school district that permitted his son Robert to attend famed Roxbury Latin School free of charge. Though the move to West Point meant that Tudor

15. A copy of the marriage certificate is in the Gardiner Papers. For discussion of Gardiner's family background, see T. A. Milford, "Advantage: The Gardiners and Anglo-America, 1750–1820" (PhD diss., Harvard University, 1999); R. H. Gardiner II and W. T. Gardiner, eds., *Early Recollections of Robert Hallowell Gardiner, 1782–1864* (Hallowell, ME: White and Horne, 1936), 189; and James McLachlan, *American Boarding Schools: A Historical Study* (New York: Charles Scribner's Sons, 1970), 90. McLachlan lists "Robert H. and F. Tudor Gardiner" instead of "J. Tudor Gardiner." Bancroft was a famous historian, author of the immensely popular *History of the United States,* 3 vols., 1834–1840, which was published in various editions. Round Hill School, while maintaining traditional emphasis on the classics, was reformist and had less rewards and punishments and more languages and sports (McLachlan, *American Boarding Schools,* 81). Round Hill cost $300 per year, $125 more than Harvard College. Tudor's father found the charges high (Gardiner and Gardiner, *Early Recollections,* 187, 90). See also *General Catalogue of Bowdoin College* (Brunswick, ME: Bowdoin College, 1950), 72; and George Thomas Little, *Genealogical and Family History of the State of Maine* (New York: Lewis Historical Publishing, 1909), 227.

began his college career over again—he would not graduate from West Point until June 16, 1840—the change was in the nick of time. By bad management and worse luck, Tudor's own father had lost a fortune. Twice mills operated by the eldest Gardiner burned down; in 1834 his house went up in flames. He lost the huge sum of fifty thousand dollars on the construction and operation of a paper mill. Repairs to docks on the Kennebec, speculations on steamboats, and purchases of lands for lumber operations contributed; inaccurate bookkeeping, the devastating depression of 1837, and, between 1833 and 1839, a general craze for enterprises of all sorts did the rest. After his home burned, Robert's grandfather proceeded to rebuild on an extravagant scale. Instead of a simpler homestead, he unwisely pooled his family's wish lists. The result was an elegant home he could not afford. To build it the grandfather hired architect Richard Upjohn, who put "turrets, battlements and buttresses" on a mansion encased in hammered stone. The eight thousand dollars originally planned for Oaklands grew to thirty-three thousand dollars, put politely, producing a shortfall in the cash flow. The grandfather admitted that the "most unfortunate expenditure was in my house... [which] gave a false impression of my property standing in the community and involved a very considerable addition to the family expense in order to keep up the establishment." In 1836 Robert's grandfather had to mortgage the property. By 1839 his name on the back of a note no longer carried any conviction whatsoever.[16]

Not surprisingly Tudor Gardiner feared extravagance. Of American settlers in California, he remarked in 1856, "Most of them... have been ruined by their own fault, borrowing money at enormous rates of interest (five percent a month is common) and then squandering [it] in gambling and all manner of extravagance." All this was not lost on his precocious son. At the time of Robert's birth, Tudor Gardiner had been on the frontier, in more or less constant military service, for fourteen years. Posted to Fort Leavenworth in 1841, he had thereafter been constantly on the move: in 1842 he had gone to Fort Gibson in present-day Oklahoma, then back to Leavenworth the following year, to Fort Washita in the Arkansas Territory from 1844 to 1846, was en route to Mexico in 1847, thence to Fort Snelling in 1849, to Fort Des Moines in 1850, and back to Snelling in 1851–1852. He had traversed a territory stretching from

16. Among others in Gardiner's class were future Union generals William T. Sherman, George H. Thomas, and his wife's cousin William Hays, as well as Confederate generals Richard S. Ewell and Bushrod R. Johnson (Gardiner and Gardiner, *Early Recollections,* 212–24).

the Mexican border to the upper reaches of the north-flowing Red River in present-day Minnesota, one of the three great continental river systems (the other two being the St. Lawrence and the Mississippi). In 1853 he spent a few months on detached service to map systematically and scientifically a route for the Northern Pacific Railroad. The able Isaac I. Stevens, a fellow army officer who had been appointed governor of the Washington Territory, oversaw Gardiner's scouting and surveying. It was a physically demanding, rugged existence. By June 17 Gardiner had to quit because of illness. He had suffered from exposure to rain and snow, likely hypothermia, possibly accompanied by intestinal disease and long hours in the saddle. He also had gout. Concluding sixteen years of hard duty, well might he exclaim, "My water proof cloak has been a treasure to me." But his troubles were not over. After an illness that sent him home in 1853, Gardiner embarked for his new post at Fort Tejon in California. At the time he was so sick he had to be carried on board the ship on a litter. Early in the voyage, the ship was wrecked. Saved by another vessel, Gardiner, for reasons that are unclear, was obliged to take command of the rescue ship and maintain discipline among starving passengers.[17] Fortunately, they were forced to put back into an eastern seaboard port. It was at that time that he met and then married Anne Hays West. Once again Gardiner set out for California, this time neither alone nor on a litter.

I have already noted Tudor's social and scientific interests. The Christian religion and its Anglican expression played an important part both in the elder Gardiner's personal and in his public life. In the summer of 1855 at Fort Tejon he took responsibility for Sunday services. When the Episcopal bishop, William Ingraham Kip, appointed another officer as lay reader and that officer proved incapable of reading in public, Tudor took over. "It was rather a trial at first[,] but I am getting used to it, and hope a blessing may rest upon it, to myself and to others," he wrote. And he preached as well. "I began with the bishop's sermon 'The time to serve God' which I thought appropriate for a beginning. . . .

17. J. W. T. Gardiner to Emma Jane Gardiner, May 31, 1856, Gardiner Family Papers; George W. Cullom, *Biographical Register of the Officers and Graduates of the United States Military Academy,* 3d ed. (Boston: Houghton Mifflin, 1891), 2:49, citation 1042. Francis Parkman in his journal of 1846, *The Oregon Trail* (Boston: Little, Brown, 1899), refers to "bodies of dragoons . . . [which] had passed up the Arkansas [River]" at the same time Gardiner was in the territory (287). See also Eugene V. Smalley, *History of the Northern Pacific Railroad* (New York: G. P. Putnam's Sons, 1883), 79. For the antisouthern politics of this enterprise, see ibid., 69–81. Tudor Gardiner to his sister, Eleanor, June 4, 1857, Gardiner Family Papers; "Gardiner Home Journal," *Kennebec (ME) Reporter,* October 4, 1879.

I trust it may be the means of good to some. I know that it has been a benefit to me." Even in the Episcopal Church where the right to preach was meted out grudgingly to the lower clergy and only in the late twentieth century to laity, laymen were beginning to take responsibility and fill such roles even if they were restricted to episcopally approved homilies. With the other denominations on the frontier, preaching by lay exhorters in the first half of the nineteenth century had become the rule rather than the exception. Their success was astonishing. Sometimes, however, the price was high: youthful exhorters' lack of preaching skills and challenges by their auditors respecting their authority often exacted a toll. Unprepared, unsettled, unsure of themselves, and unmarried, they suffered accordingly. Although lay participation and authority in the Episcopal Church never extended to the brigades of the ecclesiastically noncommissioned, an observant John Henry Newman remarked that lay authority was already too great in Anglican circles in the United States. Americans boast, he wrote, that "their Church is not like ours, enslaved to the civil power"; instead, their religious communities were the creatures of the laity, "and in a democracy what is that but the civil power in another shape?" One historian has noted that beginning in the 1850s with some remarkable changes, "even reversals[,] . . . laymen [were] replacing clergymen in spiritual leadership."[18] Though nothing could have been further from the ambition of Tudor Gardiner, the pattern of responsibility for worship and even preaching he maintained would be conveyed

18. Gardiner to his family, July 31, 1855, Gardiner Family Papers. He noted that "several of the soldiers joined in the responses" in the service of morning prayer according to the Book of Common Prayer. Until the 1979 Book of Common Prayer, a deacon was allowed to preach only "if he be admitted thereto by the Bishop" (Book of Common Prayer [1928], 533); not until 1967 was title 3, canon 25 changed to admit "godly persons, who are not Ministers of this Church, to make addresses in the Church, on special occasions" but nevertheless only with the bishop's permission (see Edwin A. White and Jackson A. Dyckman, *Annotated Constitution and Canons for the Government of the Protestant Episcopal Church in the United States of America, Otherwise Known as the Episcopal Church,* 2 vols. [New York: Seabury Press, 1981], 2:923). See also Nathan Hatch, *The Democratization of American Religion* (New Haven, CT: Yale University Press, 1989), 85–87; David Hackett Fischer, *Growing Old in America* (New York: Oxford University Press, 1977), 77–112; and Christine Leigh Heyrman, *Southern Cross: The Beginnings of the Bible Belt* (New York: Alfred A. Knopf, 1997), 94–98, 184, 213. Newman, "The Anglican Church," *British Critic and Quarterly Theological Review* 26 (1839), quoted in William R. Hutchison, "Discerning America," in *Between the Times: The Travail of the Protestant Establishment in America, 1900–1960,* by Hutchison (Cambridge: Cambridge University Press, 1989), 304; Kathryn Teresa Long, *The Revival of 1857–58* (New York: Oxford University Press, 1998), 72.

to his son. Robert in time would organize a veritable pride of Episcopal lay lions who in turn would lead his church along new frontiers.

As the result of his efforts in the Chumash area of southern California, Tudor Gardiner began to see some success. In 1856 he wrote optimistically to his family in Maine, "Our Indian war is over for the present, and I do not think it will be revived unless the whites commit more murders." Native Americans looked to the fort for protection, he said, and added that the "stories I have heard of outrages perpetrated by whites would be incredible were they not well vouched for." If only we would leave the Indians alone, he concluded, they would be naturally quiet. Later on at Fort Crook in Shasta County in northern California, his troops engaged the Pit River Indians in sporadic warfare. In the end, with the help of the wise Indian agent Edward A. Stevenson, peace was restored. When the news of bleeding Kansas reaching him, coupled with a breakdown of law in San Francisco, Tudor Gardiner judged that the future "of our country looks very gloomy."[19]

In appearance Robert's father was an even-featured, athletic man with a firm jaw and a prominent forehead. He was also introspective. There was something sad about the eyes. In the severe winter of 1846 he wrote to his older brother from the northwestern Arkansas border that his troop of dragoons had ridden across the Indian Territory from Fort Washita to Fort Gibson with the thermometer varying between zero and eight degrees. "My favorite castle in the air is the hope of some day or other being able to come and live among you all at home," he declared, "and be the oracle on the subject of trees, horses, and dogs." To which he added plaintively, "Will you have a spare room for a greyheaded old veteran with perhaps a leg or arm missing?"[20]

In 1859 Anne and Tudor Gardiner did in fact move back to Maine. That year another daughter was born (and died the following year); then in quick succession came three sons, two of them twins. On November 14, 1861, Tudor Gardiner, who had been on sick leave, retired from the army. But the trees, horses, and dogs would have to wait. On the same day he left the service, he became general superintendent of volunteer recruiting in Maine for the Union army. A year later he was back in uniform, this time recruiting troops as Maine's

    19. J. W. T. Gardiner to his family, July 13, 1856, Gardiner Family Papers, Oaklands, Gardiner, Maine.
    20. J. W. T. Gardiner to R. H. Gardiner II, January 22, 1846, Gardiner Family Papers.

assistant adjutant general, an assignment he held until the end of the war. At first he had the rank of major, then lieutenant colonel. Perhaps it was frustration with not being in the thick of it, perhaps the result of pain in his crippled legs, perhaps the experienced veteran wanted to impress volunteers with the seriousness of military life, but whatever the case, Gardiner proved to be a very tough recruiter. One hapless would-be soldier described Major Gardiner as a "full-blooded West Pointer" whose "red tape stuck out all over him like porcupine quills." He was accused of having "a crushing hatred for all volunteer troops," no sympathy when packs were too heavy, and little compassion when men fainted on dress parade, while "every detail under[went] the closest scrutiny." It was a recruit's complaint no doubt duplicated not a few times then and certainly since. In similar fashion his son Robert would require a great deal of himself and of others. Neither father nor son suffered fools gladly. Others described Tudor Gardiner differently, as having manners "gentle and polished; his heart kind and generous; his mind a storehouse of thought," and so on.[21] Again the same was true of his eldest son.

But Major Gardiner extended his contempt from slovenly behavior to the self-seeking politicians who were out to capitalize on the war. When, in 1864, fraud and kickbacks contaminated the system of producing quotas of draftees for the Union forces—mere names on paper without the recruits themselves—the estimable Gardiner refused to go along. He "was eloquent in his denunciation of the politician." But the price was replacement by a more pliable officer.[22] There was a sense in the family that the "rigid rules of Christian charity" demanded that they expose and counter the designs of wicked men. Robert Hallowell Gardiner III was similarly disposed, though more subtly and with respect to slothfulness rather than outright wickedness. If they could not reform the system in Maine, they could move on. In 1865 they did so, to Massachusetts, taking their values with them. Such was the atmosphere in the family of Anne and Tudor Gardiner: energy, perseverance, rectitude, religion, and of necessity, for they were poor, better financial management. But whatever their state, their son

21. During 1862–1863 Gardiner was assigned the same task of recruiting volunteers in Indianapolis. John West Haley, "Journal of John West Haley," quoted in Danny D. Smith, "Notices of John William Tudor Gardiner," Gardiner Collection; George W. Callum, "John W. T. Gardiner, Class of 1840," Gardiner Family Papers.

22. Louis Clinton Hatch, *Maine: A History*, 3 vols. (New York: American Historical Society, 1919), 2:502.

Robert was extremely fortunate in his parents. As he grew to maturity, his father detailed unusual responsibilities to him. Slowly, they increased, especially when the family fell on hard times. It was Robert who eventually took on financial and familial obligations for the welfare of his mother and his siblings. But that lay in the future.

In 1866 young Robert entered Massachusetts's famed Roxbury Latin School and spent the next four years at that second-oldest school in the United States. There his education rapidly expanded. Roxbury Latin was a free public school for those living in the area. It was just as well: the boy's parents had little or no money to spend on private education. Indeed, they had moved from Maine to 11 Hawes Street, Longwood, Brookline, for the express purpose of enlisting their son at the school. Besides being free, Roxbury Latin had a reputation for maintaining the highest academic standards. The school educated Eliots, Dudleys, Curtises, Lowells, Cabots, Cates, and scores of clergy, physicians, lawyers, and judges; among its more famous graduates in the colonial and national periods were Chief Justice of the Province of Massachusetts Paul Dudley and textile manufacturer and founder of the city of Lowell Francis Cabot Lowell. Inflated grading there was unknown. For his part, eleven-year-old Robert got the most out of the opportunity; he appreciated his teachers and spoke of them later as "having a deep thirst for truth and learning and a great capacity for instilling it in their pupils."[23]

His first year at the school was the last of headmaster Augustus H. Buck. Buck had created an intimate atmosphere. On the one hand, the headmaster was a strict disciplinarian who had no patience with slovenly work or with what he deemed mean and unworthy behavior. The unofficial motto of the school was "Work or quit." On the other hand, Buck also encouraged questions in his classroom, allowed dissent, and involved students imaginatively, giving them creative tasks in which they themselves, after due preparation, led their peers. The happy result was that they ended up teaching not only themselves but also each other. In addition, the school and its classes were small. There were sixty youngsters in six forms, or grades. While Roxbury Latin could boast only three teachers of academic courses, three more instructors, one each

23. Anna L. Shepley to Floyd Tomkins, February 16, 1965, Tomkins Papers; Robert quoted in F. Washington Jarvis, *Schola Illustris: The Roxbury Latin School, 1645–1995* (Boston: David R. Godine, 1995), 214.

for drawing, music, and military drill, made up the staff. The heavily classical curriculum would continue on after Buck himself left, ultimately to become professor of Greek at Boston University. Not only were Latin and Greek the mainstays of the place, but Headmaster Buck was also a German scholar. He introduced modern languages, then something of a novelty, into the curriculum.[24] Once again the promising Robert took full advantage of the changes.

Most of young Gardiner's time at Roxbury Latin was under the headmastership of William C. Collar, whose *First Year Latin* was regularly reissued from 1886 to 1918. The boy enjoyed the three primary teachers whom he gratefully named: "Dr. Collar, Mr. [Moses G.] Daniell, and Miss [Marzette Helen] Coburn."[25] Coburn was his French teacher. Since young Gardiner possessed both intelligence and a good ear, he picked up languages easily. Beginning with class 6, the lowest grade, and progressing to class 1, on a trimester basis, the boys were given a steady diet of Latin grammar and syntax accompanied in due course by Caesar's *Gallic War* (inevitable and boring), Ovid's *Metamorphoses*, Virgil's *Aeneid*, Sallust, Cicero, and Terrence. French began in the winter term of the second year, Greek in the fall term of the third year and ended in the last year with Homer's *Iliad*. Clearly, the best was kept until last. There was as well a heavy emphasis on Roman and Greek history, to the unfortunate exclusion of any other. With notable foresight, geography was required and taught in no less than eight terms. Arithmetic, fractions, the metric system, algebra, and geometry were regular fare. Trigonometry and physics could be elected. Botany, drawing, and music managed to squeeze their way in on occasion. Finally, along with the classics, English received the closest attention at Roxbury Latin; in every term spelling, writing, elocution, dictation, constant memorization of English poetry, and the works of Goldsmith, Milton, and Shakespeare were drummed into absorbent young minds. Throughout, the Red Queen's advice to Alice, "Look

24. Jarvis, *Schola Illustris,* 164–65. Buck took his pupils on hikes through the Boston area, stopping at places of historical interest where he would have those students whom he had assigned the task tell the others the historical significance of the place (Minutes of the Trustees, September 10, 1867, Archives of the Roxbury Latin School, West Roxbury, MA). See also *Catalogue of the Roxbury Latin School, 1871–72* (Boston Highlands: Macomber, Sexton, 1871), n.p. but overleaf; and Jarvis, *Schola Illustris,* 163, 194.

25. Collar, *The Beginner's Latin Book* (Boston: Ginn, 1886). Because Roxbury's "submaster," Moses G. Daniell, later revised the grammar, it was ultimately known as *Collar and Daniell's First Year Latin* and was used in schools all over the United States. Collar was headmaster from 1867 to 1907, Daniell was master from 1867 to 1884, and Coburn was a teacher from 1867 to 1874.

up, speak nicely, and don't twiddle your fingers all the time," was the order of the day at Roxbury Latin.

The school did its work well. Among Roxbury's graduates during Collar's administration and after were many notable educators: Edward H. Bradford, dean of the Harvard Medical School and a pioneer in orthopedic surgery; Shakespearean scholar George Lyman Kittredge; James Bryant Conant, later president of Harvard University; Remsen Ogilby, president of Trinity College in Hartford; Samuel Drury, rector of St. Paul's School in Concord, New Hampshire; Curtis W. Cate, founder and headmaster of the Cate School in southern California; Frederick Winsor, founder and headmaster of Middlesex School in Concord, Massachusetts; and many other academics.[26] As I shall show momentarily, Gardiner must be placed among them, for although his teaching career was short, his influence on education in the Episcopal Church was long and profound.

In 1869, for reasons unknown, Tudor and Anne Gardiner interrupted their eldest son's education at Roxbury Latin, uprooted the family yet again, and moved to Montreal. It was a curious decision. Robert was fourteen. No doubt leaving schoolmates in early adolescence was not easy. In Canada the family joined Tudor's brother, Robert Hallowell Gardiner II. This Gardiner had spent twenty years in the antebellum South. In Augusta, Georgia, Robert Gardiner II attempted to organize canals and railroads. He had married Sarah Fenwick Jones, a member of a prominent Savannah family whose ancestors had, with James Oglethorpe, founded the former colony. Robert and Sarah Gardiner were childless. Apparently, Tudor's brother Robert was ostracized in both North and South for divided loyalties, either real or imagined. Amid the growing sectional strife the couple found it difficult to continue to live anywhere in the United States and moved to England, though they ultimately settled in Canada.[27]

But that was not all. Robert Gardiner II, "Uncle Hal" to the family, was an irresponsible high stepper. He had charming manners and expensive tastes, quite the opposite of his brother, Tudor. Uncle Hal liked fine clothes and fashionable European watering holes. In addition, he squandered both his own inheritance from his father—such as it was—and that of his wife in questionable ventures,

26. Harry Lewis and David Mittell et al., comps., *Quinquennial Directory: The Roxbury Latin School, 1645–1995* (West Roxbury, MA: Publishing Concepts, 1995).

27. Henry Richards, *Ninety Years On* (Augusta, ME: Kennebec Journal Press, 1940), 228.

among which was a racecourse. He ended up encumbering the family's hapless Oaklands estate with no less than five mortgages.[28] Young Robert H. Gardiner III would later have his work cut out for him trying to generate sufficient income to save the family home from foreclosure by creditors. That Robert III did it at all remains something of a miracle of financial acumen. In the meantime, the contrast between the brothers, Uncle Hal and Tudor, or for that matter between Uncle Hal and his nephew, could not have been greater.

Young Robert gained insight into the effects of disorder and divisiveness not only from his father's political experience recruiting troops in Maine, not to mention the colonel's turbulent years in the West, but also from the plight of his aunt and uncle. He learned discipline at Roxbury Latin. In the meantime, in Canada in the late 1860s he attended a Canadian high school, from which he graduated in 1871 at age fifteen. Secondary education in Montreal was then divided into two systems: English-speaking Protestant and French-speaking Catholic. No doubt Robert went to an English-speaking school, though he could have managed the French equally well. While in Montreal he was also confirmed in the Anglican Church.[29]

In 1871 Tudor and Anne Gardiner along with their growing family reversed course and moved back to Boston. By this time the father's suffering from rheumatism and gout had greatly increased. Once again in Massachusetts, their eldest son was given an extra year of schooling at his beloved Roxbury Latin. In the fall of 1872 he entered Harvard College. There he performed outstandingly: during his freshman year he secured honors in Greek, took the highest second-year honors in both Greek and Latin, and in 1876 "was awarded the only Latin part at Commencement."[30] He graduated with honors, eighth out of a class of 142, and was second on the list of Phi Beta Kappa. His Harvard commencement was the first held in Sander's Theatre in Memorial Hall, just completed. Appropriately, Gardiner commemorated the faithfulness and service not only of the university's Civil War dead but of its present graduates and faculty as well.

Among his classmates at Harvard were eight former Roxbury Latin students, a good representation though by no means the largest. During their four years notable changes occurred at the college, some due to actions by the class itself,

28. Danny D. Smith to the author, October 16, 1999, Woolverton Correspondence, Gardiner Papers, Archives of the Episcopal Church, Austin, TX.
29. Draft of letter by Floyd Tomkins to Anna L. Shepley, February 24, 1965, Tomkins Papers.
30. Little, *Genealogical and Family History,* 227; Jarvis, *Schola Illustris,* 342–43.

others by the administration. Hazing of students was abolished, the famed humor
magazine the *Lampoon* was founded, and the elective system was introduced into
the curriculum. When Gardiner graduated on June 26, 1876, A.B., cum laude,
he was twenty years old. A photograph of him at this time shows an unpreten-
tiously dressed and self-contained youth with a prominent forehead, distinctive
nose, generous mouth, and firm chin. The eyes are reflective and keen, and
without his father's sadness. The picture is one of striking timelessness and
modernity, as if, despite the plastered hair, parted in the middle, he might quite
suddenly turn and speak in a way wholly congruent with the viewer's own time a
century and more later. The man's expression and his simple, subdued clothes
convey modesty. He was not a social lion or an academic show-off, nor were his
friendships reserved for the chosen few. One associate of later years recalled that
"he magnified his office, and so far as it could be done effaced himself."[31]

Generally, the class distinguished itself in later life. Besides Gardiner, there
were more than fifty lawyers, twenty-three businessmen, seventeen physicians,
ten professors, seven clergymen, and the rest in other occupations. Among the
more distinguished was Gardiner's close friend Francis Cabot Lowell, judge in
the U.S. district court and then of the circuit court, both of Massachusetts.
Lowell was also an overseer of Harvard College. The class of '76 produced
politicians and diplomats: Congressman Henry S. Boutell, later ambassador to
Switzerland, and Frederic J. Stimson, ambassador to Argentina and then to Brazil.
There were several academics: Charles Bell (chemistry), University of Minnesota; Adoniram J. Eaton (the classics), McGill University; Harold Ernst, M.D.
(bacteriology), Harvard Medical School; Benjamin O. Peirce, Harvard's Hollis
Professor of Mathematics; Percival Lowell, director of the Lowell Observatory
and professor of astronomy at MIT; Eugene Wambaugh, a longtime teacher at
the Harvard Law School; Charles Witherle, M.D. (neurology), Bowdoin College; and finally Charles F. Thwing, president of Western Reserve from 1890 to
1921, to name a few.[32]

Both then and later Gardiner was capable of prodigious amounts of detailed
work. He was patient and thorough: "On trains he always had his writing

31. *Harvard Class of 1876: Seventh Report of the Secretary* (Boston: Merrymount Press, 1901);
[George H. Randall], editorial in *Saint Andrew's Cross,* August 1924, 324. The school with the
most graduates at Harvard was Phillips Exeter Academy, followed by Dixwell's, Noble's, and the
Boston Latin School.

32. *Quinquennial Catalogue of Harvard University* (Cambridge, MA: Harvard University,
1930), 292–95.

materials and (keeping copies of his letter by use of carbon pads) he conducted much of his correspondence away from his office. He was never idle." And he was thorough. At Oaklands he caused a vista to be cut through the forest, "looking down the Kennebec River from his house. . . . [He said] that for two years he had planned that view before a tree was touched." The influential Bishop William Lawrence of Massachusetts noted as well that Gardiner always carefully thought out his duties "as a trustee of large properties" in the commonwealth and that he "followed these duties in an orderly way up to the limit of his time and ability; this done he left the rest to the Lord." In the interstices he did not fume or fuss or appear worried about how things were going. When some proposal in which he believed was rejected, he remained cool, refused to rattle the machinery or show scorn or bitterness, but smiled genially "as though he was saying to himself, 'Too bad you could not see the right [solution] of this matter. But I'll try again another day, and then perhaps you will.'"[33] At times such cheerful self-confidence was both annoying and puzzling to his adversaries. It carried with it a touch of disdain. Occasionally, he could sound rather ponderous.

Characteristically, he ignored the taste police and remained his own man. When others failed to act, he seized the initiative. He put his talents to good use and took it on himself to translate into English important articles published abroad in French, Latin, or Italian; his German was a bit weak. He wrote letters in Latin to Roman Catholic prelates and for that purpose mastered both ecclesiastical Greek and ecclesiastical Latin.[34] With the exception of his assistant, Ralph Brown, none at the American end of the movement for Christian reunion, and probably elsewhere for that matter, could equal him in quick and accurate translation. He often arbitrated between Protestant Ciceronian Latin as taught in English and American schools, on the one hand, and medieval Roman Catholic Latin employed by the church, on the other. He well knew that a wrong word might harm relations with the Vatican, though he was not above criticizing at least one Roman Catholic scholar as "perhaps sometimes a little careless." He went on to remark to his trusted friend Hughell Fosbroke, "My experience with ecclesiastical Latin has been somewhat limited, but I had not gathered the impression which Professor Merrill [of Harvard University] asserts so positively,

33. Ibid., 325, 327–29.
34. Richard H. Hale Jr., *Tercentenary History of the Roxbury Latin School, 1645–1945* (Cambridge, MA: Riverside Press, 1946), 21.

that, in using Latin, you must have a perfectly clear meaning in your mind."
Slyly, Gardiner added, "I thought ecclesiastical Latin was especially arranged to
conceal thought."[35] When it was necessary and even when it was not necessary,
he consulted his friends in the Harvard College language departments to make
sure he was correct in his own translations and in those of others.

In less consequential ways, Gardiner also showed forethought and independence, even nonconformity. When he found himself secure financially, he did
not take up the sports of the rich: in those days sailing, tennis, golf, or even
sportfishing. He preferred working on his farm. "I . . . don't take much interest,"
he wrote to schoolman Endicott Peabody, "in the modern craze for athletics."
Even when he became head of the Episcopal Church's organization for men
and boys, the Brotherhood of St. Andrew, he did not, as so many were doing at
the time, associate Christian faith with manly sports or muscular Christianity.
For Gardiner, Jesus went not to a gym class but to a cross. On the other hand,
when it came to the formality of the elite, he invariably conformed. Samuel
McCrea Cavert declared, "My picture of him is that of a quiet man, not given
to much speaking but giving an impression of great personal dignity, and decisive
without seeming aggressive." At one time Gardiner remarked self-deprecatingly
to an eminent theological professor, "I am only a plain layman, unadorned except
for a modest A.B. which is valued only as a record that a good many years ago I
had a certain capacity for passing examinations even on subjects of which I knew
very little." His daughter-in-law wrote of him: "He never wasted words on triv-
ialities that got nowhere. He reached people's hearts. He was apt to quote, 'The
less he said the more he heard, / Who would not be that wise old bird?'" The
daughter-in-law thought the little poem described Gardiner himself "in a
homespun way that he would have liked." Homespun or not, Bowen, the English butler, brought him lunch each day in his Pemberton Square law office.[36]

For the first two years out of college Robert Gardiner put to work his skill
with languages, honed at Roxbury Latin and Harvard. He taught French, first

35. Gardiner to Fosbroke, November 5, 1918, Robert H. Gardiner Correspondence, on
microfilm at the General Theological Seminary, New York.
36. Gardiner to Peabody, April 21, 1908, Endicott Peabody Papers, Archives of Groton
School, Groton, Mass.; Clifford Putney, *Muscular Christianity: Manhood and Sports in Protestant
America, 1880–1920* (Cambridge, MA: Harvard University Press, 2001); Cavert to Floyd Tomkins,
July 27, 1964, Tomkins Papers; Gardiner to William Adams Brown, July 2, 1917, Robert H. Gar-
diner Correspondence, 1910–1924, World Council of Churches, Geneva, Switzerland; E. Gardiner,
*Golden Memories,* 20; Tomkins-Shepley notes and correspondence, October 1964, Tomkins Papers.

at a newly chartered, in 1853, Episcopal college, DeVeaux, at Suspension Bridge (Niagara), New York, and then back at the Roxbury Latin School itself. In both places he was an "usher," or assistant teacher. It was not an uncommon way to begin a career for young men who had not made up their minds on a profession. As a teacher, he was kindly toward the boys but not reluctant to put his stamp on his charges. Without hesitation he instituted classroom prayers. "In front of him," on his first day teaching, recalled a family member, "was the traditional desk with its (then) traditional cane—for those were the days of corporal punishment in schools. Before speaking . . . he broke the cane and threw its pieces in the waste basket. Then 'We will say the Lord's Prayer,' [he] said. . . . A hand was raised, an impertinent voice called out, 'We don't pray here, mister.' Robert Gardiner . . . repeated 'We will say the Lord's Prayer,' and, so the story goes, they said it."[37] Nor did his persistence in what he saw as the welfare of Roxbury Latin cease with his teaching stint. In later life, from 1903 until his death in 1924, he played a central role in the school as a trustee and eventually in 1917 as president of the board of trustees. He interested himself in every aspect of the school's life and more than any other single person in his time ensured the continuance of its high academic reputation. He was alternately called "the savior of the School" and "the principal architect of the School's future."[38]

In 1878 Gardiner entered Harvard Law School where he stayed two years. The death of his father in September 1879 forced him to drop out in order to support his widowed mother, an unmarried sister, and adolescent twin brothers. Once again the family was in straitened circumstances, cut off from any funds. Incredibly enough, Anne's widow's pension for her husband's military service was not granted until 1887—and then it was through the perseverance of her eldest son.[39] He had in fact assumed the role of leader of the family. Gardiner went to work at the same time continuing his law studies. He did so under the direction of two remarkable men. The first, James J. Storrow, was regarded as one of the most discriminating attorneys of the day. He was also deemed "a

37. Laura E. Wiggins, "An Address Presented to Christ Church, Gardiner, Maine, on November 1, 1974," Tomkins Papers, 2. Wiggins incorrectly states that Gardiner was the headmaster of the Roxbury Latin School.

38. Jarvis, *Schola Illustris,* 389.

39. Tomkins Papers, file marked "John W. T. Gardiner, OWW 29587." The claim for a pension had been put in in 1880 by Anne Gardiner; depositions were made by R. H. Gardiner III in 1883 and 1884 ("Wid, 20,053"), but the pension was not approved until February 19, 1887.

thorough Episcopalian." The other, a family friend, William Minot, was a successful tax and real estate trust attorney in whose professional steps Gardiner followed. The young man was admitted to the Massachusetts bar in 1880. Thereafter he managed some private real estate trusts. He had entered a lucrative trade and before long was an occupant of Barristers' Hall, a prestigious office building close to the Old Courthouse on Pemberton Square where the Massachusetts Supreme Judicial Court met. Like his slightly older contemporary on that court in the 1890s, Judge Oliver Wendell Holmes, Gardiner was not content to accept the dignified though uninspired life that lay before him. But his independence was not at first apparent.

On June 23, 1881, Robert Gardiner and Alice Bangs were married at Trinity Church in Boston. To perform the ceremony the bride's family did not choose Phillips Brooks, then at the height of his fame, but the High Church bishop of Massachusetts, Benjamin Henry Paddock. Apparently the best, or so they thought, was none too good. Alice Bangs's family was old New England, older than the Gardiners; they had come over to Plymouth Plantation in 1623.[40] The Bangses had been yeomen farmers, merchants, and eventually lawyers and judges. Alice's father, Edward Bangs, had married Anne Outran Hodgkinson who, though English born, was a descendant of stern deputy governor Thomas Dudley, who was the father of Anne Bradstreet and one of the founders of Harvard College.[41] Edward Bangs was a prominent and successful Boston attorney and a graduate of Harvard College in the class of 1846.[42]

The Bangses' daughter, Alice, had a mind of her own. Against the wishes of the wealthy Bangs family, she insisted on marrying young Gardiner.[43] Despite his ability and prospects, the groom had no money. Alice was undeterred. The wedding came off. Subsequently, she took pride in the frugality they had to practice in their first years together. A woman of wit and gaiety, Alice Bangs Gardiner loved conversation and social life, including the gossip of Back Bay Boston. She had a light touch, sometimes humorous, sometimes poignant.

40. Dean Dudley, *History and Genealogy of the Bangs Family in America* (Wakefield, MA: A. W. Brownell, 1896), 9.

41. Samuel Eliot Morison, *Builders of the Bay Colony* (1930; reprint, Boston: Houghton Mifflin, 1958), 326. Dudley lived near the Harvard Yard in a "great house" that Governor John Winthrop thought too luxurious.

42. Dudley, *Bangs Family*, 264. Gardiner's mother-in-law, Anne Hodgkinson Bangs, was descended from Governor Thomas Hinckley of Plymouth Colony (1680s).

43. E. Gardiner, *Golden Memories*, 21.

Complementing her expansiveness was a lively intelligence, and if at times she did not want her husband to be quite so much the solid, resolute burgher, she respected him and made her own qualities complement rather than oppose his own. In addition, throughout the marriage she often expressed tender love for her grave and resolute husband. The Gardiners had five children: Robert Hallowell IV, born 1882; Alice, born 1885; Sylvester, born 1888 and died 1889; Anna Lowell, born 1890; and William Tudor, born 1892.

From the lessons of the frontier to famed Roxbury Latin, Harvard College, and beyond, Gardiner and his family saw education as an opportunity and an adventure. New Englanders esteemed, relished, and enjoyed scientific, literary, and religious learning. Whether he was under Headmasters Buck and Collar, a teacher in his own classroom at Roxbury Latin, during his stint at the Harvard Law School, or engaged with Storrow and Minot, he soaked up, sorted out, and stored what he had learned. Though his memory was excellent, he was not, like his contemporary Theodore Roosevelt, a prodigious cataloger of details. Rather, Gardiner grouped and then analyzed around a central and dominating set of beliefs what his mind had absorbed. That center was deeply Christian. It was also analytical, not so much of faith's relationship with science or culture as with theology itself. At the same time, through his expanding Christian commitment, he came to the conclusion that in the light of their profession of faith, church people ought to continue studying and deepening their knowledge of their heritage. To that end he maintained a lifelong interest in the ugly duckling of seminary curricula, Christian education. Gardiner wanted seminary students to trouble their heads about how best to get across to children and to mature laypeople the church's beliefs, especially the great doctrines but also its history. He thought no one-hour-a-week course on educational theory could replace hands-on knowledge by the clergy of Sunday-school materials. If the body of Christians was to be sound in heart and mind, it had to concentrate on what it taught at the parish level. Church people had to learn their Christian A, B, Cs. The tradition, Gardiner reasoned, must be passed along, practically, without delay, and not vamped up into something more decorous or new-fashioned. Second only to his contribution to the reunion of the churches, his labors in behalf of Christian education at all levels of the church emerge from the pages of the journals of the Episcopalians' General Conventions. Take away the integument of their parliamentary language and their dry-as-dust reports, in the second decade of the twentieth century an astonishing accomplishment shows its face. To say that religious education in this period had been "relegated to pious spinsters and teen-age girls," that it "was a decaying thing . . . moribund," as one historian has written, is to ignore the facts, not to have read the record, and, worse, to have failed to see how, beginning as far back as Catharine Beecher, many of those Episcopalian spinsters had proved to be tough cookies. In 1913 Gardiner wrote to his friend Archbishop Enos Nuttall of the West Indies that the church's General Board of Religious Education (GBRE) had been doing admirable work in the Sunday schools. It was not the half of it: "All the general educational efforts of the Church have now been consolidated under its management, and it will have charge . . . of [all] general parochial education in the way of Bible classes and the like, of religious education in the secondary schools and in the colleges and universities, and it will have a relation, the scope of which is not yet determined, to the matter of theological education."[44]

The lawyer from Maine did not himself write Sunday-school or any other lessons. But he took charge of the reform, saw to it that others wrote the materials, and carefully scouted the territory. Of course, such interests went as far back as his school-teaching days. There were more immediate antecedents, however: in 1904 he was appointed to the church's Joint Commission on Sunday School Instruction, in 1907 he was reappointed, and in the same year he was elected a trustee of the General Theological Seminary. The Joint Commission in 1907 urged the seminaries to give more adequate training to students in Christian education for the young and determined to send its report to every clergyman and Sunday-school superintendent in the church.[45] The report was accompanied by a sixty-page appendix of existing courses, statistics on teacher training, presentation aids, plans, problems, and a bibliography. The Joint Commission sought to strengthen the religious bond between "the teacher and his pupils" and in Gardinerian cadences to raise up "the honor and joy of helpfulness."[46]

44. George E. DeMille, *The Episcopal Church since 1900* (New York: Morehouse-Gorham, 1955), 125; Gardiner to Nuttall, December 13, 1913, Gardiner Correspondence. Beecher became an Episcopalian in early 1863 (Kathryn Kish Sklar, *Catharine Beecher: A Study in American Domesticity* [New Haven, CT: Yale University Press, 1973], 260–61). In that same year Beecher completed her influential *Religious Training of Children in the School, the Family, and the Church* (New York: Harper and Brothers, 1864); see pp. 248–49, 254–55, 282–83, 328–45, 364–77, 380–88 for her views of and involvement with Christian education in the Episcopal Church.

45. *Journal of the General Convention of 1904*, 205–6; *Journal of the General Convention of 1907*, v, 250, 469, 250.

46. *Report of the Joint Commission of the General Convention on Sunday School Instruction, 1907* (Philadelphia: George W. Jacobs, 1907), app. O, 71.

Those on the commission and, after 1910, on the reconstituted GBRE included men with whom Gardiner would work closely in the years to come: able bishops whom he respected, such as presiding bishop Ethelbert Talbot (central Pennsylvania), Chauncey Brewster (Connecticut), David H. Greer (New York), Thomas F. Gailor (Tennessee), and the future bishop of California, Edward L. Parsons; and laymen Nicholas Murray Butler, president of Columbia University, and George Wharton Pepper, a prolific member of the University of Pennsylvania law faculty and future U.S. senator. Gardiner had by 1910 become secretary to the new board. The GBRE was to have "executive powers to promote and develop and extend Sunday School work."[47]

At the convention of 1913 Gardiner presented the GBRE's report: twenty-six diocesan boards of Christian education had been formed; all but fourteen diocesan conventions had accepted the new responsibilities;[48] a standard Sunday-school curriculum had been formulated, together with a course of teacher training; a correspondence school for teachers had been organized; and a central office had been established under the leadership of William G. Gardner (no relation) as general secretary, Lester Bradner as director of parochial education, and a full-time traveling general secretary for collegiate education, Stanley Milbourne.

The parochial curriculum Bradner worked out with the aid of an advisory committee turned out to be immensely popular "because it emphasized the Church as an institution, but did not favor peculiar or extreme brands of churchmanship. . . . [It] combined information with social ideals, and a heavy Biblical content." By dint of its excellence, for the next forty years this curriculum dominated the church's Sunday schools. The GBRE in 1913 also reported that sixty thousand copies of five pamphlets on religious education had been mailed and a book of methods for promoting missions through education prepared. The convention considered the subject of Christian education so important that a joint session of the House of Bishops and the House of Deputies in

47. *Report of the Joint Commission of the General Convention on Sunday School Instruction, 1910* (Providence: F. H. Townsend, 1910), 25; *Journal of the General Convention of 1910,* 279.

48. There were sixty-eight dioceses in 1913 and twenty missionary districts in the American West; if twenty-six dioceses had Christian education departments and all but fourteen dioceses had signed on, that means 79 percent of the church was committed. However, if the twenty missionary districts are counted as "dioceses" for a total of eighty-eight, which seems unlikely, then, if there were only fourteen abstentions, 84 percent of the church was on board. Whichever way, the new curriculum was a resounding success. By 1919 eighty-nine dioceses had boards of religious education, a figure that shows as well Episcopal growth in the six-year period following 1913.

New York's Cathedral of St. John the Divine was addressed by two leading bishops, Gailor of Tennessee and Greer of New York, and by the youthful Pepper.[49]

Smack on the heels of the 1913 convention, Gardiner was made vice president of the GBRE. Since the church's presiding bishop was the president with responsibilities for the national church as well as for his own diocese, the man from Maine was left virtually in charge. He took it. Gardiner and his colleagues organized four educational departments: parochial education; secondary education, that is, Episcopal church schools; collegiate education, in which department Gardiner served directly; and theological education.[50] In 1916 the organizers announced that their "Christian Nurture Graded Material for Sunday School Lessons" series was now ready to use and had in fact already reached five hundred parochial teachers. In addition, in that same year the GBRE published and sent to all bishops, priests, and lay deputies a volume describing the plan and purpose of the board's efforts, *Church Ideals in Education.* In it they declared that educational leadership was "the most pressing need of the Church to-day," for in the past twenty-five years "the communicants of the Church have increased by 100 per cent"; that teacher training should take place at the parochial, diocesan, and provincial levels; that a unified educational program for the parish should pave the way for membership in the Brotherhood of St. Andrew and other youth organizations; and so on. *Church Ideals in Education* concluded with reports from the educational boards of the denomination's provinces. The report of the diocesan board of religious education in Maine had as its chairman the rector of Christ Church, Gardiner![51]

When Gardiner's first would-be biographer finished reading the report of the GBRE for 1919 in the *Journal for the General Convention* of that year, he penned to himself a note, "This is a fine example of Robert Gardiner's practical methods of getting things done." The accomplishments were inspiriting: a new parochial education series was now in use by many teachers throughout the church, a

---

49. Nelson Rollin Burr, *The Story of the Diocese of Connecticut* (Hartford, CT: Church Missions Publishing, 1962), 319–20; *Journal of the General Convention of 1913,* 299, 56.

50. Among Gardiner's immediate colleagues in the work were William E. Gardner, GBRE's general secretary; William Fellowes Morgan, treasurer; Charles H. Boynton, traveling secretary; and Lester Bradner, director of parochial education (see *Journal of the General Convention of 1916,* 224, app. 18, 527–30).

51. Episcopal Church, Department of Christian Education, *Church Ideals in Education* ([New York, 1916]), 21, 38–39, 81, 157, 211.

program of recruiting high school students for the ministry was being presented, and an inquiry into the education of all clergy ordained during the triennium 1916–1919 had been made, including "their age, residence, early training within or without the Church and their attainments in college and in Theological Seminary." After reporting that surveys of vacancies, ministerial needs, and clerical salaries in three of the church's provinces had been completed, Gardiner and his colleagues warned that in light of the revealed deficiencies, "the educational advance of the Church must be uneven and seriously hindered." The warning had been heeded, the report declared. As a result, at Cornell University, Iowa State College at Ames, and the Alabama Polytechnic Institute at Auburn chaplaincies had been started; significantly, all three institutions either had strong agricultural departments or were themselves agricultural and mechanical schools. Manifestly, the GBRE meant to broaden the makeup of the ministry to include candidates from nonelite, rural areas of the United States.[52]

At the same time the board authorized the National Student Youth Council, which aimed to "bind together all student Church organizations in colleges and universities, to give them a program of work and worship." Concern was manifested that the church had lost organizationally too many institutions of higher learning; it was directed that support be given "to enhance the University of the South, Kenyon and St. Stephen's which alone . . . remain . . . connected with the Church." Lest any elite Episcopalian boarding schools slip away, the GBRE secured the release of the longtime headmaster of St. Mark's School in Southboro, Massachusetts, the Reverend William Greenough Thayer. As well as being a respected headmaster, Thayer was an articulate and intellectually superior history teacher.[53] His job was to visit, survey, and consult with other headmasters and to "report to the Church the financial, educational, and religious condition of our Church Schools and to plan together how they may contribute best to the Church and Nation." For the rest, the report saw "experts and leaders" heaving into view, diocesan and parish "secretaries of education" appearing, councils and groups organizing "for study and experiment," the best "literature and materials" becoming available to the whole church, summer schools flourishing, and the publication of a monthly journal, the *Leader in Religious Edu-*

52. Floyd W. Tomkins, "*Journals of the General Conventions,* 1904, 1907, 1910, 1913, 1916, 1919, 1920," notebook 9, Tomkins Papers, 1919, n.p.; [Gardiner], "Report of the General Board of Religious Education," in *Journal of the General Convention of 1919,* 522–23.

53. McLachlan, *American Boarding Schools,* 263. Thayer sometimes put the fodder too high in the rack for his students, it was noted.

*cation.* Finally, and here Gardiner's hand is evident, the GBRE had "cooperated with other Communions and religious organizations: the Federal Council of Churches, the Council of Church Boards of Education, the College YMCA and YWCA, and the Sunday School Council." Best of all, everything had been accomplished "without deficit."[54] It was a nice touch, no doubt due to the wit and capacity of those pious spinsters.

54. Report, *Journal of 1919,* 523–24.

# Two

### ❧✝❧

# The Social Gospel's "Ham and Pickle Eaters"

## *Boston, 1893–1909*

Robert Gardiner blended an older Anglicanism with the Social Gospel and, increasingly, with worldwide catholicity. His family's allegiance to the colonial Episcopal Church in Maine led him at times to nostalgia for a bygone era when Gardiners ruled the roost. But that backward glance did not render him blind to the realities of his own day. As will become apparent, he combined his faith with democratic impulses and with an increasing concern for the plight of immigrants to America's booming industrial cities. Initially a hesitant, conservative Social Gospeler who believed that his church pretty much as it was could solve the problems of poverty, he increasingly moved in a more progressive direction toward additional legislative remedies. At the same time, his acceptance of underclass minorities broadened considerably and issued in a new ecumenism. His awareness of the interrelatedness of the reform institutions and aspirations of his day led him in fresh and imaginative directions. Such are the subjects of this chapter.

In February 1893, Robert Gardiner wrote a short piece for *My Neighbor,* the publication of Boston's Episcopal City Mission. The article was prompted by what, among other things, the author saw as the clergy's lack of missionary zeal with respect to poverty-stricken immigrants and their condition in the slums. In response to their plight in 1888, the City Mission had been founded by the clergy and laity of the Diocese of Massachusetts. They did so because "our methods of Church work are not equal to the emergencies of our time and place. . . . [T]he Clergy are overworked, the parishes undermanned in regard to workers . . . and the money is not forthcoming."[1] Despite the fact that Episcopal priests themselves wrote the remonstrance, Gardiner chose to ignore the diocese's recognition of the social crisis and reproved the ministers for slothfulness. In addition, he claimed that they lacked trust in their own laity. The clergy, he judged complacently, had not donned the hair shirt of suffering and pain. Worse, they were inept. The laity were indefectibly more skillful: "The efficiency of the layman in the service of Mammon is twice, at least, that of the clergy in the service of God." The layman in his workplace, Gardiner continued, had a chance to study people superior to himself: in the rush-hour rodeo, "he has to be through breakfast and at his work early in the morning, . . . put his whole strength into his work all day . . . till it is done." Work and not talk were his duty. By inference the clergyman was undisciplined; *feebleness* was the unfortunate word that Gardiner chose to describe ministerial behavior. The clergyman had no one to whom he must account and, as Gardiner reiterated the theme again in 1895, did not work hard enough.[2] If practice flagged behind the faith of either clergy or laity, to which ministers and to which laymen he was referring, he did not offer to say. Though his criticisms were probably taken to encourage less socially concerned priests to get a move on, they were cheap shots.

Of course, he recognized exceptions to clerical sloth and ineptitude: "The greatest inspiration [to others] of Phillips Brooks' life was," he averred, "the sight of the eager gladness with which he gave himself to his work, utterly, without stint or thought of self." In the cult of activism, young men such as Gardiner were full of combat and enthusiasm to fight for the good. Clergy, he declared, are "put there to set forth in that neighborhood the splendor of God's everlasting Gospel." Reverting to military images, the thirty-seven-year-old then demanded that the minister preach a crusade, drill his company, "charge the enemy at the head of his troops." If he does so, "he will soon find he will have to run faster to keep his heels out of the way of his soldiers."[3] With time, such censoriousness would abate.

---

1. Quoted in David Dillon, "Mission in an Urban Diocese," in *The Episcopal Diocese of Massachusetts, 1784–1984,* edited by Mark J. Duffy (Boston: Episcopal Diocese of Massachusetts, 1984), 30.

2. Gardiner, "The Church's Work for Laymen," *My Neighbor* 2:4 (February 1893): 7; Gardiner, "The Future of the Episcopal City Mission," *My Neighbor* 4:7 (May 1895): 9.

3. Gardiner, "Church's Work," 10; Arthur Mann, *Yankee Reformers in the Urban Age* (Cambridge, MA: Harvard University Press, Belknap Press, 1954), 234; Gardiner, "Church's Work," 8.

In the meantime, Gardiner networked. At first in the 1880s and '90s he did so locally. As a Christian layman he began naturally enough with the parish church. In fact, he founded one. In 1882 the Gardiners moved out of Boston's inner city. Like the rest of the elite, they did not want the poor in their backyard. Although the Yankees' descendants were remarkably successful in preserving their hold over Beacon Hill and the fashionable Back Bay area, one commentator notes that many bought country residences in the townships of Brookline and Longwood and in "the sylvan community" of Chestnut Hill where they would not have to rub elbows with immigrants.[4] The Gardiners chose Chestnut Hill and built a house on land owned by John Lowell, an overseer of Harvard College and a judge on the U.S. circuit court. Other prominent families, Coolidges, Saltonstalls, Lees, and Lymans, were likewise midcentury settlers in that arboreal refuge. Nearby was a Unitarian chapel that had fallen into disuse. When in 1890 the judge's mother, Katharine Bigelow Lowell, gave the land and building to be an Episcopal parish incorporated under the Diocese of Massachusetts, Gardiner and others, including Judge Lowell, stepped up to the plate. They named their parish the Church of the Redeemer. At the time some fifty or sixty people attended services.[5] For rector, they called upon Dr. Henry S. Nash, professor of the New Testament at the Episcopal Theological School in Cambridge. They were not about to open themselves to the possibility of either disappointment or boredom: Nash, who had a homely face, was a "deeply spiritual character, with the added gift of a marvelous sense of humor." He was a social reformer and by all accounts a superb preacher: "I heard him preach once when I was a boy at Groton [School]," wrote John Richards. "I still remember that his was one of the great sermons I have heard."[6] Nash accepted and remained rector until 1903, all the while teaching at the Episcopal Theological School.

4. Betty G. Farrell, *Elite Families: Class and Power in Nineteenth-Century Boston* (Albany: SUNY Press, 1993), 30.

5. Philip E. Burnham and Donald E. Bitsberger, "Church of the Redeemer, Chestnut Hill," in *Episcopal Diocese,* edited by Duffy, 482; Mary Lee, *A History of the Chestnut Hill Chapel* (Boston: History Commission of the First Church of Chestnut Hill, 1937), 37. For these and other figures, see notes, Church of the Redeemer folder, Floyd Tomkins Papers, Archives of the Episcopal Church, Austin, TX.

6. Mrs. F. Gorham Brigham, "The Church of the Redeemer," Church of the Redeemer folder, Tomkins Papers. For the Church Social Union, Nash wrote tracts: *Is There a Social Question for America?* and *The Reality of the Social Problem;* see *Publications of the Church Social Union* (Boston: Office of the Secretary, 1897), 22, 23. For Nash's preaching, see Richards to Floyd Tomkins, March 4, 1965, Tomkins Papers.

In the same month the church was donated, September 1890, Gardiner was sworn in as both warden and treasurer. He took entire charge of the altar, preparing it for worship each Sunday, even cutting the bread for the Holy Communion—into squares without crusts. In addition, very early Sunday mornings he drove his horse and carriage to Cambridge to pick up Dr. Nash. After the services he drove Nash home. Thereafter, in a steadily increasing list of appointments to influential local positions, Gardiner served both his community and his diocese. In the process he turned his attention to the greater metropolitan area of Boston. At the same time he was establishing himself as an attorney. Concurrently, he became concerned for the social and religious welfare of the less fortunate. Gardiner was also one of the founders and then chairman of the executive committee of the Republican Club of Massachusetts, vice president of the Massachusetts branch of the National Consumers League, and president of the local Brotherhood Council of Boston. In his legal and business activities he was a director of the Arlington Mills and the Webster and Atlas National Bank and trustee of the Boston Real Estate Trust and the Hotel Touraine Trust, to which he later added a directorship in the Tampa Electric Company.[7] Managing trusts left him free to pursue other interests, among them reform measures. As already described, in 1917 he saved his beloved Roxbury Latin School from extinction. Overall, he represented the major change in the United States from traditional farming and mercantile trading to acting as an attorney for the newer profitable businesses such as banks, railroads, and utilities. From that base he might, as others did, have entered politics. He did not. Instead, it was to his church that he gave his greatest attention. In the course of the decade of the 1890s he became a member of the Standing Committee of the Diocese of Massachusetts, treasurer of the Episcopal City Mission, and treasurer of the Diocesan Board of Missions for Massachusetts and later for Maine. After 1900, when he moved his legal residence to Maine, he was seven times elected a lay deputy to the Episcopal Church's triennial General Convention. At Christ Church, Gardiner, he served as either junior or senior warden from 1901 to 1924.[8] In those years he continued to maintain a home and a law office in Boston.

7. *Boston Evening Transcript,* October 3, 1904; *Churchman* (Milwaukee), October 8, 1904; obituary for Gardiner, *The Episcopal Church Annual, 1925* (New York: Church Pension Fund, 1925), 82–83.

8. John Richards, *A Continuation of the Story of Christ Church* (Augusta, ME: Kennebec Journal, 1962), in *Christ Church, Gardiner, Maine* (Gardiner, ME: Reporter-Journal Press, 1893), 54–59.

If Gardiner worked hard for the parish churches to which he belonged, he was also quite possessive of them. He came by it naturally. Beginning in colonial times with Dr. Silvester Gardiner, the leader of the family regularly played first fiddle at Christ Church. When the parish was without a rector his grandfather, the first Robert Hallowell Gardiner, had conducted services himself, organized and superintended the Sunday school, guaranteed half of the cost of a new building, and gave the organ "and five or six tombs which he had built." He also donated the park fronting the church. The Gardiners had an almost baronial feeling of ownership. For Robert Hallowell Gardiner III, shared kinship and a sense of place had become fundamental. At Christ Church on May 30, 1920, in an anniversary address of welcome at the centennial celebration of the Diocese of Maine, he remarked on his own "deep and sacred associations which have centered in this city and its venerable Church for four generations before me." In 1754 his grandfather's grandfather, he related, had "acquired individual title to the territory... [and] set about establishing the Church." On his entailed estate—which included the parish—the old Silvester Gardiner had sought to perpetuate a system of tenants "under the benevolent rule of his descendants, submitting themselves to the Rector and Squire for the time being, ordering themselves lowly and reverently to all their betters."[9] Not surprisingly a Loyalist, in 1776 the doctor lost his fortune and fled to England.

"With all my heart," continued Robert Gardiner a century and a half later in the address, "I rejoice that his dream failed of fulfillment," that the entail was broken, and that "the new spirit then beginning to stir in America" abolished class distinctions. His ancestor's dream was, he surmised, contrary "to that true democracy which Christ came to establish." Yet the great-grandson found a sense of responsibility in the old order that "we are in danger of losing, now that entrance into the ranks of privilege comes largely from the acquisition of wealth." If the old order evinced an icy charity in which the poor man gathered the crumbs from the rich man's table, "even that was better than the [present] bitter struggle between rich and poor," between capital and labor, in which each person tries "to wrest from the other as much more as possible."[10] Although some nostalgia remained for the old rural squirearchy, Robert Gardiner crafted a broader ideological perspective. He had, in fact, educated himself in the urban

---

9. [Marguerite Ogden, ed.], *One Hundredth Anniversary of the Diocese of Maine, 1820–1920* (Boston: Merrymount Press, 1920), 60–62; Gardiner, "Address of Welcome," in ibid., 107, 109.
10. Gardiner, "Address of Welcome," 110.

affairs of industrial capitalism. And he read both sides, including Mary Simk-hovitch's *City Workers' World in America* (1917) and John Leitch's *Story of Industrial Democracy* (1919).

He believed in the principle of noblesse oblige. It was an expression that he himself used without apology. To be sure, it was not his only motivation, but it served to sharpen an innate sense of responsibility as well as command. As a result he was early on tucked in with some strange political bedfellows. Gardiner in fact became treasurer of the Church Social Union. That very liberal organization had been founded by socialist Congregational minister turned Episcopalian W. D. P. Bliss and by Vida Dutton Scudder of Wellesley College. Bliss, a some-time Marxist, used his membership in the Socialist Labor Party and its *Workmen's Advocate* "to recruit members for his Society of Christian Socialists." Scudder kept a red flag draped over her prie-dieu and wanted to combine Marxism and Christianity. As she explained: "The air was full of a ferment of thought in Boston in the Nineties." Scudder first joined Bliss's Church of the Carpenter: "Robert Woods, Harry Lloyd, and Mr. [George] McNeill and I were of this congregation. Not only did we worship together, singing with special zeal the Magnificat, but we had wonderful suppers, true agape, when . . . we feasted on ham and pickles in hope of imminent revolution."[11] The Church Social Union's executive committee boasted the pioneer in institutional church building, W. S. Rainsford of St. George's Church in New York City; Richard T. Ely, the outspoken progressive who was in favor of the socialization of national monopolies on natural resources;[12] and Gardiner's own rector, Professor Nash. Bishop Frederick Dan Huntington was president of the Church Social Union as well as president of the Church Association for the Advancement of the Interest of Labor (1887).[13] George Hodges, dean of the Episcopal Theological School, was secretary, while Bliss became its traveling gadfly. Gardiner joined these ham-and-pickle eaters with their red flags. But he was not a Marxist, and it is doubtful that he ever read Karl Marx's writings.

11. Jacob H. Dorn, "'The Oldest and Youngest of the Idealistic Forces at Work in Our Civilization': Encounters between Christianity and Socialism," in *Socialism and Christianity in Early 20th Century America,* edited by Jacob H. Dorn (Westport, CT: Greenwood Press, 1998), 5; Scudder, *On Journey* (New York: E. P. Dutton, 1937), 165.

12. Robert T. Handy, "Editor's Introduction," *The Social Gospel* (New York: Oxford University Press, 1966), 210.

13. W. D. P. Bliss, ed., *The New Encyclopedia of Social Reform* (New York: Funk and Wag-nalls, 1908), s.v. "Church Association for the Advancement of the Interests of Labor."

In their ongoing effort to tidy up the past, historians of the Progressive Era have by and large noted four, and possibly no less than five, different attitudes within the larger Christian ethos of those in the United States concerned with "social Christianity." First, there were the radical Marxist socialists who sought the reconstruction of society from the ground up through public ownership of the means of production (Bliss and Scudder among others in the Episcopal Church).

Second came the theologically liberal progressives, metaphysical idealists who saw God as immanent in the unfolding historical, cultural, and social process. They believed that science and philosophy were normative for theology and, most important as it turned out, for biblical criticism. They sought to bring about gradual social and economic change through education and through influencing legislation (Ely and Huntington in the Episcopal Church, George A. Gordon and Washington Gladden among the Congregational Churches, and many others). They were in favor of public ownership of some industries and means of production.

Third, there were the conservatives who sought primarily the regeneration not just of individuals but of the church itself through mission and settlement work.[14] Here was probably the largest group of reformers, and the early Gardiner is to be found among them. The group also included Henry M. Torbert, Charles Henry Brent, and Gardiner's older contemporary in the Episcopal Church, William Reed Huntington; there were others, notably Presbyterian Arthur Judson Brown and Methodist John R. Mott.[15] They went along with moderate biblical criticism such as that of Charles A. Briggs but were more churchly in their theology than the liberals: the *church,* not efforts at lobbying the halls of Congress for social legislation, would advance the kingdom of God.

Finally, there were those on the Right, two major groups: the so-called higher-life theologians, on the one hand, and most recently the "purity reformers," on the other.[16] The first, the higher-life people, shared many social aspirations

14. I follow here Robert T. Handy, *Undermined Establishment: Church-State in America, 1880–1920* (Princeton, NJ: Princeton University Press, 1991).

15. See Robert T. Handy, *A Christian America: Protestant Hopes and Historical Realities* (New York: Oxford University Press, 1971), esp. 128–39.

16. Grant Wacker, "The Holy Spirit and the Spirit of the Age in American Protestantism, 1880–1920," *Journal of American History* 72:1 (June 1985): 45–62; Gaines M. Foster, "Conservative Social Christianity, the Law, and Personal Morality: Wilbur F. Crafts in Washington," *Church History* 71:4 (December 2002): 799–801.

and attitudes with liberal theologians such as institutional designs "to meet the medical, educational, recreational, and spiritual needs of the urban poor." They may be distinguished from the conservative church-related reformers by their emphasis on individual conversion, baptism by the Holy Spirit, faith healing, anticipation of the Second Coming of Christ, and the authority of religious experience apart from the sacraments and even from scripture and the creeds. Prominent among many were Dwight L. Moody, Baptist Adoniram Judson Gordon, and Congregationalists Reuben Archer Torrey and Gardiner's friend the anti-creedal Newman Smyth.[17] Smyth plays a prominent role in this study. Though the liberal theologians and their conservative allies were later to part company with the higher-life theologians into irreconcilable modernist and Fundamentalist camps, early on they often shared eschatological views and for a while swam together in the mainstream. Gardiner at times seemed to straddle the two groups. A short while before his death in 1924, he thought he "was degenerating into rank modernism," as he wrote a friend, and that it "was rather amusing, for I am supposed on the whole to stand for good old-fashioned conservatism."[18]

Somewhat different from the higher-life people were the purity reformers, who bypassed emphasis on individual conversion. Whereas the purity reformers gave lip service to social legislation, they were primarily interested in stopping Sabbath breaking, gambling, divorce, intemperance, drug abuse, and the mailing of obscene materials.[19] Notable among the purity reformers were Wilbur Crafts, Episcopalian canon at the Cathedral of St. John the Divine in New York; Canon William Chase; Josephine C. Bateham of the Department of Sabbath Observance of the Women's Christian Temperance Union; Senator Henry W. Blair of New Hampshire; and Craft's own Reform Bureau. Members of the Knights of Labor, the American Sabbath Union, the National Reform Association, the American Anti-Saloon League, the Christian Endeavor Society, and others now seem in many cases to have been ahead of their time. In such causes as drug (opium) abuse, Episcopal bishop in the Philippines Charles Henry Brent, who will figure prominently in this account, gave considerable time as a presidential appointee to the Opium Commission, initiating the movement to control international

17. Wacker, "Holy Spirit," 51, 56, 57.
18. Phillips Brooks preached for Moody in the latter's revival of 1877 (A. V. G. Allen, *Phillips Brooks, 1835–1893,* 2 vols. [New York: E. P. Dutton, 1900], 1:325–26); Gardiner to Canon H. N. Bate, April 24, 1924, Robert H. Gardiner Correspondence, 1910–1924, World Council of Churches, Geneva, Switzerland.
19. Foster, "Conservative Social Christianity," 807–11.

opium distribution and proposing to Theodore Roosevelt the convening of the Opium Conference held in 1907 in Shanghai, China. At the same time attempts to stop violence and pornography in the movies greatly concerned Canon William Chase. Then, last but by no means least, came the Pentecostals in the first decade of the twentieth century. Gardiner, as we shall see, saw them as an important part of the developing American religious scene, and, though he was unable to follow up sufficiently, the mere fact of his attention is noteworthy. To what extent may Pentecostals be seen as part of the increasingly complex "social Christianity" of the Progressive Era? Certainly, Pentecostal community building and fellow feeling among that growing population should lead to some subtle and nuanced studies of the kind of social amelioration they achieved.

All the groups here too tidily and briefly enumerated believed in the coming rule of the kingdom of God. For his part Gardiner, as I shall show, began among the conservatives and moved to a more progressive stance. At the same time he rubbed elbows with the Marxists. There is no evidence that he ever took up the causes of the purity reformers, nor did he himself ever engage in the kind of lobbying the halls of legislatures and of Congress that, albeit for very different ends, the purity people shared with the progressives. But Gardiner also parted company with other conservatives, so called, when they emphasized individual conversion. For him, as we shall see, whatever happened to the individual came as a result of involvement in and appreciation of the corporate character of the church. He was a church reformer first, a social reformer second. Put differently and more accurately, he wanted to reform the church in order that it might become a leaven for the advancement of the kingdom of God in human affairs. But the kingdom idea was to be a true progression and not a cloak for maintaining the status quo. Gardiner was well aware, as he wrote Frederick Lynch of the Federal Council of Churches, that the lay delegates to the Episcopal Church's General Convention were hardly representative. They "are taken from older men, who are more rigid and more deeply convinced of the divine right of property."[20] Nor in his desire for fairness was he hoping for the restoration of past glories so much as looking to unanticipated future improvements in equity. Eschatology rather than nostalgia motivated him. In addition, Gardiner's religious spirit, his personal anchorage in prayer and sacrament, was basic to his conviction that the church must play an increasingly ameliorating role in human affairs. Histo-

20. Gardiner to Lynch, October 6, 1922, Gardiner Correspondence. The Federal Council of Churches had just issued a report of the steel strike that was critical of the steel companies.

rians neglect aspects of personal religion in the Progressive Era and elsewhere to their readers' loss. Among these Progressives, personal piety and social outreach went hand in hand to an extent that can no longer be assumed.

Because of this combination of characteristics across the Episcopalian spectrum, and no doubt elsewhere, political and ideological divisions did not seem to matter that much. At least for a while in the 1890s, they were less acute. Improbable as it may seem, at the time Republicans like Gardiner cheerfully rubbed elbows with leftist radicals and Marxists. Future fault lines of course existed, and in the United States they were partly political and partly methodological. Although they were still there in the early Progressive Era, the contiguous seismic religious plates were not in violent opposition. In the Church of England potential divisions among social Christians were more along churchmanship lines, between the followers of Arnold, Stanley, Maurice, Freemantle, and other so-called broad churchmen, on the one hand, and the Anglo-Catholics of St. Matthew's Guild on the other.[21] In the American Episcopal Church this particular disjunction was less prominent, if it existed at all. Rather, a division—in this case, really, a difference—manifested itself between the more analytical social-science orientation of Robert A. Woods and the practical and theological solicitudes of Henry M. Torbert and his assistant, Charles Henry Brent, both of St. Stephen's Church in Boston, of which Woods was a member. This distinction appears to have cut across the four or five Social Gospel categories described by present-day historians.

At St. Stephen's Church and among their allies in the Church Social Union, the word was practical amelioration, including legislative action in behalf of the destitute. Somewhere rattling around in the more political middle between the parish priests and the social scientists was W. D. P. Bliss. Taken together, Boston's Episcopalian reformers and their friends in the Social Union (Bliss, Scudder, Huntington, Ely, Rainsford, Torbert, Brent, and Gardiner) constituted an interesting and not always stable mix. The answer to the question of how and why that particular goulash, containing as it did such a variety of opinions, still proved nourishing lies in part with the Christian principles that constituted its basic stock. As participants expressed their concerns in Christian language and unsentimentally provided the nutriment of social action, they were determined to make a difference in the lives of those who suffered as a result of immigration

21. Christopher Oldstone-Moore, "The Forgotten Origins of the Ecumenical Movement in England: The Grindelwald Conferences, 1892–95," *Church History* 70:1 (March 2001): 78.

and the Industrial Revolution. How successful they were is another matter. The intent was there, and both unselfishly and selfishly they put a great deal of time into implementing their concerns. In the process, Christian principles made other differences pale. For a time at least, the tent ropes, to change the metaphor, of the Church Social Union were long enough to include people with different solutions to urban industrial "problems."

In the broader Episcopal Church there was a similar reluctance to pronounce who was right and who was wrong. Bishop Franklin Spencer Spaulding of Utah argued openly for socialism, for the abolition of capital, for common ownership and operation of the materials of production, for equal shares of the common dividend, and for human rights before property rights. Though often engaged in lively debate, Spaulding "did not repel those who did not agree with him." Similarly, though more confrontational, was the Reverend Irwin St. John Tucker, a distant cousin of Gardiner, who was editor of the *Christian Socialist.* That journal was underwritten by the wealthy Episcopal layman William H. Cochran, who believed that "the highest duty of the millionaire is to make the future rise of Millionaires impossible." A high churchman and graduate of the General Theological Seminary then "deeply tinged with red," Tucker immersed himself in the Hebrew prophets, the church fathers, and Karl Marx. He was joined in the small, noisy, and politically radical Christian Socialist League (1911) by low churchmen, among whom was Brooklyn's John Howard Melish.[22] For his part, Gardiner wished to convert individuals to the cause of social betterment for the poor. He did not mount a campaign to aid progressive legislation or to bring on a revolution. Differences of opinion failed to rupture common efforts, however.

One way or another all saw the need first of all to educate their own kind. "In true Boston fashion," remarked Scudder, "our chief activity was the publication of pamphlets, some of them mighty good." The pamphlets, of course, were not written for the immigrants but by white Anglo-Saxon reformers from the Back Bay and the suburbs for their foot-dragging brothers and sisters. All the authors supported the settlement-house movement in the church. All read Jane Addams's *Spirit of Youth and the City Street* (1910). Despite their differences, members of the Church Social Union acted in concert as the educational wing

22. John R. Sillito, "'A Spiritual and Moral Socialism': Franklin Spencer Spaulding and Christian Socialism, 1901–1914," in *Socialism and Christianity*, edited by J. H. Dorn, 117, 112, 130 (quoting Charles Lewis Slattery); Jacob H. Dorn, "'Not a Substitute for Religion, but a Means of Fulfilling It': The Sacramental Socialism of Irwin St. John Tucker," in ibid., 144–45.

of the church's larger charitable efforts. As has been perceived elsewhere, "Bliss and his co-workers hoped to put an end to the squabbling among contending social reformers, and unite them in one grand Christian socialist movement."[23] I will have more to say about theology in a subsequent chapter, but it is enough to point out now that Scudder, Bliss, and Gardiner in particular looked to the theological inspiration, as we shall see, of the English High Church bishop Charles Gore, whose emphasis on the Incarnation was to have a long reach. And then, of course, they inspired each other.

But first what were the "hidden" motives of these reformers? Were they afraid of moral decay? Of the loss of their own prestige and power through anarchy and even revolution? "The possibility exists," maintains one historian, "that the ministerial efforts to improve slum life and eradicate immorality were simply palliatives that prevented meaningful reform and merely assuaged the guilt of those who benefited from the new materialism." Were they afraid of the new immigrants and their strange languages and cultures? Certainly, the betterment of those forced to dwell in slums was not unconnected with their "Americanization." One historian has recently pointed to the connection between nostalgia for a bygone New England heritage and its accompanying nativism with the settlement-house movement specifically in mind. Interpretations "of a fabled Puritan/Yankee past consign[ed] ethnics to the cultural periphery," he contends, portraying Irish, Italian, French Canadian, and Portuguese immigrants "either as underminers or... as passive recipients of the real New England's authentic traditions." Gardiner himself declared that "the Church needs a great congress of her laymen of all classes... in a common effort to realize their responsibility as the backbone of the Church." So far so good. He then went on to call upon his compatriots "to shape the character and destiny of our hundreds of immigrants."[24] It did not occur to him or to many others at the time that those same immigrants would want to shape their own character and destiny in the free land to which they had come. Indeed, they had grabbed the reins of their own buggies already. But then again, was "Americanization" such a bad idea? Many older Americans did and do rejoice to see representatives of minorities step up

23. Scudder, *On Journey,* 168; Mann, *Yankee Reformers,* 92.
24. Jack Tager, "Social Reform in Boston," in *Massachusetts in the Gilded Age,* edited by Jack Tager and John Ifkovic (Amherst: University of Massachusetts Press, 1985), 197; Joseph A. Conforti, *Imagining New England: Exploration of Regional Identity from the Pilgrims to the Mid-Twentieth Century* (Chapel Hill: University of North Carolina Press, 2001), 248–54, esp. 252–53, 315; Gardiner, editorial in *St. Andrew's Cross,* October 1907, 6.

to the national lectern with a resolute eye and confident syntax, whether accented or not, and, knowing very well the law, deliver their lines accordingly.

Christian motives in the settlement movement must not be brushed aside or ignored.[25] The possibility and surely the probability exist that these "Social Gospelers" had specifically Christian reasons for doing what they did and that behind the political realities with which they wrestled and the other motives that accompanied them lay an explicit and shared faith on the basis of which they acted as they did. By the end of the century, especially among clergy, academics, and lawyers, a dissatisfaction arose with the inherited wisdom that their primary function was "still to rationalize, uphold, and conserve the existing order of things." However much they were needed and however much their services were paid for by the captains of industry, lawyers like Gardiner were trained to see "things with more disinterested eyes than [the businessmen] did." At that time lawyers and Christian leaders in the United States were traditionally called upon to set public agendas, speak out on moral issues, and generally be the wise men of the community. Such men did not want to be called, as Gardiner's friend Francis Lynde Stetson was, "the attorney general of J. P. Morgan."[26] Valuing their independence, both men turned to public service. The arena in which they performed that service was the church. Did they do so simply to satisfy a personal need for applause? Or did they sense that while in the new century knowledge came, wisdom lingered?

There were, to begin with, the stated principles of the parental English body, the Christian Social Union, of which Charles Gore was a founder: first, that Christian law was the ultimate authority in social matters; second, a commitment to study and to educate others on how to apply moral truths to the social and economic problems of the day; and, third, to "present Christ in practical life as the living Master and King, the enemy of wrong and selfishness, the power of righteousness and love."[27] Members were expected to pray "for the well-being of the union at Holy Communion." Intercessory prayer was strongly urged—and prac-

---

25. An example of the latter is Camilla Stiver, *Bureau Men and Settlement Women: Constructing Public Administration in the Progressive Era* (Lawrence: University Press of Kansas, 2000), 47–65.

26. Richard Hofstadter, *The Age of Reform* (New York: Vintage, 1955), 154, 162; *Dictionary of American Biography* (New York: Scribner's 1943), s.v. "Stetson, Francis Lynde."

27. Bliss, *Encyclopedia of Social Reform*, s.v. "Christian Social Union." See also Paul T. Phillips, *A Kingdom on Earth: Anglo-American Social Christianity, 1880–1940* (University Park: Pennsylvania State University Press, 1996), particularly p. 126 for general background reasons for their concern and response.

ticed. The idea was, for Gardiner at least, to reconcile labor and capital in the foremost pledge to accomplish "the reconciliation of classes." All took it. But, as Scudder commented, "Only a very few of us at that time wanted classes, to be not reconciled, but abolished." Such differences, as I have noted already, did not cause divisions. Anglo-Catholic Episcopalians, such as Scudder, worked closely with more Protestant churchmen like Phillips Brooks. Brooks was in fact for her the "noblest of American religious leaders," a man of "gracious teaching," and "one of the first to have faith in the new enterprise [of settlement houses] and to become a generous subscriber." As late as 1921 the conservative Gardiner had no hesitation declaring that he was reading Vida Scudder's *Social Teachings of the Church Year*. All of them were committed to more than pothole patching and guard-rail repair. They were also realistic and fair-minded, as Scudder's hard-nosed service to the Consumer League amply illustrates.[28]

Expressions of Christian faith that sprang from a desire to fulfill the second half of the Great Commandment—love of neighbor—were not mere rhetoric. Certainly, nowhere in the systems of orthodox or Sumnerian economics or Spencerian sociology was there mention of such Christian principles as sympathy and helpfulness toward the poor and cooperation for their betterment.[29] Yet those attitudes were themselves the stuff of history. And purveyors of the Social Gospel stated quite simply these principles of their faith. In doing so they changed popular attitudes and "more or less eliminated the category of the unworthy poor... [marking] an incredibly important transition in Protestant philanthropy." Could it be, moreover, that Hodges and others did so on the basis of a hard-won prophetic eschatology made all the more urgent by the needs of the hour? And should they not be taken at their word and their motivation accepted for what it was and not reduced to something else? Robert Gardiner maintained consistently that if he and his generation did not attempt to quench people's physical needs, then "the Incarnation is but barren dogma, a dry theological abstraction."[30] Into that ideological unity he and many others made their way.

28. Scudder, *On Journey*, 380, 36, 72, 135; Gardiner to Ferdinand Blanchard, March 8, 1921, Gardiner Correspondence; Dorothy Schneider and Carl J. Schneider, *American Women in the Progressive Era, 1900–1920* (New York: Doubleday, 1993), 72–73.

29. Mann, *Yankee Reformers*, 78.

30. Jonathan A. Dorn, "'Our Best Gospel Appliances': Institutional Churches and the Emergence of Social Christianity in the South End of Boston, 1880–1920" (PhD diss., Harvard University, 1994), 126; Gardiner, "Future of the City Mission," 10.

Behind their concern and hastening its implementation lay the ugly events accompanying the Industrial Revolution: the Railroad Strike (1877), the Haymarket Affair (1892), the Pullman Strike (1894), and the searing knowledge transmitted by Jacob Riis and others of how the "other half lives." Through such tidings middle- and upper-class Americans were coming face-to-face with social unrest and desperate poverty. And then in the late winter of 1893 came the initial collapse of the Philadelphia and Reading Railroad that "sparked the pyrotechnic contraction" of the economy. The terrible depression of that year, the worst to date in the nation's history, had begun. A little more than a year later, in June 1894, 156 other American railroads also lay flat. All went into the hands of receivers, including the Boston and Albany (New York Central), which was the wealthiest corporation in the most densely populated state in nineteenth-century America. Significantly, Robert Gardiner would serve on the board of directors of that railroad.[31]

Massachusetts was, per capita, the most industrialized state in the nation. By the last third of the nineteenth century in Waltham, Lawrence, Fall River, and Lowell (where Gardiner was also a director of the Lawrence Manufacturing Company), Irish and French Canadian immigrants were followed by blacks, Norwegians, Swedes, Russian Jews, Portuguese, Greeks, Sicilians, Poles, Lithuanians, Syrians, Chinese, and Italians, changing the face of the commonwealth forever. In 1900 Boston proper had a city population of 560,892, of which 197,129 were foreign born. The greater metropolitan population of Boston was 2 million in 1900, of whom more than two-thirds were either first- or second-generation immigrants. Already in 1890 the Irish in the city proper outnumbered old-line Americans and thereafter began to enjoy increasing political clout. By 1920, 73 percent of the city's total population were immigrants or the native-born children of immigrants. New England itself by 1895 was 70 percent foreign in either birth or parentage, more Catholic and Jewish than Protestant.[32]

31. Douglas Steeples and David O. Whitten, *Democracy in Desperation: The Depression of 1893* (Westport, CT: Greenwood Press, 1998), 32; Jack Tager, "Massachusetts in the Age of Economic Revolution," in *Massachusetts in the Gilded Age,* edited by Tager and Ifkovic, 7; *Harvard College: The Class of 1876, Tenth Report, June 1926* (Norwood, MA: Plimpton Press, 1926), 67.
32. Stephan Thernstrom, *The Other Bostonians: Poverty and Progress in the American Metropolis, 1880–1970* (Cambridge, MA: Harvard University Press, 1973), 16, 22. See also Frederick A. Bushee, "Population," in *The City Wilderness: A Settlement Study* (New York: Houghton Mifflin, 1898), edited by Robert A. Woods, 36–37; Jack Tager, *Boston Riots: Three Centuries of Social Violence* (Boston: Northeastern University Press, 2001), 145.

The living conditions for most of these immigrants in Boston's Gilded Age were appalling. Squalid tenements were often made from what had been larger homes; diseases such as typhoid and tuberculosis were prevalent, as were illiteracy, drunkenness, and depressed wages. In such slum conditions a sick person was an isolated person; accident rates in the factories were high; hours of work excessive—sixty hours a week in the textile mills; unemployment spelled total financial insecurity; and class fissions along religious and ethnic lines hardened. The New England descendants of the Puritans were the first in the nation to cope with the recurring cycles of boom and bust brought on by an unrestrained plutocracy.[33] That they were themselves part of that plutocracy goes without saying. That they undertook to cope with social and economic ills is to their credit. They, of course, had the tools with which to set about the task. As one historian has commented:

> Most, if not all, of the intellectual sources that influenced Protestantism towards a new social theology were not just present, but were prominent in Boston: modernist thinking and social ethics courses at the seminaries, progressive periodical literature, socialists, several strong charity traditions, and a vibrant network of social clubs and discussion groups. In few other places was the ground so fertile for social Christianity.[34]

Boston was also the most expensively governed city in the United States, its per capita running costs more than twice the average of eighty-six leading American cities. In the post–Civil War period several hundred secular and religious charitable, philanthropic, and relief organizations emerged in the greater metropolitan area in astonishing numbers. Chief among the public municipal organizations were the City Hospital (1864), a floating hospital for women and children (1894), and the People's Palace (1906), with its employment, legal aid, and medical bureaus, its baths, rooms, gymnasium, public hall, and library.[35]

---

33. Tager, "Age of Economic Revolution," 12, 13, 21; Alexander Keyssar, "Social Change in Massachusetts in the Gilded Age," in *Massachusetts in the Gilded Age,* edited by Tager and Ifkovic, 138–43; Tager, "Age of Economic Revolution," 6.

34. J. A. Dorn, "'Our Best Gospel Appliances,'" 7.

35. From 1894 to 1904 the average yearly expenditure of the City of Boston was $27,354,416, exclusive of payments on funded and floating debts; its per capita expense was $35.23, whereas that of New York was $23.92 and Chicago $11.62. See *Encyclopedia Britannica,* 11th ed., s.v. "Boston." For additional analysis, see John F. Woolverton, *The Education of Phillips Brooks* (Urbana: University of Illinois Press, 1995), 27–30.

Boston was at the time generally acknowledged to be both the pioneer and the most advanced city in social outreach in the United States.[36] Despite their minority status—some would say because of it—the Protestant churches played a key role. So indeed did the emerging Irish political machine.

With growing awareness of the human destitution on their doorsteps and in their backyards, the city's leaders systematized their many philanthropic organizations. They did so under the umbrella of the Associated Charities. In addition, at the end of the century denominational headquarters, parish churches, and already existing philanthropic organizations as well as individual prophetic figures rose to the challenge. Roman Catholic charities included St. Elizabeth's Hospital and St. James Church, with its flourishing parochial school and young men's sodalities; among Protestants, the Congregational City Missionary Society, the Clarendon Street Baptist Church, the South End's Berkeley Temple (Congregational), and the Morgan Chapel (Methodist) were the most outstanding.[37]

Leaders such as the tireless publicist for the poor Frederick B. Allen created at the Episcopal City Mission a remarkable number and variety of organizations: a convalescent home, Mothers' Rest; prison visitation; the Rescue Mission for transients and alcoholics, which provided work, fresh clothes, food, and counseling; the Sailors' Haven—a favorite of Gardiner; St. Mary's Free Church for Sailors; and the Girl's Friendly Society, which taught trades and homemaking. For the single and worst depression year, April 1894 to April 1895, the Episcopal City Mission registered 7,310 "exploring calls," 6,490 home visits, 3,762 to the sick in the hospitals; there were 613 visits to prisoners, 2,747 to ships in the harbor, and as a result 28,192 sailors stayed at the Sailor's Haven. So well known was Gardiner that many of them would call on him at night at his home for help of one kind or another. The City Mission gave out nearly a thousand Bibles and prayer books; it served 4,564 meals, gave free lodging, befriended immigrants, and even found employment for the poor. Other parishes and settlement houses did likewise.[38] The Episcopal Church was highly successful because

36. Jacob A. Riis, *The Making of an American* (New York: Macmillan, 1902), 252, 388.

37. Woods, *City Wilderness*, 207, 208, 214. J. A. Dorn, in "'Our Best Gospel Appliances,'" treats the Berkeley Temple and the Morgan Chapel in detail, as well as the Episcopalian St. Stephen's Church and the Church of the Ascension.

38. Tomkins Notes, Episcopal City Mission folder, Tomkins Papers. Dillon, in "Mission in an Urban Diocese," catalogs other Episcopal churches and organizations: Church of the Ascension, St. Cyprian's Church, Roxbury (African American), St. Francis Chapel (Italian), St. Ansgarius Church (Swedish Americans), the Church Home for Orphans and Destitute Children, South Boston, the Church Home for the Care of Children, St. Monica's Home (African American

it had fewer older and diminishing parishes to worry about and "apparently unending resources available to bishops and rectors."[39] As a result it could plant new churches wherever they were most needed.

Above all in importance for Gardiner was the brainchild of Bishop Phillips Brooks, St. Stephen's Church, which Brooks had placed under the authority of the Episcopal City Mission. Represented by its clergy, Henry M. Torbert and Charles Henry Brent, St. Stephen's was to become the third church that had a profound theological influence on Gardiner. Brent was to remain, as we shall see, Gardiner's friend and confidant for the next thirty years. Later on in letters, they addressed each other with the most familiar and affectionate designations—for those days—their last names. Despite Brent's elevation to the episcopate, the salutations between them remained "Brent" and "Gardiner." It was a friendship of equals. When the former was elected bishop of the Philippines in 1901, Gardiner was one of three people he sought out for advice on whether to accept or reject the offer. "Robert Gardiner came to speak to the [St. Stephen's] Brotherhood of St. Andrew this evening," Brent recorded in his diary. "I consulted with him. He considers the opportunity [of going to the Philippines] to be glorious. After conferring with him about the situation at St. Stephen's, I wired Bp. Hall that that ought not to hold me."[40]

For the decade of the 1890s St. Stephen's provided both Gardiner and those who worked there in Boston's South End with "an experiential meaning and spiritual import" and "began to reshape the very fabric" of their faith. Torbert and Brent did so first by placing at the center of their activities a service of intercessory prayer that became central for the workers at the parish. As its numbers swelled and "the floodgates opened . . . they released a torrential flow of imagination and organization."[41] All the while the church remained rooted in prayer. It was a lesson Gardiner insisted upon among those who, from 1910 on, were involved in the work of the World Conference on Faith and Order.

-------

women and children), St. Martin's House (for manual training), House of Mercy (rescue and relief of "fallen women"), St. Luke's Convalescent Home, Roxbury, the Church Service League (to draw together women's work), Vida Scudder's Denison House, and the Stanhope School (agricultural training), to name some of the outstanding.

39. J. A. Dorn, "'Our Best Gospel Appliances,'" 103.

40. Brent Diary, October 10, 1901, Charles Henry Brent Papers, Library of Congress, Washington, DC.

41. J. A. Dorn, "'Our Best Gospel Appliances,'" 101. Torbert died of typhoid fever on September 29, 1901; in October of the same year Brent accepted his election as bishop of the Philippines (Brent diary, container 52, Brent Papers).

The second lesson he learned from St. Stephen's was the centrality of the doctrine of the Incarnation. The parish had hung a little tin cup next to its ice-water fountain. In proffering the cup, church workers believed they "participated vicariously in Christ's life and, in fact, resurrected His ministry."[42] By performing works of mercy, they declared, they ministered to Christ himself. Both the giver of cold water and the recipient completed the circle of scripture by following its clear sense (Matt. 25:35). Christ was present, incarnate, it was claimed, not in the church's machinery but in the Word of God and in the "new" sacrament of service. The doctrine of the Incarnation underwrote their lives. As God was incarnate in Jesus of Nazareth, so analogically he became present in the works of mercy his followers performed. A mysterious power resided, they held, in acts of kindness performed in his name. It did not occur to them as it has to many today to find God "incarnate" in moments of private enlightenment along the path of life's journey. The Incarnation informed self-giving rather than self-enhancement. With a degree of objectivity and literalness those connected with St. Stephen's Church, whether parishioners or supporters, intended to act out the implications of the biblical injunctions respecting love of God and neighbor. This they did. They called that action social justice. It was, as Vida Scudder affirmed, the first mark of the faith of St. Stephen's churchgoers.

Intercessory prayer, the Incarnation, and social justice carried over into other institutions. Without that trinity the Social Gospel in the Episcopal Church cannot be understood at its deepest. Its simple devotion led to a strong desire for unity with Christians of other traditions. For Scudder, prayer became the lodestar of the laywomen's Society of the Companions of the Holy Cross. Acknowledging the influence of "my rector, Mr. Brent, as he then was called," she remarked that "several women . . . connected with the nascent Settlement Movement joined the Society, and insensibly our intercessory life took a special character, till we became first and foremost pledged to prayer for social justice and for the unity of Christendom." And these laywomen, companions, as they were called, kept financial and institutional matters in their own hands. Even when it came to worship and meditations, remarked Scudder slyly, "we often dispensed with the clergy."[43] Later on, Gardiner was to find unstinting allies among these women. They in turn influenced and supported him in their shared concern for prayer, social equity, and Christian unity. Gender appears to have played no role at all.

---

42. J. A. Dorn, "'Our Best Gospel Appliances,'" 95, 100.
43. Scudder, *On Journey*, 232, 380, 379.

In the meantime, in 1897 Gardiner wrote an important essay for the Church Social Union, "A Lawyer's View of the Function of the Church." In it he described the nature of the church. Throughout, he kept in front of his readers the local parish, its members, not forgetting himself. What, he asked, were his duties as a Christian toward others around him? For parishioners, there was no fudging obligations, no "standing aloof from their neighbors," no excuse for not being engaged locally, no passing by on the other side of the neighborhood street. The great commission, "Go ye therefore and teach all nations, baptizing them in the Name of the Father, and of the Son and of the Holy Spirit, teaching them to observe all things whatsoever I have commanded you" (Matt. 28:19–20), bound individuals into a union with the head, Christ. Members of the church "cannot help being like him in all the acts of our life." And then came the key sentence of the essay, "Let us turn our love for Him and our love for each other into *service*." That service began in the local parish church with the "duty of setting up within its limits a visible Kingdom of Peace and Righteousness and Love." So far, we might say, so trite. In truth he took the church's familiar language intensely and seriously. He wanted others to do so as well. Using himself as a model, he found that he was "so in the habit of hiring [others and having] his work done for him that he forgets Christ's law of personal service." Gardiner would not let anyone off the hook, least of all members of the Church Social Union. "We," the educated elite, "have not felt it right to waste our talents in the drudgery of helping our actual individual neighbor."[44]

Like his fellow reformers, Gardiner thought the first step in fulfilling the demand for personal service was self-education. He sought to "study ethics and history and economics" and to "infuse them with Divine Love without which they are but dry bones." Although he judged prejudicially and incorrectly that social wrongs were not as widespread in the United States as in the Old World, nor, "except in a few great cities, as deeply seated," he was well aware of the "great sin of the unjust conditions of society." He wanted immigrants and laborers to "have a decent place to live and work in and earn fair wages."[45]

Education, however, was not enough. For too long, he maintained, he and his associates had "played with the Social Union." They had "read their papers, sometimes with glowing consciousness of our virtue in caring for its questions."

44. Gardiner, "Lawyer's View," in *Publications of the Church Social Union,* May 15, 1897, 13 (emphasis added), 19, 14.

45. Ibid., 20, 19. See also Richard T. Ely, *Social Aspects of Christianity and Other Essays* (New York: Thomas Y. Crowell, 1889), 77.

At other times they dispensed with the readings because they judged that they already knew they were superior to those of their own class who had no social conscience at all. The "exquisite luxury of sentimental sympathy with those who are ground into the dust by conditions which cannot affect us" was an emotion that to their discredit had been enjoyed by the reformers. What, he asked, had they really done to help? The answer he laid on was rhetorical: "Nothing most of us. Nothing in the eye of God or man." Rather, he charged, they should see "that there be no foul tenements, no soul-destroying saloon, no house of prostitution, no man starving for want of work within the sound of the bells of our Church." But it was, as in his castigation of the clergy two years previously, simply not true that they had sat on their hands, as their act of founding the Episcopal City Mission in 1888 proves.[46]

Be that as it may, the responsibility for others was corporate as well as individual. What was the purpose for which Christ founded the church? Gardiner asked. Why did he "endow it with perpetual succession, with universal authority, with grace and duty of ministering the Sacraments ordained by Him and of preaching His Gospel"? Not for the purpose of enhancing private religion, not to build "a cloud kingdom" for the favored few, the spiritually exalted. Nor did Christ command his disciples to "discuss abstract or philosophic theology" but to "teach the nations the definite and practical observance of the things that he had commanded, and the great bulk of those things relate to the social conditions of this world." Still, for Gardiner, the conviction remained strong that the basis of social responsibility was individual morality. "Even where the new stress on reform of the corporate life was welcomed and affirmed as necessary," explains one historian, "it was not uncommon to find individualism at the root of such receptivity, in the form of the belief that private virtue was the only sure foundation of public weal."[47] The transformation from an individual gospel to a social gospel was not really complete. But was the combination of the two undesirable? Only if personal piety were used as an excuse for ignoring social wrongs could "individualism" prove unwholesome to the common good.

The accusation does not fit Robert Gardiner. His thought was more subtle than the either-or of private versus public Christianity. Into his argument for personal service in a social gospel, Gardiner wove other themes and authorities,

---

46. Gardiner, "Lawyer's View," 13; Henry F. May, *Protestant Churches and Industrial America* (New York: Harper Brothers, 1949), 182–85; Mann, *Yankee Reformers*, 90.

47. May, *Protestant Churches*, 12; Thomas Sieger Derr, "The Political Thought of the Ecumenical Movement, 1900–1939" (PhD diss., Columbia University, 1972), 48.

communal ones. As this was to be a lawyer's view of the church's function, he invoked Sir William Blackstone's *Commentaries on the Laws of England* (1765–1769), a summation of which had been published in the United States in 1804 under the title *Common Law*. Its four volumes were a ready reference and guide for busy attorneys. Before midcentury there would be an additional fifteen versions of *Common Law* that hosed off Blackstone's monarchical Toryism for the benefit of American readers. Had Gardiner read fellow Boston attorney Oliver Wendell Holmes's Darwinian challenge to the entire edifice of Blackstone? Holmes's *Common Law* was published early in 1881, and it had shaken the legal establishment by raising doubts about the possibility of discovering immutable principles transmitted in natural law by divine will. Instead, Holmes appealed to evolution, experience, and history rather than to logic, tradition, and God. Force, not value, would now, as Holmes hoped, dominate jurisprudence. It was not to be entirely so.[48]

With respect to the nature of corporations, Gardiner made use of Blackstone; he then applied the English jurist's thought to the nature of the church and to its function. He began his essay by questioning the claims of some Episcopalians to the effect that other denominations that did not maintain the apostolic succession of bishops were schismatic. The fact of schism was one thing; its occurrence was clear enough from history. However, the guilt of schism "may be rather on the Church which has failed to execute its Founder's purpose than with those who have not united with it." The fault of schism, he determined, lay not so much with the Presbyterians, independents, Baptists, and Methodists who in succeeding decades and centuries had left the mother Church of England as with Anglicans themselves who had become schismatic. Their privilege and duty had been "to preach good tidings to the poor, to heal the broken-hearted, to preach deliverance to captives and recovery of sight to the blind, to set at liberty them that are bruised, to preach the acceptable year of the Lord, its estate in the love and presence of Him who is always with it." Then came the conclusion: palaces, episcopal seals, and "the inventory of our estates in Probate Court"

---

48. See, for instance, Allen C. Guelzo, *Abraham Lincoln: Redeemer President* (Grand Rapids, MI, and Cambridge, England: William B. Eerdman's, 1999), 77; and Liva Baker, *Justice from Beacon Hill: The Life and Times of Oliver Wendell Holmes* (New York: HarperCollins, 1991), 249–58. Gardiner's references to and appeal to history would seem to indicate that Holmes's ideas had influenced him to some degree; it is inconceivable that Gardiner should have been ignorant of *The Common Law*, which created a sensation, but I have found no direct references to the book.

are not the measures of true worth, "but . . . the record in heaven of the sacrifices we have made for others."[49] Such propitiations seemed to him few and far between.

Did he mean to say that the presence of bishops, priests, and deacons in itself was a hindrance to advancing the Gospel? Such government was "a marvellously efficient instrument for spreading the Kingdom of Christ"—but a kingdom founded on the "social law of Christ" and not "on temporal power." Enter Blackstone. The Vinerian professor of law at Oxford had argued that the durability of society rested on the foundation of corporations. Voluntary assemblies were one thing, corporations another. The one lasted only so long as there was common agreement; the other had rules in law that had binding force generation after generation. For the church, those rules were "the historic creeds, the perpetual succession of the threefold ministry, and the unfailing use of the Sacraments as ordained by the Church's Head." Were the "new sects" unorthodox in doctrine? Had they, in fact, abandoned the creeds? And was not the threefold ministry subject to more than one interpretation? Were there not Protestants with high views of both church and sacraments? What was a corporation anyway? Was it real or fictional? Or something in between, people who arrange themselves or were arranged in a certain order or system? If the order was man-made, then the corporation could be changed. If it was God mandated, then no single hair of its head could be clipped. But what if it was a mix of the two, divine and human? Who was to make a determination in that case? On the godward side, matters might be fairly clear, but on the man-made side of things, what might be considered convenient and proper changes or alterations?[50] To these questions Gardiner did not give answers in his article, but he offered hints that would be developed later as his thinking progressed.

In "A Lawyer's View" he began by relating Blackstone's description of the nature of a corporation to the church. When people are united in a corporation, Gardiner declared, quoting the English jurist, "they and their successors are then considered one person in law, as one person they have but one will," and by its authority can establish rules of conduct, order, privileges, immunities, estates, and possessions "in perpetuity. . . [with] no new conveyance to new successions." Finally, all individuals "were but one person in law, one person that never dies." When he applied this to the church, he spoke in the cadences of

49. Gardiner, "Lawyer's View," 3, 7, 8.
50. Ibid., 4, 6.

Johannine theology: all who "have accepted the free grace of God, who shall hereafter accept it, are but one person in Him who for their sakes conquered Death, 'that they all may be one, even as Thou, Father art in me and I in Thee, that they may be one in us.'"[51] In his high Anglicanism, Gardiner rejected what he saw as the "unrestrained license of the majority" that was free "to carry [Christians] in any direction within or beyond the purposes . . . of the corporation." Liberty, for Gardiner, was paternal, severe, and restrained; it was to be enjoyed by subserving the self to the community, by taking the doctrine of the church with utmost seriousness, and by living under its "law." At the heart of the law was love; love in its turn was the equivalent of duty, service, and sacrifice."[52] Liberty was a privilege granted to those who committed themselves to Christ and his church. Thus, for Gardiner, there was a powerful impetus—and seriousness—to bring individuals into communion with the church's head. Here alone was true liberty, and it was at the heart of the corporation that spoke and acted as the one divine Saviour had spoken and acted.

For the assemblies of those churches that more nearly represented the American temper, liberty was natal, always being born again in revivals, conventions, and camp meetings; liberty was the right to reach a consensus in conformity not with communal law but with eschatological expectation. From the experience of arriving at that consensus, be it in a religious awakening or in a congress of the people, came the church's and the state's authority. Deference to the corporation's fixed discipline and its hierarchy was replaced by the right of free individuals to devise, live within, and alter if need be those freely arrived at social contracts to which they had given their allegiance. As a result Jonathan Ploughboy felt free to whoop it up—who could resist the temptation?—to shock visiting English butlers and those they served. Popularly, but only so, had Americans

---

51. Ibid., 5–6. Gardiner declared that Blackstone's second, third, and fourth attributes of a corporation, namely, the right to sue and be sued, the right to purchase lands, and the right to have a common seal, did not belong properly to the kingdom of God, which was not of this world (6). See 1 John 5:11 with respect to eternal life as well as John 17:6–11, 22–23, and 14:20.

52. Gardiner, "Lawyer's View," 14. Although Gardiner was free to compare the church to a corporation, it must be said that the two are by no means similar. There are three things inherent in the term *church*: first, the life (including the teaching), death, and resurrection of Jesus Christ as recounted in the Bible; second, the Great Commandment (Mark 12:29–31); and third, the Great Commission (Matt. 28:18–20). A corporation, on the other hand, has no such intrinsic components; it is a legal term and has no meaning except what the legal system assigns to it. See John T. Noonan Jr., *Narrowing the Nation's Power: The Supreme Court Sides with the States* (Berkeley and Los Angeles: University of California Press, 2002), 75–76.

rejected the "'corporation spirit'—in which laws [as they adjudged] were enacted for the benefit of the powerful and were enforced by the caprice of magistrates, masters, overseers, and churchwardens. They are themselves a source of insecurity."[53] In the world of practical affairs, if men and women did not speak and act as Christ would have had them do, the liberty that rested at the heart of the divine community was, they felt, abused. All equally had sinned and fallen short of the glory of God, kings, queens, and bishops as well as the rustics. On the other hand, all were susceptible to those good influences emanating from the provenance of grace.

Had Gardiner forgotten this? Not necessarily. However much an older Anglicanism pervaded his family's tradition—and the Gardiners had never been anything but Anglican—he sought to discover basic principles, to go behind the cultus of the Church of England, of the state-run establishment, and of inherited denominational practices to discover more basic principles and relate those to the divine corporation. Increasingly, he came to determine that that "corporation" was in fact the universal church. That the basic principles turned out to be biblical is no surprise. He then proceeded to interweave them with the thought of Blackstone. The corporation of the church was thenceforth to be free from laws enacted for the benefit of the powerful and was to come into its own and flower in effectuating "Christian" laws for the benefit of those who were powerless. Inhibiting procedures and customs could be laid aside—in fact, must be. In particular, the Gospel was to be social in the sense that it sought to lift up those who were down. As a corporation dedicated to this end, the church being one person was to act as one, unified.

And the individual? Oneness with God in Christ, he stated in 1897 in a sort of lawyer's ethical and theological brief, involved each person in further obligations. They were nurtured within a community with a tradition, a liturgy, and a way of reasoning and behaving. Obligations began locally, in a parish church, in a Sunday school. Parishioners incorporated their community, so that in a legal fashion each member individually escaped personal liability for the parish's legal obligations. But there was a deeper and more demanding responsibility for the individual Christian, a moral obligation "to make the personal liability of each of its members not a thing to be avoided but a means of grace." As Christ accepted both legal and personal liability "once and for all men in the mystery of the Incarnation and the Atonement," so personal liability was to be assumed by his

---

53. Alan Ryan, "A New Vision of Liberty," *New York Review of Books,* July 5, 2001, 44.

followers in behalf of others, and "not one throb of pain would we forego if more and more we are His and bring by means of [personal liability] the world to Him."[54] The charter of the church was love, not for the self but for others.

Gardiner also wanted to relate the church to democracy. Though he was not wholly incorrect, his Whig bias got him into trouble historically. He announced that the "Church of England stood among the foremost in the fight for the great charter of liberty and equality for the English race in Magna Charta." It was the first victory, he added, "'of the masses over the classes.'" Surely, it is true that English kings thereafter "came to be regarded as under some law greater than that of their own making."[55] But his assertion that the nobles at Runnymede represented the masses says more about his thinking than about the significance of the event itself. In the crisis of 1215 the papal church had sided with the "absolute" monarchy (King John was in fact a vassal of Innocent III), rather than with the nobility or the emerging common-law tradition. Thus, the claim that the church stood for liberty is false.[56] Though he clearly thought he was employing it, Gardiner's purpose was not historical accuracy. He believed in democracy. He wanted his Episcopal Church to occupy a significant position within that democracy, which meant as well within the larger stream of Christianity in the nation. Was not his denomination indigenous, progressive, and democratic? By 1897 he believed, or wanted to believe, it was all three. The church had changed, or in the United States had been forced to change. Then how should it comport itself in this new situation? What about tradition? However that large question might be answered, he was clear in his own mind that in the young country the church was free to shape its own character, attitude, and destiny. In that assurance, he was closer to William White's *Case of the Episcopal Churches in the United States Considered* (1782) than to the high church

54. Ibid., 9.

55. Ibid., 5. The Magna Carta was a victory for both the classes and the masses, for the rule of law over tyranny, either royal or papal. Thenceforth, the king could not proceed against any free person in his realm except by the due process of the common law, whatever its institutions might be. The tyranny of King John was "a manifestation of the absence of law" (R. W. Southern, *The Making of the Middle Ages* [New Haven, CT: Yale University Press, 1953], 109). Gardiner was considerably less accurate when he spoke of the "Church of England" instead of the "church in England," a point still of some contention among Anglicans. See Robert J. Janosik, ed., *Encyclopedia of the American Judicial System,* 3 vols. (New York: Charles Scribner's Sons, 1987), s.vv. "common law and common legal systems," "due process of law."

56. *Encyclopedia of the Judicial System,* ed. Janosik, s.v. "trial by juries and grand juries." Jury trial replaced trial by ordeal, which latter the clergy not only supervised but by which they profited from fees collected from the ordeals themselves and their bribed verdicts.

ecclesiology of Samuel Seabury as expounded in that Connecticut churchman's *Discourses on Various Subjects* (1793).[57]

But political and theological questions hung in the air. Should the church support socialism? If so, what kind? For Gardiner, those who advocated political and legislative involvement in such a course might also be avoiding the demand for personal service. Still the questions persisted. Should there be an equal division of property? Property had, he claimed, nothing to do with the socialism Christ preached. What then? To be sure, Christ commanded a "socialism" that "the common law has partly crystallized into the maxim that you shall not use the property God has given you to injure another." Property, when acquired, Gardiner declared, should be used so that "all may be helped by it toward the ideal God means for every man to reach." Although he acknowledged the "complicated relations flowing in these modern days," the solution to the acquisition of great wealth and the resulting conflicts between labor and management lay with the church itself. "Christ's socialism does not seek to destroy property except so far as [the ownership itself] leads men to forget Him and wrap themselves up in self" — in which case, is destruction permissible? Jesus, in fact, "taught the sacredness of property used in his service by commending the man who with his five talents gained another five for his lord."[58]

What lay behind Gardiner's thinking was awareness of the enmity against the railroads that existed among industrial laborers and farmers and the resulting threatened destruction of property. The events surrounding the failures of the railroads, already alluded to, stood in the background of his 1897 paper for the Church Social Union. His father had helped to survey for the Northern Pacific Railroad in the 1850s, and the son by 1897 was a director of the Boston and Albany. He came by his interest in railroads naturally. In the essay for the Church Social Union he quoted the unchallenged decision of the circuit court in Wisconsin in the case of *Farmers' Loan & Trust Co. v. Northern Pacific R. R.* of April 6, 1894.[59] Property, it was declared in the decision in that case, was sacred. The strikers, whose salaries had been cut 10 to 20 percent as a result of

57. Gardiner, "Lawyer's View," 17. White's tract was nontheological and practical and addressed the issue of how to unite thirteen Episcopal churches; Seabury was theological and briskly unchurched other denominations (in his unpublished "Lectures upon the Catechism," ca. 1770, 39, 42, General Theological Seminary Library, New York).

58. Gardiner, "Lawyer's View," 11, 12.

59. Ibid.; *Farmers' Loan & Trust Co. v. Northern Pacific R. R.,* 60 F.1st, 803–24 (Wisc. Cir. 1894); Shepherd, *Federal Citations,* 80:803.

the depression of that year, had threatened to destroy locomotives, cars, tracks, and the telegraph unless they were compensated for their losses.[60] Acknowledging that the "aggregate power of combined labor is perilous to the peace of society, and to the rights of property," the court declared that the matter was no longer open to controversy. The judiciary had an obligation, it was stated, to "restrain threatened trespass involving the immediate or ultimate destruction of property, working irreparable injury, and for which there would be no adequate compensation at law."[61] Gardiner read these words. Apparently, neither he nor the court thought that the government had an equal obligation on behalf of the public to regulate the rates and services, the manipulation of which had brought sizable profits to the owners at the expense of the farmers and ranchers. A railroad-friendly judiciary turned a blind eye to such shenanigans and to the Interstate Commerce Act (1887) that was already in place, making regulation of railroad practices possible.

What appealed to the Boston attorney, however, went beyond the immediate issue. He had approved of the judge's reasoning that "'rights grow out of and are limited by duties,' as was said by Judge Jenkins." The rest of the decision spun out the court's deliberation and was in close keeping with Gardiner's own views; it was absurd to say that "one may do as he will with respect to the rights of others" or that liberty was the exercise of unbridled will. Rights and interests were subordinate to public duty. But, of course, the argument cut both ways. The property of the laborers—their work and their agreed-upon pay or the purchases of the ranchers and farmers—was threatened just as much as the locomotives and the boxcars. The Northern Pacific Railroad had done as it willed with the rights of others. But Gardiner did not see it this way. He wanted no "elaborate socialistic legislation." Jesus Christ, he averred, "preached no Gospel of political organization or of associations to secure the amendment of statutes." Those statutes had the character of Old Testament law, of "the Old Covenant necessary to the preparation of an ignorant, undisciplined race for the free acceptance of the highest, because voluntary law of righteousness." Christ came to fulfill in the new the promise of the old. Rather than waiting for some human "law-giver to perfect the statutes," he believed that "only by regeneration of the individual could His kingdom be established." He wanted to

60. The Northern Pacific was in 1894 in receivership—for the second time. See Eric Foner, *Reconstruction: America's Unfinished Revolution, 1863–1877* (New York: Harper and Row, 1988), 512.
61. *Farmers' Loan & Trust Co.,* 60 F.1st at 809, 810.

educate "gradually inspiring public opinion...till legislation seemed to come spontaneously, or did not come at all simply because there was no need for it."[62]

Not all of his fellow Episcopalians in the Church Social Union agreed with his defense of property or with his gradualism. A prickly Vida Scudder argued that whereas property "is then as sacred as the most sententious conservative conceives, we must learn to reverence it more, not less deeply as civilization goes on." But Scudder had an ace up her sleeve. She then quoted Karl Marx's *Communist Manifesto* to the effect that the immense majority of humanity had no property at all, to which she added: "In a society in which every tenth man still dies a pauper, outcries concerning the sacrosanct rights of property ring strangely on the ear." Socialists sought not to destroy but to fulfill. "We want to strike the word 'private' [from the text] that the full force of the noun 'property' may be realized." Property privileges should no longer be restricted to the few, she argued. To be sure, for Scudder, gradualism might well be commended, "a process which can be carried on as slowly as wisdom dictates," but it would be "for the socialization of wealth-producing wealth." The influential George Hodges did not go as far. Nonetheless, he too thought that the state should perform more than the negative function of keeping "off thieves and robbers . . . [and] interest itself in a positive way in forwarding the universal welfare of man." Hodges wanted inspectors to enforce laws relating to sanitation, regulation of hours, working conditions, housing, lighting, water supplies, and "cheap rates of transportation." For him, "the wealth of the state is in the health and happiness of the people," and that happiness involved trade unionism, boards for arbitration, profit sharing, municipal ownership, and the "nationalization of telegraphs, telephones, railroads, and mines."[63]

Alongside these colleagues, Robert Gardiner appears timid. He did not at first advocate social legislation; Christians had their own means at hand, the church. Better use it unapologetically, resolutely, and compellingly. But his insistence on creating change through the church itself was not a means of preserving soft berths and fancy privileges elsewhere. He did not fear "creeping socialism" or the "welfare state." Indeed, he spoke of the "day of Democracy, toward which civilization has been struggling from its earliest dawn, often through blood and fire." Democracy was the "instinct deeply implanted by God in the hearts of all men that they may be fit to be His friends, brothers of His Son and of one

62. Gardiner, "Lawyer's View," 12, 15.
63. Scudder, *Socialism and Character* (Boston: Houghton Mifflin, 1912), 290, 292, 293; Hodges, *Faith and Social Service* (New York: Thomas Whittaker, 1896), 167, 168, 170, 172.

another in His Son." Men and women were made free—"free to share in His purposes of Love, or free, if we will, to thwart and postpone them."[64] Democracy was the business of the church, and the church really mattered. "It is not that democracy is a new creation which is affecting the Church," he wrote. "Democracy is the product of the Church." The spirit of democracy began with the Incarnation; he was not exactly clear as to why this was so—was it perhaps because in Christ men and women were now friends of God and not servants and so had a say and a vote? Did the dictum "one 'man,' one vote" apply also to the persons of the Trinity? "I am sure the Holy Spirit is moving in this matter," Gardiner claimed, "and very powerfully." Especially, it might be added, in the church unity movement that had sprung up in the United States! He neglected to point out that the government of the Roman Catholic Church was based not on democratic principles at all but on those, as its name implies, of the imperial Rome of the Caesars! Nothing new there: all are "subject to the particular cultural and social logics of what one might call their 'host culture.'"[65]

Gardiner assumed that democracy and Christian faith went hand in hand. It was up to humankind to realize both. They were to influence each other, he advised, toward brotherhood, sisterhood, and practical neighborliness. In the failure to realize these goals Gardiner faulted both capital and labor in industrial America: "Trusts and Labor Unions have thought primarily of their own power, [and] the advancement of their own interests." Attempts to check the taking of extreme profits on the part of the few by means of the income tax and inheritance taxes were "at best mere palliatives, not cures or preventives, of social disease." Labor too was to blame: "strikes or threats of strikes . . . cause not merely the upsetting of business but widespread suffering for the necessities of life." There had been little reflection given, he maintained, to "the fair distribution of the earnings of business." Unions insisted on their right to the "brute force of strikes," whereas capital "still hopes that strikes may be made unlawful, so that Labor may be forced to continue to serve." Now was the time to proclaim "the New Commandment of Love."[66]

And in his own sphere he not only proclaimed that commandment but also acted on its urgings. Gardiner's means were not large nor his purse crowded, said one, but "in many a home he will be remembered for the thoughtful and

64. Gardiner, "Address of Welcome," 113.
65. Gardiner to George William Douglas, June 23, 1913, Gardiner Correspondence; Peter W. Williams, "'Does American Religious History Have a Center?': Reflections," *Church History* 69 (June 2000): 390.
66. Gardiner, "Address of Welcome," 109.

tactful way in which the rent has been met, or the insurance premium has been payed, or the doctor's bill quietly confiscated."[67] He practiced what he preached.

In hindsight, whether the churches had either the will or the influence any longer to realize the potential of the new commandment of love is beside the point. Certainly, Gardiner and others in that hopeful generation thought that they had both. But what is of no little interest is that by demanding they do so, he placed himself on the path mapped out by his contemporary John Dewey. That American guru distinguished between the ideal (the classical mode of thought) and the modern. In classical philosophy, he had written, "the ideal world is essentially a haven in which man finds rest from the storms of life, it is an asylum in which he takes refuge from the troubles of existence with the calm assurance that it alone is supremely real." But now the belief that knowledge was active and "operative" had taken hold, and the ideal realm was no longer aloof and separate. "It is rather that collection of imagined possibilities that stimulates men to new efforts and realizations." It was an exact fit: Gardiner's idea of the church was not that it was an asylum from stress but that it was a school where current events were to be examined for nothing less than reshaping the world. Although the new commandment of love remained the ideal, it was to be treated as "a possibility capable of realization *in* the concrete natural world, not as a superior reality apart from that world."[68]

Gardiner was concerned over the tensions between the few and the many, between capital and labor, between the unions and industry. In the next decade he moved beyond his initial reluctance to support reform legislation. By 1908 he was recommending to those in his circle of associates a series of weekly lesson papers on pressing social questions. The papers were published by the American Institute of Social Service, an organization devoted to "industrial and social betterment" founded by Josiah Strong and William H. Tolman. Gardiner specifically recommended to his constituents that they read the institute's papers on "child labor, prison reform, [and] housing . . . [that give] not only the facts but also what is the teaching of Christ bearing on these facts"; he ended by declaring that the papers made "good material for discussion and action."[69] What that action would be will be told in the next chapter.

67. [Randall], editorial, 325.

68. Dewey, "Changed Conceptions of the Ideal and the Real," quoted in *Pragmatism and the Political Economy of Cultural Revolution, 1850–1940,* by James Livingston (Chapel Hill: University of North Carolina Press, 1997), 197.

69. Bliss, *Encyclopedia of Social Reform,* s.v. "American Institute of Social Service"; Gardiner, editorial in *St. Andrew's Cross,* September 1908, 837.

In the decade before the outbreak of World War I, Robert Gardiner emerged in the Christian world first as a denominational leader, then as a national and finally as an international figure. Increasingly after 1904, he came to seek certain things on a world scale. The first was at least the facing, if not the overcoming, of ethnic and racial prejudice. He wanted more and more to include immigrants in both the church and the nation and, albeit haltingly, minority groups, particularly African Americans. This goal of incorporating the new, the strange, and the repudiated, as shall be shown presently, was neither immediate nor innate with him. He had his prejudices. They tended to wedge uncomfortably at first between his principles and his actions. Once he had come to know the people in the suspect races, groups, and churches, however, he quickly changed his mind. Inclusiveness was something he learned as he went along, not something he came by naturally. Its roots were in the Social Gospel and may even stretch back both to his family's days on the frontier as well as to his own years in French Canada.

The Social Gospel then had two emphases: first, the inclusion of minorities, of the "new" and the different, and, second, the amelioration of their suffering. The one spoke to the Christian life, the other to the church's work as nourishing that life. In point of fact, the work of improvement had come first, that of inclusion second; the one grew out of the other. As Gardiner and his friends moved into the slums, they got to know the latest immigrants and their conditions. They then came to see those new arrivals as human beings and, in varying degrees, as fellow Christians. Nor did Gardiner leave off being so concerned. Through his work with young people (discussed in Chapter Four) and the Federal Council of Churches (Chapter Five), he came to participate in the Life and Work Movement that spun in orbit with that of Faith and Order in the new ecumenical universe; both of them were spin-offs of the larger cooperation of the Progressive Era, and, coming together in 1948, they resulted in the birth of the World Council of Churches.

Toward the end of his life, Gardiner's interest in bringing his faith to bear on social problems was evidenced by his participation in the American section of the Life and Work Movement, that branch of the ecumenical movement that dealt with the relation of Christian faith to society, politics, and economics. At the request of Archbishop Nathan Soderblom of Sweden, he was invited to lecture at the Olaus-Petri Foundation of the University of Uppsala. Though he declined, believing he was more needed in the United States as the Great War wound down, he continued along with Soderblom to coordinate the two proposed Christian world conferences, the one on social and economic issues, the other on theology and church order. Both took place after Gardiner's death, the first in 1925, the second in 1927.

In 1922 in the New York City meeting of the American section of Life and Work he was one of three Episcopalians appointed; thereat he was elected to the executive committee, of which he eventually became chairman.[70] He was also chairman of the Committee on the Church and Social Service. In 1923 at the American section's Philadelphia meeting, he chaired the Committee on the Church and Economic and Industrial Problems. In January 1924 he was elected to the International Committee of Life and Work.[71] As he wrote to his friend Edwin T. Palmer, Anglican bishop of Bombay, "The vital importance of social and industrial questions" must cause the church to steer "the social revolution which seems impending all over the world" along paths of peaceful development and harmony. If the conference on Life and Work was going to be more than a "pleasant meeting of a number of gentlemen who have extemporary ideas on important subjects," he advised Presbyterian Arthur Judson Brown, "... we ought to be carrying on a very wide correspondence ... to select speakers and topics and to get papers thoroughly prepared as was done before Edinburgh."[72]

The second goal he sought was church unity, the major topic of this study, and, third, a catholic and sacramental understanding of the Christian community. Along these three paths, social, ecclesiological, and theological, he moved concurrently and with increasing resolution. In the meantime, he had struck a blow for reform in his own church: first in Christian education, then in easing the plight of the poor and, as I shall show in the next chapter, in youth work, and finally in interdenominational relations. Ultimately, he emerged as an international Christian leader. He had a forehead of brass. He needed it, for he was aiming at nothing so much as world reformation along Christian lines. In his goals, however far-fetched they may seem today, he offered hope and purpose to his contemporaries. He was a Progressive with a wide and daring plan.

70. Gardiner to Charles Henry Brent, March 17, 1922, Gardiner Correspondence.
71. Minutes of the Life and Work meetings, notebook 1, 21–23.
72. Gardiner to Palmer, December 14, 1920; Gardiner to Brown, December 14, 1921; see also letters to Brown, December 21, 1921, March 15, 1922, and April 14, 1924, all in Gardiner Correspondence.

# THREE

❧✝❧

## Parliaments and Brotherhoods

### *Chicago, 1893*

At the end of the nineteenth century three events in Chicago helped to shape Robert Gardiner's life. The first and more general was the World's Parliament of Religions at the World's Columbian Exposition of 1893. There the Swiss American scholar Philip Schaff delivered his famous and, as it turned out, last address, "The Reunion of Christendom." It was as if this important church historian had written a programmatic essay for his younger contemporary Robert Gardiner. So exactly did Gardiner follow Schaff's lead that it is tempting to claim direct influence. Alas, there is no proof. The best that can be said is that given Schaff's renown and the Boston attorney's growing commitment to reunion, it is likely Gardiner either read the speech or knew of its contents, but no more can be said. What is significant is that both Schaff and Gardiner went against the received wisdom of the time: either voluntary federalism or organic church unity but not both. Schaff and Gardiner disagreed; they saw the value of exploring both paths simultaneously, indeed that the one anticipated the other.

In his address, Schaff urged the restitution of the undivided church. As a first step he called for a federation of the churches in the United States. A decade and a half later, in 1908, the Federal Council of Churches was formed with thirty-two denominations numbering 18 million Americans. Robert Gardiner was to play an important role in that organization. When, again and again, his denomination refused to join, he maintained an Episcopalian presence in its governing body. Gardiner, like Schaff himself, would go well beyond the idea of federation.

The second event of significance was the founding in 1883 at St. James Church in Chicago of the Brotherhood of St. Andrew, an Episcopalian organization for men and boys. Gardiner was to become president of the brotherhood in 1904. The third event was the appointment in 1910 of the Episcopal bishop of Chicago, Charles P. Anderson, as Gardiner's immediate superior in the church unity movement. I will deal with the first two events in this chapter, the third in the next.

But first, the World's Columbian Exposition in the great new midwestern city provided the context for each of these three events and created for them, even in that still-frontier town, an atmosphere of accomplishment and authority. If Bostonians breathed the air of self-satisfaction, citizens of the Windy City exuded braggadocio. With its waterways and battery-driven motor launches, the Chicago fair aspired to nothing so much as to be crowned "the Venice of the Western World." Shortly before noon on May 1, 1893, President Grover Cleveland rose to address the opening ceremony. The occasion marked the four hundredth anniversary of the landing of Christopher Columbus in the New World. On that May morning the president looked out over a sea of some 350,000 to 500,000 faces of happily shouting, crushing, muddy-shoed citizens (final paving in front of the dignitaries' stand had yet to be completed). Choristers sang the "Columbian Hymn," and the U.S. Senate's blind chaplain, the Reverend W. H. Milburn, proclaimed a "sabbatic year for the whole human race" with such zeal that the crowd, thinking he was giving a speech, rather than praying, cheered. An epic poem, a Wagnerian overture, and the customary congratulations by the fair's director finally gave way to the president's speech. At that moment, "the sun, as if to give nature's blessing to the proceedings, burst forth from behind the clouds, bringing the fairy-like marble palaces and shimmering lagoons to life as the nation's leader faced the resounding cheers and sea of waving handkerchiefs." At the close of his remarks, Cleveland pressed a golden button (actually, a gilded telegraph key): immediately, fountains erupted, banners unfurled, bells and whistles sounded, cannons boomed, two hundred terrified white doves fled skyward, the band struck up "America," and, notwithstanding that she was the "most respected woman of her day," Jane Addams's purse was snatched. In more ways than one, Chicago had arrived. "When myriads of electric lights pierce night's sabled mantle and shed their opalescent rays upon the sapphire waters of the lagoons," caroled the Shepp brothers, "it presents a fairy scene of inexpressible splendor reminding one of the gorgeous descriptions in the Arabian Nights when Jabau al Raschid was Caliph."[1]

The Columbian Exposition was not only arresting but international as well. The event has been described as a watershed in U.S. history, a new beginning, a stepping forth onto the world stage of the first new nation among the great powers.[2] Covering nearly seven hundred acres, the fair was the largest ever staged.[3] It was also a cultural event that revealed two opposing sides of the American mind and attitude. The replication of this division was not at all in the minds and purposes of those who financially underwrote the venture. In a time of fierce national rivalries Chicago's business interests sought to celebrate capitalism, their city, and the United States of America, more or less in that order. The architects made sure that visitors would respond with corresponding awe: the buildings were corporation Roman. In Chicago in 1893 academic classicism triumphed over American spontaneity. It need not have, and it is just here in the fabric and stuff of the fair, in its physical shaping, that the opposing sides emerged. The city's celebrated architect, Louis Sullivan, "called for a native expression in architecture, a 'national style' answering to 'the wishes of the people, and ministering to its conceptions of the beautiful and the useful.'"[4]

Sullivan's national style provides a helpful analogy to Robert Gardiner's attitude and mode of operation in those institutional reforms he would undertake in the next twenty years. For the Chicago fair Sullivan wished to build from the inside out, to develop an architecture that grew out of "American realities" and "would be in keeping with the spirituality and character of the American experiment."[5]

1. R. Reid Badger, *The Great American Fair: The World's Columbian Exposition and American Culture* (Chicago: Nelson Hall, 1979), xiii; James W. Shepp and Daniel B. Shepp, *Shepp's World's Fair Photographed* (Chicago and Philadelphia, 1893), 9, quoted in Louis C. Hunter and Lynwood Bryant, *A History of Industrial Power in the United States, 1780–1930* (Cambridge: MIT Press, 1991), 209.

2. Henry Steele Commager, *The American Mind* (New Haven, CT: Yale University Press, 1950), 41. A more convincing case is made by Warren Zimmerman, *First Great Triumph: How Five Americans Made Their Country a World Power* (New York: Farrar, Straus, and Giroux, 2002), 8–9, for the years 1900 to 1909 as the watershed in U.S. history.

3. David F. Burg, *Chicago's White City of 1893* (Lexington: University Press of Kentucky, 1976), xii.

4. Alan Trachtenberg, *The Incorporation of America: Culture and Society in the Gilded Age* (New York: Hill and Wang, 1982), 226.

5. George Cotkin, *Reluctant Modernism: American Thought and Culture, 1880–1900* (New York: Twayne, 1992), 139.

His ideas did not fit the received wisdom, however; they were too newfangled. Unobstructed expression gave way to imposed authority. Spontaneity was smothered by symmetry of form and by monumentality. These proved to be the ingredients in "an effort to incorporate contrary and diverse values under the unity of a system of culture in support of a system of society."[6] Sullivan's idea of building from the inside out, of variety and of improvisation, remained to be picked up later by others.

The exposition's architectural symmetry of form was not in truth a *unity* of system at all so much as an outward uniformity of spectacle. The one invited contribution; the other asked for deference. Along these same lines but in a very different milieu, Gardiner too argued persuasively for contribution, this time by the churches toward a new "world's fair." Uniformity was imposed and required a submission in which fairgoers became spectators. A unity that grew from within invited participation. Conformity accompanied the one, freedom the other. Henry Adams put the difference in economic terms: "The American people had hesitated, vacillated . . . between two forces, one simply industrial, the other capitalistic and mechanical." In Chicago's exposition, Adams lamented, all "one's best citizens, reformers, churches, colleges, educated classes, had joined the banks to force submission to capitalism." There was no avoiding it, the "law of mass"—Oliver Wendell Holmes's force—ensured the victory of capitalism and submission to its power. Still, "of all forms of society or government, this was the one [Adams] liked least." Andrew Carnegie put it more bluntly: the exposition was "too Frenchy" and "most pretentious."[7]

Nevertheless, until the fair closed and Chicago's winter weather set in, the impression made by the pavilions and their surroundings was sensational. "The noble group of buildings, white against the blue of the lake," wrote Robert Morse Lovett, recalling the summer of 1893, was in its "unity of design a symbol of the co-operation which was the secret of Chicago's success." The exposition, at a cost of twenty-seven million dollars, was the triumph, he continued, of the feudal barons who had made the city great. For Lovett, a young professor at the University of Chicago, "the contrast between [the exposition's] artificial glory and the squalor of the real city was appalling." Lovett, like Adams, though in social, not economic, terms, saw both forces at work, the imposing and the

6. Trachtenberg, *Incorporation of America,* 216.
7. Adams, *The Education of Henry Adams* (Boston: Houghton Mifflin, 1918), 344; Louis M. Hacker, *The World of Andrew Carnegie, 1865–1901* (Philadelphia: J. B. Lippincott, 1968), 370.

imposed upon. Presumably, he would have wanted those living in modest communities or even in Chicago's squalid tenements to have had their say in the exposition. Native expression and style, the inward character of the culture, would not down. "American Indians," as they were then called, were permitted, however patronizingly, to exhibit their "savage" culture. African Americans were not. After all, what *culture* had they? The ragtime musician Scott Joplin, who arrived at the fair to play "jig" piano, or "cakewalks," found no place to relieve himself save at the Haitian Pavilion on the Midway, managed by an indignant Frederick Douglass.[8] Still, black people came and so did American jazz. Thereafter, a vibrant African American art, both in its simplest workaday form and later in its polyphonic complexity, caught the ear of a nation as completely as anything else in the new century. It had no rivals.

In the first week of May, just as the fair was opening, panic gripped the New York Stock Exchange. By the end of the year 642 banks had failed, railroads went into receivership, and the nation experienced the worst depression in its history. Uncertain income, farm failures, industrial layoffs, and an eroded hope of finding new work caused many to despair and some to take their own lives. With high imports, gold outflows through greenback redemption, and a declining treasury reserve, cheerless reality gainsaid the Dream City.[9] Still, there was success—and results of far-reaching significance. Both the recognition on the part of Sullivan, Adams, and Lovett of the "wishes of the people" and the desperate financial situation that engulfed them in early 1893 were to have a profound effect on Robert Gardiner and were to guide him into that camp in American society that stood for unity by free and open contribution, on the one hand, and for the alleviation of economic distress, on the other—in Christian terms, true ecumenicity and a social gospel. We have already examined his activities with respect to the latter; the following chapters will substantiate the former.

Of all the gatherings at the exposition for this and that, the World's Parliament of Religions was conspicuous and ascendant. It drew more attention than its

8. Lovett, *All Our Years* (New York: Viking Press, 1948), 53, 54. Douglass and Ida B. Wells wrote a tract, "The Reason Why the Colored American Is Not in the World's Columbian Exposition," quoted in John E. Findley, *Chicago's Great World's Fairs* (Manchester: Manchester University Press, 1994), 28.

9. Douglas Steeples and David O. Whitten, *Democracy in Desperation: The Depression of 1893* (Westport, CT: Greenwood Press, 1998), 33–37. Only the Great Depression of 1929 and thereafter surpassed that of 1893. See also Neil Harris, introduction to *The Land of Contrasts, 1880–1901,* edited by Neil Harris (New York: George Braziller, 1970), 26–28, 346–47, 354–55, with specific reference to poverty, inequality, and the Chicago exposition (32).

only rival, the women's World's Congress Auxiliary. The Parliament of Religions upstaged assemblies of educators, authors, architects, historians, labor leaders, and scientists. (The subject of evolution was addressed in the parliament, not in the scientific conference.) Religion's prestige at large expositions, however, was temporary. Eleven years later, at the St. Louis World's Fair of 1904, the honors for publicity and attendance passed to the International Congress of Arts and Sciences. Much as the later congress of 1904 represented an attempt to sum up for the new century the totality of academic disciplines, so the parliament of 1893 represented a summary of the nineteenth century's interest in so-called comparative religion.[10] The organizers sought, as the motto of the parliament declared, "To unite all Religion against irreligion, [and] to make the Golden Rule the basis of this union." Accompanying that confident aim was the equally prospective belief of the chairman, John Henry Barrows, that whereas "religion, like the white light of Heaven, has been broken into many-colored fragments by the prisms of men," the very fact of the parliament, Barrows warbled, will "change this many-colored radiance into the white light of heavenly truth." To that end, day after day, papers were read by ministers, bishops, swamis, and other wisdom merchants. Lecturers marched up to the podium, spoke their lines, and then sat down again. There were no panels for discussion, no questions from the floor, no respondents, no comments from the chair. But curiosity and colorful costumes brought packs of visitors to the four thousand–seat Hall of Columbus. From scarlet-robed James Cardinal Gibbons to the saffron-and-white-clad Hindu theists, the frequenters expected variety and novelty and got them. For nineteenth-century Americans, the outside world, particularly that of the Far East, was still exotic. "Fundamental and important differences . . . in the way people behaved were more apparent in daily life" in 1893. Not only did these sahibs and patriarchs from abroad "still live in rich and complicated settings of ancient faith," but they also adhered to those faiths and practices as much as the avatars of American Methodism.[11] To Westerners, the foreign and the unaccustomed retained their ability to astound.

10. William R. Everdell, *The First Moderns: Profiles in the Origins of Twentieth-Century Thought* (Chicago: University of Chicago Press, 1997), 219; Joseph M. Kitagawa, introduction to *The History of Religions: Essays in Methodology*, edited by Mircea Eliade and Joseph M. Kitagawa (Chicago: University of Chicago Press, 1959), 2.

11. Louis Henry Jordan, *Comparative Religion: Its Genesis and Growth* (Edinburgh: T. and T. Clark, 1905), 197–200, quoted in Kitagawa, introduction to *History of Religions*, 3; Barrows, "The History of the Parliament," in *The World's Parliament of Religions*, edited by Barrows, 2 vols.

But the goal of a single white light of heavenly truth did not emerge out of the many-colored radiance of the event. Just the opposite: teaching *about* many religions eventually displaced either belief in one alone or belief in one out of many. The line of march from the spiritual wine tasters at the Chicago fair to religion as an academic study, to the disestablishment of the Protestant phalanx, and eventually to its deconstruction in university circles might have been anticipated in the very format of the parliament itself. It was not. Although no open debate on issues dividing different religions or even Christian denominations took place, touchier subjects were not altogether shunned. Criticism (by Asians) of Western missionary methods, disapproval of economic inequality at home, objections to misconceptions of Judaism, expostulations on religion and race, and remarks on gender relations all received their day in court. Throughout, interest remained high. On the last day seven thousand jammed the World's Parliament of Religions in two vast halls. Still, not all religious groups chose to attend. To the chairman's rhetorical question, "Why should not Christians be glad to learn what God has wrought through Buddha and Zoroaster—through the sage of China, and the prophet of India and the prophet of Islam?" the archbishop of Canterbury replied, "Why should they?"[12] With the important exception of Princeton Theological Seminary's Benjamin B. Warfield, conservative Christians stayed home.[13] Baptists withdrew because the exposition was open on Sundays.

Had they anticipated the future impact of Vedanta philosopher Swami Vivekananda (Narendranath Datta), those who stood aloof might have found further cause for alarm, even flight. Vivekananda, "the one who exults in a clear conscience and in discernment," took advantage of every opportunity afforded by the luxuriant growth of religious pluralism. With his superb bearing, swarthy features, "princely raiment" that he varied adroitly, and rich American friends, this "first missionary from East to West... opened up new vistas of expanding life and religion to thousands" of the earnest and the impressionable.[14]

---

(Chicago: Parliament Publishing, 1893), 1:3; J. M. Roberts, *Twentieth Century* (New York: Viking Press, 1999), 14, 15.

12. See, for instance, Barrows, *World's Parliament,* 2:812–13, 1:75.

13. See Grant Wacker, "The Protestant Awakening to World Religions," in *Between the Times: The Travail of the Protestant Establishment in America, 1900–1960,* by William R. Hutchison (Cambridge: Cambridge University Press, 1989), 257–58.

14. Amit Chaudhuri, "The Suborning of Saffron: How Hinduism Became a Rich Man's Religion," *Times Literary Supplement,* March 31, 2002, 14; Wendell Thomas, *Hinduism Invades*

In spite of the fact that the "thousands" turned out to be a few score wealthy sophisticates, Vivekananda became a larger-than-life figure, a notable symbol of the expanding American consciousness of world religions. And the nice part about it was that men and women could join the Vedanta Society and still remain loyal Episcopalians or Presbyterians. After all, did not every religious prophet preach the same message? To that perennial American question Robert Gardiner would give an emphatic No. Millionaire physician, Social Gospeler, and socialist Episcopalian J. G. Phelps Stokes thought otherwise. Taking full and officially unanticipated advantage of the much-flaunted Episcopalian comprehensiveness, he "ventured into many other Protestant faiths and nondenominational Christian movements" as well as into Hinduism, Buddhism, and Islamic Sufi mysticism. Wherever he worshiped, Stokes sought, in a tongue-tying phrase, the "One with in and as All That is."[15] To make sure that membership in the Vendanta Society and all the rest did not jeopardize his designation as "a member in good standing" at Grace Church on New York's lower Broadway, the amiable and conscientious Stokes checked out his moves with his Episcopal rector. Could it have been that the Vedanta Society was attractive to this rich young man because, whereas Christianity has often quarreled with the enjoyment of riches, Hinduism rushed to embrace the West's benefits?

If the parliament was not, as was extravagantly claimed, "the greatest event so far in the history of the world" or the "most important occurrence since the birth of Jesus," it served notice that Americans were ready to be entertained by faiths that had yet to play in Peoria. Whereas Swami Vivekananda was par excellence the exotic presence, Philip Schaff was deservedly the most respected. It was Schaff who "delivered the great irenic address on the churches of Christendom before the World's Parliament of Religions." The speech was at once a statement of its author's profoundest hope and the last public statement that he bequeathed to those who succeeded him. Before the year was out Schaff was dead. As a result the speech's significance was even greater. Against a background of oohs and aahs and the parade of dignitaries, Schaff delivered carefully crafted

_America_ (New York: Beacon Press, 1930), 77. It has also been noted that "the World [_sic_] Parliament of Religions . . . changed the entire landscape for Buddhism in America" (Charles H. Lippy and Peter W. Williams, eds., _Encyclopedia of the American Religious Experience,_ 3 vols. [New York: Charles Scribner's Sons, 1988], s.v. "Buddhism").

15. Robert D. Reynolds Jr., "Millionaire Socialist and Omnist Episcopalian: J. G. Phelps Stokes's Political and Spiritual Search for the All," in _Socialism and Christianity in Early 20th Century America,_ edited by Jacob H. Dorn (Westport, CT: Greenwood Press, 1998), 205, 216.

sentences under the title "The Reunion of Christendom." Unlike the other speeches, his was a call to action, not astonishment. He upheld a desirable truth: the coming together of those who professed one Lord, one faith, one baptism. He was not making an appeal for mere tolerance.[16] To be sure, many had spoken before of uniting divided denominations; a few, such as Episcopalian William Reed Huntington, would later speak of organic union within the American scene.[17] Under Huntington's inspiration, first the Episcopal Church in America and then the Anglican Communion as a whole, in 1886 and 1888, respectively, had laid down the conditions under which they would unite with other churches and traditions. The Anglican stipulations for reunion were acceptance of the holy scriptures as the Word of God, the primitive creeds as the rule of faith, the two sacraments ordained by Christ himself, and the episcopate as the keystone of governmental unity. On the last point, the final text (Lambeth Conference of 1888) read: "The Historic Episcopate, locally adapted in the methods of its administration to the varying needs of the nations and peoples called of God into the unity of His Church."[18] Schaff set a very different course, one that Robert Gardiner would follow: for both men there would be no prior conditions of the sort required by Huntington and other Episcopalians, no ultimatums, only the basic biblical principle that God was in Christ reconciling the world to himself. That alone would be enjoined on those participating in interchurch activities. All else—including Anglicanism's beloved "historic episcopate"—was to take a back seat.

The reunion of Christendom, Schaff argued, presupposed "an original union which has been marred and obstructed but never wholly destroyed." He noted the existence already of such an agreement on fundamental articles of faith

16. Alfred W. Momerie, quoted in Burg, *White City*, 281; Don Herbert Yoder, "Christian Unity in Nineteenth-Century America," in *A History of the Ecumenical Movement, 1517–1948*, edited by Ruth Rouse and Stephen Neill (Philadelphia: Westminster Press, 1967), 246. In a different but related context, see C. John Sommerville, "Post-secularism Marginalizes the University: A Rejoinder to Hollinger," *Church History* 71 (December 2002): 848–57, esp. 854–55.

17. See Huntington, *A National Church* (New York: Charles Scribner's Sons, 1898); and John F. Woolverton, "William Reed Huntington and Church Unity: The Historical and Theological Background of the Chicago-Lambeth Quadrilateral" (PhD diss., Columbia University, 1963). For federal union, see, for instance, Elias B. Sanford, *Origin and History of the Federal Council of Churches of Christ in America* (Hartford, CT: S. S. Scranton, 1916).

18. John F. Woolverton, "Huntington's Quadrilateral—a Critical Study," *Church History* 39: 2 (June 1970): 198–211. For variations on the wording of the "four points," see "Text of the Chicago-Lambeth Quadrilateral, 1886/1888," *Anglican Theological Review*, supp. series, no. 10 (March 1988): vii.

necessary to salvation: Christ, the head of the church; God manifested in Jesus Christ, that is, the Incarnation (which would become Gardiner's central doctrine for unity); and for Schaff—much too optimistically, as it turned out—an already agreed-upon unity of scholarship on the creeds, the exegesis of scripture, and historical studies. These, he insisted, though formerly "subservient to apologetic and polemical ends," are "more and more carried on without prejudice and with the sole object of ascertaining the meaning of the text and the facts of history." Moreover, he found in the American scene the kind of atmosphere most conducive to Christian union. On the one hand, there was religious "liberty and equality before the law"; on the other hand, the evil of divisions, antagonisms, and (competitive) interferences at home and on the missionary fields abroad was "beginning to be felt more and more." The cure must begin, Schaff averred, where the disease of disunity had reached its crisis stage and where the church was freest to act, "for the reunion of Christendom, like religion itself, cannot be forced, but must be free and voluntary."[19] Like Sullivan's architectural principle, the logic of unity for the churches must grow from the inside out.

Schaff divided the Christian Gaul into three parts: the Greek and Slavonic peoples of the Orthodox churches, the "Latin races of Southern Europe and [South] America" who were Roman Catholic, and "the Teutonic races of the North and West" who were Protestant. Although the description was far too simple, it was his hope that all the divisions of Christendom would, "in the providence of God, be made subservient to a greater harmony." Beginning with North American Protestantism, where once the sin of schism abounded, he predicted that the grace of future reunion would much more flourish. Schaff believed that "variety in unity and unity in variety is the law of God . . . [and] we must expect the greatest variety in the Church of the future." In the meantime, he warned, those "who believe in the ultimate triumph of their own creed and form of government or worship . . . are all mistaken and indulge in a vain dream." He challenged the Episcopalians: their "historic episcopate" was a stumbling block to the rest and would "never be conceded by them if it is understood to mean the necessity of . . . Episcopal ordination in unbroken succession." Schaff wanted a liberal construction placed on the episcopate as "locally adapted," broad enough "to include the 'historic presbyterate' which dates from the apostolic age and was never interrupted." Or perhaps, he mused, Episcopalians would

19. Schaff, "The Reunion of Christendom," in *World's Parliament,* edited by Barrows, 2: 1192, 1193.

"drop [the historic episcopate] altogether as a term of reunion."[20] Whatever they decided, one thing was sure: they could never arbitrarily impose it on others. Once again his warning would bear fruit.

But Schaff was not through. Union must include the Greek and Roman churches. Imaginatively and with seasoned wit, he suggested that the pope, "under the inspiration of a higher authority, should infallibly declare his own fallibility in all matters lying outside of his own communion and invite the Greeks and the Protestants to a pan-Christian council in Jerusalem where the mother-church of Christendom held the first council of reconciliation." In a spirit of humility and of listening to the others that Gardiner would himself urge on his own people, Schaff called for "a restatement of all controverted points . . . [that] shall remove misrepresentations, neutralize anathemas pronounced upon imaginary heresies, and show the way to harmony." Again optimistically, he thought that grammatical and historical exegesis would bring out the "real meaning of the writer instead of putting in the fancies of the reader." Proof texting on all sides for polemical purposes was out. The study of history—"'with malice toward none but with charity for all'"—was in "as a means of correcting sectarian prejudices and increasing mutual appreciation." Such an investigation would, he believed, bring the denominations closer together in "a humble recognition of their defects and a grateful praise for the good that the same Spirit has wrought in them."[21] Skillfully, Schaff wove together belief in historical evolution with natural evolution and concluded that his listeners should be afraid of neither. Had not Christ himself in the twin parables of the mustard seed and the leaven endorsed what every historian now accepts? Every evolution must have a beginning; God's power was displayed even more wonderfully in the gradual process.

In the meantime, before reunion, there must be the cultivation of the irenic spirit, cooperation in philanthropic endeavors and in missions, and the "duty and privilege of prayer, that his disciples may be one in him, as he is one with the Father." As we shall see in the rest of this study, Robert Gardiner echoed Schaff, even to the necessity of the Johannine high priestly prayer to the Father that "they may be one even as we are one" (John 17:22). The similarity of attitude and even of language is remarkable. Yet whereas Schaff called for a "federal or confederate union" resembling the "political confederation of Switzerland,

20. Ibid., 1194, 1195.
21. Ibid., 1196, 1198.

the United States, and the modern German Empire," Gardiner seventeen years later took the final step toward the great church historian's ultimate goal, organic union. In the meantime, he was—and remained—determined to play a role in what became the FCC. In a particularly perceptive essay, one historian has suggested that the council "functioned as an 'established church.' . . . It embodied in a single institution the authority, interests and activities of a religious establishment incorporated only in denominations. . . . It also served, like any other established church, as a symbol of basic values, a constant reminder to the faithful of their duties to God, church, and society."[22] While certain nonestablishment churches such as the Society of Friends, Seventh-Day Baptists, and others were members of the FCC, a significant number of churches refused at first to join, and some never did: the Southern Baptist Convention, most Lutherans, the rapidly emerging Holiness and Pentecostal churches, and until 1937 the Episcopal Church. But for Gardiner and his friend George Hodges, both of whom served in leadership positions, the influence of the FCC toward greater ecumenism was considerable. At council meetings they rubbed elbows with leaders of thirty-three other denominations. As well as representing and summing up the Protestant establishment, the FCC was an invaluable training ground for discovering the United States and for forging ideological unity. It was also a place where Gardiner could and did further his own purposes.[23] Still, the Episcopal Church refused to join.[24] Whereas William Reed Huntington disapproved of the organization because it appeared to make federalism a substitute for "organic" unity, Gardiner did not. He would serve on both its executive and its administrative committees for the rest of his life.

At the end of the century, Chicago was not only the scene of the World's Fair with its declaration of America's national prestige but also the place where a new Episcopalian lay organization took hold, prospered, and served as a model for other American denominations. That organization also shaped Gardiner's attitude and career in the larger Christian world.

22. Ibid., 1199; Yoder, "Christian Unity," 256; Robert A. Schneider, "Voice of Many Waters: Church Federation in the Twentieth Century," in *Between the Times,* by Hutchison, 97.

23. John A. Knight to Floyd Tomkins, August 24, 1965, Floyd Tomkins Papers, Archives of the Episcopal Church, Austin, TX. Gardiner presided in 1912 at a public meeting in Chicago of the FCC, titled Youth and Christian Unity. The major speaker was Thomas A. Marshall, vice president of the United States.

24. George E. DeMille, *The Episcopal Church since 1900* (New York: Morehouse-Gorham, 1955), 66. The Episcopal Church regularly refused membership until 1937.

James Lawrence Houghteling was the son of one of Chicago's feudal barons. After graduation from Yale in 1883, Houghteling returned home to become active both in his father's banking business and in the family's parish, St. James Church. Not content to teach a Bible class as many young businessmen then did, Houghteling founded the Brotherhood of St. Andrew, which "in 1883 epitomized late nineteenth-century lay evangelism." He was twenty-eight. Starting with a group of twelve young men at aristocratic and prestigious St. James, Houghteling forged a national and in a short time international movement within Anglicanism. It paralleled the older YMCA, Mott's Student Volunteer Movement (1888), and the World Student Christian Federation (1895). The cumulative influence on the ecumenical movement of these organizations is still a rich field of investigation.[25] All sought "the evangelization of the laity by the laity." In the BSA, it was declared that, as the apostles Andrew and Philip had gone to find others and bring them to Jesus (John 1:40–51), so its early members—all about seventeen years old—would set forth to bring a brother or a friend within sound of the Gospel. They did so with marked success. Not only were the Houghtelings people of "deep religious sentiment," but, more important, young James was able to instill dedication and excitement in those around him. As a result, the BSA became an outstanding example of communal joie de vivre. It was the first of its kind, was copied by other denominations, and stood in sharp contrast to the academic and literary "fin de siecle spirit of deep pessimism . . . of ennui, languidness, and depression," the symptoms of American nervousness that "had become the defining affliction of modern times."[26]

From a group of eleven boys meeting on November 30, 1883, the brotherhood grew within the year to forty; by 1886 there were parochial chapters at work in thirty-six additional parishes. Modest enough for a starter. The year before, Houghteling created an advisory council and enlisted an impressive array of public figures: William T. Stirling, vice president of the Illinois Steel Company; William S. Rainsford, the influential rector of St. George's Church in New York City; G. Harry Davis, judge of the court of common pleas in Philadelphia; H. D. W. English, an insurance executive, conservationist, and chairman

25. Rima Lunin Schultz, *The Church and the City: A Social History of 150 Years at St. James, Chicago* (Chicago: Cathedral of Saint James, 1986), 135; Ruth Rouse, "Other Aspects of the Ecumenical Movement, 1910–1948," in *History of the Ecumenical Movement*, edited by Rouse and Neill, 601.

26. Edward Duff, S.J., *The Social Thought of the World Council of Churches* (New York: Association Press, 1956), 21, 136, 138. Cotkin, *Reluctant Modernism*, 144.

of the Pittsburgh Civic Commission who became president of the BSA; John F. Stiness, chief justice of the Rhode Island Supreme Court; and John W. Wood, editor of the famed *Spirit of Missions*.[27] By 1887 there were 115 chapters with a total membership of more than two thousand men and boys. Ten years later the brotherhood had become an international movement within Anglicanism with groups in England and Japan; thereafter, additional chapters were added in China, Alaska, and Hawaii, to be followed in 1908 by thirteen more brother-hoods in other places.[28] By 1906 there were seventeen thousand young men and boys in more than twelve hundred senior and junior brotherhoods.[29] Two years before that, Gardiner became the president of the movement. In order to hold the American brotherhoods together, he appointed four traveling secretaries to assist him, and with their success he added a fifth in 1908. Gardiner himself was "continually traveling all over the country."[30]

What was the character of the fellowship? It asked its members to repeat the example of Andrew and bring a brother "to Christ." Besides the missionary motive, the BSA had two rules: the first was prayer, which included worship; the second was the rule of service. Gardiner picked up on the first rule at once. Throughout his life he was committed to and insisted upon regular prayer for himself and for those he led. He sought and obtained for his men and boys a "Week of Prayer" at the beginning of Advent in 1908. It was to be "for the spread of Christ's Kingdom." In the planning of the special week, he wisely involved the young people themselves. "If by earnest prayer and careful thought," he declared extravagantly, "we will all make careful preparation, God, the Holy Spirit, will make this the greatest week in the Church's history since Pentecost." The Holy Spirit, he went on to assert, did not cease inspiring people at the end of the apostolic age. He then enjoined daily prayer and regular attendance at the Holy Eucharist.[31] As president of the BSA, Gardiner combined evangelical zeal with high church sacramentalism.

27. Edward H. Bousalls, "A Retrospect," *St. Andrew's Cross,* September 1904, 361, quoted in notebook 7, Tomkins Papers. See also "Prominent Men of the Brotherhood Convention," *Church Militant,* October 1902, 4.
28. Gardiner, "The Week of Prayer," *St. Andrew's Cross,* October 1908, 7. The additional loca-tions were the Philippines, Puerto Rico, Cuba, Mexico, the West Indies, the Canal Zone, France, Germany, Italy, Africa, Persia, Australia, and New Zealand.
29. *St. Andrew's Cross,* February 1906, 349, quoted in notebook 7, Tomkins Papers, 1416.
30. *St. Andrew's Cross,* December 1908, 144; January 1909, 297.
31. Gardiner, editorial in ibid., July 1908, 702–3; February 1906, 347.

Gardiner's language about bringing people to Christ, his supplications for the spread of the kingdom, and his confidence in the inspiration of the Holy Spirit had the pungency of the revival tent. At a distance his clichés gush, seemingly employed to win converts by their fervency alone. The "Brotherhood idea," however, was different: "It is as far as anything can be from 'exciting' a young man's emotions frequently or at all." A member of the fellowship was to exert "personal influence in the quietest and most natural way on the men who are closest to him." Appeals to the emotions "I know to be dangerous, and there goes with it," he continued, "a more or less unconscious and certainly unintentional exclusiveness—as of saying, 'we are the ones'—which is fatal." What he termed derisively as the "missionary spirit" of one-upmanship clashed with that of the brotherhood: the former implies, he judged, "that you have got something which the other fellow has not, and asserts your conviction that he needs it." This puts the owner of that spirit "in a false position from the start, by affronting the democratic sense of the other fellow." In the BSA's idea of service to the sick and hungry, "the difference between your condition and theirs is obvious, and there is no affront." As a result Gardiner was "somewhat skeptical" about the methods of the more obviously revivalistic Northfield Conferences of Dwight L. Moody, though otherwise "I see the good [in Northfield], and it is very good—even admirable."[32] Such was the inverted enthusiasm of most Episcopalians.

At times Gardiner sounded moralistic. He spoke to his young men and boys about being free from sin. He declared that "only by self-mastery, only by the voluntary putting on the Lord Jesus Christ can we emancipate ourselves from the lusts of the flesh, the weariness of the world and the snares of the devil." It was all pretty standard stuff for those days. But he was not above criticizing the administration at Harvard of President Charles W. Eliot and Dean LeBaron R. Briggs who made the mistake, Gardiner claimed, of stopping with personal virtue. Their "aim is comparatively low, for they are content with improving the morality of the College, and so long as their influence does not extend beyond mere morality, they are not giving the men they influence any permanent inspiration and guide." Gardiner was not trying to turf out the "depraved." Morality by itself, he maintained, did not take a person very far or last very long. The man

---

32. Gardiner to Endicott Peabody, October 26, 1900, April 17, 1909, Endicott Peabody Papers, Archives of Groton School, Groton, MA.

from Maine had other fish to fry, theological ones that he was to serve up in the coming years. He insisted on the classical expressions of Christian faith, on the importance of the creeds, and on sound theology springing from them. The resurrection of Jesus Christ, he told his brotherhood, "made an absolutely new world. After the first Easter [the disciples] were absolutely new men." Creeds were vital, "for they rest on the great fact of the Incarnation, the centre of all true life, individual, social, or national." He taught the union of wills with God. From it came love, "burning, eager, impatient indomitable, not static"; it would "recreate the world."[33]

The second rule of the BSA was service. Here Gardiner's previous experience as a Social Gospeler in Boston's Episcopal City Mission and in the Church Social Union came into play. He wanted "weekly lesson papers on pressing social questions—child labor, prison reform, [and] housing."[34] He specifically mentioned the essays issued by Josiah Strong and William H. Tolman's American Institute of Social Service.[35] Once again, as in *Our Neighbor*, he spoke in the *St. Andrew's Cross* of the conflict between capital and labor. This time he was more innovative. He wanted his young readers to help "destroy the greed of the trusts and [that of] the poorer anarchists." He still placed his faith in the power of Christian brotherhood to accomplish the task. He spoke with contempt of the "increasing and soul-destroying luxury of the rich and [at the same time] the sordid desire of those who are not rich to heap up wealth." As before, the "consecration of the individual to the personal service of the God of righteousness and peace and love" was his repeated theme.[36] This time he added Strong and Tolman to it.

Consecration did not shut out action. Members of the BSA were expected to provide help across a broad spectrum, often small things, but not unimportant. For example, notices went into urban hotels: "Travelling men who are sick or in trouble are invited to call on the Brotherhood of St. Andrew" together with information about how to reach whoever was locally in charge that day. Brothers were to help in hospitals, assist the destitute, and encourage the weary. In 1907

---

33. Gardiner, editorial in *St. Andrew's Cross*, July 1905, 379; Gardiner to Peabody, October 26, 1900, Peabody Letters; Gardiner, editorial in *St. Andrew's Cross*, April 1907, 427; July 1907, 629–30; May 1908, 566.

34. Gardiner, editorial in *St. Andrew's Cross*, September 1908, 836.

35. W. D. P. Bliss, ed., *The New Encyclopedia of Social Reform* (New York: Funk and Wagnalls, 1908), s.v. "American Institute for Social Service." The American Institute of Social Service had been founded in 1902 and combined in its publications factual descriptions of social conditions together with Christian teaching bearing on the issues involved.

36. Gardiner, editorial in *St. Andrew's Cross*, November 1905, 141; July 1907, 629.

Gardiner rejoiced that the Episcopal Church, because of the brotherhood, "is now preeminent in placing Services within the reach of the unfortunate in jails, prisons and penitentiaries, in hospitals, homes, refuges, asylums and alms houses." If Christ came to Boston, he would go to those places first, "the mansions of sorrow and pain." Gardiner wanted his young men to take the church's message "to the down-trodden . . . the suffering and oppressed."[37] He held up the Christlike figure of Edward L. Atkinson, the reforming priest at Boston's Church of the Ascension from 1895 to 1901. Gardiner had known the man personally; Atkinson was "that gallant young knight of the cross" who rejoiced in his work in the slums of Boston. Atkinson had started a brotherhood chapter at the Church of the Ascension.[38] The young man bore, wrote Gardiner, "the sins and sorrows and distresses of the hundreds and thousands who came to him from all parts of a great city, yet [he was] always full of courage, hope, and enthusiasm." He carried the burdens of many, and those ever after counted him as a friend. Members of the BSA should do likewise. In the pages of the *St. Andrew's Cross* Gardiner recommended a biography of Atkinson, who had drowned in 1902.[39]

What confronted a young man entering the brotherhood was a military-like organization. BSA leaders greeted young men and boys arriving at church; these "lieutenants" were stationed in the aisles.[40] Under them were the "privates," usually one or more to a pew. "Quartermasters" kept the pews filled with hymn books and invitation cards. Those entering the brotherhood pledged to pray daily and to bring others into the movement's Bible-study classes. Inductees received certificates of membership, printed prayers, and a summary of the objects and recommendations of the brotherhood. And then there was the *St. Andrew's Cross* to which members were expected to subscribe. It was made clear from the start that the BSA existed not to propagate itself but "to revitalize the spiritual life of the laity of the whole church, and arouse and mobilize them to greater personal effort for Christ and his Kingdom."[41] Later, Gardiner would push the

37. Ibid., July 1904, 321; May 1907, 493.

38. Jonathan A. Dorn, "'Our Best Gospel Appliances': Institutional Churches and the Emergence of Social Christianity in the South End of Boston, 1880–1920" (PhD diss., Harvard University, 1994), 262.

39. Gardiner, editorial in *St. Andrew's Cross,* November 1906, 79; Charles Lewis Slattery, *Edward L. Atkinson* (New York: Longman, Greens, 1904). For a more critical view of Atkinson, see J. A. Dorn, "'Our Best Gospel Appliances,'" 258–67.

40. Clifford Putney, "Men and Religion: Aspects of the Church Brotherhood Movement, 1880–1920," *Anglican and Episcopal History* 63:4 (December 1994): 461.

41. Editorial in *Witness,* September 4, 1947, 3.

idea of revitalizing the laity and insisted that "the Church needs a great congress of her laymen of all classes, that they may come together in a common effort to realize their responsibility as the backbone of the Church." If, he continued, the brotherhood has no such vision, "it has no right to exist." In effect, he sought to create a "Men's Auxiliary" comparable to the "Women's Auxiliary." He wanted the laity as never before to "take their place in the councils of the Church." But he insisted that the brotherhood existed for the church and that clergy and laity work closely together. With the BSA he hoped to build up "in each diocese a body of laymen who would be personal followers and supporters of the Bishop and therefore be very much more valuable in their own parishes."[42]

How elitist was the Brotherhood of St. Andrew under Gardiner's watch? Although its leaders cooperated with the YMCA and the Student Christian Movement (SCM), unlike its Methodist imitator (the Brotherhood of Andrew and Philip), the BSA did not become interdenominational; it did not take in young men of churches other than the Episcopal. Partly, the reason was no doubt snobbishness but also a sense of ecclesiastical apartness that was the legacy of high church colonial–New England Anglicanism. That religious bequest was built upon by nineteenth-century high churchmen, leading one recent historian even to claim that, "as any student of theology can attest, Episcopal theology has always marched to a drummer far different from that of the rest of Protestantism."[43] Be that as it may, Episcopalians had a tendency to bolt the door and keep out the nonclubbable. So, as Gardiner recognized, did others. The same come-outer tendency, he believed, obtained when the Moodyites said, "We are the ones," to the exclusion of the spiritually unwashed. As he questioned the self-importance of born-again Christians, so he came to throw doubt upon high-plumed Episcopalian attitudes.

Along with his rejection of denominational proscriptions, he tried to break down the barriers that maintained them. The Social Gospel's emphasis on the kingdom of God caught his imagination. More and more that larger supremacy must become "the controlling motive of our lives"; when this happens, he went on, "the divisions which now hinder the progress of the Kingdom will disappear, and we shall recognize that the Holy Church Universal is, and must be, one;

42. Gardiner, editorial in *St. Andrew's Cross*, October 1907, 6, 15; August 1907, 698; May 1907, 493; Gardiner to Methodist bishop L. W. Burton, March 30, 1915, Robert H. Gardiner Correspondence, 1910–1924, World Council of Churches, Geneva, Switzerland.

43. Robert Bruce Mullin, *Episcopal Vision/American Reality: High Church Theology and Social Thought in Evangelical America* (New Haven, CT: Yale University Press, 1986), x.

for it is the one body of the one Lord." His thinking about Christian reunion was beginning to take form. It was already a combination of the evangelical and the catholic, the "kingdom" idea, on the one hand, and the "sacramental idea of the church . . . [and its] sacramental teaching," on the other. If he believed that the sacramental church was better represented by the Episcopal Church, the dominion of God, he knew, took in all Christians. Acting on that last belief, he corralled representatives of the seven largest denominations for his Week of Prayer in 1908. He would have the BSA "resolved to use all Christians of every name, in every part of the world to observe the first week in Advent next as a season of special prayer for the Kingdom."[44]

But the democratic kingdom needed an assist from the patrician junto. Gardiner began to carry on a correspondence with an increasingly potent figure in American education, Endicott Peabody, rector and headmaster of Groton School. So popular among the wealthy had Peabody and his school become that in 1892 Gardiner "entered" his son William Tudor there, even though the boy would not be old enough to attend for another decade. Later he confessed to Peabody, "I never meant to send a child of mine to a boarding school, but I shall send this young man to Groton without any hesitation or regret." The following year he began patiently to enlist Peabody in the cause of the BSA: "It is a good while since I plagued you, and you must be getting lonesome." He wanted "the rector," as Peabody was known, "to expound the Brotherhood idea." Evidently, he was successful, for by the spring of 1907 Peabody got recent graduates to attend a BSA gathering: "I'm glad your boys liked the College Conference. Everyone else did, and I guess we have really gotten the ball started." Later, Peabody asked his older friend for a history of the BSA: the rector wanted to preach a sermon "telling [students] something about the Christian Endeavor Society, the Student Volunteer Movement, the Layman's Forward Movement, and the St. Andrew's Brotherhood."[45]

There was a breadth and inclusiveness to these protagonists. Both were socially

44. Gardiner, editorial in *St. Andrew's Cross,* May 1908, 566; Gardiner to Peabody, November 6, 1907, Peabody Letters; Gardiner, "A Twentieth Century Crusade," *St. Andrew's Cross,* November 1908, 77–78.

45. Gardiner to Peabody, October 15, 1901, March 11, 1902, May 4, 1907, Peabody Letters; Peabody to Gardiner, January 10, 1910, Peabody Letters. The Christian Endeavor Society had been founded in 1881 by Congregationalists in Maine; it was interdenominational and international. The Laymen's Forward Movement was Episcopalian and was later shortened to simply the Forward Movement, its purpose the publication of daily devotional materials.

and ecclesiologically democratic for their class and day. At Gardiner's urging, Peabody had joined the Church Social Union. But that was not the only influence on Groton's rector; earlier, the future schoolman had been strongly impressed with the English cleric Charles Kingsley and the latter's "enthusiasm in connection with social problems." Both Gardiner and Peabody were progressives. In the 1930s Peabody sided, not uncritically, with his former pupil Franklin D. Roosevelt, turning aside in coolly measured tones those of Groton's rich who believed the president was a national menace and a "traitor to his class." Likewise, in their progressivism neither Gardiner nor Peabody wanted the church to isolate itself from other Christian denominations on campuses and elsewhere. And so they encouraged cooperation with larger movements. On the other hand, they stood by "institutional religion," as Peabody put it, and believed "that the [Episcopal] Church has a most important work to do among the colleges."[46]

Gardiner frankly wanted to enlist in the church those who would be the elite leaders of the rising generation. But between the clubs, secret societies, and fraternities on Ivy League campuses, on the one hand, and the attractions of such society hangouts as Long Island, Newport, and the North Shore of Massachusetts Bay, on the other, the task was not always easy. At Harvard Gardiner deplored the "'gulf' that stands between Mt. Auburn Street and the Yard," that is, between the elite and the poorer students. Still, he was upbeat and thought the segregation could be overcome. He even criticized Peabody for saying that "Harvard is 'one of the least democratic institutions in the country.'" Gardiner, however, was himself not above criticizing his alma mater and confessed at one point that the college needed "above all things the spirit of the Brotherhood of St. Andrew, but I know of hardly any place where less of that spirit is found." He wrote Peabody of his discouragement: "I have not really succeeded in interesting anyone in or out of College who represents the privileged classes. . . . [T]hese privileged boys need to be reached in some way which shall be more permanently effective than existing methods."[47]

But the BSA was growing rapidly and could very well do without them. It was attracting middle-class young men and boys. The brotherhood's council included youth from Houghteling's Chicago but also from colleges in other

46. Gardiner to Peabody, October 15, 1901, Peabody Letters; Frank D. Ashburn, *Peabody of Groton: A Portrait* (New York: Coward McCann, 1944), 38, 344–45; Peabody to Gardiner, October 13, 1915, Peabody Letters.

47. Gardiner to Peabody, May 4, 1905, October 22, 1900, March 27, 1907, March 11, 1902 (for elitism), Peabody Letters.

cities throughout the country: Savannah, New Orleans, Louisville, Detroit, Bismarck, Helena, Colorado Springs, San Francisco, and Seattle, to name a few.[48] Nor were the elite the only ones on Gardiner's wish list of fresh faces; he wanted the church to touch those "whom she has seldom reached in the past." He singled out African Americans, noting in the *St. Andrew's Cross* "the feeling of shame throughout the Church at the inadequacy of her efforts to minister to the negro and the universal desire to discharge this peculiar responsibility more thoroughly." In the same year he read Booker T. Washington and W. E. B. Du Bois's Bull Lectures, *The Negro in the South* (1907). He spoke as well of having "colored chapters" of the BSA. Nor was he reluctant to warn young white southern gentlemen for whom chivalry and hospitality were everything that "gentility is not a matter of wealth or fashion, of mental training, or of clothes. No matter how obscure, poor, humble," a man is a gentleman "if he be sober, chaste, honest." As Jesus rejoiced, he continued, so the disciples of the brotherhood must be glad and eager "to help the poor and the weak and the down-trodden, seeing and reverencing in every man he meets the image of God." Elsewhere he commended "our constant mingling on terms of perfect equality with all sorts and conditions of men."[49]

Despite the shame he felt about white treatment of blacks, from 1904 onward Gardiner took no part in the Episcopal Church's debates in its General Conventions over providing African American bishops for black communicants and parishes.[50] In light of his BSA stand vis-à-vis the "colored chapters," it is a curious omission. In 1907 the idea was promoted of black suffragan bishops who would serve black congregations; such a one would have a seat in the House of Bishops but no vote in a diocesan convention and no right of succession to another post within his own or any other diocese. Individual dioceses were to choose their own men. It was understood that these bishops would supervise work among blacks only. Maine's delegates, Gardiner among them, voted in the affirmative. This proposal became church law, though most African American

48. Others were Tarboro, North Carolina; Cleveland; Los Angeles; Kirkwood, Missouri; and Nashville. Still, of the forty-six members of the council, nineteen, or 41 percent, were from the northeast corridor; this was perhaps inevitable, as well over half of the Episcopal Church resided in the Northeast.

49. Gardiner, editorial in *St. Andrew's Cross,* April 1909, 552; October 1907, 6; October 1905, 38; December 1905, 210.

50. The issue was a complicated one. See David Reimers, "Negro Bishops and Diocesan Segregation in the Protestant Episcopal Church, 1870–1954," *Historical Magazine of the Protestant Episcopal Church* 31:3 (September 1962): 231–42.

Episcopalian leaders opposed it. Such bishops would clearly be second-class citizens in the church. African American leaders wanted a black missionary district with separate but equal rights to send their bishops and delegates, clerical and lay, to the church's General Convention where they could vote with everyone else. It was not to be. When in 1913 a racial missionary district was suggested that "shall occupy the same relation to the General Convention and have the same rights of representation" as other missionary districts, Maine's lay delegates voted in the negative, Gardiner again among them.[51] It is likely that he, as it was with other white northerners, did not want the church permanently divided along racial lines. It could not have been anything but a hard choice, however.

How hard? African Americans in the Episcopal Church, given the circumstances of their lot, wanted a separate missionary district, equal or unequal. At least they would have their own diocesan bishop and be able to manage their own affairs. The idea of a suffragan, or "suffering bishop," as the black priest George Freeman Bragg called such a one, was opposed by Episcopalians of his own race.[52] A majority wanted full equality. When Gardiner and his colleagues invited other churches to join in preliminary discussions for the World Conference on Faith and Order, they did not include African American churches. In the midst of negotiations with the powerful Southern Baptist Convention, the issue of whether to include black Baptist churches arose. "The question of the Colored Baptists may be a difficult one," Gardiner commented to William Manning.[53] Did Manning know of any white Southern Baptists with whom the matter could be checked out? Gardiner at least knew that the black Baptists were "quite strong numerically," to which he added the dismissal, "but otherwise I suppose they are not very important." He was at best ambivalent, at worst prejudiced, and perhaps somewhere between them crafty. He had one solution for the BSA, another for the Episcopal Church as a whole. It made no sense. He was clearly inconsistent. The age may not have been propitious for the inclu-

51. *Journal of the General Convention of 1907,* 370, 518–22; *Journal of the General Convention of 1913,* 342, 482–85.

52. Reimers, "Negro Bishops and Diocesan Segregation," 234–35. A black diocesan would per force have a vote in the House of Bishops, as would clerical and lay representatives in the House of Deputies.

53. Gardiner to Manning, February 27, 1911, box 2, ms. M316w, St. Mark's Library, the General Theological Seminary, New York. Gardiner to F. J. Hall, March 1, March 21, 1911, Gardiner Correspondence.

siveness he seems deliberately to have skirted, but when is it? Certainly, the ignorance of how others lived and thought was astonishing. It was an attitude shared by many other white Americans of the Protestant establishment.

What was Gardiner's and the BSA's relationship to the highly charged issue of immigration to the United States? Was the BSA open to the children of Orientals and eastern Europeans? Boston was the political and intellectual center of the Immigration Restriction League (IRL), founded in 1894, and of anti-Catholic and anti-Semitic movements "dedicated to restricting immigration from Eastern and Southern Europe." Significantly, Gardiner did not join the restrictionist movement of his fellow Bostonians Senator Henry Cabot Lodge and Lodge's fire-eating son-in-law Congressman Augustus P. Gardner. Organizing Lodge's IRL were Prescott F. Hall, Robert DeCourcy Ward, and Charles Warren. They, in turn, commanded a powerful fraternity of Boston restrictionists, leading citizens such as Robert Treat Paine and his son of the same name, both of Trinity Church; Leverett Saltonstall and Henry Lee; John Fiske, philosopher, historian, and popularizer of both Darwin and Herbert Spencer; and George S. Hall and Samuel R. Capen, both of the Municipal League of Boston. Most of these men "had wearied of the burdens of humanitarianism."[54]

Their fatigue was caused by the depression of the 1890s that had "sparked the first serious effort [in the United States] to restrict immigration from Europe."[55] In Congress a literacy test became the means of restricting immigrants from southern and eastern Europe. (In the broader picture, similar tests were used to keep African Americans from exercising the right to vote.) Five presidents vetoed a succession of literacy acts aimed at immigrants and passed by Congress until on February 5, 1917, the Senate overrode that of Woodrow Wilson. Thereafter, the humanitarian impulse slowed to a crawl and came to a halt with the Johnson-Reed Act of 1924. The provisions of that notorious bill of goods "ensured that those new arrivals who were still allowed to enter, in the self-congratulatory words of the immigration commissioner, once again 'looked exactly like Americans.'"[56] This act, often called the Quota Act, established a nativist system for

54. Thomas Muller, *Immigrants and the American City* (New York: New York University Press, 1993), 30–31; Barbara Miller Solomon, *Ancestors and Immigrants: A Changing New England Tradition* (Cambridge, MA: Harvard University Press, 1956), 104.

55. Christopher Jencks, "Who Should Get In?" *New York Review of Books,* November 29, 2001, 57.

56. See *Williams v. Mississippi,* 170 U.S. 213, 220 (1898), which declared literacy tests (against African Americans) do not deny equal protection of the laws guaranteed by the Fourteenth and

excluding undesirable foreign nationals and prohibiting all immigration from Japan.[57]

There were even leading Social Gospelers in Boston who supported the policies of the IRL: Robert A. Woods, Brahmin Joseph Lee, and many in the Association of Charities who "found it difficult to reconcile the existence of different ethnic groups with the formation of a distinctive [American] nationality."[58] Eugenics wedded to Lodge's IRL played subtly on the psychology of nationhood, so that even Gardiner spoke in terms, as I have shown, of the "Americanization" of immigrants. Moreover, Lodge's fancy footwork made the IRL appear prolabor when it announced its desire to protect American workers from the cheap wages paid fresh arrivals.[59] But the issue was more racial than economic. "There is little evidence that immigration caused unemployment, as many American workers feared, but there is evidence that it impeded the growth of blue-collar workers' wages." The IRL was also anti-imperialist at the turn of the century. It was a stand that appealed to more socially concerned elements.[60] Highly respected educators were also members of the IRL: Harvard's A. Lawrence Lowell, William DeWitt Hyde of Bowdoin College, and John R. Commons of the University of Wisconsin. Lowell, for instance, urged the Harvard Corporation in 1922 to adopt a quota system in order to solve the "Jewish problem."

More in keeping with Lowell than with the socially concerned restrictionists were the grumpy lamenters of a lost heritage. Among these was Harvard professor Barrett Wendell, "whose [Bostonian] identity was secured by the use of two last names" and who was certain that "'We Yankees are as much things of the past as any race can be.'" Augustus P. Gardner straddled both camps and gave special meaning to prejudice when he declared that "all immigrants are un-

---

Fifteenth Amendments. See also *Pope v. Williams,* 193 U.S. 621 (1904); *Nixon v. Herndon,* 273 U.S. 536 (1927); *Smith v. Allwright,* 321 U.S. 649 (1940); George M. Stephenson, *A History of American Immigration, 1820–1924* (New York: Russell and Russell, 1964), 149; and Matthew Frye Jacobson, *Whiteness of a Different Color: European Immigrants and the Alchemy of Race* (Cambridge, MA: Harvard University Press, 1998), 78.

57. Michael Martin and Leonard Gelber, eds., *The New Dictionary of American History* (New York: Philosophical Library, 1965), s.v. "Quota Act of 1921." The Johnson-Reed Act was variously supported by the Ku Klux Klan.

58. Solomon, *Ancestors and Immigrants,* 143.

59. Ibid., 117.

60. Jencks, "Who Should Get In?" 57. Jencks cites the work of Claudia Goldin and Gary Libecap, eds., *The Regulated Economy: A Historical Approach to Political Economy* (Chicago: University of Chicago Press, 1994), 223–57. See also Solomon, *Ancestors and Immigrants,* 120.

desirable." Most, however, were content to excoriate "members of debased Latin and Slavic races."[61]

The opposition to the IRL fielded an equal number of prominent Bostonians. The most impressive foe of the anti-immigration forces was Harvard's famed president Charles W. Eliot. Eliot declared flat out, "The more Italian immigrants the better."[62] Not surprisingly, he was joined by William Lloyd Garrison, for whom the United States remained an asylum for the downtrodden. There were also William James and Josiah Royce of Harvard's Philosophy Department and leading citizens of Boston such as Thomas Wentworth Higginson, Unitarians John Graham Brooks and Edward Everett Hale, and the socially concerned editor of the *New England Magazine* and the *International Library,* Edwin D. Mead. Among influential women, Emily Balch, author of *Our Slavic Fellow Citizens* (1910), and above all Chicago's Jane Addams stood by free immigration. Addams's Immigrants' Protective League (1908) sought to extend to newcomers all of the fundamental outlines and tenets of American society.[63] Generally, those "important elements in the business community [of Boston] continued to press for an open-door immigration policy."[64] Some did so for reasons of principle; others because they wanted cheap wage labor. The issue was complex, to say the least.

Close friends of Robert Gardiner and supporters of the BSA were assimilationists, among them his teacher in the law James J. Storrow; his rector during the 1890s, Henry S. Nash of the Episcopal Theological School; the school's dean, George Hodges; as well as Gardiner's associate at St. Stephen's Church Vida D. Scudder. Besides their Christian faith and the ethics of inclusion that sprang from it, they and others "retained the old democratic faith that the illiterate immigrants would be assimilated and become good Americans." And just there lay the irony. Whereas Christian faith might be one thing, becoming an American could be quite another. The liberals, Gardiner, Scudder, and others, failed adequately to distinguish between the two; the difference was slurred

61. Joseph A. Conforti, *Imagining New England: Exploration of Regional Identity from the Pilgrims to the Mid-Twentieth Century* (Chapel Hill: University of North Carolina Press, 2001), 210; Solomon, *Ancestors and Immigrants,* 139. See also Richard M. Abrams, *Conservatism in a Progressive Era: Massachusetts Politics, 1900–1912* (Cambridge, MA: Harvard University Press, 1964), chaps. 2–3.

62. Solomon, *Ancestors and Immigrants,* 187.

63. Angela Howard Zophy, *Handbook of American Women's History* (New York: Garland, 1990), 696:280–81. See also James Weber Linn, *Jane Addams: A Biography* (Champaign: University of Illinois Press, 2000), 359.

64. Thomas J. Curran, *Xenophobia and Immigration, 1820–1930* (Boston: Twayne, 1975), 124.

over, even confused. In 1905 Gardiner trumpeted to the BSA that God had blessed America: "Nowhere else in the world is it so open to a man to make himself all that God hopes and means him to be. . . . [We must] do our part in bringing every American citizen . . . to the recognition of his deepest duty and great privilege."[65] So spoke the Protestant establishment. It did not occur to him that the immigrant man or woman might not need to be brought along by others and was perfectly capable of recognizing opportunity without their aid.

In fact, newly arrived citizens had already themselves recognized their duty to the United States and their privilege within it to maintain their own cultures and churches and to vote into office their own candidates. While bringing others willy-nilly into the Anglo-Saxon world became the big, audacious, and un-examined goal for social reformers, when the educated but nonetheless slum-dwelling Italian immigrants in Scudder's Circolo Italo-Americano proved less interested in Dante and picnics than in Giuseppe Mazzini and Antonio Gramsci, she was puzzled. For their part, the Italians "found the process of Americaniza-tion vulgar and degrading." Scudder and, despite his disavowals, to some degree Lodge himself disliked the "peasant class" of Italians. In this respect at least, Gardiner proved more democratic. He urged—too optimistically, as it turned out—that the BSA develop many more chapters for Italians, "for thousands have left the Roman Church after their arrival on our shores." Throughout, he sought "to make America the veritable Kingdom of God."[66]

Nor was he unwelcoming to Asians. When it came to the Chinese, Gardiner lauded the Harvard chapter of the BSA whose "new idea"—actually his own—was to make friends with Asian students and to bring them into the brother-hood. Chinese Harvardians for their part were not slow to respond. They Sino-cized their Caucasian classmates by teaching them Mandarin Chinese! Gardiner seems to have missed the humor in the reversal of roles. When the BSA hand-book was translated into Mandarin for use in Hawaii and elsewhere among Chinese followers, he publicly asked his young followers, "Why not use it in the USA as a means of introducing yourself to Chinese in your city?" to which he added blandly, "We ought to take more interest in the stranger in our midst."[67] What emerges from a study of his attitude toward blacks, southern Europeans,

65. Ibid., 122; Gardiner, editorial in *St. Andrew's Cross,* July 1905, 376.

66. Solomon, *Ancestors and Immigrants,* 165; Jacobson, *Whiteness of a Different Color,* 60; Gardiner, editorial in *St. Andrew's Cross,* May 1910, 552; July 1905, 379; December 1905, 210.

67. Gardiner, editorial in *St. Andrew's Cross,* October 1910, 24; May 1910, 522. Chinese stu-dents were one of the groups exempt from the Chinese exclusion acts, as Prescott Hall himself

and Asians in the BSA is that although the organization sought a high degree of commitment, discipline, and self-forgetfulness for the good of the whole, it was different from the Soviet "New Man" or the Aryan "Blond Beasts" of the Hitler Youth or the Jewish sabras. More Athenian than Spartan, the BSA did not seek "homogeneity, and the obliteration of self," allied as those were in many cases with ethnocentricity.[68] Gardiner, in fact, welcomed other cultural contributions, even while he thought American democracy provided the best of all possible worlds. Increasingly, as he later discovered other churches and their faiths both in the United States and abroad, his tent ropes lengthened and his prejudices receded. But the origin of that generosity in the first decade of the twentieth century lay with the brotherhood.

Although there is no record that Gardiner ever explicitly spoke against literacy tests for either immigrants or African Americans, given his mildly progressive, reforming orientation it hardly seems possible that he would have supported restrictions on the rights of either group. We do know that he was quick to blow the whistle on those who sought the "salvation of the few" with the curtailment of civil liberties in the wartime federal sedition law and during the Red Scare of 1919–1920. "Even in America, boasting itself for more than a century as the land of the free, we have witnessed with equanimity, if not with horrid joy, the oppression of conscience and the destruction of free speech." In 1920, following raids by the "department of Justice on the 'reds,'" Gardiner, as president of the Harvard Liberal Club of Boston, organized a banquet to promote freedom of speech. The next day the *Boston Herald* editorialized that the club "had spoken the long-needed word of sanity to an overwrought and excited public opinion."[69] Coming as they did from a man for whom liberty was held to be restrained and limited, such words and actions were all the more telling.

Gardiner's politically liberal credentials were also attested by his reaction to

---

noted in *Encyclopedia of Social Reform,* ed. Bliss, s.v. "immigration." Gardiner's interest in China may have been generated by his cousin Henrietta Gardiner, who became a missionary to Hankou in 1916 (Jennifer Peters to Anne F. Bloy, February 25, 1998, Brotherhood of St. Andrews folder, Gardiner Correspondence).

68. Bernard Wasserstein, "Toothbrushing for Zion," *Times Literary Supplement,* March 1, 2002, 8.

69. Cushing Strout, *The New Heavens and New Earth: Political Religion in America* (New York: Harper and Row, 1974), 251–52; Gardiner, "The Harvard Liberal Club of Boston," *Harvard Graduates' Magazine,* December 1920, 230. In the spring of 1918 the House passed by only one negative vote an unlimited statute that made a crime of seditious libel. Wilson held the belief that the right of free speech ceased when war was declared.

larger issues such as the Versailles Treaty, which he scorned. He spoke openly of the "iniquities of a treaty" that "has sought to reduce to hopeless slavery a great nation [Germany], sinful though it may have been, yet whose industry and ability and thoroughness had so greatly helped to promote learning and science."[70] In 1918 he became one of the founders and treasurer of the Foreign Policy Association, or as it was at first called the League of Nations Association, the purpose of which was to promote U.S. entry into the league. Gardiner and Brent shared a common point of view: in the summer of 1923 the bishop confided to him about his own role on the league's advisory board on narcotic drug control.[71]

Throughout the years he was president of the BSA, Gardiner became more and more occupied with the reunion of the churches. As in the case of the Social Gospel, here too was a forward-looking cause; in fact, in the Progressive Era, both constituted the cutting edge of American Protestant life. As one astute observer later reflected: "It is hard for us to-day [1951] to realise how novel, how bold, and how difficult it was forty years ago, to plan a conference of representatives of divided churches."[72] If a conference was difficult, actual reunion was Herculean. Nonetheless, the idea persisted. Ever since William Reed Huntington's *Church-Idea: An Essay toward Unity* (1870), the matter of how and on what basis Episcopalians would unite with other denominations had been in the air. At the General Convention of 1886 in Chicago, Huntington's four points—scripture, creeds, the two sacraments, and the episcopate—had been accepted by the delegates with changes in wording only.[73] Then in 1888 the

70. Gardiner, "Address of Welcome," in *One Hundredth Anniversary of the Diocese of Maine, 1820–1920,* [edited by Marguerite Ogden] (Boston: Merrymount Press, 1920), 114.

71. See Bruce W. Jentleson and Thomas G. Paterson, eds., *Encyclopedia of United States Foreign Policy,* 2 vols., s.v. "Brent, Charles Henry"; for Gardiner's participation in the association, see *Who Was Who,* 14 vols. (1943; reprint, Chicago: A. N. Marquis, 1962), 1:135; Brent to Gardiner, May 2, 1923, Gardiner Correspondence. Brent was already an international figure in the antidrug effort, having served as president of the International Opium Commission.

72. Leonard Hodgson, *The Ecumenical Movement: Three Lectures* (Sewanee, TN: University of the South University Press, 1951), 9–10.

73. Huntington's original four "points" were as follows with the 1886 changes in parentheses: "the holy scriptures (of the Old and New Testaments) as the (revealed) Word of God; the primitive creeds as the rule of faith (the Nicene Creed as the sufficient statement of the Christian faith); the two Sacraments (baptism and the Supper of the Lord ministered with unfailing use of Christ's words of institution and of the elements ordained by him) ordained by Christ himself; the (historic) episcopate, (locally adapted in the methods of its administration to the varying needs of the nations and peoples called by God into the unity of his church) as the keystone of

Chicago Quadrilateral, as it became known, was accepted by the entire Anglican Communion at its Lambeth Conference of that year.[74] But it was Huntington's subsequent book, *A National Church* (1898), that was to prove even
more significant and took the course of reunion further. Despite its title, in *A
National Church* the author went beyond nationalism and in the most important statement in the book declared: "We cannot avoid that conclusion, save by
taking the ground of nationalism in religion as a temporary expedient, a policy
forced upon us by the necessities of the present, and destined in due time, unless
indeed the course of this world be meanwhile interrupted by the personal coming of the King, to merge in the larger *eccelsia* in which are to be gathered all
the nations of the earth." Privately, Huntington revealed to a friend his disillu-
sionment with "all these big gatherings of . . . 'pan'-this and 'pan'-that" (presumably including the Lambeth Conferences); they were but faint sketches "of
some real council with powers, destined to meet at some time future and draw
Christendom together . . . with both clergy and laity given the right to vote."[75]
These statements, the one public, the other private, were prophetic of what
Robert Gardiner would spend the rest of his life working toward.

Gardiner began in the pages of the *St. Andrew's Cross* to enlist his young
men: "Let us pray," he wrote, "that . . . our brothers in the Holy Church Universal who now call themselves by names seeming to separate them from the
historic Church, may seriously take to heart our unhappy divisions." What did
he mean? Was the "historic Church" to be equated with the Episcopal Church?
Or were those brothers of other denominations only "seeming" in Episcopalian
eyes to separate themselves from "the Holy Church Universal"? Whatever the
answer, he wanted young people to set aside "all unessential matters of opinion
on their part and ours [that] we may unite and offer to our Lord in the one Faith
and through the one Baptism, the mighty army which he means us to be." The

---

governmental unity." See John F. Woolverton, "The Quadrilateral and the Lambeth Conferences,"
*Historical Magazine of the Protestant Episcopal Church* 52:2 (June 1984): 95–109, esp. 98, 102,
103 for subsequent variations in wording.

74. Ibid., 103. The Lambeth Conference made significant additions. The following was added
to the first point: scripture "as containing all things necessary to salvation, and as being the ultimate rule and standard of faith." And the following was added to the second point, that both
creeds, the Apostles' and the Nicene, would be included, "the Apostles' Creed, as the Baptismal
Symbol; and the Nicene as the sufficient statement of the Christian faith."

75. Huntington, *A National Church,* 12; Huntington to Catherine Meredith, March 27,
1908, William Reed Huntington Papers, Episcopal Divinity School, Cambridge, MA, quoted in
Woolverton, "Huntington and Church Unity," 263.

next spring, he and Houghteling called a meeting—again in Chicago—of the officers of the laymen's brotherhoods from mainline denominations. Their purpose was to appoint a planning committee for the time, place, and scope of an interbrotherhood conference. Gardiner was elected to chair the committee. The next month, April 1908, he urged BSA members to get in touch with laymen in other local churches. The lesson may have come late for some "that ecumenical successes required educational labors at the grass roots." For him, it came early. It would continue into the Faith and Order Movement. In May he assured his readers that the more they made Christ's kingdom the controlling motive of their lives, the more "the divisions which now hinder the progress of the Kingdom will disappear, and we shall recognize that the Holy Church Universal is, and must be, one, for it is the one body of our Lord." A year later, in February 1909, he addressed a national convention of the YMCA and told them that the Week of Prayer (in Advent of 1908) "has drawn us close to our brother Christians." Then in the summer of 1910 Gardiner held what was to become a recurring event: a small conference at Oaklands of prominent adults—citizens of Maine, as it turned out, including the president of Bowdoin College. Their purpose was to talk about conducting an international church conference.[76]

From nationalist to internationalist: the move culminated in an extraordinary adventure that took this Boston and Maine attorney to the heart of Europe on the brink of World War I. His horizons had been broadening, as had those of others in the "revolution in communications" that marked the turn of the century but came too late to avert disaster. Whereas railway, telegraph, and stamped postage all required international cooperation, when it came to political cooperation among nations, late-nineteenth-century Europe "produced no solid instruments of . . . diplomatic mediation." Since the Roman Catholic Church had lost its pan-European authority, others tried to step in. In 1899 the usually rash and hasty Czar Nicholas II decided to convene an international conference to limit armaments and to frame an international court for settling disputes between nations. He was not alone. Beginning with the (American) Ecumenical Missionary Conference in New York (1900), the International Christian Movement in Tokyo (1907), and such events as the World Missionary Conference in Edinburgh (1910), others acted as well, unconsciously, to fill the void left by

76. Gardiner, editorial in *St. Andrew's Cross,* June 1907, 562; April 1908, 496; Edwin S. Gaustad, "The Pulpit and the Pews," in *Between the Times,* by Hutchison, 34; Gardiner, editorial in *St. Andrew's Cross,* May 1908, 566; February 1909, 344–45; August 1910, 778.

the demise of Roman Catholic authority. But common Christianity in Europe "found an easier expression in philanthropy" than in united political and religious pressure.[77]

Gardiner sought to achieve both ends. He came to believe that the universal church must think on a world scale and make a difference by reuniting its own divided forces and at the same time create a peaceful community of nations. He argued that the church had a larger role to play than looking out for its own interests and those of its constituents. As early as September 1914 he foresaw that in the postwar period, "if a military despotism is established there will surely come a revolution as soon as there is strength to revolt. If we are not ready with our whole strength to guide that revolution by Christ's law of peace and righteousness . . . the forces of evil will prevail and all that was first in the French Revolution will be multiplied a hundredfold. If democracy wins we must be ready to guide that too." He was prescient about the danger of postwar dictatorship as well as about the eventual triumph of democracy, if not the inevitability of revolution. Time and again he called for "united prayer for guidance"; unity was essential "in this the greatest undertaking before the Christian world *for the whole world*." Until the body of Christ is visibly one, "there can be no hope that his law of peace will govern the world." In 1918 he held that "nothing can be obtained of permanent value either in the direction of visible Church unity or of permanent peace—international, social and industrial— until we have prepared the way on substantially the lines of the World Conference movement." A great international conference would "convince and convert mankind." Realistically or unrealistically, he judged that "if the world is to endure, we must have a new order of things from top to bottom."[78] In Gardiner's case, Christian internationalism and the reunion of the churches had not yet been metamorphosed into the more modest, domestic "ecumenical movement." The two—church unity and international unity—were for him positive forces that would cast a light upon the dark intractabilities of history. Or so he hoped. Because he and his colleagues held out such hope, they attracted able men and

---

77. John Keegan, *The First World War* (New York: Alfred A. Knopf, 1999), 12, 17, 13.

78. Gardiner to Peter Ainslie, September 1, 1914; to William T. Manning, August 23, 1915 (emphasis added); to Edward S. Talbot, bishop of Winchester (Church of England), February 5, 1918, Gardiner Correspondence. Military despotism was overthrown in Russia—by communism. Christian guidance there had no chance at all. The subsequent military despotisms of Italy and Germany did not prove susceptible to revolt, much less Christianity, though in Germany at the end of World War II the anti-Nazi underground had a Christian flavor.

women to their cause. On the other hand, they had first to deal with those who lacked their Wilsonian idealism and who only dimly discerned what they—and particularly he—saw so clearly.

At the beginning of the twenty-first century, such focused and highly general aspirations are in short supply. They seem strange to us. They have been replaced by the particularism of the New Left and its many causes such as the crusade for the survival of the snail darter, by therapeutic self-absorption, by an ahistorical spirituality, and by the political and religious fundamentalism of the radical Right.[79]

In the meantime, Gardiner's health had not been good. In October 1909 at the national convention of the BSA, he was unable to fulfill his presidential duties, was "confined to his rooms in the headquarters hotel, and later on his physician's advice . . . [had] to leave the Convention and return to his home." Fearing overwork, his friends resolved that he should take six months' vacation. Gardiner wrote them that his "illness at Providence was only a temporary return of an old trouble which I have had ten years or more before I was elected" president of the BSA (which would be either 1893 or 1894). What the illness was is undetermined. The December issue of the *St. Andrew's Cross* declared that "Wednesday evening [October 13], the day the convention opened he was quite unwell. . . . He made a brave attempt to remain at the Convention." The journal went on to claim that although there was nothing serious about the illness, "he was in considerable pain." Did he suffer from heart trouble? We only know that he was overworked and that he smoked; from his Anglo-Catholic friend B. Talbot Rogers, he once received this jocular note: "My opinion of you is that you are not a heretic, but you have an unhealthy fondness for cigarettes and the miasmic atmosphere of Uncatholic Associations. I love you just the same and of course shall do all I can to rescue you from the dangers with which your soul and body are ensnared."[80]

79. See, for instance, Todd Gitlin, *Twilight of Common Dreams: Why America Is Wracked by Culture Wars* (New York: Metropolitan Press, 1995).

80. Editorial in *St. Andrew's Cross,* November 1909, 73; December 1909, 164; Rogers to Gardiner, December 4, 1913, Gardiner Correspondence.

# FOUR

❧✝❧

## Faith and Order's Troubled Beginnings

*Edinburgh, 1910*

Shortly after the death in 1909 of Episcopalian leader William Reed Hunting-ton, church unity received fresh attention when a group of twenty-four Episcopal bishops, presbyters, and laymen met at St. Thomas's Church on Fifth Avenue to memorialize Huntington and "to promote Christian Unity at home and through-out the world by the method of research and conference."[1] Early January of the following year saw the first formal meeting of this new voluntary society, the Christian Unity Foundation (CUF), its incorporation in July 1910, and a gift of ten thousand dollars from St. Thomas's parishioner R. Fulton Cutting. As well as Cutting, members of the board of the CUF included people with whom this study is concerned, Bishop Charles Anderson of Chicago; John M. Glenn of the Sage Foundation; George Wharton Pepper, general counsel to Governor Gifford Pinchot of Pennsylvania; and William J. Shiefflin, president of the Citi-zens' Union. Both the foundation and its money soon dried up. When another similar group was to put the Episcopal Church officially on the road to reunion, voluntary societies, at least those in search of Christian unity, became a thing of the past.

In the meantime in downtown New York in early January 1910, a smaller group comprising Robert Gardiner, nine other laymen, and six clergy were

---

1. Joseph R. Jeeter Jr., "The Christian Unity Foundation," *Historical Magazine of the Protes-tant Episcopal Church* 44:4 (December 1975): 451, 461–67.

meeting at Trinity Church on Wall Street. Among the laity were William M. Grosvenor, prominent journalist and editorial writer for the *New York Tribune;* Gardiner's friend New York attorney George Zabriskie; and Admiral Alfred T. Mahan, author of the famous book *The Influence of Sea Power on History, 1660– 1783* (1890). The clergy were represented by Social Gospeler James O. S. Huntington of the Order of the Holy Cross and Henry S. Nash of the Episcopal Theological School in Cambridge; the group had also corralled Loring W. Batten, the inspiring teacher and scholar of the Old Testament at the General Theological Seminary.[2] Their host was William T. Manning, rector of the famed parish at the head of Wall Street. The future lay with these men, not with the CUF.

The conferees issued a statement that sought to lay out common ground for reunion. Their words marked a departure from emphasis on personal salvation to that of the corporate nature and purpose of the church. Beginning with the doctrine of the Trinity and its "fellowship"—the word used throughout—of Father, Son, and Holy Spirit, they moved to God's fellowship with humankind in the act of creation and in the subsequent incarnation in Jesus of Nazareth; that fellowship involved the believers in communion both with God and with each other as well. "This fellowship," with God and with each other, they wrote, is "so far above our natural state that by our strength we cannot attain unto it." The Holy Spirit created it; it is an "outward and visible embodiment... [of] the Holy Catholic Church." In strongly Christological language they went on to speak of the communication of Christ's life, made available in baptism, expressed in the Apostles' and Nicene Creeds, and continued in "the Holy Communion as instituted by Christ Himself." Such a corporate act of worship calls for "some minister, who bears Christ's commission[,] to preside in the assembly"—in fact, dictates "a continuing priesthood." Those called to that special ministry derive their strength from the "priesthood of the Lord Jesus Christ [who] abides in the whole fellowship." Authority for those who so preside in the circle of the faithful comes from Christ "by the outward sign and means of ordination... effected from sub-apostolic times by the laying on of the hands of the historic episcopate and prayer." The signers declared that if such a min-

---

2. Mahan was also the author of *The Harvest Within: Thoughts on the Life of the Christian* (Boston: Little, Brown, 1909). For a good biographical sketch of Mahan, see Warren Zimmerman, *First Great Triumph: How Five Americans Made Their Country a World Power* (New York: Farrar, Straus, and Giroux, 2002), 85–122, esp. 88, 101–11, 120–22. Powell Mills Dawley, *The Story of the General Theological Seminary: A Sesquicentennial History, 1817–1967* (New York: Oxford University Press, 1969), 308.

istry was universally restored, it would be "an effective bond."[3] Philip Schaff would have been disappointed. The "historic episcopate" of the Chicago-Lambeth Quadrilateral remained in place. Despite their fresh use of the word *fellowship,* the signers stuck to the party line. Then came Edinburgh.

The World Missionary Conference, held in the royal burgh, Scotland's capital, was a high point of the Progressive Era. Chaired by American layman John R. Mott of the SCM, the proceedings at Edinburgh marked the coming of age of a grassroots movement in the New World of students, women missionaries otherwise denied access to professional schools, idealistic ministers, theologians, and church leaders. These cultural exporters of American social values of democracy and missionary fervor joined their more academic European partners in the early summer of 1910 in a momentous international gathering. Once again, as in the case of Chicago's World's Parliament of Religions, the format of the conference left something to be desired. The organizers gave speakers only seven minutes to address the audience. Each day there were fifty speakers, three hundred in a week. When the turn came for Charles Henry Brent, American Episcopal bishop in the Philippine Islands, the great assembly had already been in session for eight days. Even though audiences in 1910 were used to drinking deeply at the homiletic Pierian spring, the thirst for oratory at the conference was no doubt approaching satiety. As a result attention was thin to all but the most pressing matters. Remarkably, Brent at once gained more than a polite hearing. He wowed them. Forty years later, layman Joseph H. Oldham, the chief organizing secretary of the conference, left no doubt that the Philippine bishop's remarks "made an immediate and indelible impression." Oldham declared, "I have the clearest recollection" of what he said. Oldham should have. At that moment, the possibility arose that Brent would repudiate the principle that the organizers had "for two years been discussing and defending with people of all sorts" and upon which the meeting was based: the guarantee that no one would wield an ax in the primeval forests of theology and ecclesiology. The assembly itself was made possible by an agreement not to discuss any divisive issues of doctrine, creed, or polity. Had the bishop raised such matters in the name of church unity, Oldham knew "the conference would at once disintegrate."[4]

This first worldwide assembly of missionary societies and officially appointed

3. "The undersigned . . . in unofficial conference at Trinity Chapel, New York . . . 27th and 28th of January 1910," leaflet, Gardiner Collection.

4. Oldham to Ruth Rouse, April 22, 1950, Edinburgh 1910 folder, Floyd Tomkins Papers, Archives of the Episcopal Church, Austin, TX.

delegates from separate and dissimilar fellowships was "more nearly a body authorized to speak for the Churches than any of the gatherings which had preceded it."[5] The stakes were high. Practical cooperation was the only subject permitted. The organizers wanted "a new comprehensiveness in the understanding of Christian co-operation." The basis of their coming together, Oldham judged, was "thought out on its merits" in full awareness not only of the Church of England's Anglo-Catholic wing but also of those in the Presbyterian Church of Scotland, in the United Free Church of Scotland, and in German missionary societies, wherever there were those who held "distinctive tradition[s] of their own, which they valued highly, and were not prepared to surrender or compromise in order to undertake tasks in common."[6] Such cooperation was new in 1910, and though some held aloof, many genuinely wanted to turn their deliberations to good account.

The impulse for cooperation was strong. Its antecedents lay with the Social Gospel, the missionary thrust that accompanied it, and the evangelization of the laity by the laity in the Student Christian Movement. Thenceforth, through the realization of "catholic unity," "united service," "devotional fellowship and mutual counsel," as the simple language had it, an increasing number of Christians sought to "promote the application of the law of Christ in every [practical] relation of human life." Perceptibly, the participants were moving from a conception of the church as the gathering of saved individuals whose unity was spiritual and not necessarily visible in ecclesiastical organization to a conception in which the still-separated bodies began to understand each other as parts of a corporate whole. Discipleship, mission, and service wrought the change. The next step was to understand that social cooperation and missionary cooperation would eventually manifest themselves, not only in the common enterprises of daily life but also in thought, structure, and polity. As one historian has judged, the individualistic idea of the church corresponded to an individualistic concept of salvation in an otherworldly kingdom. Thinking of the church as a single corporate body—in the world, not out of it—fitted "appropriately with expecting the work of salvation and the triumph of the Kingdom to take place in and

5. Kenneth Scott Latourette, "Ecumenical Bearings of the Missionary Movement and the International Missionary Council," in *A History of the Ecumenical Movement, 1517–1948,* edited by Ruth Rouse and Stephen Charles Neill (Philadelphia: Westminster Press, 1967), 357.

6. Oldham, "Edinburgh 1910 and the International Missionary Council: Comments on the Chapter by Professor Latourette," Edinburgh 1910 folder, Tomkins Papers, 9, 7, 8.

through the social process." As one commentator has written of the Progressive Era in general, if there was "no conviction that deliverance for all [humanity] was at hand, there was at least the conviction that the commonality of mankind was a noble and imaginative project."[7] Those seeking church unity shared in this hope. With common beliefs that already to some degree united Christians, the premise was that if their collective capacities could lead to an improved and more humane society, then inevitably they could and ought to improve themselves and lay a foundation for the reunion of their separated bodies. Such a result, they believed, was both desirable and achievable.

One hundred years later, when "pleasures and addictions and evanescent communities galore [are] to be found under the big tent of popular culture," this earlier longing for human solidarity in one community seems visionary, even laughable.[8] In the early twenty-first century, attachment to those who most resemble ourselves is given priority. In a pluralistic age, we seek comfort and support within discrete circles, whether in "chat rooms" on the Internet or in other like-minded groups. The men and women of 1910 would have found alarming our "commonality lite" with its enticements to present personal satisfaction and its transient cultural crusades. Theirs was a more persistent vision of the future, a deep belief in the universal philanthropy of the human, and for many a Christian project. Individual "philanthropy" and spirituality took a back seat. So did the kind of cynicism so predominant in current circles of power.

Under the leadership of Mott and perpetuated by Oldham, the Edinburgh conference "for the first time made provision for the implementation of its purposes." Oldham would be the continuing secretary with authority to carry out the wishes of the conference. But that was not all. In his brief remarks, it was Brent who challenged the delegates and took them that memorable further step, the one toward examining their differences in thought and structure. In doing so, he wielded no ax against the trunk of any tree. In that significant moment Oldham "was naturally all ears." Summarily, the bishop stated in his

---

7. From the 1905 Carnegie Hall conference of twenty-nine denominations that led to the founding of the Federal Council of Churches, quoted in Ronald C. White and C. Howard Hopkins, *The Social Gospel: Religion and Reform in Changing America* (Philadelphia: Temple University Press, 1976), 200; Thomas Sieger Derr, "The Political Thought of the Ecumenical Movement, 1900–1939" (PhD diss., Columbia University, 1972), 59; Todd Gitlin, *The Twilight of Common Dreams: Why America Is Wracked with Culture Wars* (New York: Henry Holt, 1995), 85.

8. Gitlin, *Twilight of Common Dreams,* 86–87.

diary, "Spoke at the morning session on promotion of unity. Laid stress on our relations with the Roman Church. A difficult task but well received. Men of every type and creed came to me by scores and thanked me. It was most moving." But "relations with the Roman Catholic Church" was not what others heard. Though no copy of Brent's remarks survives, Oldham outlined the three points he had heard the bishop make "with the utmost clarity and with the force of his remarkable personality." First, and it was here that the Scotsman breathed a sigh of relief, Brent did not challenge the nontheological basis of the Edinburgh Conference itself. He remained true to the principle of avoiding any statements, not to mention disputes, about faith and order. Second, he stated that "questions which were excluded from [Edinburgh's] purview were none the less of such crucial importance that in another context and by different people, they must be openly and freely discussed." Third, he promised that upon return to the United States he would take steps to initiate an effort to make possible the examination of those questions. "I am quite certain," Oldham continued, "that the Faith and Order Movement was born in the decision which Bishop Brent made and announced during the days of the Edinburgh Conference."[9]

The next day Brent addressed the conference in the time set aside for longer speeches of an hour or more. "The hall was crowded to the doors, about 3000 people," he recorded in his diary. "I fear I did not rise wholly to the occasion, but I spoke simply and the people listened. God's sufficiency made up for my insufficiency." He then took the train to London to dine the next day with Prime Minister Herbert Asquith. It was high style all the way. Brent, Mott, Oldham, and others in the Anglo-Saxon Christian world were welcomed in the halls of power. The American bishop was invited to the homes of such people as Lord Ardwell, the Scottish judge and distinguished free churchman, keenly interested in religious affairs; he spent a morning with Ronald Munro-Ferguson, viscount Novar, privy counselor, and junior lord of the treasury; and he conversed with the most outstanding figure in Scottish life, Lord Balfour, eight years in the third Salisbury cabinet and lord rector of the University of Edinburgh. He rubbed shoulders with the cautious but influential archbishop of Canterbury

9. Oldham, "Edinburgh 1910," 9; Brent diary, June 21, 1910, Charles Henry Brent Papers, Library of Congress, Washington, DC; Oldham to Rouse, April 22, 1950, Tomkins Papers. Canon Tissington Tatlow of the Church of England stated at the same time: "Oldham's memory is shared by me" (Tatlow to Rouse, May 9, 1950, Robert H. Gardiner Correspondence, 1910–1924, World Council of Churches, Geneva, Switzerland).

Randall Davidson, himself a Scot. In between, Brent played golf and "became intimately acquainted with every bunker."[10] But it was all very bracing.

From the Edinburgh assembly of 1910, the first modern assembly of world-wide churches, Brent went to the General Convention of the Episcopal Church meeting that October in Cincinnati, Ohio. Shortly before, he recorded in his diary, "At the morning Eucharist there came vividly before me the possibility of a World Conference on Faith and Order." And he meant *world* conference. Given his previous entry of June 21, that such a gathering would include the Roman Catholic Church was unequivocal. We must, as he wrote six months later, create a "movement toward unity." Beyond pious talk, safe ultimatums such as Anglicanism's Chicago-Lambeth Quadrilateral, or Edinburgh's limited cooperation, the times called for action on a grander scale with more audacious goals. They were embarking, Brent observed, "on a perilous sea. . . . [T]he risks involved are extreme." Nor was he sure of the seaworthiness of his own church. It was, he judged, too divided into warring factions. Brent was convinced that in the Episcopal Church neither the Anglo-Catholics nor the Evangelicals should get control of the journey toward unity. Other churches would be watching, Protestant, Orthodox, and Roman. If Episcopalians moved along internal partisan lines, "we might either have a schism [if the Anglo-Catholics got control] or else lose the distinctive character of the Church [if the Evangelicals preponderated]." The question hung in the air: Was the Episcopal Church disciplined enough, theologically and ecclesiologically, to convince others that together they could accomplish the task of Christian reunion? Conversely, was it free enough from abstractions and rules that might appear to provide certainties but whose "recitation . . . boxes the facts into established categories"? Was it convincing enough to lead others through uncharted waters? Brent was not sure. The dangers of bitterness during World War I, on the one hand, and party spirit in the Episcopal Church, on the other, were to weigh on his mind. He wrote, "It is easy enough to fall into the trap in which Elijah was caught and say that we are no better than our fathers; probably we are not, but we should show as much courage and as much hope in the face of world disaster and inner discord as Luke XXI seems to require of the disciple."[11]

10. Brent diary, June 22, 25, 1910, Brent Papers.
11. Ibid., September 5, 1910; Brent to Gardiner, March 22, 1911, Robert H. Gardiner Correspondence, container 19, Brent Papers; John T. Noonan Jr., *Narrowing the Nation's Power: The Supreme Court Sides with the States* (Berkeley and Los Angeles: University of California Press, 2002), 144; Brent to Gardiner, February 3, 1916, Brent Papers.

With this Gardiner agreed; he bemoaned the fact that Evangelicals "have now formed a league ready to declare war on . . . the American Church Union," an Anglo-Catholic lobbying organization founded shortly after the English Church Union (1859). He added derisively, "The great body of the church is without any interest in the dispute." Later, Brent confided to Gardiner, "Our mouths are full of criticisms. We are forever telling others what ought to be done, whereas our own course is confused and very frequently stupid. I am inclined to use some strong language, but knowing your objection to it, I will refrain." This Anglo-Catholic bishop and former postulant in the monastic Society of Saint John the Evangelist confessed to "a hopeless feeling . . . when I take up [the journal] the Living Church." In that high Episcopalian publication he observed a "seeming pleasure in what I would call raw controversy[;] its destructive criticisms and its carping tone make for neither unity nor good will."[12]

Episcopalian leadership had its difficulties. Brent saw that his denomination would be sticking its neck out, "acting corporately and risking her all." Leaders then must move "with precision, with fearlessness, and with that faith which conquers all things." As he did not care for controversy, neither did he enjoy those bishops "who consider they have high ecclesiastical privilege and stand very near the throne of God." Such a one "behave[s] like a bantam cock crowing out his pride on a stump." Gardiner too singled out members of the General Convention's upper house: "Each of them thinks he is absolutely infallible, and it is impossible for one hundred infallible men to do business together." To Brent, Gardiner confessed what he saw as a lack of serious leadership in the Episcopal Church: "We are altogether too self-complacent and egotistical, thinking that the eyes of the world are on us, whereas if we do not take that leadership pretty soon, I believe we shall be left on one side altogether." The two were in accord, prickly, not mincing words. Brent was the indispensable inspirer, Gardiner increasingly well known "as the pulsing heart of the faith and order movement."[13]

At the Cincinnati convention Brent made two speeches on church unity, one on the eighth of October before the Women's Auxiliary at the presentation of their United Thank Offering, the other "before the great Missionary Mass Meet-

12. Gardiner to Brent, March 13, 1916; Brent to Gardiner, December 28, 1922, January 17, 1923, Brent Papers.

13. Brent to Gardiner, March 22, 1911, Brent Papers; Gardiner to George Gilbert, November 11, 1913, Gardiner Correspondence; Gardiner to Brent, May 4, 1911, Brent Papers; Frank E. Sugeno to the author, July 10, 1997, Sugeno folder, Robert H. Gardiner Collection, Archives of the Episcopal Church, Austin, TX.

ing in the evening of Oct. 11." In the first he spoke of the Philippines as "a battle-ground for unity." His experience there taught him that "a disunited and competing Christendom [was] woefully inadequate to the evangelical task." Such international experience also convinced him, as he told the women, that the "Body of Christ is one. . . . No Christians can break that unity, no man living can put another out of the Body of Christ." The wonder was not that people should fight for unity; "the wonder is that they do not fight" for it. At the missionary meeting he reiterated his stance: "Let us look on Christians of other names as Christians in deed and in truth, and treat them accordingly." To defame the name of another church was for him "a grievous sin." He then threw down his challenge: "Other Christians will not be won to unity with us if we merely stand on an exalted platform and ask them to come up to it." He wanted his listeners to "adopt the principle of the Incarnation and make the interests of others our interests." Episcopalians should lay aside some of their "distinctive characteristics in trying to gain the unity which our Lord meant for His Church." He was cheered, as one reporter wrote, again and again. "His frank and fearless attitude seemed to give strength to others."[14] Not everyone huzzahed, however, and many considered him an Ishmaelite and not a true Hebrew from among the twelve Anglican tribes.

Two days later, on October 13, Trinity Church's William Manning offered in the House of Deputies a resolution setting up an official commission "for the consideration of questions pertaining to the Faith and Order of the Church of Christ, and that such committee, if it deem such a [World] Conference feasible, shall report to this Convention." What so far has remained unknown is that Brent, Gardiner, and Philadelphia attorney George Wharton Pepper together approached Manning and invited him to make the motion.[15] "Always quick to see the importance of a suggestion of that kind," Manning accepted and "offered the resolution." Six days later the New York rector reported to the lower house that in the mind of the committee "the time has now arrived . . . to lay aside self-will . . . in all lowliness and singleness of purpose . . . [and] place ourselves

14. Floyd Tomkins, notebook 9, "Journals of the General Conventions," 7, 8, Gardiner Collection; Eugene C. Bianchi, S.J., "The Ecumenical Thought of Charles Henry Brent," *Church History* 33:4 (December 1964): 448. See also *Churchman,* October 15, 1910, 573.

15. *Journal of the General Convention of 1910,* 309–10, quoted in notebook 9, Tomkins Papers, 8. The conclusion is made by Floyd Tomkins on the basis of correspondence between Gardiner and Zabriskie, July 1917, notebook 1, Tomkins Papers, 16. Brent had sought the advice of the two lawyers.

by the side of our fellow Christians, looking not only on our own things but on the things of others." The world conference should be for study and discussion of the problems that separated Christians, "without power to legislate or adopt resolutions." Such a conference would be, he declared, the next step toward reunion. His peroration expressed Episcopalians' "grief for our aloofness in the past, and for other faults of pride and self-sufficiency which make for schism."[16] Manning then called for respect for the convictions of those who differed as well as for recognition of those matters in which they agreed.

The Cincinnati convention had taken a highly important step forward. That day the *Boston Herald* reported that "two great conventions met at about the same time, the deputies, lay and clerical of the Episcopal Church in Cincinnati, and the delegates of the Congregational Church in Boston." The article went on to record the degree of seriousness about reunion of these two denominations. Episcopalians, the *Herald* continued, had formed a committee to consider plans for unity and to call a world's convention on the lines of the great Edinburgh missionary assembly. "Everyone is coming to realize the importance of pulling together." The *Herald* reported that there was "a deep enthusiasm for the resolution." The Joint Commission Appointed to Arrange for a World Conference on Faith and Order consisted of seven bishops, seven priests, and seven laymen. Its chairman was Bishop Charles P. Anderson of Chicago. Others included J. Pierpont Morgan; Brent; George Zabriskie, who became treasurer; Seth Low, former president of Columbia University and reform-minded mayor of New York; Associate Justice Horace H. Lurton of the Supreme Court of the United States (who soon dropped out); Pepper; and at the bottom of the list, Robert H. Gardiner, secretary. No one, the newspaper reported, "can accuse such a body of men of fostering a mere dream." What the *Herald* and other papers neglected to point out was that the Disciples of Christ at their General Convention in Topeka, Kansas, had, on the very same day, October 19, 1910, taken steps to create a similar commission on Christian unity within their own denomination.[17] That made three.

16. Edward L. Parsons to Tomkins, March 15, 1951, Tomkins Papers. The immediate issue was the use of the phrase "The Lord Jesus Christ as God and Saviour" that appeared in the resolution and was to be the defining phrase for participating churches (*Journal of the General Convention of 1910,* House of Deputies, October 19, 1910, 377–78; see also notebook 9, Tomkins Papers, 9).

17. *Boston Herald,* October 30, 1910, 7; on the same day, October 30, an identical article appeared in the *New York Times,* 1. For a complete list of commission members, see *Joint*

Within the next few months the Joint Commission organized itself, dividing into committees: one, Plan and Scope, in effect the executive committee, chaired by Manning; one on literature; and one on finance. Gardiner served as secretary both for the Joint Commission and for the Committee on Plan and Scope. He was also a member of the subcommittee on finance where Francis Lynde Stetson, Morgan's lawyer and senior partner in the prominent New York law firm Stetson, Jennings, and Russell, was a key player. Thirteen of the twenty-five members of the Joint Commission came from the Boston-to-Philadelphia corridor—five from New York City alone. The rest came from Chicago (three), Ohio (two), Wisconsin (two), and one each from California, the Philippine Islands (Brent), Tennessee, Vermont, and Virginia. As a result of Episcopalian, Congregational, and Disciples of Christ action, fourteen other American denominations appointed commissions to join in the planning for the world conference. Taking the lead, the Episcopalians' Joint Commission then passed resolutions appointing subcommittees to contact the archbishops and metropolitans of the Anglican Communion, the Roman Catholic Church, the Old Catholic churches, and Eastern Orthodox churches, and to reach all other Protestant communions.[18] On behalf of the subcommittee on finance Stetson announced on December 15, 1910, that "Mr. J.P. Morgan had deposited with J.P. Morgan & Co., subject to the check of Mr. Stetson, the sum of one hundred thousand dollars without limitation."[19] The process by which such untried steps were taken sounds smooth enough. It was not. From the start there was trouble, first among the Episcopalians themselves, then with other denominations.

---

*Commission Appointed to Arrange for a World Conference on Faith and Order* (published by the commission, March 20, 1911), 5–6, Gardiner Collection; Charles H. Lippy and Peter W. Williams, eds., *Encyclopedia of the American Religious Experience*, 3 vols. (New York: Charles Scribner's Sons, 1988), s.v. "ecumenical movement"; and Tissington Tatlow, "The World Conference on Faith and Order," in *History of the Ecumenical Movement*, edited by Rouse and Neill, 407–8.

18. [Gardiner], *The World Conference for the Consideration of Questions Touching Faith and Order* (printed for the commission, 1913), 6; Moses King, comp., *Notable New Yorkers of 1896–1899* (New York: Bartlett, 1899), 88; *Report of the Committee on Plan and Scope* (printed for the committee, 1912), 7, 9–11.

19. The sum of $100,000 in 1910 is equivalent to about $2 million plus in 2005 currency; this figuring is based on $1 in 1860 being worth $14.83 in 1989. Though Jean Strouse in her microbiography *Morgan: American Financier* (New York: HarperCollins, 1999) treats Morgan's much larger donations of $200,000 in 1887 to St. George's Church, Stuyvesant Square, and his $500,000 to the Cathedral of St. John the Divine in 1892, she fails to mention this smaller but significant contribution, which would have added a new dimension to her discussion of Morgan's religion.

While public attention was still high and focused Gardiner wanted the Joint Commission to act. Speedily. He agreed with Yale's Congregationalist professor Newman Smyth that "we should create at once the impression that something is doing." Later, he would urge caution and a more deliberate pace, but at the starting bell, there was need to convince the irresolute. The subject of a world conference, he continued, "is so vast that it will be important to get men thinking about it a long time before we have definite suggestions." Few saw, as did Brent and Gardiner, the magnitude of the undertaking. In order to send invitations they had first to track down the addresses of all denominational headquarters, their leaders, and their principal publications, not only in the United States but worldwide as well. Surprisingly, it was not an easy job. Only by 1919 was Gardiner able to tell John R. Mott that "the weary work of invitation has been substantially completed." Still, by the end of the first full year, in a thorough, detailed letter to Mott, he was able to announce the considerable progress that had been made. Gardiner ended with a warning: "If I make myself too prominent, I shall destroy any little influence I may have." At the same time that they were inducing other churches to set up commissions paralleling their own, the Episcopal commissioners themselves faced internal tasks: they had to choose a central location for correspondence and publications, lay plans to educate their own clergy and laity on unity, initiate regional conferences around the world for discussion of the subject, appoint deputations to visit Rome and the Eastern churches, and finally set up a representative interdenominational "Continuation Committee" to take over the actual work of convening the conference. As Gardiner saw at once, it was a monumental undertaking. "The deeper I get into the work, the more I see there is to do," he wrote Chairman Anderson, "and, to speak quite frankly, it is evident to me . . . that the majority of the members of the Commission do not by any means begin to appreciate the variety and extent of the problems before us." He told Manning a few days later that members of the commission had to be convinced that "there is a good deal more to be done than issue invitations to a Conference as we might to a dinner."[20]

20. Gardiner to Stetson, December 6, 1910; to Manning, December 5, 1910, August 23, 1915; to Anderson, January 16, 1911, June 1, 1917; to Francis J. Hall, October 10, 1912, Gardiner Correspondence; to Manning, April 8, August 9, 1913; Manning to Gardiner, May 5, 1914, Bishop Manning Correspondence, boxes 1 and 2, St. Mark's Library, General Theological Seminary, New York, NY; Gardiner to Mott, November 4, 1919, December 18, 1911; to Anderson, December 17, 1910; on the "vastness of the undertaking," see Gardiner to A. C. A. Hall, May 12, 1914; to Manning, December 21, 1910, Gardiner Correspondence.

One of the very first things they had to do was draw up a statement of purpose. In early November 1910 Gardiner sought Brent's advice. He then arranged a small meeting of Manning, himself, and the absolutely essential figure of Mott, founder of the World Student Christian Federation, masterful presider at the Edinburgh Conference, and chairman of its Continuation Committee.[21] Gardiner envisaged that the three would come up with the text of a statement containing wording suitable for the prerogative-conscious archbishops of the Church of England "and of some other letters," he added cryptically, presumably referring to additional European and Eastern churches. The New World must not appear to be upstaging the Old. These texts would then be presented for the approval of the Committee on Plan and Scope at its December 15 meeting in New York City.[22]

It was not to be. The composition of the statement was put off. Delays were, of course, inevitable. In the meantime, Gardiner practiced the art of the possible. "Prayer, publicity and patience in ourselves and in our brethren are the three things which seem to me to be essential now," he confided to Stetson early in the new year. "Whether it takes one year or five to prepare the statement is to my mind quite immaterial, so I really think I can claim to be disposed to move quite as slowly as anyone else." But he was not convincing, and by the end of March 1911, Pepper told him to calm down. Nonetheless, he could not resist urging that the Roman Catholics be brought into the process immediately; he noted that it would be "seemly that we should seek their aid at the outset and by seeking it, we will make it very much easier for them to participate." Besides, once Rome was on board, the Protestant communions "will have to come [in] in a much more cordial spirit than some of them have been in the habit of displaying toward Rome."[23]

If he was quick to mark Protestant suspicion of all things Roman Catholic, Gardiner's own clannishness eventually stared him in the face. I have already noted his on-again, off-again attitude toward African Americans in his own

---

21. Latourette, "Ecumenical Bearings," 356.

22. Gardiner to Manning, November 4, 1910, Gardiner Correspondence. Gardiner got Mott into the planning very early; see Gardiner to Mott, November 8, 1910, ibid. So as not to alarm Manning that a Methodist would be initially contacting English archbishops, he added, "I don't think it would be especially appropriate to have Dr. Mott's opinion on that point." Presumably, Mott would be asked to contribute to the texts "of some other letters."

23. Gardiner to Stetson, January 10, 1911; Pepper to Gardiner, March 28, 1911; Gardiner to Stetson, January 10, 1911, Gardiner Correspondence.

church. He displayed the same prejudice about blacks outside it: as we have already seen, African American Baptist churches were ignored by the unifiers. As he wrote Manning in March 1911: "My own feeling is that we can properly leave the Colored Baptists out for the present." And so they did. When American Lutherans failed to take much interest in the world conference movement, he became patronizing: "Personally I do not take very much interest in them, but, of course, it is important that we should have their cooperation." He showed characteristic Anglican blindness to the churches of the American revival tradition, in this case the Disciples of Christ:

> On account of their ignorance of theology and lack of the historical sense and that strong self-opinion which comes from ignorance, I should think they would be almost the most difficult of all bodies to bring into any real and permanent unity. Of course, this does not apply to Dr. [Peter] Ainslie and a few others almost as remarkable as he, but they are so far in advance of their main body that I do not believe their leadership would be very effective.[24]

The robust self-confidence of the evangelical bodies disturbed him. He had feared for some time, as he wrote Manning, "that we shall have a good deal of trouble with our Baptist friends." They were "considerably impressed of late with their numerical strength." With some distaste he went on to say that Baptists "seem to retain more strongly than any of the other Protestant bodies the old militant spirit of the Reformation period." Nonetheless, over the objections of Bishop Anderson, he insisted that invitations go out, not just to the major Protestant denominations but to the small ones as well. At first, Gardiner's hauteur extended as well to the Orthodox. "You have to know your Greek Priest pretty well," he casually advised Manning, "before you can trust him. There is one in Providence [Rhode Island] who is, I believe, all right, but when I met him last May he knew no English; probably he had acquired it by this time, however." Given the nature of the American scene, he supposed they would have to include the "Polish bishop," but he was less than enthusiastic. Adventists, he presumed, "are not especially educated theologically and would therefore not be much interested in . . . the Conference."[25]

24. Gardiner to Manning, March 27, 1911, April 14, 1913, November 9, 1911; see also September 26, 1911. See Anderson to Gardiner, August 2, 1911, and Gardiner to Anderson, August 7, 1911, Gardiner Correspondence.
25. Gardiner, to Manning, February 27, 1911; to F. J. Hall, March 21, 1911, Gardiner Correspondence.

Discovering America took time. But he stuck with it, and his disdainful attitudes began to fall away. But first, he had trouble with his own denomination. Within it he was determined to sound bells, blow whistles, make a nuisance of himself, and do his best "to preach discontent with our achievements...[for] unless we think we have not accomplished a great deal, we shall not be likely to be more active and energetic in the future than in the past." He wanted constantly to plan ahead. For the sake of Christian unity, he stood ready to give every ounce of strength he could spare from his other duties, for "I consider [the world conference] the greatest opportunity that has been offered to a man for many centuries." He held the belief that "the whole world is yearning for real and vital Christianity; that means unity and without unity there can be no real Christianity." He was also a busy trust lawyer and had other responsibilities. "As I ventured to hint to you in New York the other night," he wrote Chairman Anderson in December 1910, "my business is one of the largest of its kind in Boston, besides which I have numerous responsibilities to my Diocese and Parish which I cannot neglect." Three years later when the federal income tax was passed by Congress, he wrote Stetson that with the "tremendous [new] burden of applying the Income Tax to my trusts, my time will be more completely filled than ever, and I sometimes wonder how I can get through the next winter." He would "economize every moment." Only at the end of 1918 did he retire from his legal practice.[26]

But he had no intention of giving up his work with the Joint Commission. Gardiner judged that what the commission needed was a "general secretary," that is, one with executive power. Himself. If he was humbled by the task that he believed God had placed before them, he was also not averse to political maneuvering. To Newman Smyth, who thought that unity could be achieved without much fuss, he admitted that the Episcopal commission had not yet gotten together and found itself. "We do not realize that in an important and complicated undertaking like this, there must be one executive head.... [T]here are several of us trying to run the machine and a number of other[s] who think they could run it a great deal better." And there had to be a central office "where copies of all correspondence... should be kept and tabulated." Heads of committees must

26. Gardiner to B. Talbot Rogers, July 31, 1911; to Reginald Weller, November 17, 1914; to Manning, December 5, 1910, January 13, 1911, February 27, 1913; to Stetson, January 10, May 1, 1911; to Anderson, April 24, August 7, 1911; to F. J. Hall, July 20, 1911; to Rogers, December 31, 1910; to Zabriskie, December 18, 1914; to Anderson, December 17, 1910; to Stetson, November 6, 1913; to Rogers, December 19, 1918, Gardiner Correspondence.

stay in periodic touch with the secretary and he with them, and so on, but in the first few years of the Joint Commission's work it all had to be ironed out, and that was not easy for a group of volunteers who had not worked together before. When in March 1914 the Joint Commission had been incorporated and a constitution adopted, it was stated that the secretary was to have custody of the records of the commission, conduct its correspondence, oversee publication of documents, serve as assistant treasurer, and appoint assistant secretaries.[27]

Gardiner wanted a businesslike division of responsibilities among the officers, but not so inflexible as to dampen incentive. He wished for order and simplicity. When Stetson suggested that an additional trust company in New York City hold and disburse Morgan's funds, Gardiner wrote to Talbot Rogers that they were not used to so much red tape in New England. "As it is, we are to some extent duplicating each other's work," he wrote Manning, "and we are not working together as efficiently as we might." In a note he had struck before, he contrasted his own business efficiency with the "usual leisurely course of procedure in the Church." From the beginning he spelled out what he meant in a stream of letters. He wanted "consecutive thinking," advance planning, "promptness," and the opportunity to "thrash matters out more" in their meetings. He wrote to Bishop Boyd Vincent of Diocese of Southern Ohio that conversations were superior to letters. Above all, he wanted people to listen to each other, to take in different points of view.[28] He took the advice himself, and ultimately "the respect that he showed other traditions gained for him the respect and the trust of church leaders throughout the world."[29] He was forever trying to "persuade our brethren . . . to mingle with [other denominations] and get to understand them." He declared to one Roman Catholic leader, "We are confident that if we can only get together in friendly conferences, we shall learn to know each other," that they "should convene small gatherings of influential ministers and laymen." At the same time, he recognized that "three hundred leaders will never accomplish anything until they get their respective Communions

27. Gardiner to Smyth, February 13, 1911; to F. J. Hall, July 20, 1911, Gardiner Correspondence; *Minutes of the Meetings of the Joint Commission Appointed by the General Convention of 1910 to Bring About a World Conference on Faith and Order* (printed for the members of the commission, May 1914), 76.

28. Gardiner to Rogers, November 16, 1910; to Manning, February 3, 1911; to Rogers, July 31, 1911; to Smyth, February 13, 1911; to Anderson, April 24, August 7, 1911; to Manning, June 11, 1911; to F. J. Hall, March 29, July 27, 1911; to Zabriskie, December 4, 1912; to Vincent, February 9, 1912; to Stetson, January 10, 1911, Gardiner Correspondence.

29. Frank E. Sugeno to the author, March 6, 1997, Sugeno folder, Gardiner Collection.

stirred deeply."[30] The lawyer from Boston and Maine had little time for those in high ecclesiastical office who wanted to go it alone and who saw life as a stately procession accompanied by endless ovation.

Early in 1911, he heard a rumor that due to time constraints Anderson might resign as chairman. It was a solution to be hoped for. "Bishop Anderson," he wrote to theologian Francis J. Hall, "seldom answers and I presume seldom reads letters." Two years later he confided to Manning, "I do not see that there is anything that you and I can do about it. . . . [T]here must be a great deal of valuable information piled up on Bishop Anderson's desk in Chicago." He was glad to have all letters to Anglican bishops go out from Anderson's office: "I think that is a desirable thing to do . . . [for a letter from him] will have very much more weight with the other Bishops than if it purported to come from me." He was, however, not prepared to sit by and see nothing happen. As Talbot Rogers caustically remarked, on an ecumenical world tour Anderson liked to "deliver the invitation, make a speech, and run along, getting home as soon as possible." To hasten the happy eventuality of Anderson's departure in January 1911, Gardiner called for a "thorough discussion of the machinery of the Commission" and the responsibilities of the officers at the next meeting of Plan and Scope. Increasingly, the bishop of Chicago was unable to fit meetings into his schedule. That being the case, however, resignation from the presidency of the Joint Commission would appear logical and desirable. And Anderson—"His Humility," as George Zabriskie called him—had unfortunately a monarchical view of the episcopate; the secretary did not.[31] The one wanted to impose unity from the top down; the other sought first to interest and engage everyone, clergy and laity alike, on the local level. Their differences were profound.

30. Gardiner to Rogers, March 31, 1914; to L. F. Schlathoelter, February 16, 1912; see also to Herbert Kelly, January 29, 1915; and to Reginald Weller, July 13, 1913, Gardiner Correspondence.

31. Gardiner to Hall, March 13, 1911; to Mott, December 18, 1911, April 9, 1914; to Manning, June 9, 1913, January 18, 1911; Rogers to Gardiner, November 13, 1919; Gardiner to Stetson, January 4, 1911; Zabriskie to Gardiner, July 25, 1919, Gardiner Correspondence. See also Anderson to Gardiner, January 30, 1913, December 29, 1915, February 7, 1916, Gardiner Correspondence. For Anderson's inattentiveness, see Gardiner to Manning, May 9, 1911; and Pepper to Gardiner, February 16, 1912, in which Pepper states that Brent "shares my regret that it does not seem possible for the chairman and the secretary to hit it off better." See also Gardiner to Manning, January 23, 1922. In fairness to Anderson, his great interest while bishop of the Chicago diocese was building a cathedral and centralizing diocesan social and ecclesiastical work in episcopal hands. He sought to emulate the heads of corporations and build an empire. See Rima Lunin Schultz, *The Church and the City: A Social History of St. James, Chicago* (Chicago: Cathedral of St. James, 1986), 163, 168–80, 192–98, 201–2.

Although Gardiner wanted the officers' positions defined both on the commission and on Plan and Scope, when Talbot Rogers, another Anglo-Catholic of national note, fancied an even more detailed description of the secretary's role, Gardiner smelled a rat. "Dr. Rogers is anxious to have the functions of the various officers carefully mapped out in detail," he wrote Francis Lynde Stetson. "Apparently he thinks that certain letters can only be signed by a Bishop, others by a presbyter and perhaps," he added, "he would think there might be some which would not be of much consequence which might be signed by a layman." Two months later, he confided to George Wharton Pepper, "Many of the brethren, at the last meeting [of the Joint Commission], seemed to be very much disturbed at the possibility of the Secretary writing any letters to anybody." Given the volume of mail generated by the world conference movement, the idea of making such distinctions, thought Gardiner, was totally impractical; the commission would simply have to trust its own. He let it be known that officially he would not convey his personal views but reflect only those of the commission as a whole. The larger issue for some, of course, was that of having a layman serve in such a key position in the first place. Manning thought the secretary "ought to be in Holy Orders and if possible a Bishop." Gardiner contended otherwise: "On the general question as to whether the secretary should be a Bishop, Presbyter, or a layman, I don't think it matters," to which he added the afterthought, "I think it happens far too frequently that a Bishop is limited in his horizon to his own diocese."[32] Whether such a supposedly low ceiling was a limitation is arguable.

But the political reality was that as a layman he had to fight for a voice and a place in the movement. He admitted, "I run counter to the Fond du Lac notion [that is, Anglo-Catholic, after the Diocese of Fond du Lac] that a layman must not take the lead in such matters and must not even write certain kinds of letters." Such an attitude was "an unwarranted extension of the doctrine of the grace of Orders." Anderson wanted all formal letters of the commission to go out from his diocesan office. When they did so, Gardiner was quick with praise for their contents. For his part, the bishop of Chicago pompously reminded his Down East secretary that "dignified ecclesiastical procedure and taste" dictated that only a bishop could address another bishop. "The Orthodox, Old Catholic, and Roman Catholic Churches can only properly be approached in a matter of

---

32. Gardiner to Stetson, January 4, 1911; to Pepper, March 27, 1911; Manning to Gardiner, October 6, 1911; Gardiner to Rogers, December 24, 1910, Gardiner Correspondence.

this kind through the Episcopal order." "Many of them," Anderson continued, "would regard anything else as bordering on the discourteous." Gardiner may have been head of the Brotherhood of St. Andrew, but "that was a lay organization." The Joint Commission was different. There he did not "have much to do . . . with such Catholic communions as we are dealing with." For his part, Gardiner doubted the wisdom, as he wrote to his friend Pepper, of seeing "the official correspondence left in the hands of our distinguished President." As for religious figures being addressed by a mere layman, he observed to Manning, "I have had plenty of correspondence with larger ecclesiastical dignitaries than the Bishop of Chicago and they have never taken any offense." Six days after Anderson's May 1911 broadside, Gardiner replied coolly, "I ought to say to you frankly . . . that I quite resent the tone of your letters." He granted that the bishop was no doubt under "considerable pressure and writing in considerable haste. . . . [N]evertheless I venture to think that a little more consideration and courtesy would not be out of place." "Of course," he concluded with impeccable irony, "busy men cannot spend much time in verbose politeness."[33]

But Anderson was not alone in questioning the prominent place held by the lay secretary. As Gardiner wrote a now-converted Rogers, "The Commission is so terribly afraid of having anything done, especially if it be done by a layman, that I suppose I shall get into serious difficulty. However, I am quite ready to go to the stake." Two months later, he confided to Lord Hugh Cecil, marquess of Salisbury, "In my private opinion, if anything effective is to be done in the direction of Unity, it must be strongly supported, if not practically initiated by the laity." He added significantly that laymen and laywomen "from the great body of the Church . . . ought, as in primitive times, to feel a greater responsibility and to have an active share in its government." As he let fall to Archbishop Enos Nuttall of the West Indies, "A number of very distinguished lawyers and other laymen cheerfully gave up three weeks of their time [at the church's General Convention] and displayed as much interest as they would give to the most important business affairs." To his younger friend Edward L. Parsons, rector in Berkeley and future bishop of California, he wrote, "I am hardly shocked at your feeling that all the Bishops are not as wise as Bishop Nichols [William F. Nichols of California]." He thought that a good many were far "not only from

33. Gardiner to F. J. Hall, January 6, March 29, 1911; to Smyth, February 13, 1911; Anderson to Gardiner, May 5, 1911; Gardiner to Anderson, March 10, April 24, 28, 1911; to Pepper, March 29, 1911; to Manning, May 9, 1911; to Fosbroke, July 23, 1913; to Anderson, May 10, 1911, Gardiner Correspondence.

[Nichols's] wisdom, but it would sometimes appear even from ordinary common sense." On the other hand, Bishop Philip Rhinelander was keen on giving the executive secretary—presumably Gardiner himself—full powers to do the job: "Set him free to do it, and equip him with everything necessary and desirable."[34]

And then there was the problem of William Manning himself, who, as I have already shown, was a major player. Although he and Gardiner were always in the closest touch, they never developed much rapport. Manning had a strong personality and, as Gardiner recognized, an "adhesive mind."[35] Born in England—his family migrated in 1882 to the American frontier of Nebraska when he was sixteen—he attended the University of the South, where he came under the powerful influence of theologian William Porcher DuBose. From DuBose he acquired a pietistic Evangelicalism coupled with a high doctrine of the church based on a sacramental, incarnational theology.[36] Manning also had a Social Gospel streak as well as forcefully advocating Christian reunion. With obvious talent and competence came high visibility, first as rector of Trinity Church (1908–1921), then as bishop of New York (1921–1947). And he enjoyed the notoriety. Gardiner wrote to Stetson, "I have an evil suspicion that the Chairman [Manning] of the Committee on Plan and Scope as well as our distinguished President [Anderson] is not averse to a little personal publicity." Manning seldom took advice from others, particularly if it meant greater exertion on his part. As Gardiner confessed to Brent, he and Manning "do not work together to the best advantage, and we are not very fond of listening to each other's suggestions." Concurrently, Gardiner complained to Francis Stetson, "I cannot make Dr. Manning see the importance, of another personal interview with [James] Cardinal Gibbons that we might get him to take another step." The question was whether the time was auspicious to contact the papacy, in which effort Gibbons would be a key figure. "Doctor Manning feels as strongly that such a personal interview is unnecessary as I do that it is necessary or at least highly expedient. If we are to make progress we must avail ourselves of every opportunity to get into close relationship with the Cardinal." In the end Gardiner went

34. Gardiner to Rogers, July 8, 1911; to Cecil, September 21, 1911; to Nuttall, December 13, 1913; to Parsons, December 30, 1911; Rhinelander to Gardiner, December 24, 1914, Gardiner Correspondence.

35. Gardiner to Pepper, December 22, 1913, Gardiner Correspondence.

36. For a description of Manning's life and theology, see William H. Katerberg, *Modernity and the Dilemma of North American Anglican Identities, 1880–1950* (Montreal: McGill-Queen's University Press, 2001), 108–34, esp. 109–10.

to Gibbons himself—twice. If Manning was often slow to respond to others, Trinity's rector also took it into his head to act suddenly and independently. Fancying himself a businessman, he complained about the secretary's expenses and wanted the executive committee to approve payment of every bill. The secretary, who often spent his own money for the movement, exploded to Hughell Fosbroke, "If I can't get calmed down by the end of next week, I guess it would be well for you to squeeze out time to come and reason with me."[37]

Increasingly, as the rector of Trinity Church gained prominence, he came to see himself as the Joint Commission's most important spokesman. In the crucial spring of 1914 when the planning for the world conference was beginning to bear fruit, Manning jumped the gun and without prior consultation took it upon himself to speak to the press on the key report of the deputation to the Protestant churches of Great Britain. At the time there were 461 news releases about to be mailed. Exasperated, Gardiner wrote George Zabriskie that they needed a policy "of refusing to give anything to the newspapers until I have had a reasonable time to prepare it or . . . that a committee should be appointed to see them immediately at the close of our meeting or the next day and give them a carefully prepared statement."[38] Manning also saw himself as the defender of Anglicanism. One historian suggests that social and cultural changes disturbed him so that he turned defensive and sectarian. Increasingly, he insisted upon "apostolic succession as essential to the church's authority and identity."[39] Then in December 1915 he issued his own ultimatum to Protestants in an article in the *Constructive Quarterly.* It was a doozy. Manning repudiated "separate Churches of men's own making." He insisted that "a Priest, ordained by a Bishop, in direct succession from the Apostles, is indispensably necessary for the Celebration of the Holy Communion," that no Protestant minister "can under any circumstances be . . . allowed to celebrate the Holy Communion, without ordination to the Priesthood, at the hands of a Bishop," that "the Anglican Communion aligns herself with Catholic Christendom," and finally that there should

37. Gardiner to Stetson, May 1, 1911; to Brent, May 4, 1911; to Stetson, May 1, August 22, 1911, May 1, 1914; to Fosbroke, April 25, 1914, Gardiner Correspondence. Ten years later Gardiner was still pleading to Manning to take the lead (see Gardiner to Manning, January 23, 1922, Gardiner Correspondence). From the outset Gardiner had urged fund-raising but had been ignored; members of the commission were probably lulled by J. P. Morgan's initial gift.

38. Gardiner to Zabriskie, November 27, 1915, March 25, 1914; see also November 27, 1915, Gardiner Correspondence. For adverse reactions, see Gardiner to Stetson, September 21, 1915; and Stetson to Gardiner, September 22, 1915, Gardiner Correspondence.

39. Katerberg, *Modernity and Anglican Identities,* 115, 117.

be no Episcopalian cooperation "with the present movement for Protestant federation in America or to enter into United Protestant work in Mission fields or elsewhere."[40] Considering the delicate nature of interdenominational negotiations then in place and the author's prominence, such claims were as devastating as they were unnecessary.

Reactions were swift, predictable, and negative. Newman Smyth spoke of the "nasty spirit which Manning and others have ... shown toward Protestantism." Paul de Schweinitz of the Moravians asked if "non-episcopally ordained clergymen will for a moment take any stock in the whole Conference if they are asked to swallow such utterances?" For his part, Gardiner found de Schweinitz "red headed intellectually and physically sectarian, narrow and bigoted," as he wrote Brent some years later, "and quite sore about the Episcopal Church." Gardiner judged that the Moravian's nose was out of joint because the Episcopal Church had not recognized the validity of the Moravian episcopate. And he was right. William Adams Brown of Union Theological Seminary in New York warned Gardiner that Manning's

> personality has been so closely associated with the movement for a world conference that it is difficult not to give what he says a representative character. If the attitude which he has expressed in recent utterances toward federation movements should be shared by his colleagues of the Commission, I fear there will be little chance of securing effective cooperation of the great body of Protestants in any movement conducted under such auspices.

Gardiner, as was his wont, came right back to Brown, stating that no member of the commission had any authority to speak for the rest and that its task was limited by the General Convention to the promotion of the conference itself. It was, he added, "a little unfair that the utterances of one ... should be allowed to out-weigh the fact that several other members of the Commission have taken an active part ... in the Federal Council of Churches."[41]

40. Manning, "The Protestant Episcopal Church and Christian Unity," *Constructive Quarterly* 3 (March–December 1915): 679–96, esp. 684–86. Zabriskie defended Manning; see Zabriskie to Gardiner, August 20, 1916, Gardiner Correspondence. F. J. Hall also defended Manning: "I know of course that Dr. Smyth and others construe Dr. Manning's article as indicating the danger of sacerdotal control of the movement. This is, of course, hopelessly astray. The article simply defines the limits of the scope of our movement as seen by those who adhere strictly to our General Convention instruction" (to Gardiner, December 28, 1915, Gardiner Correspondence).

41. Smyth quoted in Zabriskie to Gardiner, December 27, 1915; Reverend Russell Cecil (Presbyterian) to Gardiner, October 1923; de Schweinitz to Gardiner, July 21, 1916; Gardiner to

Still, he was fearful and wrote Charles K. Gilbert, editor of the *Churchman* (1913–1917), of "the grave danger that Manning's course may alienate our Protestant support . . . and even check . . . closer understanding in England." It did. The Church of England's able youth leader, Tissington Tatlow, wrote that were he a Protestant, if what Manning "says is to be taken as the last word of the Anglican Communion, it is not worth the while of Free Churchmen to worry themselves to come into a conference with us." Gardiner had to reassure Canon Tatlow that Manning's remarks were "pretty nearly contrary to everything that we have promised about the World Conference from the very beginning." "Manning is impressed," he added, "with the idea that he is the leader of the Catholic party in the United States, and he has been rather confirmed in the idea of a sort of martyrdom when his diocese . . . failed to re-elect him as a delegate to the General Convention." To Francis J. Hall the secretary lamented that the *Constructive Quarterly* article was "unnecessary and unfortunate . . . and it has irritated our Protestant brethren" without having any effect on Rome or the East. "It undertakes to do exactly what we have always said we would not do, that is, lay down an ultimatum before the Conference." He believed that if Manning was entitled to insist on the episcopate, "the Presbyterians . . . are equally entitled to insist on its rejection, and the Conference is deadlocked before it convenes."[42]

But there was a more illuminating difference between Gardiner and Manning. It had to do with the role of the Joint Commission and, ultimately, of the Episcopal Church itself in the search for a suitable beginning to Christian unity. What should be their attitude? Their strategy as opposed to tactics? Should they stir their stumps and encourage education, bring about local conferences, stimulate publicity? Manning thought not. Sending out invitations was sufficient. Let others respond as they would. For their part, Episcopalian leaders would write papers and lecture on unity but otherwise mark the time with reserve. Gardiner reasoned that that kind of treacle caught few flies: "Such invitations will never be accepted until we have created in the several countries a strong interest in our movement and expectation of valuable results." As he remarked

---

Brent, November 8, 1922; Brown to Gardiner, August 8, 1916; Gardiner to Brown, August 12, 1916, Gardiner Correspondence.

42. Gardiner to Gilbert, July 21, 1916; Tatlow to Gardiner, March 18, 1916; Gardiner to Tatlow, March 18, April 24, 1916; to Hall, December 31, 1915; to Reginald Weller, December 22, 1915, Gardiner Correspondence.

to Bishop Reginald Weller, there should be "gatherings of people of all kinds for prayer and quiet devotional study led by suitable men.... [By that means] much would be done to foster a new spirit of loving sympathy." Such a course as this "sounds very simple, but, in reality it would need every bit in the way of oversight and organization as the conferences." And he wanted the conferences to report to him, for only then would he be able to learn, as he wrote G. K. A. Bell, from "a good deal of constructive criticism and advice."[43]

When after the first few months of World War I Gardiner himself drew back from advocating local conferences and sought less proactive groups, ones that would pray for peace, Weller reminded him of his original commitment, "I always hesitate to differ from you and from Dr. Fosbroke in any manner, but I really think your [earlier] paper on local conferences is an admirable one... something better than I myself could have produced." The Anglo-Catholic Weller had found the experience of a small gathering exhilarating: "The only discordant note was that of a certain Baptist minister who was tremendously fond of independence and personal liberty and apparently wanted to crawl off into a corner and have his religion to himself." Gardiner got the message. He pushed on. Christian America, he knew, was not yet behind the movement for reunion. He meant to sound reveille and confided to Zabriskie in November 1914, "We could well devote four years to educating our own Church and other Communions, especially if we could directly or indirectly accelerate [their] existing tendency... to unite the divisions in the various families." Gardiner and Father James O. S. Huntington, for whom he had affectionate regard, understood each other perfectly; both sought convocations for laity and clergy of all denominations without prior demands being made. These should be held at the grassroots level all over the country, they said. Local assemblies would, as Huntington remarked, "stiffen the allegiance of a good many of our own men" to the cause of church unity.[44]

Whereas Gardiner wanted local and national conferences held throughout the Christian world in anticipation of a great world gathering, the rector of

43. Gardiner to Weller, December 10, May 21, 1914; to Bell, April 4, 1922, Gardiner Correspondence.

44. Weller to Gardiner, October 29, 1914, March 25, 1915; Gardiner to Zabriskie, November 7, 1914; Huntington to Gardiner, March 18, 1916; Gardiner to Huntington, March 23, 1916, Gardiner Correspondence. See also Gardiner to Smyth, May 8, 1912, on Protestant unions and December 28, 1912, for the need for education, Gardiner Correspondence.

Trinity Church did not. Manning was absent from a meeting in April 1915 at which approval for a North American conclave was given the green light. The Joint Commission authorized the sending of the North American plan and program, once they were completed, to other worldwide churches. "Manning expressed great fear," wrote Gardiner to Zabriskie, "as to the suggestion of these conferences to the Communions in other countries. . . . [He] formally requested me . . . to hold up the minutes." The New York attorney responded that it was settled practice for any secretary of an organization to send out minutes. Were Gardiner to yield to Manning's wishes in the matter, the secretary could be censured. In the absence of a contrary order from the Joint Commission itself, his friend Zabriskie advised, "it . . . [is] your duty to follow the established practice."[45] The planning and the minutes sent out ultimately issued in the Garden City (N.Y.) Conference of January 4–6, 1916.

On occasion, Gardiner defended Manning. He valued "these excellent addresses of yours, and it seems to me I ought to have more" to publish. When Bishop A. C. A. Hall of Vermont reprimanded the secretary on the appointment of the New York rector as a delegate to sound out the pope about the Faith and Order conference, Gardiner backed his friend. Hall remarked that Manning was only a priest, not a bishop; he suggested that he might go to the pope as a bishop's chaplain. How could Gardiner even suppose, Hall exclaimed incredulously, "that the Pope would recognize the Rector of Trinity Church, New York as equal to a Bishop!" The secretary replied that Manning had been appointed a delegate because "it was felt that the chairman of our Executive Committee was too important a person to be merely a Chaplain of any Bishop however distinguished."[46]

Manning was not alone in his defensiveness about Anglican orders, priestly rights at celebrations of the Holy Communion, apostolic succession, and an arm's-length attitude toward Protestants. Many among the Episcopalian leadership—such as Frederick Burgess, bishop of Long Island; Richard H. Nelson, bishop of Albany; Frederick C. Morehouse, editor of the *Living Church;* Silas

45. Gardiner to Zabriskie, April 9, 1915; Zabriskie to Gardiner, April 11, 1916, Gardiner Correspondence.
46. Gardiner to Rogers, July 26, 1915; to Manning, February 13, 1913; Hall to Gardiner, June 4, 1914; Gardiner to Hall, June 10, 1914, Gardiner Correspondence. For his part, Zabriskie defended Manning's right to speak his mind: "Do Protestants expect the Pope to divest himself of popery before they will consent to confer with him on justification by Faith?" (to Gardiner, August 30, 1916, Gardiner Correspondence).

McBee of the *Churchman* (to 1912); Bishop Hall himself; and on one occasion Bishop Reginald Weller of Fond du Lac—all held similar views.[47] When in debate over the Congregational-Episcopal Concordat of 1920–1922 the Episcopal side demanded Congregationalists agree to the "sacramental efficacy" of ordination, an ever loyal but now incensed ecumenist, Newman Smyth, called the stipulating faction "the Catholic Co. Limited."[48] But the Anglo-Catholics by no means presented a united front against church reunion. There were significant exceptions, as we have already seen: Fosbroke, in his wiser moments Reginald Weller, Talbot Rogers, James O. S. Huntington, Bishop Brent, and even Professor Francis Hall.

But then in the end Gardiner, Anderson, Manning, and with very reluctant feet Bishop Hall of Vermont somehow worked it all out. They knew that they were not following well-worn trails but were traveling into an unmapped expanse. For this task their instructions from the highest authority in the Episcopal Church, the General Convention, were explicit: They were only to bring about a world conference on faith and order in which Christian differences could be freely discussed. They were not to try to settle those differences themselves. The conference was not, despite the misapprehensions of many, "concerned with the creation of a united Church out of existing denominations."[49] Only Bishop Hall failed to see the point: organic unity may have been their ideal, but it would take place only at the conclusion of their work together. And the end product might look different from what any of them had anticipated. Meanwhile, none of them was going to turn back, least of all Robert Gardiner. And so they stuck together for well over a decade, at the end of which they transferred the leadership to an international ecumenical body. All along, Manning lectured, Anderson wrote occasional tracts, while Gardiner dictated his forty letters a day. By 1922 the secretary was even signing a few of them to Manning "Affectionately yours." But such fellow feeling came neither easily nor often.

Gardiner's value to the movement increased in direct proportion to the size of his mail in both Boston and Maine. By 1914, he told Reginald Weller, forty

---

47. See, for example, for the *Living Church*, Gardiner to F. J. Hall, March 14, 1914; for the *Churchman*, Gardiner to Stetson, December 7, 1910; to George Craig Stewart, September 14, 1915; to Brent, November 11, 1922, Gardiner Correspondence. For A. C. A. Hall, see Chapter Five.

48. Smyth to Anderson, November 13, 1921, Newman Smyth Collection, Yale University, quoted in Peter G. Gowing, "Newman Smyth and the Congregational-Episcopal Concordat," *Church History* 33:2 (June 1964): 183.

49. Tatlow, "World Conference," 410.

thousand to fifty thousand letters had arrived from every part of the world "and from men of every Communion . . . [and] probably a thousand letters from Roman Catholics." He added, only half joking, "No member of the Commission knows enough about the work of my office to be able to contradict me successfully." It took a week or more, he confided to J. P. Morgan Jr., "to mail a document to my entire list which contains about fifteen thousand names." Gardiner simply kept at the job. In doing so, he made himself the indispensable center of communication and tabulation for the entire movement. As early as October 1910 the Joint Commission voted that all reports of personal conferences, "correspondence, items of news, and suggestions for the work of the Commission" be sent to him. Only the chairman of Plan and Scope, Manning, and the secretary were to deal with the press and "give to the newspapers such matters as they think wise." Certainly, the Episcopalians had to speak with one voice. But once again it was not so simple. What the Joint Commission ultimately published had to be agreed upon by a majority of its members. And they were men who represented very different points of view about the nature of the church, its ministry, its sacraments, and what constituted its unity. The temptation to delay publication or at a later date to revise and tuck in favorite phrases was irresistible. When Hall proved to be a footdragger on the Committee on Literature, Gardiner admitted to Hughell Fosbroke that he had constantly to "save planks from the shipwreck when I submit anything to the Bishop of Vermont." From one of Hall's prayers, the secretary observed with New England starch, "the Committee cut out the phrase the 'holy kiss of peace' for we feared it would be a little too oriental for general use." On the whole such Anglo-Catholics as Hall were in Gardiner's opinion "substantially Protestant, for they are continually protesting."[50]

Whereas Gardiner's own catholic theology will be analyzed in the following chapter, it is evident to anyone reading the Faith and Order correspondence that his greatest support came from a circle of high church clergy friends such

50. Gardiner to Weller, December 26, 1914. Gardiner also reported, "Thousands of letters have not been preserved which express a warm interest, but did not indicate any specific attitude of the writer" (*Minutes of the Meetings,* 63). Gardiner to Morgan, December 29, 1920; to F. J. Hall, July 20, 1911, Gardiner Correspondence; *Minutes of the Meetings of the Executive Committee of the Joint Commission* (printed for the use of the members of the Joint Commission, October 19, 1910), 6, 7, Gardiner Collection; Gardiner to Fosbroke, June 5, 1919; to Manning, February 13, 1913, September 1, 1915, March 8, 1921, March 28, 1922; to Hall, May 6, 1915; to Manning, August 30, 1915, Gardiner Correspondence.

as Brent, Rogers, Weller, and Dean Fosbroke of the General Theological Seminary where Gardiner himself was a trustee. There were, to be sure, broad churchmen such as Henry S. Nash; James Perry, "one of the ablest of our younger Bishops, a man of vision . . . and sound business and organizing ability"; and Philip Rhinelander, the rector of Christ Church, Cambridge, and later bishop of Pennsylvania. Of Fosbroke, Gardiner wrote that he "is very methodical and conscientious, a thoroughly sound, wholesome, strong man." There were other clerical allies such as Father Herbert Kelly, professor of theology at the Central Theological College in Tokyo; Edward L. Parsons, future bishop of California; and above all two Englishmen, Tatlow of the SCM in England, "my discrete and confidential friend" and Gardiner's counterpart in the United Kingdom, and Edwin J. Palmer, bishop of Bombay, single-minded and efficient, "whose enthusiasm is of the steady kind," remarked Brent, "that reaches its end."[51] With all these men Gardiner spoke freely on both theological and political matters. None in this clerical circle was defensive or sought personal notoriety; none settled back and applauded his own point of view. Each wanted to get the job done.

Not all of Gardiner's friends were clergy, by any means. There was, first of all, that brotherhood of attorneys of which he was a member: Stetson, Zabriskie, and Pepper. They were a distinguished group, committed churchmen, ambassadors without portfolios for their faith.[52] Their unflagging attention to the world conference ensured its success; without them the assembly would never have convened. They also provided the secretary with a place where he could vent his frustrations. There were laywomen in the inner circle as well; they were neither tokens nor auxiliaries, but were as accustomed to command as their male counterparts were. Gardiner came to rely on the Society of the Companions of the Holy Cross. The society, "which for several years," he informed Mott, "has taken a deep, vital, and practical interest in the question of Christian unity, is planning a large public meeting in Boston." This association of women, he told Fosbroke, "is the only organized body that has really

51. Gardiner to Bishop Ethelbert Talbot, January 6, 1923; to Zabriskie, May 12, 1916; see Gardiner to Fosbroke, April 2, 1918, April 11, 1919, as well as the prior Gardiner-Fosbroke correspondence, 1912–1916; Gardiner to Tatlow, July 9, 1913; Brent to Gardiner, June 25, 1923, Gardiner Correspondence. Tatlow was secretary of the Archbishop's Committee on the World Conference. See Gardiner to Tatlow, April 18, 1914; and to Mott, July 3, 1917, Gardiner Correspondence.

52. Pepper would be the first layman to give the Lyman Beecher Lectures at Yale Divinity School. See B. Franklin Pepper Jr., "George Wharton Pepper: 'Mens Sano in Corpore Sano,'" (bachelor's thesis, Princeton University, 1951), 23–24.

taken any practical interest in the World Conference movement, or, in fact, [in] the question of Christian unity." He urged Fosbroke to go to the companions' headquarters, Adelynrood, in Byfield, Massachusetts, and conduct their "Day of Devotion," adding, "They are most of them leading women, accustomed to getting things done, and not trained as we men have been in ecclesiastical procrastination." When Brent went there, Gardiner wrote him, "That group has always been an inspiration to me." Through his friends Vida Scudder, Helen Dudley of Denison House, and Ellen Starr of earlier Social Gospel days in Boston, he had met Mary Kingsbury Simkhovitch, founder of Greenwich House in New York City in 1902. In 1922 they served together on the Commission on Social Service, planning for the Conference on Life and Work (1925).[53]

In a letter to Professor Alice Brown of Wellesley College, Gardiner judged that getting the church to think ecumenically "must come from the laity. . . . The patience with which the Companions have listened to me time after time fills me with admiration and deep gratitude." "I wish I could get some organization of lay men," he added to Brown, "to adopt the same course" and have a committee on church unity like that of the companions. At the same time that Gardiner was enlisting these women, he had been organizing "a three-year petition campaign that garnered over a thousand signatures from priests and laymen and women in favor of allowing women to serve as deputies" to the General Convention.[54] When organizing an educational campaign for regional conferences, Charles Henry Brent, Presbyterian Arthur Brown, and Congregationalist

53. Gardiner to Mott, June 25, 1919; to Fosbroke, March 15, 1917, February 12, 1918; to Chauncey Brewster, September 9, 1918; to Mott, June 25, 1919; to Pepper, September 9, 1921, Gardiner Correspondence. For the views of the Society of Companions of the Holy Cross and on Gardiner's visits to their center, Adelynrood, see Emily Morgan, *Letters to Her Companions* (South Byfield, MA: privately published, 1944), 116, 197, 221, 261, 274, 276, 285; *Twenty-first Annual Conference of the Society of the Companions of the Holy Cross,* August 23, 1917, 3, Archives of the Society of the Companions of the Holy Cross, South Byfield, Mass.; Gardiner to Charles Henry Brent, August 10, 1922, Gardiner Correspondence; Minutes of the Meeting of the Commission on Service, March 14, 1922; and Rima Lunin Schultz, "Women's Work and Women's Calling in the Episcopal Church: Chicago, 1880–1989," in *Episcopal Women,* edited by Catherine Prelinger (New York: Oxford University Press, 1992), 20, 23.

54. Gardiner to Brown, January 23, 1918, Gardiner Correspondence; Mary Sudman Donovan, *A Different Call: Women's Ministries in the Episcopal Church, 1850–1920* (Wilton, CT: Morehouse-Barlow, 1986), 163. Donovan also suggests that Gardiner may have been influenced in this by his sister, Eleanor, who was a member of the Community of St. Mary in New York City. See also *The Twenty-third Annual Conference of the Society of the Companions of the Holy Cross, 1919* (Chicago: Presbyterian Theological Seminary), 26.

Nehemiah Boynton thought that the initial discussions should take place at small local luncheons for women and small dinners for men. Gardiner replied, "There is no reason why the sexes should be kept separate—have both lunch and dinner for both." He wanted women to become lay readers in the services of the church. "I should be very glad," he wrote Bishop Edwin Lines of Newark, "to see the word 'male' taken out of Canon 23 [sic]. . . . [But were women made] eligible as lay readers, there would be an outcry at once that they were seeking the priesthood." When a woman friend came to see George Zabriskie about getting the right to vote for vestrymen, "one thing led to another," wrote the New Yorker to Gardiner, "and I remarked that I did not believe that the suffragists (of whom she is one) aim at anything short of the priesthood." The woman responded to Zabriskie, "We ought to utilize in the full ministry the spiritual powers of women." Zabriskie was taken aback. Gardiner was not. Two months later he chided his New York friend about not having women on the Joint Commission: "I am sorry you don't want to have the full representation of the whole Church."[55]

As we have seen in an earlier chapter Gardiner did not think very highly of the efficiency of the clergy. Laymen and -women, he judged, were generally more skilled and resourceful. Despite his admiration for such clerics as James O. S. Huntington, Edward L. Parsons, Hughell Fosbroke, Reginald Weller, Tissington Tatlow, Edwin J. Palmer, and others, there was still in his attitude and in that of his lawyer friends a lack of confidence in clerical abilities. George Wharton Pepper wrote him in early 1915 that "the clergy of the PEC [Protestant Episcopal Church], taking them as a bunch, have no conception of the meaning of unity and . . . [it would be] a foolish move to make them the mouthpiece for interpreting unity." Gardiner declared he was in full agreement. If priests were to be instructed to preach about church unity, Pepper judged, "it seems to me the most we can hope to do is to limit the harm that will result." Fairly or unfairly, the future senator from Pennsylvania saw a lack of coherence, of intellectual caliber, and of moral vigor among Episcopal clergy.[56]

55. Gardiner to John Stewart Bryan, September 12, 1921; to Lines, April 9, 1919; Zabriskie to Gardiner, May 19, 1918; Gardiner to Zabriskie, July 11, 1918, Gardiner Correspondence. Gardiner should have said "Canon 21" (currently Canon 26). Despite an attempt in 1925 on the part of the House of Deputies to allow women to become lay readers (vetoed by the House of Bishops), it was not until 1969 that women could be licensed on the same basis as men.
56. Pepper to Gardiner, February 3, 1915; Gardiner to Pepper, February 5, 1915; Pepper to Gardiner, September 7, 1921, Gardiner Correspondence.

Parsons summed up attitudes in the Episcopal Church itself toward the Joint Commission: "You know how the ultra-protestant element in the Church feels that the Commission is either a mere ornament or else a tool of the extreme Catholic party." Parsons had heard "one of our sanest and ablest clergy in this diocese [California] ... attack the Commission as practically useless." It was, declared Parsons, "only one instance of a very common attitude." That attitude, he said, had some foundation in fact, for the commission did not appear to be balanced. "Everywhere through the Church Bishop Hall ... is known as a strong high Churchman." Fosbroke had been chosen as dean of the General Theological Seminary "by the extreme men ... and as for Dr. [Francis J.] Hall ... he is as a theologian the very embodiment of the 'authoritative' view of the Church." Hall was "not representative; the entire Protestant element in the Church distrusts his theology, and from my point of view they are perfectly right." A "bad strategical error" had been made, Parsons judged, and "I think men like Fosbroke would fully recognize that fact."[57]

As more and more contact with other churches proceeded in the crucial years 1910 to 1914, the secretary developed allies outside of his own denomination. Highest on his list of those in whom he placed confidence was John R. Mott. Gardiner had "great respect for his knowledge and diplomatic and administrative efficiency." When Herbert Kelly criticized the Methodist leader, Gardiner replied that he did not agree: "He seems to me the greatest man in the Christian world, and he would be a donkey if he did not recognize the extent of his power." Gardiner had a strong suspicion "that [Mott] would come into the Church if there was any place for him, but the P.E. Church in the U.S.A. would not know what to do with a man as big as he is." Early on, there was Peter Ainslie of the Disciples of Christ who grew in everyone's estimation; the ever enthusiastic and impatient Congregationalist Newman Smyth; Gardiner's good friend Arthur Judson Brown, head of the Presbyterian Board of Foreign Missions; and Presbyterians William Adams Brown, who underwent "a change of feeling toward our Church," and even the "formerly luke-warm" J. Ross Stevenson, president of the Chicago Theological Seminary and then of Princeton Theological Seminary.[58]

57. Parsons to Gardiner, February 1, 1918, Gardiner Correspondence.
58. Gardiner to J. Howard Swinstead, September 30, 1914; Gardiner to A. C. A. Hall, June 10, 1914; Zabriskie to Gardiner, June 24, 1917; Gardiner to Zabriskie, August 19, 1915; Zabriskie to Gardiner, June 24, 1917; Gardiner to Kelly, May 17, 1918; see as well to J. Howard Swinstead, September 30, 1914, for more on Mott's importance; Gardiner to A. J. Brown, May 20, 1920,

Among his Roman Catholic friends was the Reverend Edward A. Pace, a pioneering psychologist at Catholic University, first president of the American Catholic Philosophical Association, and editor of the *Catholic Encyclopedia*, and Pace's collaborator, John J. Wynne, S.J., author of *The Jesuits of North America* (1925). By 1917 Wynne was serving both on the Committee on Literature of the Joint Commission and on the North American Preparation Committee. Wynne "has been seeking to convert individual Roman Catholics to the World Conference movement," Gardiner informed Manning in 1917. Nine months later he wrote Hall that the "number of Roman Bishops and Roman ecclesiastical magazines . . . which are speaking cordially of our movement is steadily increasing." The secretary carried on a confidential correspondence for eight years with Aurelio Palmieri, editor of the leading Byzantine journal *Bessarione*. Palmieri was as well director of the Institute for Eastern Europe. He was a laicized Roman Catholic priest "in whose ability and good faith I place great confidence," said Gardiner. He later cultivated a friendship with the heroic Belgian patriot and promoter of church unity Joseph Cardinal Mercier of Malines. Gardiner also made a close and lasting friendship with the Eastern Orthodox scholar Hamilcar S. Alivisatos in Athens.[59]

But all was neither sweetness nor light. What is more, Gardiner's troubles were by no means limited to recalcitrant elements in his own denomination. He faced mistrust and truculence from leaders of other churches as well. With the heirs of an older holiness movement, the Methodists, Gardiner sometimes fared well, as in his close friendship with John R. Mott. With the more parochial in that large and powerful body, it was a different matter. Among those he sought out was Edwin Hughes, "one of the strongest of the Methodist Bishops and a young man of great promise." Ironically, Hughes argued with Gardiner

Gardiner Correspondence. See also *General Catalogue: Presbyterian Theological Seminary, Chicago* (Chicago, 1939), 128; and *Pulpit Digest* (December 1962): 24. For W. A. Brown, see Brent to Gardiner, November 3, 1922, Gardiner Correspondence. For Stevenson, see *General Catalogue of (McMormick) Presbyterian Theological Seminary, Chicago* (Chicago: Presbyterian Theological Seminary, 1939), 161.

59. Gardiner to Manning, March 2, 1917; to Hall, December 18, 1917; to Anderson, December 17, 1918; see Gardiner-Palmieri correspondence and Gardiner to Fosbroke, February 28, 1918, May 9, 1920, Gardiner Correspondence. Palmieri's name was omitted to protect his identity for diplomatic reasons from a resolution thanking him for his work with influential Catholics (Executive Committee Minutes, March 18, 1920, 141). Gardiner revealed his name to Anderson (May 4, 1920). See also Gardiner to Mercier, November 18, 1918, April 1, May 9, 1924; and particularly to Alivisatos, September 14, 1914, Gardiner Correspondence.

not over holiness and sanctification, but over ecclesiology. Hughes feared that "an institutional conception of the Church that claims for itself alone either validity or authority will stand in the way" of unity and that it would be "best for those Churches that claim apostolic succession to get together" by themselves. "In my own communion," said the Methodist leader, "I do not know of a single minister who would consider a union which involved a confession that our spiritual forefathers have not had both a valid and regular ministry." Gardiner replied, "I think it will be some years before we are ready to consider the old questions of validity and regularity of orders. . . . [T]hat controversy has done serious damage in excluding . . . the conception of the church as an organism, the body of Christ, the fullness of Him that filleth all in all."[60]

In the years to come Hughes continued his thorny correspondence. He did not think there was "the slightest hope of reunion under the auspices of your Church," and later asserted that he was "not in the least degree persuaded that we should have one Church." That had already been tried, Hughes judged, and the "memory of it is far from good." Episcopalians' attitude toward their Methodist brothers and sisters "is an utter denial of the prayer of Christ," Hughes added, "which was that his disciples should be one in their fellowship and mood." But Episcopalians would not even enter the FCC! Hughes related that when he came back from World War I, he shared a cabin with an Episcopal bishop. Being a roommate was one thing; sharing worship was another: "At the [shipboard] Communion Service on Sunday he wishes me to read a scripture which is not part of the set service while he does the rest!!" When Hughes became bishop of the Methodist Church, "Boston Area," it was almost five years before "I met Bishop [William] Lawrence. We lived within four miles of each other. I received no call, had no note of welcome. Yet I know that, after the selection of Cardinal O'Connor, Bishop Lawrence called on him promptly and then wondered why the Cardinal did not return the courtesy." Hughes saw no improvement in Episcopalian attitudes and conduct. His final word was that if all Episcopalians were like Gardiner, they would not have the "present situation" of guarded and jaundiced denominational attitudes. "Whether you know it or not," Hughes added, "you are practically always referred to as a sort of an Episcopalian exception."[61]

<hr />

60. Hughes to Gardiner, June 12, 1911; Gardiner to Hughes, June 23, 1911, Gardiner Correspondence.

61. Hughes to Gardiner, May 16, 1918, May 17, July 27, 1921, Gardiner Correspondence.

Methodist Bishop E. E. Hass of Nashville, Tennessee, objected to the leaflets sent out from Gardiner's office: they "contain a good many historical statements that some of us who have been called on to study and teach history do not believe correspond to the facts." Were they to come together, asked Hass, "on terms of absolute equality. Or are we to be met with teachings that imply that some of us have been guilty of schism?"[62]

Elsewhere Gardiner fared better. English Methodist John W. Hamilton wrote him that he believed that it would be Episcopal laymen "who would overcome this aloofness in your communion. . . . I speak freely to you because I know the breadth of your vision and the depth of your sympathies and the length of your cabletow," an apt metaphor.[63] Gardiner returned the compliment. He made other friends. Among the more durable was W. C. Bitting, corresponding secretary of the Northern Baptists who became his ally and admirer. Surprised, Gardiner found Baptists positively inclined and "eager for the fray." He also extended courtesies to Lutherans and to a number of Orthodox clergy and laity such as Archimandrite Alexopoulos, pastor of the Greek Orthodox church in the District of Columbia and a dignitary of the Orthodox Church whose position is usually defined as one in charge of a group of monasteries and in rank just below a bishop. Alexopoulos turned out to be "a warm believer in Church Unity, and thinks the Greek Church ought to cultivate relations with the Episcopal church." In 1913 Gardiner wrote to Peter Ainslie, "I have stretched my authority a little bit by inviting Mr. George A. Copp of Strasbourg, Virginia, who seems to be a Dunker (Church of the United Brethren in Christ), to come to the meeting at the Astor House on May 8th."[64] There would be others.

But the resentment of some was itself a signal that the Episcopalians had entered the public arena, were gaining attention with their ideas, and even

62. Hass to Gardiner, May 23, 1913, Gardiner Correspondence.

63. Hamilton to Gardiner, December 6, 1913, Gardiner Correspondence. In navigation, given the pitch and roll of the vessel rendering service as well as those taken in tow, there has to be maximum maneuverability in the rudder action of the towing ship and careful coordination in the progress of all of them so that the cable tow itself does not snap as the result of violently alternating tension caused by the respective positions of the vessels vis-à-vis the waves. Hamilton's implication was that Gardiner was able to bring along many in his long train in a stable, consistent manner.

64. See Bitting to Gardiner, February 14, 1913; Gardiner to Zabriskie, November 8, 1911; to Woelfkin, October 31, November 20, 1911; to Manning, November 17, 1917; to Ainslie, May 1, 1913, Gardiner Correspondence.

making progress. By the end of 1911 one hundred thousand letters and copies of the proposal for the conference had gone out from the Joint Commission to all Episcopal clergy, to all bishops of the Anglican Communion, to Roman Catholic cardinals and bishops, and to all Protestant and Orthodox leaders the world over. By 1912 Gardiner's office was not only writing in Latin, French, and Italian but soliciting replies in modern Greek, German—and Russian. He made use of the Harvard faculty to ensure correct translations of conference material into French and German. With a light touch he declared to theologian Francis J. Hall, "I have found it so difficult to acquire even a slight knowledge of the Russian alphabet that I don't believe I shall attempt Chinese." In the late summer of 1913 Gardiner enlisted the services of an assistant, Ralph Wilder Brown, a 1906 graduate of Harvard and himself an expert linguist who coached the secretary in modern Greek. Brown was to succeed his boss as secretary of the Continuation Committee in 1924.[65]

In the meantime, the virus of suspicion of Episcopalian motives was contagious. In early 1913 Eugene Camp of the Church News Association reported to Gardiner on the Foreign Missions Conference at which an Episcopalian emissary, John W. Wood, "appeared, made a short address and departed." Wood's lack of conviviality and refusal to stay for the meeting's other considerations failed to commend his ecumenical plea. To make matters worse, at the beginning of the missions conference, reported Camp, "inquiries were made, where were the Episcopalians, and on one day at one of our meetings a member took out of his pocket one of your Church Unity leaflets and held it up." A general laugh went around the room. Who did the Episcopalians think they were? Those present represented "great bodies, many times larger than the Episcopal, and giving far more money." (In 1913 the Episcopal Church had not paid its apportionment to the Home Mission Council for two years.) Camp continued, "Here was one of the smaller bodies, firing tracts from Maine about unity, and, when there was an opportunity to practice a little unity, holding aloof." Camp ventured the opinion that "until some Episcopalians are at least willing to speak to these

65. Tatlow, "World Conference," 412; Gardiner to Canon H. N. Bate (of England's Carlisle Cathedral), December 28, 1923; to Hall, August 31, 1915, Gardiner Correspondence; Tomkins, notebook 1, Tomkins Papers, 7, 49, 53. The Continuation Committee should not be confused with the Joint Commission of the Episcopal Church; the former was the overarching ecumenical committee that took over the direction of the movement for a world conference. Gardiner resigned from the Episcopal commission in the early 1920s, but retained the secretaryship in the then more important Continuation Committee.

Presbyterians, Methodists and others, tracts talking about unity are wasted or worse." What was equally damaging was the fact that "in very many quarters in New York during the week [of the conference] your efforts were made fun of, because the practice of the Episcopalians is so far, they say, from high sounding tracts." Progress, he concluded, "is making backwards." The people in those meetings, Camp reminded Gardiner, "were the leaders of Christian thought and action in all America."[66]

Gardiner kept his cool. He was well aware, he rejoined, that this haughty attitude obtained among certain members of his own church. "It will take a good deal of patience and perseverance to induce" these fellow churchmen "to see the matter [of cooperation] in its real light." He then went on to argue for "the fundamental necessity of a common life" rather than for federation. It was a short, measured response that reminded critics of the larger goal. He himself was not forever lost in admiration for his church and certainly not for its aloofness. "I have always felt," he contended to Bishop Hall, "that if the Church had really been in earnest about the Chicago-Lambeth overture, it would have done more than tack it up on the front door for those to read who wanted to take the trouble." On the other hand, he complained to William A. Smith of the *Churchman*, "I think it is rather curious that our Protestant brethren never seem to think of unity among themselves, but look only to the P.E. Church; that, in a way, is a tribute to that Church, but if they would try to unite with each other, they would find that the P.E. Church is not the only one which is difficult to deal with."[67]

When Moravian Paul de Schweinitz suggested that if Episcopalians were sincere in wanting church unity they ought to muzzle some of their spokesmen, the secretary replied that he could not muzzle anyone: "In fact . . . the idea of muzzling, which seems to me to imply some sort of compulsion, is foreign to the spirit in which our Commission is trying to approach the Conference." As late as 1923 Congregationalist Herbert P. Woodin found proposals for a world conference from the Episcopal Church that had not even joined the FCC "exceedingly hypocritical . . . if not positively ridiculous." Episcopalians "'tithe,

66. Camp to Gardiner, January 17, 1913, Manning Correspondence, box 2, Tomkins Papers. For a more positive view of Episcopalian activities, see Howard A. Bridgeman, "Do the Episcopalians Mean Unity? A Talk with Bishop Brent on the Cincinnati Proposal," *Congregationalist and Christian World* (November 19, 1910): 759.

67. Gardiner to Camp, January 31, 1913, Manning Correspondence, box 2, Tomkins Papers; to Hall, February 10, 1913; to Smith, May 4, 1918, Gardiner Correspondence.

mint, anise and cummin [over apostolic succession] but have left void the word
of God. Is it conceivable that Jesus would stand for that sort of thing?" Gardiner replied that the movement was no longer an Episcopalian affair, adding,
"Even if Episcopalians are still grievously in error, that seems to my mind a special reason why our brethren of the other Churches, to whom greater light has
been vouchsafed, should get into the conference with us as often as possible to
see if he [*sic*] could not be infected with a better spirit."[68] No reply exists.

Then there was the problem of indifference. On the eve of the American delegation's embarkation to the free churches of the British Isles (1914), Tissington
Tatlow put it succinctly—and forlornly—to his American counterpart when
he wrote: "It is uphill work in this country [England]. One or two of the Nonconformist Churches have written polite little notes saying that they do not
think they can do much toward getting their leaders together to meet the
American delegates, but if I would send them the date of the conference, they
would try to send somebody. They all think the conference is going to be held
in the United States within the next few months." Trying to get through to
Lutherans, Pentecostals, and Roman Catholics proved particularly difficult. In
these cases the problem of insouciance was compounded by a lack of esteem for
the Episcopal Church. In a brusque response to the Joint Commission's invitation, Professor Theodore E. Schmauk, president of the General Council of the
Evangelical Lutheran Church in North America and champion of confessional
Lutheranism, declared that Lutherans did not "believe that there is any unity in
the Church which is not based on principle." They could not do anything in
any event until 1913. Schmauk requested that Gardiner outline the plan and
scope of the work, "giving as clearly as you can . . . the method to be employed
and the results to be aimed at." Then he lectured, "Our branch of the Lutheran
Church is very conservative, will not yield on its principles of faith, does not
look on other Protestants as rivals, believes on acting on its own faith as a matter
of conscience, until such time, if the Lord ever brings it about, as the conscience of all Christians will be cleared to hold the same faith, and meantime . . ."
The letter ground on mechanically, far removed from Martin Luther's unbut-
toned, intellectual vigor. In reply Gardiner wondered, might not it be possible
for the Lutheran council to "appoint a committee to act with us without waiting two years?" That autumn he remarked that his "letters and our invitations

68. Gardiner to de Schweinitz, June 29, 1911; Woodin to Gardiner, May 28, 1923; Gardiner
to Woodin, June 4, 1923, Gardiner Correspondence.

were not received with any great cordiality [by the Lutherans], although there were several friendly expressions . . . [and] two or three distinctly hostile replies." One of the latter came from J. A. Morehead of the National Lutheran Council of America who was "not convinced that the organization and apparent development of the movement you represent does not give up some essential elements of the Christian religion which have found fullest historical expression in the Protestant Reformation." Morehead did not elaborate, except to remark that the " 'Faith' side of your movement for me spells things essential and the 'Order' side means things non-essential in themselves but nevertheless important from the point of view of the practical welfare of the Church." Having sounded that tentatively conciliatory note, on behalf of the National Lutheran Council of America, he declined official partnership in the Faith and Order Movement. In the meantime, Theodore Schmauk had not only kept in touch but in 1916 attended the important Garden City meeting. The secretary in turn learned from Schmauk, kept him informed about overtures to the Roman Catholic Church, and simultaneously discovered the Lutherans.[69]

Indifference also marked the response of Presbyterians. In addition to the early reaction of William Adams Brown, Gardiner's fellow conferee at the 1914 peace conference at Lake Constance, Germany, William P. Merrill, as late as 1921, was of the opinion that "Presbyterians are not very deeply interested in the discussion of Faith and Order as the basis of church unity." Merrill declared that there was an "almost universal feeling among Presbyterians" that unity would be achieved better "through co-operation in work than through discussion of Faith and Order." There were others who were not only hard to pin down but difficult to find in the first place. By 1916 Gardiner was in touch with Edwin M. Bliss of the Bureau of the Census requesting information on Pentecostal and Holiness churches. Although his interest began to extend to what has been called "*the* popular religious movement" of the twentieth century, there is no evidence that he carried on extensive correspondence after his initial inquiry, or that if he did Pentecostals ever responded. The Holiness movement and its successors in the twentieth century were powerful and multiple lay movements, "ill-accommodated to established ecclesiastical order." Drawing on both

---

69. Tatlow to Gardiner, December 24, 1913; Schmauk to Gardiner, April 6, 1911; Gardiner to Schmauk, April 10, 1911; to Gilbert P. Symons, October 9, 1911; Morehead to Gardiner, February 7, 1921; Gardiner to Schmauk, August 5, 1916, Gardiner Correspondence. Gardiner sent out eleven thousand letters to Lutheran ministers and said "many ministers desire to be entered on our mailing list."

blue-collar people as well as the marginalized, the Pentecostal movement "was the product of clashing forces within the vast and amorphous holiness movement that swept across evangelical Protestantism in the last third of the nineteenth century." Beginning hesitantly in 1906, Pentecostalism's growth was only cursorily examined in Gardiner's day; its remarkable advance took place later without benefit of formal hierarchical structures, at least not obvious ones. This is not to say either that it was ever anticlerical or that it was leaderless. Some of its most important initiators were ministers; others were laymen and laywomen. Among the clerical founders were Charles F. Parham (Methodist), Eudorius N. Bell (Baptist), Joseph H. King (Methodist), B. H. Irwin (Baptist), and Charles H. Mason (an African American Baptist); among the more famous lay leaders were the African American William J. Seymour, Sarah W. L. Palmer, A. A. Allen, A. J. Tomlinson, J. J. R. Flower, and Oral Roberts. Often, however, the lines between clergy and laity blur. But if the elders of the Church of God, for instance, could claim "that none of deliberations had been humanly constructed" and at the same time "sustain the vision of leaderlessness," the "plain truth is that the Pentecostal sky was studded with stars, luminaries of the flesh-and-blood variety, and their trajectories illumined and ordered the world around them."[70]

Aside from profound differences in style and in theology, the problem for someone like Gardiner was that there was no centrally organized group of leaders with whom he could correspond. Which was precisely the point: the wind of Pentecostal faith blew where it willed, "and you hear the sound of it, but you do not know whence it comes or whither it goes" (John 3:8). And so it was with those born of the Spirit on America's Azusa streets. Social disparities between middle- and upper-class churches and the smaller conventicles of the poor also hindered communication. The latter were suspicious of the educated and the powerful; instead of large congregations with set liturgical customs, prescribed modes of behavior, telephones, secretaries, and letterheads, Pentecostals enjoyed small, intimate, almost secret groups in which they freely expressed themselves. In addition, they were radically democratic. Baptism in the Holy Spirit, gifts of

70. Merrill to Gardiner, March 12, 1921; Bliss to Gardiner, January 27, 1916, Gardiner Correspondence; Peter W. Williams, *Popular Religion in America* (Champaign: University of Illinois Press, 1989), 144; Bryan Wilson, "Can the 'Latter Rain' Survive Consumerism?" *Times Literary Supplement,* March 29, 2002, 8; Charles H. Lippy and Peter W. Williams, eds., *Encyclopedia of the American Religious Experience,* 3 vols. (New York: Charles Scribner's Sons, 1988), s.v. "Pentecostalism"; Grant Wacker, *Heaven Below: Early Pentecostals and American Culture* (Cambridge, MA: Harvard University Press, 2001), 143, 144.

tongues, faith healing, urgent millenarianism, the restoration of primitive Christianity, and entire sanctification could set anyone clapping and singing. Such red-hot halloos had little to do with solemn rites of ordination, clerical dignity, or episcopal drapery. Neither creeds, nor sacraments, nor theological education determined Pentecostal membership in good standing. Without waiting on such profundities, God, the Holy Spirit, straightaway smote the unsuspecting. As a result the Pentecostals' early strength lay in their very organizational shapelessness. How do you pin such people down? But, of course, the actuality was more complex: in Pentecostalism there was indeed a liturgy, sacraments, education, and all the rest. Only they were different. The contrarieties were obvious to Gardiner and Brent. Nevertheless, they resolved between themselves that when it came to invitations to join the conference movement, "Even the smaller bodies ought to have proper respect if they meet the requirements." Although that touch of the patronizing remained, increasingly the two men recognized, as Charles Henry Brent put it, a unity of spirit through all the diversity of positions. "The main thing," he concluded, "is that men are thinking both honestly and thoroughly."[71]

The approach to Rome was of a different character. It called for silk-gloved urbanity. Gardiner did his artful best. "I have been having a notable correspondence with Cardinal Gasparri," he wrote Archbishop Randall Davidson of the Church of England. "It has been conducted in ecclesiastical Latin which lends itself . . . to the utterance of glittering generalities." When Gasparri wrote that "the plans of the Roman Pontiffs . . . have always been specially directed to the end that the sole and unique Church . . . should open wide its door for all . . . who desire to hear the fatherly voice of the Supreme Shepherd of souls," the secretary replied with similar emollient sentiments expressed in "Latin superlatives," as he confided to George Zabriskie. "So great is the sweetness that breathes from your letters," Gardiner cooed to the cardinal, "that we doubt not that at the reading of them all who earnestly desire the restoration of Christian unity will labor with greater effort for its accomplishment and establishment."[72]

71. Brent to Gardiner, November 3, March 19, 1923, Gardiner Correspondence.

72. Gardiner to Davidson, May 20, 1915; Gasparri to Gardiner, December 18, 1914; Gardiner to Zabriskie, February 23, 1915; to Gasparri, March 1, 1915, Gardiner Correspondence. Pietro Cardinal Gasparri was the Vatican's secretary of state. For a discussion of Rome and the ecumenical movement, see Oliver Stratford Tomkins, "The Roman Church and the Ecumenical Movement, 1910–1948," in *History of the Ecumenical Movement*, edited by Rouse and Neill, 677–93.

But the mists of sanctimony—and humbug—concealed, as we shall see later, the lurking headlands of discord.

On the other hand, some of Gardiner's correspondence with Roman Catholics was often humorous. He made contact in 1923 with a certain Abbé Lugan, editor of the liberal French Catholic paper, *Le Mouvement.* In conversation with his new correspondent, Lugan openly criticized the Roman church in the United States "as being largely Irish, to which I agreed," Gardiner wrote to Bishop G. K. A. Bell, "pointing out that it is too Italian also in Europe, and to that he gave the most cordial assent." A charmed Lugan then intimated that the Episcopalians might be invited to a proposed Roman ecumenical conference in 1925. Nothing ever came of it. Between Gardiner and the German American Roman Catholic L. F. Schlathoelter, a "distinguished theologian," relations were less indulgent. There was, in fact, some very plain speaking. At the Episcopalian's initial inquiry, Schlathoelter took off the gloves. The Joint Commission of the Episcopal Church "must prove it was appointed . . . by Christ . . . [for we] cannot submit to any purely human authority." Gardiner replied plausibly: "We are confident that if we can only get together in friendly conferences, we shall learn to know each other better and find that most of our prejudices and misunderstandings have no foundation." Schlathoelter: The conference's decisions would have to be approved by the pope. Gardiner, unwilling to take the bait: Perhaps Schlathoelter might want to read some Protestant books? Schlathoelter, bare knuckled: I cannot read Protestant books; they are all negative. Gardiner: Anglican books are used in Roman Catholic seminaries. Touché! On resuming debate three years later, Schlathoelter provided an opening: "You are taking too big a bite to be able to swallow it." Gardiner: "No communion will be asked or indeed permitted to make any surrender or compromise" and, on higher ground, if "we can have faith enough to believe that if God once brings us all to surrender our self will and our self opinion so as to manifest to the world the unity which He desires, He will give us the grace to continue." Schlathoelter, sensing danger: There is no question of surrendering "self opinion"; the pope, the bishop of Rome, is Christ's successor: "I would not like to sit aside of a man for the purpose of discussion . . . unless I knew from the start that he was in doubt." Gardiner: "A man may possess the whole truth, but state it in such a way that he irritates his hearers and closes their minds. . . . [He] must be willing to recognize the possibility—slight though it be—that he may not have comprehended so fully the whole faith as he thinks." Schlathoelter, seeking refuge, wrote: "I do not care to know what they [Protestants] teach about the matter unless it tallies with the Decrees of the Pope. . . . I, for my part, have never thought much of discussion on religious matters. If I am approached by a Catholic who starts a discussion on religious matters, I always suggest to him to make a good confession."[73] And that was that. At the Mad Tea-Party, Schlathoelter generally played a Roman Catholic March Hare to Gardiner's Alice: "It wasn't very civil of you to sit down without being invited," the March Hare announced, to which Alice replied, "I didn't know it was your table. . . . [I]t's laid for a great many more than three."

The result? "I am between the upper and nether millstone," Gardiner wrote Stetson. "About half my correspondents accuse us of being too Catholic and the other half of being too Protestant; and that is true also of those members of our own Commission who are not in active touch with us." Some Roman Catholics used the growing contact and correspondence to proselytize Gardiner himself. "In a few cases," he confided in Bishop Hall, "my replies incited a pretty voluminous effort to convert me to Roman Catholicism." Though he noted that the efforts had been made "in the most affectionate spirit," they "seem to me to be rather pathetic, for they are based entirely on the argument of the medieval scholastics," which, he judged with wry humor, "would be a terrible heresy for me to confess."[74] It was difficult trying to get all the bullfrogs into the wheelbarrow, and he was unwilling to abandon the effort and take a place himself on the lily pad of the biggest frog of all.

But generous support without stint or strings came to him from surprising quarters. The Church of the United Brethren in Christ, Dunkers or the "Plain People"—who also had bishops—were true to their name. This church, growing out of German pietism in Pennsylvania at the end of the eighteenth century under the leadership of Philip William Otterbein and Martin Boehm, became an episcopal church, following strongly Methodist polity, doctrine, and practice. Said Brother William Bell, "On every platform where I have the oportunity [sic] my voice is raised in behalf of the movement." And later: "It has my

73. Gardiner to Bell, October 27, 1923; to Schlathoelter, June 12, 1916, for the ascription; Schlathoelter to Gardiner, February 3, 1912; Gardiner to Schlathoelter, February 16, 1912; Schlathoelter to Gardiner, January 13, 1913; Gardiner to Schlathoelter, January 27, 1913; Schlathoelter to Gardiner, January 30, 1913; Gardiner to Schlathoelter, February 4, 1913; Schlathoelter to Gardiner, March 22, 1916; Gardiner to Schlathoelter, April 24, 1916; Schlathoelter to Gardiner, May 3, 1916; Gardiner to Schlathoelter, May 9, 1916; Schlathoelter to Gardiner, May 12, 1916, Gardiner Correspondence. (I am paraphrasing close to the grain.)

74. Gardiner to Stetson, July 14, 1915; to Hall, May 1, 1912; see also Paul Francis of the Community of the Atonement to Gardiner, January 10, 1917, Gardiner Correspondence.

deepest heart." Cornelius Woelfkin, the Northern Baptist professor at the Rochester Theological Seminary, felt "a prophetic instinct that this work will grow by spiritual contagion." Woelfkin was "profoundly grateful to God for the wise and deliberate manner in which you are guiding this movement." He added that that growth must be by evolution, not revolution. W. C. Bitting, corresponding secretary for the Northern Baptists, said a "hearty Amen" to Gardiner's championing the attitude of denominational humility and remarked that there were "lots of fellows in all ecclesiastical connections that strut up and down the church horizon in the main delusions that their own particular garb has been woven in heaven. I always feel like hurling a big dose of Jeremiah at all these little compass ecclesiastics wherever they are found. . . . May God bless you!" Of Cardinal Gibbons's aid and interest Gardiner wrote glowingly: "My request for advice was listened to with quick and thorough comprehension and the advice given was most satisfactory and showed a deep capacity to further a project. . . . I have seldom met a more thorough understanding of the fact that our project is fundamental." The Augustinian Aurelio Palmieri, without whom contacts in Italy and eastern Europe would have been severely limited, won Gardiner's gratitude; he remained for the American "an astonishing scholar and a man of remarkable intelligence."[75]

Whatever the praise, Gardiner was not "in favor of a Hurrah campaign for the World Conference." But from the start, in spite of the difficulties, they made progress.[76] In June 1912 a deputation of Episcopalians was sent to the Anglican churches of England, Scotland, and Ireland. By February 1913 plans were made for an informal meeting of various denominational commissions in the United States. That meeting took place on May 8 at the Hotel Astor in New York City. It included representatives from the commissions of fifteen American churches, plus Tatlow, who represented notoriously cautious Archbishop Davidson's "Co-operating Committee" of the Church of England, and

75. Bell to Gardiner, August 10, 1911, April 29, 1913; Woelfkin to Gardiner, December 11, 1911 (see also Gardiner to Woelfkin, October 31, November 20, 1911); Bitting to Gardiner, February 14, 1913; Gardiner to Stetson, October 2, 1911; to Charles K. Gilbert, November 6, 1916, Gardiner Correspondence.

76. Gardiner to Pepper, November 22, 1911, Gardiner Correspondence. See also Gardiner to the archbishop of Canterbury, October 18, 1911, January 12, 1912; to Manning, May 10, 1913; to A. C. A. Hall, January 20, June 23, 1913; Manning to Gardiner, April 23, 1914; and the Committee of Five to Manning and Gardiner, April 23, 1914, Gardiner Correspondence. The Committee of Five's task was to recommend names of representatives to contact the free churches on Great Britain.

Dean Hotovitsky, representing both the Holy Orthodox Church of Russia as well as the Russian Orthodox Church in the United States.[77] The Hotel Astor assembly appointed the deputation (Ainslie of the Disciples, Smyth of the Congregational churches, and H. W. Roberts of the Presbyterians, among others) to the free churches of Great Britain.[78] The meetings that resulted paved the way for the Church of England and the free churches of Britain to commence talks among themselves. In the same summer of 1913 members of the Episcopal Joint Commission met with the English archbishops and their staffs who promptly served the ball back into the Americans' court: responsibility for inviting the free churches of Great Britain would be up to the Americans— which was already being accomplished—and the conference itself would be held in the United States. For their part the Joint Commission had much to show for their time and effort: their initial pamphlet, a printing of 630,200, had been translated by August 1913 into Modern Greek, Latin, Italian, Russian, Swedish, German, French, Dutch, and Spanish and sent to members of thirty churches worldwide; those receiving them were by occupation, besides the clergy of the churches, 110 professors, 43 college presidents, 26 theological seminaries, and 108 colleges and universities. By the end of November 1913 the Church of Ireland and the Old Catholics of Europe had also appointed commissions, and in January of the following year Anglicans in South Africa had done the same. A hopeful Hughell Fosbroke wrote Gardiner of his enthusiasm for the Astor meeting and its subsequent accomplishments.[79]

Momentum was clearly picking up, and the first half of 1914 proved to be a high point. On March 13 William Manning informed Gardiner that thirty-six "of the leading Christian communions in the United States and Great Britain and other parts of the world are now officially committed to this great movement and a Deputation of the highest official character is shortly to make a formal

77. For the importance of this meeting, see Fosbroke to Gardiner, September 5, 1913, Gardiner Correspondence.

78. See Tatlow to Gardiner, March 30, 1914, Gardiner Correspondence, marked "Private and Confidential," in which the Englishman remarks, "The Free Churches are much more difficult to get hold of than the Church of England. They are very individualistic, and the leaders work very much each on his own lines. They have got to be laid siege to and secured one by one.... I am now hard at work in a quiet way.... I have secured the co-operation of Dr. [P. T.] Forsyth and of Dr. Selbie."

79. *Report of the Joint Commission to the General Convention of the Episcopal Church, 1913* (printed for the commission, 1913), 9–10, 12–14, 19, 21–22; Fosbroke to Gardiner, September 5, 1913, Gardiner Correspondence.

visitation to the Churches in Europe and the East in regard to it." Plans were laid for a deputation to Europe in 1914, which included John R. Mott and Gardiner himself. It was an ambitious program. The delegation planned to spend a few days in London consulting with British clergy familiar with conditions on the Continent, thence go "to Holland, Denmark, Sweden, Norway and Russia." In New York Manning conferred with the Russian Archbishop Platon who had "promised to come and see me, which is more honor than I anticipated." Platon gave Manning the names and "correct titles of the authorities in Russia with whom we must communicate." The archbishop, Manning reported, "goes to Russia next month and promises to do everything in his power to prepare the way for our Deputation and invites us to visit him in his new home in Kishineff [sic]." At the same time Manning informed the secretary, "I have had a talk with the Rev'd Sebastian Dabovitch, Archimandrite of the Servian Church. He has promised to make a list of all the Eastern Churches which, in his judgment, we ought to visit together with those whom he considered the most important individuals in each case. This list may be valuable as Dabovitch has close personal knowledge of the situation in the East."[80] In early May in New York City, Dabovitch was introduced to the committee of those responsible for planning the international conference. With them he discussed particular leaders of the Orthodox Balkan, Russian, and Near Eastern churches who were important for the delegation to contact. Gardiner took it all down:

> The Rev. Father Dabovitch, Archimandrite of the Servians, was introduced to the Committee; and in an address recommended that the deputation to Europe visit in order the Patriarchs of Jerusalem, Antioch, and Alexandria, the Primate of Athens, the Primate of Belgrade, the Servian Primate of Carlowitz in Hungary, the Primates of the Roumanian Church in Hungary and in Austria, the Archbishop of Volhynia in Russia, the Archbishops of Odessa and Vilna, the Metropolitans of Kief and St. Petersburg, and the Patriarch of Constantinople;

---

80. Manning to Gardiner, March 13, 1914, Gardiner Correspondence. The day before, Manning had presided over the truly ecumenical Advisory Committee meeting at which Peter Ainslie had read the report of the deputation to the free churches of Britain (*Second Meeting of the Advisory Committee: Report of the Second Deputation to Great Britain* [printed for the commission, 1914], 4–10). Gardiner to Thomas Robinson Hodgson of the British and Foreign Bible Society, Constantinople, May 29, 1914; Manning to Gardiner, May 5, April 23, 1914, Gardiner Correspondence. Kishinev was the Bessarabian town where on Easter Sunday (April 4) 1903 a vicious anti-Jewish pogram took place in which "some fifty Jews were killed, many more injured, and a great deal of Jewish property looted and destroyed" (Richard Pipes, *The Russian Revolution* [New York: Vintage Books, 1991], 10).

and if time permit, the Primate of Bosnia and Herzegovina, and the Primate of Montenegro. He advises traveling second class. The proper personage to approach on behalf of the Church of Armenia is the Catholicos of Etchmiadzin. He advises visiting Jerusalem first, because that is the heart of Christendom. Father Dabovitch took his leave with the thanks of the Committee for his visit.[81]

At the end of the month the secretary was writing Thomas Hodgson in Constantinople that the deputation would "arrive in London September 1st next."[82] They would then go to the continent. As if by some cruel joke, everyone's steps seemed to move toward the very city, Sarajevo, where on June 28 Archduke Franz Ferdinand, nephew of the Austro-Hungarian emperor, was assassinated by a Bosnian Serb youth. On July 21, 1914, Joseph Cardinal Mercier's secretary, Abbé Francis Dessains, wrote that the cardinal was happy to receive, unofficially, the deputation with the knowledge that conversations might "lead to further intercourse with the happy result for God's glory and [the] salvation of souls." In the same week Bishop A. C. A. Hall of Vermont threatened to resign from the Joint Commission on the World Conference on Faith and Order if John R. Mott was appointed to the deputation.[83] Within days both responses became academic.

On June 20, 1914, Gardiner sailed for Europe. What awaited him was a tragedy of monstrous proportions: the shattering of "what little unity Western civilization had to that point achieved."[84]

---

81. *Minutes of the Meetings of the Executive Committee of the Joint Commission Appointed by the General Convention of 1910 to Bring About a World Conference on Faith and Order* (printed for the committee, 1914), 51.

82. Gardiner to Hodgson, May 29, 1914, Gardiner Correspondence. Gardiner wanted a meeting in Constantinople between the American deputation and the leaders of the Orthodox Church, against which Hodgson warned because of Eastern suspicions of Anglican and Protestant proselytizing: "If your Commission were to approach the Greek and Armenian Patriarchs here through one of our English Bishops or, better still, one of the Archbishops you would obtain a favorable hearing" (July 14, 1914). Gardiner responded that the deputation anticipated only an informal and unofficial meeting in any case (July 29, 1914, Gardiner Correspondence).

83. Dessains to Gardiner, July 21, 1914; Hall to Gardiner, July 27, 1914, Gardiner Correspondence. Dessains had become a personal friend of Gardiner, who addressed him by his last name only.

84. George F. Kennan, "The War to End War," in *At a Century's Ending: Reflections, 1982–1995* (New York and London: W. W. Norton, 1996), 18.

# FIVE

❧✚❧

# War and Theology

## *Lake Constance, 1914*

Robert Gardiner's early adult years were marked by the Western European nations' expansion and their subsequent globe-circling empires. The United States too was involved in the swelling industrial growth and in the West's imperial reach.[1] In the decades prior to the Civil War, the Northern states underwent remarkable change: they looked not to the past, as did the South, but to a new age and had in fact "hurtled forward eagerly toward a future of industrial capitalism." It was precisely this American transformation to which Tudor Gardiner contributed and which was celebrated at the World's Columbian Exposition in Chicago in 1893. With the victory of the North in the Civil War, the expansion of a nation, now rendered one, proceeded rapidly westward. Eventually, at the turn of the century it crossed the Pacific Ocean. The United States was not alone. Germany had been unified in 1871, Italy in 1872 when Victor Emmanuel II entered Rome; thereafter, the expansion of Russia, Germany, France, Holland, Belgium, and Portugal followed the earlier example of Great Britain in Asia and then in Africa and "seemed to underline the growing importance of geopolitics."[2] The great Western nations, not all behemoths by any means, had for good and for ill forced the peoples of the world to think beyond

1. See Niall Ferguson, *The Pity of War* (New York: Basic Books, 1999).
2. James M. McPherson, *The Battle Cry of Freedom: The Civil War Era* (New York and Oxford: Oxford University Press, 1988), 860; Linda Colley, "Size Does Matter: How a Few Islands Won an Empire," *Times Literary Supplement,* September 20, 2002, 14.

their river valleys, borders, and islands. Some did with stunning effect. America's influence in the Pacific was challenged by the growing power of the empire of Japan. Human unification both with each other and with the peoples and cultures they had subdued but not conquered eluded the Western powers. The same failure had also marked the most ancient Far Eastern civilizations of China and Japan. Such was the very startling background to the attempted unification of Christian churches and to the age in which Gardiner himself reached maturity.

Despite two nasty Balkan wars and numerous army maneuvers by the major European powers during 1912 and 1913, not everyone in the spring and early summer of 1914 expected war to erupt throughout Europe. The conspicuous advances in the arts and sciences, the spirit of progress, the hopefulness of youth, their expectation of a new world in which the "garden city of the future seemed a realizable goal that could be reached," as one said, "in our own lifetime, replacing the grime of industry and the misery of the poverty-ridden areas," were powerfully present in the summer of 1914. Few imagined the fearful scope of the carnage about to commence. To be sure, in 1891 old Field Marshal Count Helmuth Karl von Moltke, uncle of Germany's new chief of the Great General Staff, had predicted a colossal European conflict that would go on, he judged, for seven years. A few years later, Rudyard Kipling thought along the same chilling lines. On the other hand, Andrew and Louise Carnegie sent 1914 New Year's greetings to friends, "strong in the faith that International Peace is soon to prevail thru [sic] several of the great powers agreeing to settle their disputes by arbitration under International Law." Many people as late as the spring of 1914 were equally sanguine. Archbishop of Canterbury Randall Davidson "declared himself convinced that in the situation then obtaining, the existence of the two Councils [British and German that went by the unwieldy title of the Associated Councils of Churches in the British and German Empires for Fostering Friendly Relations between the Two Peoples] was no longer absolutely necessary."[3] For Davidson, such organizations "stood for something which had already been practically secured." In Germany a leading churchman, the highly respected Friedrich Siegmund-Schultze, was optimistic about achieving the "right atmo-

---

3. Serge Obolensky, *One Man in His Time* (New York: McDowell, Obolensky, 1958), 121; David Gilmour, *The Long Recessional: The Imperial Life of Rudyard Kipling* (New York: Farrar, Strauss, and Giroux, 2002), 115–18; Joseph Frazier Wall, *Andrew Carnegie* (New York: Oxford University Press, 1970), 1008; Nils Karlstrom, "Movements for International Friendship and Life and Work, 1910–1925," in *A History of the Ecumenical Movement, 1517–1948*, edited by edited by Ruth Rouse and Stephen Charles Neill (Philadelphia: Westminster Press, 1967), 512.

sphere" for realizing peace between Europe's two greatest empires. Other church people were not so sure it could be done.

Influenced by his association with the Federal Council of Churches in America, Robert Gardiner was one of them. Thus, in addition to sailing for Europe in the early summer of 1914 as part of the World Conference on Faith and Order deputation, he was also traveling under the auspices of the FCC as a delegate to the Church Peace Union's conference. That assembly of American and European Christians was convened on the German side of Lake Constance. It was "the first international Christian conference ever held specifically in the interest of world peace." Gardiner, recently appointed to the executive committee of the FCC, was an official delegate. That February, pacifist Carnegie, adding to his already established Carnegie Endowment for International Peace (1910), had given two million dollars to his new Church Peace Union. There were other efforts toward world peace. In January the Swiss Reformed Churches invited the Christian bodies of Europe to meet at Berne for the promotion of peace, the scaling back of armaments, and reduction of the danger of war. The conference was never convened. Carnegie's support was also to make possible a meeting of La Ligue Internationale des Catholiques pur la Paix under the leadership of Joseph Cardinal Mercier. This Roman Catholic peace conference was to meet at Liège, of all places, on August 10 and 11. Like the Swiss one, this too never occurred. But Carnegie's money made possible the assemblage of the summer of 1914. The date was August 1.[4]

Gardiner's plan was to cross the Channel at the end of July, "spend six days in Paris thence four days to . . . the Peace Union Conference at Constance." Three days before the churchmen gathered, Czar Nicholas II, without the knowledge even of his minister of war, had ordered full mobilization in Russia. On July 31 both Germany and France called up their armies. On August 1 Germany declared war on Russia; the next day, Sunday the second, Russia declared war on Germany, "and the fatal chain of events was set in motion."[5] *Der tag*, the inevitable day, to use the favorite term of the younger von Moltke, had arrived.

    4. Samuel McCrae Cavert to Floyd Tomkins, July 27, 1964, Floyd Tomkins Papers, Archives of the Episcopal Church, Austin, TX; Wall, *Andrew Carnegie*, 902. See also *Annual Reports of the Federal Council of Churches, 1909–1914: Report of the Delegates*, 178.
    5. Gardiner to Tissington Tatlow, July 22, 1914, Robert H. Gardiner Correspondence, 1910–1924, World Council of Churches, Geneva, Switzerland; Richard Pipes, *The Russian Revolution* (New York: Vintage Books, 1991), 200. John Keegan, in *The First World War* (New York: Alfred A. Knopf, 1999), notes the "trigger effect of one mobilization proclamation on another" (59).

Although the war's probability was ensured by imperial economic and political rivalries, by the "creeping militarization of European diplomacy," and by poor communications among civilian leaders, their insouciance, their hollowness, and lack of control of their armies made it all but inevitable. Throughout the lands rumbled the lust for domination. If the reasons for the war remain complex, without doubt everyone was asleep at the switch. In the crucial fortnight before hostilities began, the kaiser was still on his annual three-week vacation cruising the Norwegian fjords in his yacht; the French president and his foreign minister were at sea on *La France* returning from a state visit to Russia, the British foreign secretary was off fishing, and the czar was playing tennis at his summer palace.[6]

Though they had no immediate political power, the delegates at Lake Constance were meeting for good purpose. In retrospect they appear, as has been argued not very convincingly, "unrealistic, naive, and pathetic ... [b]ut they were ... profoundly prophetic in the concerns they reflected." Surely, the great civilized European powers could be encouraged and pressured in the modern age to draw back from the brink of destruction! To this end 85 of the 153 delegates planning to attend met at Lake Constance. And they were an able group. Among the Americans besides Gardiner were Henry M. McCracken, chancellor of New York University; Swiss-born bishop John Louis Nuelson (Methodist), a former professor of ancient languages and currently American correspondent for the *Theologischer Literatur-Bericht;* Louise Carnegie's Congregational friend the Reverend Frederick Lynch, director of the New York Peace Society and secretary of the Church Peace Union; Bishop Luther B. Wilson (Methodist), president of the Anti-Saloon League; William C. Bitting, corresponding secretary for the Northern Baptist Convention; and William P. Merrill (Presbyterian), pastor of the influential Brick Church in New York, president of the Church Peace Union, and the Carnegies' friend. Lynch had planned the conference.[7]

6. T. G. Otte, "Countdown to Carnage," *Times Literary Supplement,* August 16, 2002, 24; Barbara Tuchman, *The Guns of August* (New York: Macmillan, 1962), 78; Keegan, *The First World War,* 53–55, 57, 64.

7. George F. Kennan, "The Balkan Crisis," in *At a Century's Ending: Reflections, 1982–1995* (New York and London: W. W. Norton, 1996), 192; Wall, *Andrew Carnegie,* 1014. Merrill was a future Lyman Beecher Lecturer at Yale (1922) and the author of the not quite antimilitarist hymn, "Not Alone for Mighty Empire" (1909). I am indebted to the Reverend T. Guthrie Speers for this information.

No sooner had these and others arrived on Sunday, related Canon George W. Douglas of New York's Cathedral of St. John the Divine, when a letter from the emperor's sister, the grand duchess of Baden, was delivered to Siegmund-Schultze. It warned the conferees to leave Germany immediately before the army commandeered what few remaining railroad trains were left for civilian transport. Using the duchess's letter, Siegmund-Schultze persuaded the railroad authorities to provide a special train to depart Monday at 9:30 a.m. for Holland. The hapless delegates concluded there was only one thing left to do. That evening at the very first session of the conference a telegram was sent to all European prime ministers and chancellors as well as to the president of the United States. It begged them "to avert war between millions of men, among whom friendship and common interests had been steadily growing, and thereby to save Christian civilization from disaster and to assert the power of the Christian spirit in human affairs."[8] It was a whisper of sanity made by the delegates— English, German, French, and American—in the midst of a scene of extraordinary amity and fervent prayer. Too late, their plea went unheard amid the rising pitch of the war cries.

The next morning Lynch and Siegmund-Schultze, whom Gardiner held in high regard, collected from the delegates all the German money they had, more than forty-two hundred marks, to settle the hotel bills. Fortunately, the travelers had breakfast before they left. It would be the last meal they would receive until they arrived in London the afternoon of the next day. For the fifty or so refugee delegates German authorities had provided two coaches; later, all members of the party were put into a single car in which only half of them could sit down at a time. Despite the "grilling sun of one of the century's most brilliant summers," train windows were ordered shut; soldiers stationed along the track were told to shoot into any open ones. As Lynch wrote Andrew Carnegie, "We saw all the men being taken from work and corralled at every railroad station. We saw one young man go crazy at being torn from his wife and children." At Cologne a crowd of American and English tourists filled the platform and were forcibly prevented from boarding the train. Nonetheless, the delegates rescued one young Russian family that had been pulled from another train, "the mother

8. Canon George W. Douglas to the *Churchman* (Milwaukee), September 12, 1914, 342; Karlstrom, "Movements for International Friendship," in *History of the Ecumenical Movement*, edited by Rouse and Neill, 514.

so frightened that her milk stopped." "We took them along in our party and on the steamer, Lady Barlow... found a mother with a baby who offered to give the little Russian a drink from her breasts." Worst of all, wrote Lynch, "we saw great crowds of young men... howling... for blood."[9]

When they reached Flushing in Holland, the Channel boat was already crowded with people fleeing to England, its restaurant bought out. They arrived in London with only the clothes on their backs. At the final session, held on August 5, the conferees constituted themselves the World Alliance for Promoting International Friendship through the Churches. Carnegie, then in Scotland, sent money for the Americans' passage home. Gardiner cabled William Manning about Faith and Order matters, "Deputation trip [to eastern Europe] impossible." By September 2 Manning was hoping "to hear soon that you have landed in safety. How terrible beyond all expression this outbreak of barbarism is." It was, as pacifist cabinet minister John Morley wrote to Carnegie, "Hell in full blast." On the ninth Gardiner wrote, "I arrived in New York yesterday morning and I can't tell you how glad I was to see America again." War, he wrote George Wharton Pepper, is "the fruit of the evil which lies at the root of almost all human relations."[10]

All the time Gardiner's interest in international affairs was growing, as evidenced in his library at Oaklands, where he kept such volumes as Nicholas Murray Butler's *International Mind* (1913), John M. Keynes's *Economic Consequences of Peace* (1920), and Walter Rathenau's *New Society* (1920). As much as the proposed World Conference on Faith and Order, his participation through the Federal Council of Churches in the Lake Constance assembly contributed to this interest. In 1918 he became one of the founders of the Foreign Policy Association, or as it was at first called the League of Nations Association.[11]

Simultaneously, his loyalty to the FCC continued. Since there were those Episcopalians who adamantly opposed membership, Gardiner's allegiance was

9. Gardiner to Nathan Soderblom, November 21, 1919, Gardiner Correspondence; Keegan, *The First World War,* 101; Douglas to the *Churchman,* 342; Wall, *Carnegie,* 1015.

10. Gardiner to Manning, August 5, 1914; to Ralph W. Brown, August 7, 1914; Thomas P. Brown to Ralph W. Brown, August 7, 1914; Manning to Gardiner, September 2, 1914, Gardiner Correspondence; Wall, *Carnegie,* 1014; Gardiner to Manning, September 9, 1914; to Pepper, November 5, 1915, Correspondence.

11. See Bruce W. Jentleson and Thomas G. Paterson, *Encyclopedia of United States Foreign Policy* (New York and Oxford: Oxford University Press, 1997), 2:153. For Gardiner's participation in the association, see *Who Was Who,* vol. 1, *1897–1942* (1943; reprint, Chicago: A. N. Marquis, 1962), 439; he was treasurer of the association.

not always popular in his own denomination. Already by 1913 it had gotten him in trouble, for he played a central role in the General Convention debate over whether the Episcopal Church should formally join the interchurch forum. The ensuing squabble sharpened his theological wits and deepened his commitment to reunion. The FCC is then the unlikely but key place to begin examining his theology, for Gardiner broke into the theological circle with the doctrine of the church, and the council by its very existence invited reflection on the larger issue of church order. Before discussing in detail his doctrinal convictions, it is important to see how he interacted with the new federation.

Without sacerdotal agreement, voluntary alliance for social service and moral outreach did not appeal to many Episcopalians. One of the most powerful dissenting voices was that of William Reed Huntington. This broadly respected cleric wanted more, that is, "organic," church unity as opposed to administrative cooperation for benevolent ends. "I quite understand," Gardiner wrote to the president of the Association for Improving the Condition of the Poor, financier R. Fulton Cutting, that to quite a few, "cooperation is in some way compromising and . . . that federation may be taken as a substitute for unity and so become a great impediment [to reunion]." Federation, he wrote in a long article in the *Churchman,* was "only a preparation for something better—an approach to, and not a substitute for, reunion."[12] Philip Schaff would have agreed.

Many but by no means all in the Anglo-Catholic wing of the church felt that joining the council would endanger the distinctiveness of the Episcopal Church. "One doesn't like being classified among Protestant Churches," Bishop A. C. A. Hall complained to Gardiner, "nor (this is really more important) the XXXIX Articles being reckoned as our Creed."[13] For Hall, the Episcopal Church was not a confessional church as were Lutherans, Presbyterians, and other reformed groups—for example, the Augsburg Confession for Lutherans and the Westminster Confession for English and American Presbyterians. In the Episcopal Church, evangelicals found the Articles of Religion to be a positive defense of the English Reformation and sought to make them normative for the church.

---

12. John F. Woolverton, "William Reed Huntington and Church Unity: The Historical and Theological Background of the Chicago-Lambeth Quadrilateral" (PhD diss., Columbia University, 1963), 302, 328–31. See also William Reed Huntington, *The Four Theories of Visible Church Union* (New York: John H. Smith, 1909), 4–5. Gardiner to Cutting, May 7, 1912, Gardiner Correspondence; Gardiner, "Federation," in *Churchman,* January 3, 1914, 11.

13. Hall to Gardiner, April 30, 1912, Gardiner Correspondence. Hall said "Creed," but he meant "Confession" (see below).

Anglo-Catholics, like Hall, wished to relegate the articles to a lower place because they were confessional and the church, they held, was not; liberal, broad church people, on the other hand, wanted to relegate the articles to a lower place, not because they were confessional but because they confessed superannuated things. Hall had a point. Episcopalians who embraced the FCC endangered, he believed, the distinctiveness of their church. To Hall, the secretary's view appeared to trivialize deeply held convictions and failed to recognize what was at stake when religion gets checked at the door whenever its proponents "engage in tolerant activities." Hall accused Gardiner of recklessness and indifference: "You help to foster the delusion spreading more and more among Protestant bodies that Philanthropy equals Religion and that social reform is the great business of the churches." The bishop feared that in a federation, Anglican distinctiveness would be ironed out of the fabric of communal life, the doctrine of the church lost, and much that was venerable and immemorial fade away. His views were echoed in the pages of the *Living Church:* the difficulty for Episcopalians, that journal held, "is that in accepting the platform of Federation, the Church *seems* to the world at large to have abandoned her old-time doctrine of 'the Church' and to have accepted the popular idea of 'the Churches.'"[14] Since in the United States there was no single established religious body, before the law and the Constitution, the nation, in point of fact, had nothing but "churches," however much one or more of them might claim otherwise.

And so long as they did not try to force their will on the rest of the nation, they could indeed claim otherwise. Given the fact of religious liberty in the United States, however uncharitable it might seem, Hall was perfectly justified in defending and maintaining his church, its tradition, sacraments, priesthood, and theology. To settle for anything less—and he assumed it would be less— was to him spiritless and craven. Episcopalians were free to shape their own church as they saw fit, so long, as Anglican tradition had it, as they were illumined by the Holy Spirit and informed by the Gospel.[15]

At the same time, Hall was not indifferent to the plight of the poor. The Vermont bishop approved civic and social reforms, but they were to be "under-

14. David Little (with reference to Richard Rorty), "Challenges to the New Media Order to Freedom of Expression, Freedom of Religion and Belief, and Group Rights," *Harvard Divinity Bulletin* (Winter 2001–2002): 28; Hall to Gardiner, December 26, 1912, Gardiner Correspondence; editorial, "The Church and the Federal Council," *Living Church* (December 28, 1912).

15. H. R. McAdoo, *The Structure of Caroline Moral Theology* (London, New York, Toronto: Longmans, Green, 1949), 28.

taken by *citizens* without limitation of religious belief," though with "our religion certainly inspiring us to take part in them." In the meantime, Vermont's
bishop could play hard ball. He wanted full power over the literature that the
Joint Commission published for the World Conference on Faith and Order.
He threatened to resign if he did not get it.[16] Gardiner called his bluff. The
bishop backed down.

If Hall would not admit the ministerial equality of others, that too was permissible in the American republic. "I should not say we (Rev. A. Baptist [and I])
were equally ministers of God," he wrote, "because I believe in the transmission
of an authoritative commission for the ministry which we claim to possess &
Protestant bodies do not." We cannot spuriously recognize equality with them,
and it is just this, he declared, that is commonly understood to be acknowledged
in "Union Services, exchange of Pulpits, [and] Federation[s] of Churches." Hall
referred to "[Protestants'] laxity of faith & practice with reference to the Sacraments, ministry, the great truths embodied in the creeds." The sacraments and
the ministry belonged "to the *integrity* of the Christian Religion," he maintained.
Protestants equaled "non-sacerdotal Christians." To one Wisconsin rector who
wrote the University of Chicago's liberal Shailer Matthews, "the Federal Council
stands for practical deism."[17]

Gardiner's view was different. Just as much as Hall, he held to a sacerdotal
priesthood, commissioned by Christ himself, and maintained by the episcopal
office. Priesthood and episcopacy were marks of his church. He was not about
either to downplay or to abandon them, but he was not going to smack others
across the face with the wet mackerel of ministerial superiority. That is what
Manning did in his *Constructive Quarterly* article of 1915. "Of course you and
I," Gardiner wrote the anxious Hall, "cannot conceive of anything except win-
ning back Congregationalists and Methodists and all the others to the full
Catholic Faith and Order." They had a perfect right, he judged, to maintain
such views. If other denominations were surprised that "we are not prepared to
surrender... [our] principles," then let them imagine giving up some of their
own. But that was no reason to go off in a sulk. "Our Communion is imbued
with the idea that it must take the leadership," Gardiner wrote to Talbot Rogers,
"... but leadership does not mean repelling the men you are going to lead." It

16. Hall to Gardiner, December 26, 1912; Gardiner to Manning, February 13, 1913, Gardiner Correspondence.

17. Hall to Gardiner, December 2, 9, 1913; Gardiner to Matthews, January 31, 1914, Gardiner Correspondence, in which Gardiner responds to Matthews's query about the letter.

means that we are "to retain and seek every opportunity to increase that leader-ship." Administrative cooperation and the fellowship that came with it were clearly insufficient, but "one of the best ways to reach essential unity and to persuade our brethren of the necessity of it, is to mingle with them and to under-stand them and to gain their confidence." The FCC was working in such a fash-ion, Gardiner declared. He had been "deeply impressed with the way in which members of different Communions get to understand and appreciate each other."[18] Why should there not be cooperation and even an admission of equal-ity in other realms of Christian life?

Gardiner pressed his case with Hall. "I am greatly puzzled by your saying," he wrote, "that we cannot admit 'ministerial equality.' You are so precise in the use of words that I cannot suppose you overlooked the Prayer Book distinction between 'minister' and 'priest.'" The secretary pointed out that a priest is, or ought to be at least, minister but then something more. Hall was a bishop, "but you do not hesitate to serve on a committee with Dr. Rogers lest you should seem to abdicate [thereby] your episcopal office." Gardiner did not see how the FCC's reference to the "essential oneness of the Churches" was a denial of the "One, Holy, Catholic and Apostolic Church." Those who read it this way, "if they have read at all," he wrote sarcastically in the *Churchman,* "get into a panic lest the one Catholic and Apostolic Church has been denied." He asked Hall whether he "would hesitate to speak of the churches in Vermont which are under your care for the fear that such a phrase would seem to deny either diocesan or national or Catholic unity . . . ?" To the bishop's fear of contamination by Protes-tantism, Gardiner reminded him that the FCC "does not limit its cooperation to representatives of so-called Evangelical Churches, if that somewhat vague word 'Evangelical' is to be construed as excluding Catholics." There was no barrier to Roman Catholic membership. In addition, the FCC "is distinctly for-bidden from drawing up any creed or form of government or of worship or to interfere in any way with the autonomy of any Christian body adhering to it." Gardiner saw the council, he declared, as a "practical and efficient effort for the carrying out of His [Christ's] will and purpose."[19]

18. Gardiner to Hall, February 10, 1913; to Rogers, January 3, 1913, Gardiner Correspon-dence; Gardiner, "Federation," 11; Gardiner to Rogers, March 31, 1914; Hall, December 8, 1913, Gardiner Correspondence.

19. Gardiner to Hall, November 30, 1913, Gardiner Correspondence; Gardiner, "Federation," 12; Gardiner to Hall, December 8, 1913, Gardiner Correspondence; Gardiner, "Federation," 12; Gardiner to Hall, December 12, 1913, Gardiner Correspondence.

At the 1913 General Convention of the Episcopal Church, Gardiner placed on the calendar of the House of Deputies a resolution to the effect that the church "approves the purpose and plans of the Federal Council and authorizes the Commissions of the General Convention on Christian Unity and Social Service to send . . . such numbers of delegates as the Church is entitled to"—in other words, officially to join the council. Four days later when the lower house took up the resolution, Manning, hoping to quash it, moved it be referred to the Joint Commission on Faith and Order. His motion was tabled, the vote taken, and the resolution passed resoundingly. But Manning had lied. Gardiner wrote him:

> You have put me in rather an awkward position . . . when you moved to lay on the table my resolution. . . . As I understood you, and as most of the House did, you said that the matter had been considered by the [Joint] Commission. The inevitable inference was that the Commission had decided not to take the action which I proposed; that of course was not the fact. Neither the Commission nor its Executive Committee had considered the question.

The secretary refused to go public about Manning's duplicity: "I do not want to seem to be in any position of public controversy with a personal friend like you whose earnestness and devotion to the cause I admire so greatly." If the rector of Trinity Church had exercised more restraint, he could have saved himself embarrassment. When Gardiner's resolution got to the House of Bishops, it was defeated. The bishops took the safe way out and declared for "organic unity," whether they really believed in it or not. Still, their substitute resolution permitted "without sacrifice of principle" the appointment of "representatives to take part in the Federal Council." The deputies in the lower house then rejected the substitute motion. A conference was called, but it was "found impossible to reach any agreement respecting a basis for further action by the two Houses." In the end, on a resolution from Gardiner himself, the bishops' substitute was accepted, but not without anger. The Maine lawyer played it cool, however, and suggested that "as soon as the brethren calm down a little and can see things as they are," the misunderstandings "will be dispelled."[20]

20. *Journal of the General Convention of 1913,* House of Deputies, 279, 316–18; Gardiner to Manning, December 16, 1913, Gardiner Correspondence; *Journal of the General Convention of 1913,* House of Bishops, 145–46, 357; Gardiner, "Federation," 12. The voting results are as follows: for the affirmative, thirty-nine clerical votes, forty-three lay votes; in the negative, twenty-three clerical votes, twelve lay votes.

A low churchman with whom Gardiner had served as a representative of the Episcopal Church to the FCC, John Howard Melish, wrote him shortly after the convention, "You may be interested to know that the Bishop of Chicago led the opposition in the Upper House." Melish continued: "Bishop Anderson said . . . that he proposed to fight that measure because Gardiner presented it in the Lower House against [Anderson's] advice and in the face of his disapproval expressed to him when the Commission on Faith and Order had considered the matter." Gardiner replied that he had not conferred with Anderson, "because it never occurred to me that I was under any obligation to consult him." He added that "the Commission on Faith and Order, to the best of my recollection, never considered the matter at all."[21]

The next day the secretary complained to Bishop Hall, "It is just as difficult for me to understand how anyone could have voted against the resolution which I introduced . . . as it apparently is for the majority in the House of Bishops and the minority in the House of Deputies to understand my position." He allowed that there were a few among the deputies—and by inference Hall himself?— "whose only conception of unity is absolute and minute agreement with themselves, which I take to be the essence of the Protestant attitude of mind." Clearly, the lawyer from Maine knew how to measure verbal swords. He did so, not only with his Anglo-Catholic opponents but with low churchmen as well. When Melish sought to enlist Gardiner in a return match against the bishops' 1913 substitute motion and an effort to get the church fully to participate in the FCC, Gardiner gave him a chilly reception. "Permit me to say . . . that I disagree entirely with the spirit of your letter and with most of the statements," he wrote. "I do not think that the [bishops'] resolution . . . was in the least anemic." Gardiner was "entirely opposed to fighting" opponents of the FCC in the House of Deputies. "I have never seen any valuable result from any fights in the house of clerical and lay deputies. . . . If a fight is made over the Federal Council, it will . . . simply deepen the prejudices and misunderstandings of those who are opposed to it."[22] Besides, he had other fish to fry at the 1916 General Convention, educational ones, as I have already shown. But the issue of the FCC would crop up again in 1923.

21. Melish to Gardiner, November 13, 1913, Gardiner Correspondence; editorial, "Christian Unity and the General Convention, *Churchman,* April 18, 1914, 499; Gardiner to Melish, November 17, 1913, Gardiner Correspondence.
22. Gardiner to Hall, November 18, 1913; to Melish, September 26, 1916, Gardiner Correspondence.

Gardiner had had to defend Episcopalian participation in the FCC against sharp critics. In the process he had honed his own views. Through his membership in the council he was becoming aware of the faiths of others, broadening his way of thinking beyond those of his own denomination and without, he thought, jeopardizing its cherished beliefs. He was well aware of the importance of boundaries, borders, and authorities, or in Christian terms, in doctrines, creeds, and ministries. Simultaneously, he discovered that boundaries were not static; they could move, open up, provide fresh insights. Like William R. Huntington before him, he valued principles, not the vestments in which they were paraded. Gardiner, along with the Roman Catholic Alfred Loisy, would not have the "church bury herself, immovably, in contemplation of traditional formulas, [for] if she scrutinizes and explains them, it is because she employs activity and intelligence in the faith."[23] Both men wanted to snatch their contemporaries from the realms of fancy.

But there was more. Place and kinship, even ideology, whether in Maine, New England, or in Anglicanism itself no longer sufficed for the secretary. Despite his doubtful assertion that John R. Mott might become an Episcopalian, he was learning to recognize the equally high seriousness of Peter Ainslie, Edwin Hughs, Theodore Schmauk, John J. Wynne, W. C. Bitting, Aurelio Palmieri, Hamilcar Alivisatos, and of course Mott himself. These men differed from him and did not hold dear what he cherished; like him, they had no intention of surrendering their traditions. But they were at the same time reluctant to humiliate their brothers and sisters with eye-glazing claims about their own perfections. All were coming to realize that there were other points of view, even larger vistas, on which to feast their eyes. Out of such discoveries came the increasingly strong conviction that the several protagonists needed carefully to listen to each other, learn what they might, and thereby both sharpen their own wits and even broaden their own tent ropes. These were essential first steps toward a united Christian world.

The struggle to get the Episcopal Church into the FCC was not small potatoes to Gardiner and to those who thought like him. In this struggle local efforts rhymed with the desire for a multinational Christian consensus. What is more, they contributed directly to the larger goal of international unity. The unifiers fervently believed, as Gardiner wrote to Charles Henry Brent, in the "necessity

23. Alfred Loisy, *The Gospel and the Church,* edited by Bernard B. Scott. (Philadelphia: Fortress Press, 1976), 178.

of the vital unity of the church if the world is to be saved from chaos."[24] The issue to them was that simple and that urgent.

Behind these Christian leaders and offering an intellectual framework were university men and women, academics. The differences between late-nineteenth- and early-twentieth-century theologians and religious thinkers has been analyzed, often brilliantly.[25] What has been neglected, however, is their politics, a shared concern for the world at large, for building a new, more vibrant order based on Christian or humanitarian impulses or both. If this solicitude was rather general, it was no less important for it. In the Progressive Era platoons of Christians, like Brent, Vida Scudder, Gardiner, and their followers envisioned together with such disparate commentators as Edward Bellamy, Josiah Royce, and Herbert Croly "an almost mystical community in which men made their own distinctive contributions to . . . shared goals and values . . . an 'organic' society in which individuals and groups harmoniously interacted."[26] Writing in 1887 but looking back from the imagined year 2000, Bellamy suggested (incredibly) that in the course of the century Bostonians, and presumably others as well, had ceased "to be predatory in their habits, [and] . . . became co-workers and found in fraternity at once the science of wealth and of happiness." Royce, ever the nonconformist, the self-confessed "ineffective member of committees," dedicated himself to the welfare of all peoples, "to the whole community of mankind . . . the Great Community." Early on, these Americans were joined by those in the British Isles such as McLeod Campbell, Robert C. Moberly, and above all the younger Bishop Charles Gore who won respect for his "persistent pessimism," as Gardiner put it, "coupled with an earnest and faithful determination to keep doing the best of his ability the job which the Lord had put to his hands." Campbell and Moberly provided a theological base in their arresting theory of the Atonement with its insistence on Christ's self-identification with humanity as a whole. But it was Gore who gave the most instant call for

24. Gardiner to Brent, November 25, 1922, Gardiner Correspondence.
25. Hans W. Frei, "Niebuhr's Theological Background," in *Faith and Ethics: The Theology of H. Richard Niebuhr* (New York: Harper and Brothers, 1957), 16–64, esp. 26–32, 53–61.
26. Richard H. Pells, *Radical Visions and American Dreams* (New York: Harper & Row, 1973), 6. There were, of course, those who had not the slightest interest in the religious dimension of a new order for humanity, notably in America, Jacob Riis, Upton Sinclair, William Allen White, Ida M. Tarbell, Oliver Wendell Holmes, former Lutheran Thorstein Veblen, and, despite their background in Chicago's Hull House, John Dewey and Charles A. Beard.

social flexibility in Great Britain, for peace, for the unity of Western nations, and for the harmonizing of all classes and peoples. In an impressive, even electrifying, address delivered to his diocese in 1892, Gore linked the doctrine of the Holy Spirit to "'the prophetic word,' not an antique record hard of interpretation but a living voice speaking in the events of life."[27] With an affecting challenge the English bishop showed his own mettle and thereafter made himself a name with which to reckon.

Gore's contemporary in Germany, Adolph Harnack, also dealt with "the Social Question," and spoke "of the tendency to union and brotherliness [that] is not so much an accidental phenomenon of [the Gospel's] history as the essential feature of its character." Harnack ardently believed in church unity, "was convinced that the Christian religion was the greatest force for reconciliation of men with one another," and looked forward "with keen anticipation" to the Lausanne Conference on Faith and Order in 1927. His compatriot Ernst Troeltsch insisted that politics be "brought, to a certain extent, into harmony with ethical and humanitarian conceptions . . . a recognition of the value of personality, and . . . an acknowledgment of the claims of all to the necessities of life." As for Gore, so for Henri Bergson, it was Christianity, building on the prophetic tradition of Israel, that effected the "passage from the closed to the open," from Israel to the universal brotherhood, but the first opening was due to "the Prophets of Judaism." Could philosophy have brought about this expansion? "There is nothing more instructive," was the acerbic reply, "than to see how philosophers have skirted around [the Christian influence], touched it, yet missed it." More will be said about Bergson at the end of the chapter. Suffice it to say for the moment that these intellectuals held out hope for the future, a hope that, however, had to be grasped.[28] That was the point all of them made together.

27. Bellamy, *Looking Backward* (New York: Harper and Brothers, 1959), 273; Royce, "Words of Professor Royce at the Walton Hotel at Philadelphia, December 29, 1915," in *The Philosophy of Josiah Royce,* edited by John K. Roth (New York: Thomas Y. Campbell, 1971), 406, 407; see also Royce, *Hope of the Great Community* (New York: Macmillan, 1916), 122–36; Gardiner to G. K. A. Bell, May 9, 1923, Gardiner Correspondence. Shortly thereafter, Gardiner found Gore "pretty rigid" (Gardiner to his close friend Edwin A. Palmer, March 26, 1924, Gardiner Correspondence). John Kenneth Mozley, *Some Tendencies in British Theology: From the Publication of "Lux Mundi" to the Present Day* (London: SPCK, 1952), 26; Gore, *The Incarnation: A Revelation of Human Duties* (London: SPCK, 1892), 27, 37, 38, 43, 46.

28. Harnack, *What Is Christianity?* translated by Thomas Bailey Saunders (London: Williams and Norgate, 1901), 100; Wilhelm Pauck, *Harnack and Troeltsch: Two Historical Theologians*

What was Gardiner's own theology? Three things must be said by way of answer. First, what emerges from a reading of his correspondence, his published materials, and the books about which he spoke is that he was neither a dogmatic nor a creedal theologian in the professional sense of those terms, though he came closest to the latter. Certainly, he was not a systematic theologian, if by that qualifier we mean someone who viewed Christian faith by means of a particular system of thought outside of the received teaching of Bible, church, and tradition and by means of which those fundamentals would then be expounded and indeed controlled.

Second, he read widely in the volumes recommended by the Joint Commission's Committee on Literature.[29] In his capacity as secretary, he had to approve them. Among those books that he often quoted and had obviously read with great care were Johann Adam Moehler's *Symbolik* (1832) and his earlier *Unity in the Church* (1825), Robert C. Moberly's *Ministerial Priesthood* (1898) and *Atonement and Personality* (1905), Chauncey B. Brewster's *Catholic Ideal of the Church* (1912), Herbert Kelly's *Church and Religious Unity* (1913), Aurelio Palmieri's *Theologia Dogmatica Orthodoxa* (1911), and of course Charles Gore's *Incarnation* (1892), among others. His acknowledged debt to nineteenth-century and early-twentieth-century Roman Catholic theologians is, for an American, significant, even unusual.

As his discovery of Protestant thought advanced, Gardiner came to value P. T. Forsyth, especially the latter's article "The Need for a Church Theory for Church Unity," which appeared in *Contemporary Review* (March 1917), which Gardiner reviewed glowingly in the *Churchman* (June 1917). Curiously, the secretary does not appear to have read high church Presbyterian and fellow countryman John Williamson Nevin's *Mystical Presence* to which he would have been sympathetic, nor Nevin's opponent B. S. Schneck. The works of Horace Bushnell, so influential with other Episcopalians, apparently went either unread

---

(New York: Oxford University Press, 1968), 41, 39; Troeltsch, *Christian Thought: Its History and Application,* edited by Friedrich von Hugel (New York: Meridian Books, 1957), 173; Bergson, *The Two Sources of Morality and Religion* (Garden City, NY: Doubleday, 1954), 66–67. For a more current treatment of the subject, see John F. Woolverton, "Hope Dismantled?" *Anglican Theological Review* 82:2 (May 2000): 303–20.

29. See Francis J. Hall, comp., "Bibliography of Topics Related to Church Unity," in *Minutes of the Meetings of the Executive Committee of the Joint Commission Appointed by the General Convention of 1910 to Bring About a World Conference on Faith and Order* (printed for the committee, ca. 1913), pamphlet 17, 3–23.

or unremarked, as did Charles Porterfield Krauth's *Conservative Reformation and Its Theology*.[30] Although Gardiner was not a professional theologian and so cannot be faulted for not "keeping up," his failure to include some of these figures is also a measure of the limits of high church Episcopalianism. Such minds would clearly have broadened his understanding of Protestantism and its ongoing commitment to the doctrines of the Reformation, not the least its incarnational thought in both Luther and Calvin. Most of Gardiner's reading in Anglican thought was limited, however, to the high church, Anglo-Catholic side of the theological aisle. Absent in large measure were the works of Thomas Cranmer, Richard Hooker, and broad churchman F. D. Maurice; also neglected was the American Episcopalian theologian William Porcher DuBose, although a passing reference was made to DuBose's *Soteriology of the New Testament.* The same was true of the evangelical writings of Edward A. Litton. The later so-called "Cambridge Theological Essays" and their authors, edited by H. B. Swete, are not to be found among Gardiner's references to published materials.[31]

On the other hand, he kept up with the Thomistic journal *La Ciencia Tomista* and the orthodox journals *Bessarione* and *Eirene* along with the church presses of American denominations, including his own.[32] He was also knowledgeable about biblical texts and ancient liturgies of the church and kept a copy of the *Breviarum Romanum, Biblica Hebraica,* and *Vetus Testamentum Graece* on his study shelves at Oaklands. All in all his reading tended to the high church,

30. Nevin, *The Mystical Presence: A Vindication of the Reformed or Calvinist Doctrine of the Holy Eucharist* (Philadelphia: J. B. Lippincott, 1846); Schneck, *Mercersburg Theology Inconsistent with Protestant and Reformed Doctrine* (Philadelphia: J. B. Lippincott, 1874); Krauth, *The Conservative Reformation and Its Theology* (Philadelphia: J. B. Lippincott, 1871). Nevin's influence on William Porcher DuBose has often been remarked. See, for instance, Ralph E. Luker, "Liberal Theology and Social Conservatism: A Southern Tradition, 1840–1920," *Church History* 50:2 (June 1981): 198; and Frederick Thomas Barker, "Holiness, Righteousness, and Life: The Theology of William Porcher DuBose" (PhD diss., Drew University, 1985), 97–99. See also Arria S. Huntington, *Memoir and Letters of Frederic Dan Huntington* (Boston: Houghton Mifflin, 1906), 190; Mary C. Sturtevant, *Thomas March Clark* (Milwaukee: Morehouse Publishing, 1927), 64; William Lawrence, *Memories of a Happy Life* (Boston: Houghton Mifflin, 1926), 62, 75; James McLachlan, *American Boarding Schools: A Historical Study* (New York: Charles Scribner's Sons, 1970), 253, 256; and Raymond W. Albright, *Focus on Infinity: A Life of Phillips Brooks* (New York: Macmillan, 1961), 106 and 203.

31. Gardiner to A. W. Anthony, December 28, 1916, Gardiner Correspondence; Litton, *Introduction to Dogmatic Theology* (London: Elliot Stock, 1882); Swete, *Essays on Some Theological Questions of the Day* (London: Macmillan, 1905).

32. His knowledge of modern Greek permitted him to read such publications as *Eirene;* see Gardiner to F. J. Hall, January 19, 1911, Gardiner Correspondence.

Catholic side of his tradition. The volume he often mentioned was the liberal Roman Catholic Moehler's *Symbolik.*[33] For this German priest of the Catholic faculty of the largely Lutheran University of Tübingen, symbols, that is, dogma, doctrines, hymns, and prayers, were not secondary to interior faith and conviction but were identical with that which they expressed. For church historian Moehler they were in fact infallible decrees. Inner faith and its outward expression went together. The Christian lived her life in God in a visible community without the loss of individuality. This community was based on love emanating from Christ, embodying his living will in Holy Scripture and the church, an association characterized by harmonious and again infallible interworkings. Doctrines such as that of the Incarnation were essential symbols, but the Roman Catholic hierarchy, including the papacy, pertained to the realm of the function of the church. Moehler's interpretation of the church's organization and its authority did not commend him to the Vatican. It was too lyrical by far. Since he wanted to deal with Protestantism fairly, Moehler also avoided debate on points of ecclesiological differences and confined himself to dogma. That too cost him with his superiors. On the other hand, Moehler contributed positively to the search for unity. He saw Christ's influence among Protestants. If he did not hold out much hope of reunion in his own lifetime, he meant to draw attention to "the cause of Divine truth, especially in its living manifestation in Christ Jesus, who should alone be the object of our love." All this the lawyer from Maine read and appreciated. Although there are no direct quotations from Moehler's works in Gardiner's letters, both avoided controversy and meant to build bridges. At the same time, like Moehler, Gardiner held creeds, doctrine, and prayer in high esteem.[34] That he appreciated the internal signification and worth of others' faiths reflects Moehler's desire to see Christ's influence in Protestantism. As we will see momentarily, however, he also absorbed some of the German's less convincing opinions.

33. See, for instance, Gardiner to L. T. Schlathoelter, January 27, 30, February 4, 1913, Gardiner Correspondence; and Johann Adam Moehler, *Symbolism,* translated by James Burton Robertson (New York, 1844). The irenic Roman Catholic—and Hegelian—Moehler influenced formulations of the doctrine of the church, including those of the Oxford Movement's R. I. Wilberforce, and possibly the Russian Orthodox Alexei S. Khomiakov; there were others who were critical, such as J. W. Nevin, Philip Schaff, and P. T. Forsyth.

34. Moehler, *Symbolism,* trans. James Burton Robertson (New York: Crossroads Publishing, 1997), 5, 261, 258–59, 305, 304. Moehler's distinction between the church's essence and "the exercise of public functions" got him in trouble with the hierarchy, about which he decided rather offhandedly "to make a few remarks" (5–6, 11–12, xvii, xxix).

Third, the pattern of Gardiner's theology was to some degree idiosyncratic. Whether he was commenting on the kingdom, the church, creeds, sacraments, or ministry, in each case he flensed the blubber and went for the most basic principles. Only after he had carefully thought through those principles would he permit himself or others—which was seldom—to tackle the thornier issues that divided Christians. He put this method of redaction to use persistently. The reiteration of old controversies, he surmised, would simply divide the churches further. By going back to broader principles of Christian life and thought, he sought to avoid the addictive liquor of polemics, especially if a new spirit of well-affected and sincere listening was utilized. It was these "first principles" that needed to be examined, "because it is only in the light of these that the things which are to them subordinate and accessory can themselves rightly be discerned." As he wrote frankly to Peter Ainslie, "Vagueness is intentional on our part, because we do not intend to reach definite conclusions until we have the approval of substantially the whole of Christendom; until then everything is tentative."[35] As we shall see, he then went on to relate his core principles to the immediate behavior and comportment of both individuals and churches. He carried out this theological program under the ensign and superintendence of the cause for which he labored, the advancement of Christian unity.

Gardiner's theological program began with the doctrine of the Trinity. "The unity we must seek," he wrote in 1914, "is the absolute unity of being of and in the Blessed Trinity." Later he elaborated, "How can any man or men, however wise and saintly, devise unity such as that for which our Saviour prayed?" The task was "to make Christians one, not in each other but in God." And "the unity which God wills for us is as that of the Blessed Trinity"; it was then of the very nature of the Godhead. Clearly, it was not a human option, but a divinely or-dered communion, mandated by Jesus Christ himself. "We can not make that unity; we can not even mar it, for it is given by the grace of God." We can only strive to keep it from being obscured by our quarrels. There it was in scripture, and specifically in John 17:11–23. Gardiner had the passage incorporated in "An Office Preparatory to the Holy Communion" that the Commission issued for universal use by the churches.[36] Three times in John 17 the great bell sounded

35. A Layman [Gardiner], *The Conference Spirit,* pamphlet 19, March 6, 1913; Gardiner to Ainslie, December 20, 1913, Gardiner Correspondence.

36. Gardiner, "Creed, Life, Unity," *Christian Union Quarterly* (April 1914): 117; Gardiner, "Christian Unity," *Living Church* (May 20, 1916): 87; *A Manual of Prayer for Unity* (printed for the commission, 1915), 12–13.

for the gathering of disciples into the oneness of the Father and the Son: "That they may be one even as we are one" (verse 11); "that they may all be one, even as thou, Father, art in me and I in thee" (verse 21); and "that they may become perfectly one, so that the world may know that thou hast sent me" (verse 23). None of those sanctified were to be lost; they were instead to be "sent into the world" as the Father had sent the Son.

Time and again in his correspondence over a twenty-three-year period, Gardiner emphasized the doctrine of the Incarnation as the basis for participation in the world conference. As he wrote Anson P. Stokes in 1912, "Apart from the fact of the Incarnation I see no reason for Christian unity nor any prospect of its permanence. . . . [It is] the manifestation to humanity of the Life of God in whom we live and move and have our being." He wondered if liberal preacher Harry Emerson Fosdick "could name any instance where before the Incarnation any one ever protested against the evils of child labor or public corruption." Gardiner thought that Christians should be "seeking to live the life of God Incarnate and not simply to get a front seat in the Heavenly synagogue." The Incarnation, he claimed, was produced not "by the niceness of man's thinking but by the power of God's coming." The Incarnation was "external," and "its externality avails to lift man out of himself." Human effort may at times bring a person to a higher morality, "but it cannot lift him *out of* himself (nothing of our own can)." The presence of God was his gift to us. The official statement of the Joint Commission was and remained that the world conference was open to all communions that accepted "our Lord Jesus Christ as God and Saviour." That, of course, contained the Incarnation in its insistence on the divinity of Christ. Gardiner preferred the shorthand reference to the doctrine itself and read the commission's statement in that manner. As he wrote A. C. A. Hall, "It seems to me that they were quite right in restricting . . . membership to Communions which believe in the Incarnation and this seems to me an intelligent and justifiable line of inclusion, which, as you say means also a line of exclusion." And "Gospel of the Incarnation" could and should be preached with "irresistible power." There was then a seamless quality to his thought: emphasis on the Incarnation led directly to all of the other matters in Christian life, for "when we talk about the Church we are talking about the extension of the Incarnation." The problem was, as he saw it, that Episcopalians "do not expound that in such a way that it can be understood by people who are not familiar with the question."[37]

37. Examples are as follows: Gardiner, "Notes on Newman Smyth's Paper," n.d. but ca. June 1914, Robert H. Gardiner Collection, Archives of the Episcopal Church, Austin, TX; Gardiner

Why did he not focus on the Atonement? The answer is probably that Christ's sacrifice on the cross involved an admission of sin on man's part and its result: an embarrassing guilt. It was easier to kneel in adoration at the manger in Bethlehem than to travel the road to Golgotha. Moreover, it was hard to imagine the institutional and academic leaders of mainline Protestantism and their wealthy benefactors gathering at the foot of the cross to hear with any particular relish the words addressed to each of them singly, "Sinner, beloved of God."[38] In 1900 they were traveling in a different direction, hurrying to build the American Zion—with Rockefeller money—where none had stood before.[39] The cross did not seem to them to be the actual place their Zion was ordained to rise. In addition, focusing on legal transactions between God and man, or between God and the devil, the Atonement had already given rise to too many conflicting theologies. However conceived, a great deal of ink had already been spilled over the doctrine, and Gardiner wanted to avoid unnecessary debate. "The history of the doctrine of the Atonement," he wrote, "is a long and often sad story of the efforts of finite minds to explain and to limit the methods of God's love and mercy and justice." For its part, the Incarnation avoided contention and discord, was comforting, reassuring, seemingly neutral about human sin, even uplifting. The battles over the Incarnation had mostly ended by the fourth century. Of course, there were the Unitarians, but in their "mental calm . . . they insisted on no doctrine but taught, or tried to teach, the means of leading a virtuous, useful, unselfish life which they held to be sufficient for salvation." Let others slush, puff, and sweat with unruly Christian dogmas; Boston, remarked Henry Adams, had solved the universe.[40]

---

to Manning, November 1, 1914, April 28, 1915; Gardiner to Tissington Tatlow, April 18, 1914; to W. C. Bitting, November 14, 22, 1919, Gardiner Correspondence; Gardiner, "Christian Unity," 87; [Gardiner], "The Conference Spirit," 25; Gardiner, "Federation and Unity," *Churchman,* June 16, 1917, 713; Gardiner, "The American Council for Organic Union," *Churchman,* February 21, 1920, 12; Gardiner to Stokes, September 23, 1912; and to George William Douglas, June 23, 1913, Gardiner Correspondence. See also *The World Conference for the Consideration of Questions Touching Faith and Order: The Objects and Methods of Conference,* pamphlet 28, April 8, 1915; resolution in *Joint Commission Appointed to Arrange for a World Conference on Faith and Order* (Boston: Merrymount Press, 1910), 3; Gardiner to Hall, December 12, 1913, Gardiner Correspondence; and Gardiner, "The American Council for Organic Union," 2.

38. The image is that of Reinhold Niebuhr from class notes at Union Theological Seminary, New York City, 1957–1958.

39. Conrad Cherry, *Hurrying toward Zion: Universities, Divinity Schools, and American Protestantism* (Bloomington: Indiana University Press, 1995), 1–2.

40. [Gardiner], "The Conference Spirit," 27; Adams, *The Education of Henry Adams* (Boston: Houghton Mifflin, 1918), 34.

With Gardiner, however, matters were different. He did not speak of the Incarnation apart from the cross of Christ. In his 1916 report to the Joint Commission, he stated that the attempt to unite Christians could be realized only "in the one living Body of the Lord, both God and man, incarnate, crucified, buried, risen from the dead and ascended on high, living today and the Head over all things." The philanthropy of the FCC "is to be found in the facts of the Incarnation *and* Atonement." In 1923 he wrote to his friend Edward Palmer, bishop of Bombay, that "the excesses of Modernism, Anglo-Catholicism, Liberalism, and all other 'isms' which are now so rampant" keep people from seeing "the one Lord on the Cross in Whom alone can Unity be found." Closely following Robert C. Moberly's *Atonement and Personality*, Gardiner assumed a "reverent agnosticism" about a specific theology of the cross. It was a curious expression, one probably meant to allow for multiple interpretations. A Christian's insight into the meaning of the Atonement, he wrote, "may be adequate. That it should be exhaustive is inconceivable."[41]

He was at pains to remind his readers that the faith was not a matter of sticking to "some vague abstraction which can never give us life"; we deal, he contended, with a person "on his cross, lifted up that he may draw all men to him." Later—and significantly after his British son-in-law was killed at Gallipoli—he wrote movingly to Quaker Rufus Jones: "What we need individually and socially is to bring home to ourselves the absolute necessity and the redemptive power of the deepest love, which in some mysterious way is close kin to pain." That way, he concluded, "was God's way with us and the one He means us to choose in our devotion to Him and to each other." But the times were dark: Christ on his cross "is obscured by the smoke and dirt of battle and the world cannot see him." A month and a half later he iterated in more nuanced fashion: love was the root of true humility, obedience the absolute forgetfulness of self, "the eager, glad surrender of self to another without thought of reward or return." He had hit upon the New Testament understanding of love as incautious, uncalculating action undertaken for the sake of others. It was what the kneeling penitent, the pilgrim, even the curious or the merely puzzled could not fail to recognize as on Good Friday she contemplated the free sacrifice of Jesus Christ. Gardiner had come a long way from his claim in 1912 that the Atonement was

41. [Gardiner], "Report by the Secretary," in *The World Conference* (printed for the commission, 1916), 17; Gardiner, "Federation," 2 (emphasis added); Gardiner to Palmer, August 11, 1923, Gardiner Correspondence.

a "mystery almost impossible for the human mind to comprehend" and whose interpretations have "often repelled the mind of men from the acceptance of the fact of the Incarnation."[42]

And what of the Holy Spirit? Here he turned again to scripture, especially Ephesians 4. The references in that epistle to "the unity of the Spirit in the bond of peace" (verse 3), the reality of the "one body and one Spirit" (verse 4), and the not-to-be-grieved "Holy Spirit of God in whom you were sealed for the day of redemption" (verse 29) were woven into the cloak that early Christians drew close around their lives. Under the promptings of the Spirit, said Ephesians, each man and woman would put on what became those characteristic qualities of life so at odds with the Roman will to power: lowliness, meekness, patience, forbearing one another in love, respecting each other's gifts. This, they believed, was the key to reality. When it came down to the matter of individual deportment, such qualities both appealed to and supported those who wore them. Exotic doctrine bred simple fellow feeling and marked a potential change in human nature itself, "a power of conscience which pagan teaching had not recognized."[43]

Ephesians knew—and if they had forgotten the author of the letter to them would jog their memories—there was but one body "and one Spirit [animating that body] . . . one Lord, one faith, one baptism, one God and Father of all who is above all and through all and in all" (4:6). No one, it seems, was to be "lowered to the level of the Philistines." All of them felt they were "exploring a deep mystery step by step . . . [in company with] fellow explorers along a route which required high moral effort." Theirs was not a theology of "converted sheep and unregenerate goats." In the early Christian "democracy," there was "no partiality" in the face of Jesus Christ between husband and wife, master and slave, parents and children (5:15–6:9), for he who was master of all was also slave to all. Paul had announced "the world's first egalitarian society," as one freshly minted study has it. And that announcement "has to mean freedom from all human rules and conventions." Customs, we are told, were of no consequence to the cosmic Christ. "In nothing was Paul more radical than in separating accidents from essentials." In this spirit the secretary wrote Jesuit father John J. Wynne, "I wish we could meditate a little oftener and a little more deeply

---

42. Gardiner to Rufus Jones, March 30, 1916, Gardiner Correspondence; Gardiner, "Christian Unity," *Living Church* (May 20, 1916): 87; Gardiner to Stokes, September 23, 1912, Gardiner Correspondence.

43. Robin Lane Fox, *Pagans and Christians* (New York: Alfred A. Knopf, 1987), 314.

on the IV Chapter of Ephesians. As it is, it slides over most of us."[44] It had obviously not coasted past Gardiner.

Throughout that fourth chapter breathes the liberality of the Holy Spirit who lavished individual gifts on the Ephesians, taught and animated them in the evolution of their intrepid community. There saints got themselves ready "for the work of ministry, for building up the body of Christ" (verse 12). In the unity of the Spirit why should they fear the winds of childish doctrine or even their own diversity? Gardiner shared with the Evangelicals of his day a sense of the present power of the Holy Spirit, not as an impersonal force but as a soul-stirring influence in the lives of individuals and in the collective life of the church. Did he believe in baptism by the Holy Spirit? Certainly. But not apart from the sacrament itself. Without it, the validity of religious experience was ephemeral. That experience must for him include the common faith and practice of the church. Worse, if charismatic gifts were not anchored and maintained in faithfulness to the received tradition of the body of Christ, they could lead to personal arrogance and spiritual one-upmanship. Gardiner would play no such games. He was also not overwhelmed by an interest in the dynamics of a private "higher life" but in the corporate life of the people of God nourished by creed and sacraments.

Unity, moral effort, democracy, and recognition of diversity of gifts: these were the qualities that he discerned in the earliest Christian community. He echoed his close reading of Ephesians when he put forward the "imperiousness of the call to Christian unity which will convince the world that Christ was sent by God." At the same time, he spoke of the "manifestation of that diversity which comes from life and from the liberty wherewith Christ made us free." Lest there was any doubt that they had to act "in firm assurance of the guidance of God the Holy Spirit," he caused Ephesians to be added to the Joint Commission's *Manual of Prayer for Unity*.[45] He also composed "A Litany of the Holy Ghost." Characteristically, the litany was marked in the margin "Anonymous. Modern."[46]

44. Marcel Proust, *Remembrance of Things Past,* 2 vols. (New York: Random House, 1934), 1: 54; Fox, *Pagans and Christians,* 317; Henry Rack, "The Fairer Sects," *Times Literary Supplement,* March 8, 2002, 33; Thomas Cahill, *Desire of the Everlasting Hills: The World Before and After Jesus* (New York: Doubleday, 1999), 148; Gardiner to John Joseph Wynne, S.J., September 27, 1917, Gardiner Correspondence.

45. Gardiner to Tissington Tatlow, December 14, 1914; to L. H. Roots, July 10, 1913, Gardiner Correspondence; Gardiner, "Christian Unity," 87.

46. *A Manual of Prayer for Unity,* 26–30. Whether Gardiner himself contributed to this is not known; certainly the use of verbs in the litany: *renew, shed abroad, inflame, bear, lead, teach, fill,*

Along with the Gospel of John, Ephesians was his scriptural companion. And the engine that drove his reading of both was restitutionism, the desire to recapture the freshness of early Christian experience. "We must strive with all our might to recover the true meaning which in primitive days," he wrote, "made theological terms symbols and revelations of the life of God incarnate in humanity."[47]

How did this theology work itself out in terms of the immediate, daily thought and carriage of Christians? With respect to his personal religious development, three matters appear. First, he made passing but not unimportant reference to an aesthetic appreciation of nature. Nature, at least along the Kennebec, was a means that led to a greater sense of the divine presence. He wrote: "In the beauty of fields and trees and river and sky there dawned upon me the glimmering of the perfect beauty my later years have found." He never argued, however, from the sunsets and the woodchucks to that presence; Maine winters generally froze out such temptations.[48]

Second, the more specific Christian faith that became part of his character was not a static condition. It involved activity on the believer's part. Gardiner often used the word *surrender* to describe the Christian's relationship to God: "surrender to the Father's will," "surrender of self to the one Life." "Faith," he wrote in 1916, "is that surrender by man to his Saviour." It was not "a matter of mere opinion or of finite attempts to delimit the methods and purposes of the Infinite, but the real and vital union with Our Lord." That union was brought about by the Holy Spirit who was always active and creating a "living organism" in the world, the church. Under the guidance of the Spirit, "the life of God incarnate is continuous and all-pervading, shared by all who are members of Him." Union with God was facilitated by prayer, "not the conventional prayer which has contented many of us for so long a time, but the soul-compelling prayer which shall induce us to surrender our wills and open our minds to

---

and *hasten* were characteristic of his writing but no doubt of others' as well. Still, his spirit fairly breathes throughout it. The rest of the *Manual* was the work of the Reverend H. B. St. George of Nashotah House.

47. See, for instance, Gardiner to Herbert Kelly, January 19, 1918, Gardiner Correspondence, in which he merges the Ephesian emphasis on individuality and community which is "true democracy" with the Johannine commandment to love one another; A Layman [Gardiner], *Prayer and Unity,* pamphlet 15, January 3, 1913, and December 25, 1920.

48. Gardiner, "Address of Welcome," 107; he seems here to reflect an Augustinian neoplatonic point of view. See, for instance, Carol Harrison, *Beauty and Revelation in the Thought of Saint Augustine* (Oxford: Clarendon Press, 1992).

guidance." Prayer "opens the door to the presence of the Holy Spirit." There was no use talking about Christian unity, he declared to Tissington Tatlow, "until we are willing to make some approach toward Christian fellowship, and the only real approach to that is through such prayer as shall make us absolutely one with each other in Christ." Gardiner wanted everyone in humility to "wait upon God in silent expectation of His Voice." He insisted to William Manning on "the necessity for prayer as preparation" for the meetings of those planning the World Conference on Faith and Order. And he was "firmly convinced that God was guiding the movement."[49] To him supplicants must first go; then and only then could they work out the form.

The progression: guidance by the Holy Spirit, faith, surrender, prayer, was then not only an individual act but a corporate one as well. "We need the intense personal conviction of immediate relation to God ... to be rooted personally in the personal Christ," he wrote. "But now," he declared in the third way his theology was worked out, "as the world grows smaller and men are more closely related to one another, the [understanding of the] corporate aspect of our religion is the special need." Denominational as well as personal egoism had to be overcome. Gardiner decried the "establishment of our own [denominational] opinions, the glorification of self, the victory by the absorption or subjugation of all others[,] of mere partisanship, thinly disguised under the name of *our* Church." With P. T. Forsyth, he insisted that Christians were to look beyond the denomination—or, as he hoped, within—for "what Church there is in it, [for as] denominations settle in and grow egoistic they lose their converting and saving power." He agreed with Anglicans like A. E. J. Rawlinson and with Ugo Janni, the Waldensian pastor-theologian, when the Italian looked for "a new synthesis of the truths common to the various systems and those which are held separately among them." Churches often "mistake narrow uniformity for Catholicity." Any denominational expression of faith in God was not something to be closely guarded, for the faith one holds may be only "a phase of the Catholic Faith" that may need, "for true Catholicity, to be complemented." On

---

49. Gardiner, "Christian Unity," 87; Gardiner, "Address of Welcome," 113; Gardiner to A. G. Mortimer, October 20, 1911, Gardiner Correspondence; [Gardiner], "The Conference Spirit," 25; Gardiner to Mortimer, October 20, 1911, Gardiner Correspondence; [Gardiner], *Report of the Joint Commission to the General Convention of the Protestant Episcopal Church, 1913,* pamphlet 23, 5; Gardiner to Tatlow, December 11, 1914; to Manning, November 9, 1911; see also to Manning, August 23, 1915; to Peter Ainslie, August 25, 1915; to L. T. Schlathoelter, May 17, 1916, Gardiner Correspondence.

the other hand, Gardiner recognized that "there are those to whom positive dogma is not important." With these people he disagreed. In addition, he believed that Protestantism and Roman Catholicism were complementary and that each could not avoid tracing its own life in the light of the other. Gardiner came to believe that there was destined to be a new form and union of Christians in the world that did not yet obtain and that would come about, in so far as all of them surrendered to God's direction, through their joint efforts. Many Roman Catholics, he mistakenly believed, looked to a united American Protestantism "as their hope for the future." Were that Protestant union to come about, the Roman attitude would no longer "be that of demanding unconditional surrender and the thousands of Romans all over the world who are eager to turn their backs on medievalism will take courage."[50]

Chauncey Brewster's *Catholic Ideal of the Church* seems to have informed the thinking of a majority of the members of the Joint Commission for the world conference. In particular, the book nourished Gardiner's mind. To it he gave unstinting praise: "The more I read it, the more I admire it," he declared. Brewster's essay would give "conclusive evidence that we are not trying to swallow up other Communions." That the church of the future, as it was led by the Holy Spirit, would even involve surrender of cherished denominational icons and the emergence of a new form was Brewster's assumption.[51] Like faith, hope had its sharp side. Gardiner, like the bishop of Connecticut, recognized, in Brewster's words, that "the ideal is not yet realized. The Church here on earth is far from being the perfect realization of the Kingdom of God." No single denomination or tradition should make such a claim. Nonetheless, the "divine ideal in process of realization is found in a visible [universal] Church with its outward sacramental signs of the inward and spiritual . . . , a society of the sons and daughters of God" founded by Jesus Christ himself. The one divine life "flows forth from Christ to all the parts." Perfect agreement among those parts was not necessary.

50. Gardiner, "Creed, Life, Unity," 112; Gardiner, "Federation and Unity," 714. The article is a review of Forsyth, "The Need for a Church Theory for Church Unity," *Contemporary Review* (March 1917). Ugo Janni, "The Reunion of the Churches," translated by Gardiner, *Living Church* (September 4, 1915): 664. Janni went on to quote with approval Anglican bishop and New Testament scholar A. E. J. Rawlinson's assertion that "each [Christian] division attests some neglected portion of Christian truth necessary to the just balance of the whole." Gardiner, "Anglicanism and Reunion," *Churchman,* December 9, 1916, 774; Gardiner to Ainslie, September 1, 1914, Gardiner Correspondence.

51. Brewster, *The Catholic Idea of the Church* (New York: Thomas Whittaker, 1913); Gardiner to Hall, February 3, 10, 1913; see also to Pepper, September 9, 1921, Gardiner Correspondence.

"Unity is not destroyed while all cherish the divine object of worship, the common faith, the sacraments of unity, 'one Lord, one faith, one baptism,'" as Ephesians had it. The church from which those words came was guided and governed by the Holy Spirit and was "in purpose and essential character, universal." And it spread everywhere. In fact, the test of apostolicity for Brewster was universal mission, and he reminded his readers that "Apostle means one sent forth." But throughout the book Brewster drew attention to what the church was and could become, to "that great Body of the future which shall be at once one with the organism of the past and also larger and richer and nobler far than any particular Church of to-day." He appealed to Christian hope, to "the light from afar of the holy city, having the glory of God." But the oneness did not rule out manifoldness. Unity was "inward and essential . . . vital; it is the oneness of a common life wherein the parts grow together."[52]

That growing together meant the development of what became known as "the conference spirit" that was made effectual in this case by corporate submission to God's higher authority. That authority superseded quotidian appeals to denominational tradition. Such a spirit led to "genuine and sympathetic study of other men's ideals and aspirations," encouraging them to publish their own principles of faith, to "meet each others' minds and find out the best thing to do" and not display a "desire to maintain one's own position." The conference spirit had its opposite in party spirit. While the conference spirit was developing outside of the Episcopal Church, Gardiner wrote Charles Henry Brent, "all trace of it seems to be disappearing inside." Certainly, the world conference would eventually entail "full consideration of those things in which we differ as well as to those things of which we are one," but that was not the place to begin. He insisted first on positive understanding of what others held dear. To understand, he maintained, "is to love; to love is unity. . . . Our task will not be fulfilled by any human concordat." We must, he declared, "prepare the way so that the Holy Spirit may restore that unity which will enable all who are members of Christ to receive together the Bread of Life." In the process, he assured the Greek Orthodox scholar Hamilcar Alivisatos, "we have no idea of asking or allowing any surrender or compromise of any part of the Catholic Faith." Indeed, he believed that unity would be brought about by a synthesis "of all that is valuable in the positions of various communions."[53]

52. Brewster, *Catholic Ideal*, 5, 6, 9–10, 13–14, 16, 31, 19; also 20–28.
53. [Gardiner], "The Conference Spirit," 10, 19; Gardiner to Hall, February 10, June 23, 1913; to Brent, March 13, 1916, Gardiner Correspondence; [Gardiner], "The Conference Spirit," 9;

If Gardiner had his say, there would be no ultimatums to inhibit open participation. "The ultimatum," he judged, "is a relic of the reign of brute force . . . [and] must be abandoned." Churches must not "begin the process of realizing unity by means of ultimatums." Specifically, Anglicans were not to start talking church unity on the basis of the Chicago-Lambeth Quadrilateral. Gardiner made it plain that the commission appointed by the 1910 General Convention was not empowered to speak officially for the Episcopal Church on matters of doctrine or discipline but to be a catalyst for the calling of a world conference on church unity. To bring up the Quadrilateral "or something of that nature . . . would provoke controversy." Whereas Gardiner, as we have seen, wanted "no infringement of the principles of any Church," he did not want the Joint Commission to contribute to any volume of denominational position statements that "would inevitably repeat the Chicago-Lambeth Quadrilateral, or something of that nature, and that, again, would provoke controversy." For the time being he thought it best "to publish short essays or addresses, seeking to develop the desire for union and expounding its nature."[54]

In the meantime, he roped Anglican theologian Herbert Kelly of Tokyo's Central Theological College into writing a detailed essay, "The Object and Method of Conference." Controversy, wrote Kelly, consisted "essentially of instruction and its purpose is agreement; the essence of discussion is inquiry, and its purpose is to understand."[55] Kelly added specific recommendations to Gardiner's conference spirit: discussions should be leisurely; ample time should be allowed participants to develop or modify their ideas; criticism must be encouraged by the person being criticized; if criticism is not permitted, then something may be held back; pledges must be given and received: one must fully explain one's own position and have a desire to understand that of others; and so on. If Kelly's prescriptions were somewhere between easy-steps-for-little-feet and the counsels of perfection, it is well to remember that *conflict resolution* was then, if not an unknown technique, an untalked-of term. Neither Kelly's

---

Gardiner, "Report by the Secretary of the Progress Made in the World Conference Movement," in *North American Conference, Garden City, Long Island, N.Y., January 4–6, 1916,* pamphlet 30, 21; Gardiner to Alivisatos, September 14, 1914; to Stewart, September 14, 1915, Gardiner Correspondence.

54. Gardiner, "Christian Unity," 87; Gardiner to Ainslie, December 20, 1913, Gardiner Correspondence; Gardiner, "American Council for Organic Union," *Churchman,* February 21, 1920, 12; Gardiner to Ainslie, May 23, 1913.

55. *The World Conference for the Consideration of Questions Touching Faith and Order: The Objects and Methods of Conference,* pamphlet 28, April 8, 1915, 8.

prescriptions nor current group processes have proved to be a trump card for solving society's ills. For Gardiner, the conference spirit was part of the nature and work of the church itself. Here again he displayed loyalty to basic principles wedded to sharp political instincts. He wrote to Bishop Alfred Harding of Washington, D.C.: "Of course, especially in this matter of Christian unity, one finds it difficult to take any point of view except his own, but it seems to me that the clear fact of the Incarnation and its implications leads to the Catholic doctrine of the Church, then of the Sacraments, and lastly of orders. Ministers invariably begin with the question of orders and generally reach a dead-lock at once." He desired that these principles should engage ordinary people, not just theologians and academics. He called for local conferences. Brent was in full agreement: only by this means would people in local churches "know what we are aiming at & then when their imagination has been kindled will give their interest & make their great contribution without which all else... will be futile." Except for occasional letters back to Gardiner, there are few statistics to show success or failure. In two Midwest Disciples of Christ local unity conferences at which the major denominations were present, 125 were reported in Cincinnati, Ohio, 250 in Springfield, Illinois. These were all-day affairs of clergy and laity; it is worth noting that those who attended called for smaller conferences in other towns and cities.[56]

There were more formal aspects of Gardiner's doctrine of the church. He spoke first of the kingdom of God: the Incarnation was effected in order that Christ "might lead humanity to the establishment of His Kingdom of peace and righteousness and love." He thought that Christians, as he wrote philanthropist and advocate of interfaith cooperation Anson Stokes, were often "very likely to confuse the object of that Kingdom with the means by which it is to be established." Had he implied that the church was merely an instrument to be used for other ends, however great? Though he could well have, Gardiner did not. The church was Christ's contemporary, incarnate "body" on earth. The problem was that "we do not expound that in such a way that it can be understood by people who are not familiar with the question." As Jesus himself had

---

56. Gardiner to Alfred Harding, November 28, 1916, Gardiner Correspondence; see also Gardiner to S. D. Chown, general superintendent of the Methodist Church in Canada, January 12, 1921; and to W. H. Frere, bishop of Truro, August 5, 1921, and variously throughout the entire correspondence; Brent to Gardiner, October 6, 1915, Charles Henry Brent Papers, Library of Congress, Washington, DC. See also Finis S. Idleman to Gardiner, May 2, 1923, Gardiner Correspondence.

served the cause of the kingdom, so the Christian community must do so. There was no question: the rule of God came first. But the church was more than an instrument for the justice and righteousness demanded in that kingdom; it was in fact a long, continuous, and visible extension of the divine trinitarian life itself as first confronted in the Incarnation. The church was Jesus's "visible form, His permanent or renovating humanity, His eternal revelation." Through the power of the Holy Spirit, God dwelt in his community, "a manifestation of the outward reality of the invisible body of Christ." All Jesus's promises, all his gifts, were bequeathed to it. Significantly, in the light of papal claims, Gardiner argued that those promises and gifts had gone to "no individual as such since the times of the Apostles."[57]

Even with such a caveat, his high Anglican definition had its problems, but then again, so did the view that the church was simply a fellowship of the like-minded. In the one case, the difficulty was accounting for sin, not to mention contingency, in the holy commonwealth; in the other case, it was that of showing there was anything holy about the church at all. Did Gardiner think that the church was sinless? Hardly. His belief that the Christian community on earth was the extension of the Incarnation, as he wrote fellow Anglican George Craig Stewart, "is not inconsistent with the acknowledgment that, so long as the Holy Spirit speaks through human mouths, His message will be limited, or even strained almost to distortion." Characteristically the Maine lawyer refused to sniff out lurking subversives. "It seems to me," he continued to Stewart, "that the maxim that you must love the heretic but hate the heresy is an extremely dangerous one." Who was he to "presume to pronounce anything heresy?" Besides, he added it was impossible for human nature to avoid personifying the heresy in the heretic. In the final analysis they must never forget that "the object of Christian unity," as he wrote to Hughell Fosbroke in 1918, "is the manifestation of Christ to the world." Anson Stokes had complained about the Joint Commission's "unduly restrictive dogmatic text for those who would unite with it [the World Conference]." Stokes and his wealthy friend William Jay Schieffelin,

57. Gardiner to Stokes, September 23, 1912, Gardiner Correspondence. The implication is that the church and its good works stand under the judgment of the kingdom; see Eric Anderson and Alfred A. Moss Jr., *Dangerous Donations: Northern Philanthropy and Southern Black Education, 1902–1930* (Columbia: University of Missouri Press, 1999), 198. Gardiner to A. C. A. Hall, December 12, 1913; to F. J. Hall, February 25, 1911; to Hughes, June 23, 1911; to A. C. A. Hall, December 12, 1913; to Tatlow, October 1, 1919; to Schlathoelter, June 12, 1916; to Melish, January 20, 1913, Gardiner Correspondence.

who had been the lone dissenter from the theological language of the first unofficial conference on unity at Trinity Church in January 1910, wanted cooperation and good works without dogmatic fuss. For Gardiner, on the other hand,
"dogma not merely explains but mediates [the] experience" of Christians.[58]

For Gardiner, the church then was a *gemeinschaft,* a common possession, a
communion, not a *gesellschaft,* a social gathering such as the International Beer
Tasting Society. Such gatherings were made up of individuals who sought personal satisfaction either in tasting different types of beers, liturgies, or spiritual-
ities or in meeting their friends, or all four. In the church, he argued, no one
can be concerned with her own salvation, for only when "the individual loses
himself in the collective Life of the Body of Christ, he can find salvation."[59] We
have already seen such an understanding in his use of Sir William Blackstone and
that jurist's distinction between a corporation and a voluntary assembly. A corporation logically and chronologically preceded its officers, not they it.

What, he asked, is the nature of that body? It was visible, not invisible, a band
of men, women, and children, the "primary social institution within which
one lived and moved and had one's being," not "a secondary institution cherished
for its instrumental value ... a place where one might find services for enhancing the quality of one's life." But then within the visible solidarity, there were
many gifts given and not all alike. Again with the memory of Ephesians in the
background, he asked Tatlow, should they not try to "keep clear in our minds
the distinction between unity and uniformity, so as to allow room for the diversity which is the mark of true unity, as it is of all true life?" The community for
the sake of which the individual merged her life not only allowed but in the
Ephesian sense also encouraged diversity as one of its marks. The church was a
"true democracy ... the visible manifestation of that surrender which enables ...
[the individual] to reach fulfillment and freedom." There was to be a democratic
balance between the individual and the community. Of course, there had to
be leaders. As Gardiner wrote Methodist bishop Edwin Hughes, "To my mind,
the conception of the church as a divine organism is that of pure democracy,
needing of course special officers or special organs for the performance of
special functions." But he worried about the decennial meeting of Anglican
bishops at Lambeth, "lest it should be supposed that the resolutions or conclu-

58. Gardiner to Stewart, September 14, 1915; to Fosbroke, September 3, 1918; Stokes to
Gardiner, September 19, 1912; Gardiner to Tatlow, March 20, 1916, Gardiner Correspondence.
59. Tara Sheets, ed., *The Encyclopedia of Associations,* 3 vols., 35th edn. (Detroit: Gale Group,
1999) 1:2158; Gardiner to Frederick D. Kershner, June 14, 1916, Gardiner Correspondence.

sions of that body, eminent as it is, are formal and official pronouncements of
the Church." He advised American clergy and laity to look upon them as informed opinions only. For his part, as he wrote Edward Talbot, bishop of Winchester, he could not "help being firmly convinced that the voice of the priesthood and of the laity is necessary to the complete expression of the will of the
Church."[60]

Together with the church went the creeds. The Episcopal Church's "preser-
vation of the historic creeds has been of the utmost importance," he insisted to
liberal low churchman John Howard Melish. It was still so "amid the tendency
to exalt social service and to think that it does not matter what you believe so
long as you are fairly good and do a little good." He found that people objected
to creeds because they thought such statements were not related to daily life.
He countered: "Perhaps it could be suggested that a man's faith is not merely
intellectual but the rock on which his life and character are built." He thought
that church people should discuss the "nature and function of a creed" rather
than "immediately take up the Apostles' and Nicene Creed." Necessarily preliminary "to unity is the acceptance of a definite and positive creed." There was
no getting away from affirmations; "even agnosticism and materialism are creeds,"
he averred. There was "altogether too general a notion that the Catholic creeds
must be thrown over and that for them we must substitute opinions." Gardiner
clearly distinguished between creed and confession. Too many people confuse
them, he advised Mott; they think "the Creed means only the complicated
Post-Reformation statements like the Thirty-nine Articles." The one was the
"standard instruction of the Church and the reason for its existence as a Church,"
whereas the other was based on the "idea that each Christian must be an expert
theologian." Protestants, "in their efforts to phrase tests for each other, . . . have
built Augsburg and Westminster Confessions, Thirty-nine Articles, and the like
to which they have transferred the loyalty due to the historic creeds." Christian
unity, he went on, was "oneness in life, not in minute verbal or philosophical
agreement."[61] Such comments hid a false assumption, and, as I shall show,
lacked historical appreciation.

60. Frank E. Sugeno to the author, ca. 2000, Sugeno folder, Gardiner Collection; Gardiner
to Tatlow, January 19, 1918; to Kelly, January 19, 1918; to Hughes, June 28, 1911; to Edward S.
Talbot, bishop of Winchester, October 23, 1915, Gardiner Correspondence.
61. Gardiner to Melish, April 14, 1914; to E. J. Pace, April 3, 1923; see also to F. J. Hall,
March 22, 1911; to George William Douglas, June 23, 1913; to Mott, August 22, 1922; and to
Kelly, April 3, 1920, Gardiner Correspondence.

Gardiner's moderate pietism and back-to-the-basics approach led him to declare that statements of ecumenism ought to be constructed "for evangelistic purposes and not for theologians." When Francis J. Hall got theologically heavy-handed, Gardiner suggested to A. C. A. Hall that "the Catholic conception of the visible Church could be adequately presented . . . [in] . . . a much larger, freer, and more fundamental way than is found in such papers as Dr. Hall's." He urged the bishop of Vermont as chairman of the Committee on Literature for the Joint Commission to publish a clear statement of the Anglican position for all the other denominations to read and then invite them to state with equal clarity the positions of their own churches. We "should take up the nature of Christian Faith and the need of a creed, using the word in its historic sense, as distinguished from the Thirty-nine Articles," he wrote, "and that then we should undertake to set forth the Catholic conception of the Church." He was not an anti-intellectual negativist, but sought to go behind theology, "to recover the true meaning which in primitive days made theological terms symbols and revelations of the life of God incarnate in humanity."[62] As we shall see presently, however, it led him into unnecessary rejections.

When it came to the sacraments, especially to the Eucharist, Gardiner believed that development of "the true Catholic doctrine of the Sacraments" should precede discussion of "the sacerdotal question," that is, the priesthood. Christians shared "in the life and purpose and hope for mankind of God Incarnate in the Person of the Son." That life was quickened by the "special means of grace administered through the sacraments." The church itself where the sacraments were administered was a divine creation, its basic principle "the Life of God Incarnate," its message the "Gospel of the Incarnation." Indeed, when the faith of the church, that is, the surrender of mankind to God and his Christ, is manifested, "the Incarnation is completed." Sacraments came first, yet we "talk about God as if the sacraments were ordained that we might have priests. If we put the sacraments first, I am sure our [Protestant] brethren would gradually be brought to recognize them as fundamental to the perpetuation of the Christian life."[63] If he took on Anglo-Catholic misconceptions, he also fronted on liberal Evangelicalism.

62. Gardiner to Fosbroke, September 3, 1918; to Hall, December 14, 1912, Gardiner Correspondence; A Layman [Robert H. Gardiner], *Prayer and Unity,* pamphlet 15, December 25, 1920.

63. Gardiner to F. J. Hall, March 13, 1911, Gardiner Correspondence; Gardiner, "Federation and Unity," 714, 713; Gardiner, "The American Council for Organic Union," 12; Gardiner, "Christian Unity," 87; Gardiner to Rogers, July 8, 1911, Gardiner Correspondence.

Here once again he locked horns with Melish. For the rector of Holy Trinity Church, Brooklyn, the Holy Communion "had no life" of its own; "only as the Christian takes that truth and applies it to life, has the Sacrament any value." Gardiner replied, "I do not read my Catechism quite as you do." Was not the church's distinctive teaching "as to the Sacrament of the Holy Communion . . . that it is the fullest and deepest life, a sacrament surely of fellowship with other Christians but also with God?" Following Herbert Kelly's *Church and Religious Unity,* Gardiner complained that "those who receive the sacrament without recognizing the double aspect of that fellowship fail to receive a very great part of its value." The invisible body of Christ, ever becoming sacramentally visible, endowed its members with the guidance of the Holy Spirit, bringing them into "real and vital union with our Lord." He wanted first to emphasize the benefits bestowed in the Holy Communion. How Christ was present in the eucharistic action in the elements of bread and wine was not the point. Nonetheless, Gardiner held to a "Real Presence": it is "an infinite mystery altogether above our finite comprehension and that we must accept our Lord's words of institution literally, although we cannot understand them, in the full confidence that by such acceptance we shall receive the inestimable benefits which he promised."[64]

He thought the way to approach the thorny and contentious subject of the ministry was "to develop that true Catholic doctrine of the Sacraments." The priesthood, he commented to his friend Tatlow, "is simply a corollary dogma to the life-giving knowledge of God." To F. J. Hall he argued that "the whole question of the ministry should be subordinate to that of the Church." It follows as a "logical necessity" to a "truly Catholic conception of the Church," which in its turn was "absolutely contradictory to papal infallibility." Too often when, for their part, Anglo-Catholics used the words *Catholic* and *Catholic priesthood,* "they are essentially partisan in their attitude and habits of thought." It was not too much to say, he crackled, that in a sense "they are not entitled to the use of the term 'Catholic' at all because they do not feel or display that trust of the Church which is after all the basis of the Catholic conception." Those who failed to see that the church preceded all of its parts "seem to me to be lacking in a conception of the dynamic force of Orders and the other Sacraments of the Church and in their position that Bishops, priests, and laymen who do not

---

64. Melish to Gardiner, January 3, 1913; Gardiner to Melish, January 20, 1913, Gardiner Correspondence; the reference is to Herbert Kelly, *The Church and Religious Unity* (New York: Longman's, Green, 1913), chap. 4; Gardiner to Schlathoelter, June 27, 1916, Gardiner Correspondence.

agree with them are not Orthodox." As he wrote Alfred Garvie of New College, Oxford: "While the church universal is divided, no ministry is strictly full as being the act of the whole body. If that is so, the readiness of Anglicans to accept a further, fuller commission is by no means an empty gesture of good will, and such readiness on the part of Anglicans might well be followed by Free Church-men." He then went on to spoil the point by saying that episcopal, presbyterial, and congregational polities were already represented in the American Episcopal Church. If such a claim might not wash with American Presbyterians and Con-gregationalists, when an admiring Garvie wanted Gardiner to lecture the arch-bishop of Canterbury and his clergy on how the American Episcopal Church held three polities in its quiver, the lawyer from Maine noted that "it is a rather delicate matter for an American to suggest to an Englishman, especially the head of the established Church, that there may be features of the American Church which would be useful."[65]

Again and again he insisted that the question of orders was involved with the conception of the church and its sacraments. On the other hand, he also stated, contradictorily, that when the world conference actually convened, he wanted the question of orders "discussed at once." This did not in fact occur, and future generations wisely followed Gardiner's more consistent lead and painstakingly discussed first the more general topics of "church" and "ministry." He was hope-ful that "we are again reaching the conception that the priesthood resides in the whole Church and not simply in individuals who are from time to time the organs through which the Church exercises its priesthood." When Lord Halifax sought to bring together the Roman and Anglican churches around the conception of orders, Gardiner wrote Joseph Cardinal Mercier that perhaps reunion between the two was not as simple as Halifax thought and that he hoped that "out of it [the discussions] would come the visible reunion of all who profess and call themselves Christians, in the movement for a World Conference on Faith and Order." He followed up with a letter to Charles Henry Brent: "Halifax's efforts to get recognition of Anglican orders from Rome . . . seems to me to be simply a superficial patching up of differences which will remain really very deep." He wanted no narrowing of the question of orders and instead thought of the con-ference as a place to have a "thorough discussion of it from the very foundation,

65. Gardiner to Hall, March 13, 1911; to Tatlow, March 20, 1916; to Hall, March 13, February 25, 1911; to Garvie, December 11, 1923, Gardiner Correspondence.

which would be illuminating to all of us—Anglicans, Romans, Easterns, and Protestants."[66] Nor was that all.

In March 1914 he wrote to Methodist bishop Lewis Burton, "I think we are beginning to see more and more clearly that the fundamental question is not the Historic Episcopate but the conception of the Church"; as in the case of the priesthood, so in that of the episcopate, he observed with ice-cold accuracy, it derived from a greater reality. He placed the current "monarchical conception" of the bishop's role over against that of the early church. He also believed that there was "very little difference between Presbyterianism and Episcopacy" in "primitive practice." It was in the Middle Ages, he advised Methodist bishop Edwin Hughes, that "the monarchical conception of the Episcopate" grew up. "We are in some danger of transferring that conception to this country," he continued, "but one of the results to be accomplished by this World Conference, I hope, will be to get rid of that monarchical conception." A month later in the same year, 1911, he wrote Talbot Rogers that one trouble with the Church of England is "that it suffers the monarchical conception of the Episcopate which is not sound Catholic doctrine and which makes the Episcopate seem a rock of offense to our brethren." Time and again he placed the "Catholic" concept of the episcopate over against the "monarchical." The latter "fosters egotism in our Bishops" and presents a conception offensive to others. Though he acknowledged to his Baptist friend W. C. Bitting that "probably most of us in the Episcopal Church believe the Episcopate is a necessary factor in the reunion of Christendom," he knew that it would be only one view submitted to the World Conference on Faith and Order. Nor must it be allowed to dominate discussions of either church or ministry. "I hope that those who hold to the Apostolic Succession will do a little more deep thinking about it," he wrote to conservative Presbyterian William B. Smylie of the United Presbyterian Church. "Some give the idea that it consists of a succession of quasi-magical touches. My idea is that the important point is the continuity of the Church." "I think that the Episcopal Churches have always made a mistake in talking about Apostolic Succession," he wrote Bitting; "the fundamental and permanent doctrine to my mind

66. Gardiner to Tatlow, October 30, 1916; to Alfred Harding, November 28, 1916; to Charles Anderson, December 26, 1917; see also Gardiner to Walter Hooton, November 22, 1917; Gardiner to F. J. Hall, February 25, 1911; to Mercier, November 8, 1922; to Brent, March 2, 1923; to Gilbert White, February 13, 1917; to William DeVries, February 9, 1917, Gardiner Correspondence.

is the continuity of the Church which is the body of Christ, the Episcopate being the symbol or evidence of that continuity." That did not mean accepting what he termed "blind views of the ministry of members of other communions." He believed that the overwhelming body of opinion "is fast coming to recognize that God is not shut in to a particular ministry, but has been free and always will be free to act through men whom He had called to His service, whatever their ministry may be."[67]

Implicitly and explicitly he counted himself the heir first of the Evangelical Movement in Anglicanism. He noted how his parish and diocese "shared in the Evangelical awakening to missionary activity, a reflex of the preaching of Wesley and Whitefield, which first roused the Church to life and power." Then came the "Tractarian movement which deepened and extended the missionary motive by giving the Church the consciousness of its universal and corporate responsibility as the Body of Christ." In sum, he wrote to his friend George Wharton Pepper, "I am proud of being an Episcopalian, for on the whole I think the Episcopal Church recognizes more clearly than any other [church] that Christianity is above all a religion of perfect freedom, and that it manifests that absolute unity in great diversity which is the essence of any real life and especially of the Christian life."[68]

Gardiner rejoiced that the Episcopal Church held to "the transmission of an authoritative commission for the ministry, which we claim to possess & Protestant bodies do not . . . the authority to minister Word & Sacraments in Christ's name." Many mistakenly believe that participation and cooperation with ministers of other denominations implies equality of authority, and "it is *this* which is *commonly understood* to be acknowledged in Union Services, exchange of Pulpits, [and] Federation of Churches." Yet for Gardiner the shoe was often on the other foot. For their part, Episcopalians had failed to realize their potential. The problem was basically theological: most clergy had no sense of corporate

67. Gardiner to Burton, March 25, 1914; to Hughes, June 23, 1911; to Rogers, July 8, 1911; to F. J. Hall, June 23, 1911; to Bitting, November 4, 1919; to Smylie, February 26, 1924; to Bitting, November 22, 1919; to Hughes, April 22, 1918, Gardiner Correspondence. Gardiner recommended books by Episcopal bishops and others: F. J. Kinsman, *Principles of Anglicanism* (1910); Chauncey Brewster, *The Catholic Ideal of the Church: An Essay toward Christian Unity* (1912); Robert C. Moberly, *Ministerial Priesthood* (1898).

68. Gardiner, "Address of Welcome," 112; Gardiner to Pepper, September 9, 1921, Gardiner Correspondence. He was critical of the Evangelical emphasis on conversion of *individuals* and in general "our individualism in the United States" (Gardiner to Ainslie, June 20, 1918, Gardiner Correspondence).

sinfulness, "that we are none of us really ready for the complete surrender of all that we have and all that we are to the proclamation of the Gospel, as was the case in the first years after the first Pentecost."[69]

Robert Gardiner's discovery of denominational America remained incomplete. Despite his appreciation of John R. Mott, Peter Ainslie, Edwin Hughes, Theodore Schmauk, P. T. Forsyth in Scotland, and others, and his recognition of their ministries, time and again he displayed a lack of comprehension of the faith of Protestants. The list of their shortcomings was long: they fail to appreciate the Eucharist, their laity has lost interest in theology, and when they do take an interest, they want "absolute and minute agreement with themselves which I take to be the essence of the Protestant attitude of mind." As he wrote Tatlow in the spring of 1914, "the great danger in this country at any rate is that very many Protestants think the Incarnation can now be disregarded." Thus, they believe that "the only Church is the invisible Church and that no form of visible unity is possible or to be desired." He singled out Adventist bodies: they "are not especially educated theologically and would therefore probably not be much interested in our preliminary discussions or perhaps even in the Conference."[70] Had he read Calvin's *Catechism,* his belief that Protestantism was individualism run amok would have been tempered, though not for long, given the current fashion in most of nineteenth-century America; for Calvin, the church preceded the individual and her particular gifts.[71] When in 1911 the Episcopal rector of Trinity Church in Boston, Alexander Mann, held that increasingly Protestants felt the necessity "of a definite and positive faith and the conception of the visible Church," Gardiner was "more and more convinced that he is wrong." As we saw in an earlier chapter, he thought Baptists simply expounded the old militant Reformation themes; the significance of the high calling of seventeenth-century English Baptist congregations each to write its own confession of the faith eluded him. In general, Protestants only objected to things.[72]

69. Gardiner to Pepper, September 9, 1921; to A. C. A. Hall, December 2, 1913; to Pepper, September 9, 1921, Gardiner Correspondence.

70. Gardiner to Melish, January 20, 1913; to Stetson, March 18, 1914; to A. C. A. Hall, November 18, 1913; to Tatlow, April 18, 1914; to F. J. Hall, January 5, March 21, 1911, Gardiner Correspondence.

71. Karl Barth, *The Faith of the Church* (New York: Meridian Books, 1958), 135.

72. Gardiner to F. J. Hall, March 22, 1911; to Stewart, September 14, 1915, Gardiner Correspondence.

In addition, Gardiner made nothing of the Christology of the preached Word, the "means by which the power of God is made present in the midst of His people." The understanding that God addresses the congregation through the words of the faithful preacher was not his to appreciate or enjoy. Nor did he perceive, as he might have, that God was incarnate in the words of the preacher every time he entered the pulpit. Preaching for him did not have a "sacred function."[73] He failed to notice that the New Testament was shot through with references to the declaimed Word: "We preach Christ crucified," Paul pointedly wrote to the Corinthians (1 Cor. 1:23). In words that can hardly have escaped Gardiner, P. T. Forsyth had declared, "The Sacraments are not Christ's one legacy. They are not the kind of act in which the Church rises and rests. Its unity is created by the one Gospel and not by the several sacraments; these are but the modes of the published Word, which is the sacred thing in all sacrament." This first-line theologian whom Gardiner admired then went on to emphasize the role of the church in words of which the American would have wholeheartedly approved: "The regeneration it [the church] preaches is *the* moral issue of the world."[74] But unless the Word was spoken, no one would ever hear the Gospel, much less respond to it. Gardiner missed that simple truth. On the other hand, through exposure to theologians such as Forsyth, his mind began to change, and by 1920 he was in fact agreeing with Alexander Mann that there was "more and more of a tendency among Protestants . . . toward recognition of the Church as an organism." He assured the Roman Catholic Father L. F. Schlathoelter, "I can give you plenty of Protestant books which are very positive and which do a great deal of building up" of the church.[75] P. T. Forsyth's volumes were among them.

But it was on the wisdom of the sixteenth-century Reformation confessions that he had the most difficulty awarding any credit. Confessions, he surmised, were by nature sectarian, inspired by suspicion: the fathers of the continental and English Reformations "doubted each other's comprehension of the facts and dogma's of Christianity." As a result, they phrased tests for each other, "developed differences and built Augsburg and Westminster Confessions, Thirty-nine Articles, and the like, to which they have transferred the loyalty due to the his-

---

73. James F. White, *Protestant Worship and Church Architecture* (New York: Oxford University Press, 1964), 36.
74. Forsyth, *The Church and the Sacraments* (London: Independent Press, 1917), 60, 102.
75. Gardiner to Tatlow, October 1, 1919; to Schlathoelter, February 8, 1913, Gardiner Correspondence.

toric creeds." When the eunuch said to Philip, "I believe that Jesus Christ is the Son of God," the Apostle did not cross-examine him before he baptized him. "Christian unity is oneness in the Life, not in verbal or philosophical agreement," Gardiner declared.[76] In that statement he was surely correct, though then he failed to appreciate, much less show, the line of march from such life to scripture, to creed, to confession, and to delineate their similarities of purpose.

Whatever insights may have escaped the lawyer from Maine, the compelling faith that he had developed over the years was to sustain him in future disappointments during the dark months of the Great War and its disillusioned aftermath. Curiously, the character of that faith became most apparent when he was reproving, rightly or wrongly, those who clung to the Thirty-nine Articles and the Westminster and other confessions. The question in his mind was which came first, the divine person or the theological protocol? Should believers sing their "Nearer, my God, to thee" as descant to the church's theological plainsong, or was the theme in fact the believers' faith and the confession the counterpoint to it? For Gardiner, the revelation of God was of a person with whom human wills united. Believers must first grasp the "eternal Reality... the *foundation* of our Creed... the *Life* of God." Through prayer and the sacraments that divine life instructed, ordained, impelled, and, Gardiner believed, swept along all who fell under its spell. Seldom did confessions stir up faith. It was God himself who did that, who inspired his people. For Gardiner, the order of these events of faith and its expression was of the utmost importance: movement, development, the pace and tread of the divine footfall preceded the fixity of theological statements. With approval he quoted Henri Bergson, "There are no means of reconstructing the mobility of the real by means of fixed concepts." Becoming, not being, was the "real"; things in the making, not things made, demanded attention; "not self-maintaining states, but only changing states exist."[77]

---

76. Gardiner to Kelly, April 3, 1920, Gardiner Correspondence.

77. Gardiner, "Creed, Life, Unity," 115 (emphasis added); quoting from Bergson, *Introduction to Metaphysics,* translated by T. E. Hulme (New York: G. P. Putnam's Sons, 1912), 68, 65. For a helpful discussion of Bergson's elan vital, emerging vitalism, and evolutionary thought, see, for instance, Eric C. Rust, *Evolutionary Theologies and Contemporary Theology* (Philadelphia: Westminster Press, 1969), 87–93. For the larger context of the thought of Bergson and others like him, see Langdon Gilkey, *Naming the Whirlwind: The Renewal of God Language* (Indianapolis: Bobbs-Merrill, 1969), 53–54.

That Gardiner bought into such an evolutionary life philosopher is not surprising. So had his much admired protégé Forsyth, follower of John Calvin. Whereas Forsyth propounded a theology of the cross, Gardiner sought to have his fellow Christians comprehended by Christ in his ongoing incarnation in the church and ultimately in the world itself. He was arrested by "the fact of *God* incarnate in Jesus Christ." Early Christians had been so moved and as a result "had made the life of Christ their own." Although the American never, like Bergson, rejected the transcendent, he also saw clearly that God in his immanence as well as in his transcendence was not to be bounded by any stationary ecclesiastical statutes respecting faith and order. Denominational claims, be they papal, episcopal, or confessional, must take a back seat. Litigious terms and fat contentions would give way to the conference spirit, or so he hoped. Christians were commanded to go to God first and then work out the form. Gardiner reproached his brothers and sisters for preferring "to define God and His methods instead of giving ourselves to Him."[78]

"Dogmatism," Bergson had continued, as quoted by Gardiner, "in so far as it has been a builder of systems, has always attempted this reconstruction" in order to turn the mobile into the quiescent. Both men, Bergson and Gardiner, declared that too often, in Bergson's words, "we place ourselves in the immobile order to lie in wait for the moving thing as it passes, instead of replacing ourselves in the moving thing itself, in order to traverse with it the immobile positions." As Gardiner stated the matter, we have adopted "a perverted use of the words 'dogma' and 'doctrine'"; the one was the Greek, the other the Latin for *teaching,* and that teaching was about the activity of God incarnate in Jesus Christ. Early Christians had "listened to that teaching and made the life of Christ their own."[79]

How did they do it? In the development of character, that is, in an act of the will, Gardiner replied. He found this answer in the writings (at least in those he read) of Bergson, of Friedrich von Hugel, and of his friend Charles Henry Brent. All three affirmed the primacy of intuition, feeling, and volition. Maturity in the faith or, for that matter, even unconscious awareness of it involved a "mingling of styles," of *sublimitas* and *humilitas,* both of which were

78. See John H. Rodgers, *The Theology of P. T. Forsyth: The Cross of Christ and the Revelation of God* (London: Independent Press, 1965), 270–71; Gardiner, "Creed, Life and Unity," 115 (emphasis added);

79. Bergson, *Introduction,* 67.

rooted from the beginning in the character of Jewish-Christian literature; [it was] graphically and harshly dramatized through God's incarnation in a human being of the humblest social station, through his existence on earth amid everyday people and conditions, and through his Passion which, judged by earthly standards, was ignominious; and it naturally came to have . . . a most decisive bearing upon man's conception of the tragic and the sublime.

Von Hugel would have understood the sense of this modern commentator's claim when he—von Hugel—wrote that Jesus of Nazareth "came among us, so unspeakably rich and yet so simple, so sublime and yet so homely, so divinely above us precisely in being so divinely near." The response of the individual believer involved for von Hugel not merely reflection but also action "of part of himself against other parts, of himself with or against other men, with or against this or that external fact or condition."[80]

Through such activity the Christian also, but not incidentally, grew to her real self and her "own deeper personality." She is then in a position to be fed by the Mystic Sense. When for his part Brent used the term *mystic,* he did not have in mind, however, the usual notion of the soul's fusion with Absolute Reality, or its subjection to visions, voices, or profound bodily or psychic change; mysticism for Brent was not the communion of the alone with the Alone. Quite the contrary, the mystic sense of which he spoke was a means of "finding a more excellent way" *in the affairs of the world,* one that "promises ultimately the best social results." Brent spoke of "boldly submitting propositions for improvement to the social conscience." The former slum priest in Boston had not changed; he believed that "Better to-morrows are obtruded on poor to-days, partly by virtue of the fact that the Mystic Sense is naturally in constant contact with the ideally best." Brent's Christian anthropology ended not in ecstasies but in the humdrum notion of "good character and its cultivation," which meant avoiding the suspicion (at least) of self-interest.[81]

All of this Gardiner read and absorbed. Like his mentors Brent and von Hugel, he too maintained there was such a reality as spiritual evolution; like them, he

80. Erich Auerbach, *Mimesis: The Representation of Reality in Western Literature* (Princeton, NJ: Princeton University Press, 1953), 41; von Hugel, *The Mystical Element in Religion* (New York: E. P. Dutton, 1909), 26, a book Gardiner had studied and absorbed.

81. See, for instance, *Encyclopedia of Religion and Ethics* (New York: Charles Scribner's Sons, 1961), s.v. "mysticism"; Brent, *The Sixth Sense: Its Cultivation and Use* (New York: B. W. Huebsch, 1912), 69, 70, 72.

also held out hope for a universally rewarding future. He was able to take these vague but noble ends and turn them to practical use and implementation through the institutions at hand. That was his role and his work. In them he never lost his theological bearings derived from these men or stumbled in the arduous task of implementing their insights. Throughout, he maintained a steady drumbeat for what appeared to him to be the ideally best.

# Six

꒒✛꒒

## Improbable Center of a Worldwide Movement

### *Gardiner, Maine, 1914–1924*

For the next ten years Gardiner, Maine, was the unlikely hub of the Faith and Order Movement. At its center was Robert Gardiner. He was an uncommon common man: old shoe, not given to embroidered discourse; in a way "Down East," a Maine squire and farmer who lived in his stone manor house with its high ceilings and grand staircase. There he enjoyed a triple inheritance: Oaklands itself, his parish church, and the town on the Kennebec that bore his family's name. With all three went a sense of ownership and command. Still he put on no airs with anyone; his neighbors agreed that he was the genuine article. From the town of Gardiner he commuted to that other "hub" of the universe, Boston, and there to his house on Beacon Street and to the law office in Pemberton Square. Before and after World War I he traveled across the Atlantic on the *Aquitania* and other fancy ships, but Gardiner, Maine, always remained central.

Did his choice of locale make him something of an isolated figure in his time? By no means. As we have already seen, mail reached him there in vast quantities. By 1917 the Post Office Department had to build a larger—and more expensive—building to take care of the correspondence and printed materials that came to and from Gardiner, Maine.[1]

---

1. Danny D. Smith and Earl G. Shuttleworth Jr., *Gardiner on the Kennebec* (Dover, NH: Arcadia Publishing, 1996), 109.

Close to the town and its post office was Oaklands itself. The house had been inherited by Robert Gardiner in 1886. At the time he was thirty-one years old. Alice Gardiner transformed Oaklands into a handsome establishment, staffed by servants trained in the grand manner. In addition to the domestic comforts supplied by his wife, however, Gardiner had other satisfactions: He liked to get into old clothes and swing a scythe in the fields along with the hired hands. He "loved nothing better than working on the farm, starting the day when the men did, helping with haying, clipping hedges, logging... or harvesting apples." He might even be found in town trimming the hedges around Christ Church. Elsewhere when it came to dress, he insisted on decorum. Once, an eager Maine state YMCA secretary suggested at a summer rally that the men might take off their coats. Gardiner liked neither the suggestion nor the resulting shirtsleeves. He "finally yielded but, as it seemed to me," recalled a friend, "with a great deal of discomfort. Such things were not done at the Oaklands."[2] The hay fields were one thing, a formal meeting quite another.

The question hung in the ecclesiastical air: what better headquarters could there be for advancing international Christian unification than Gardiner, Maine? The answer was a lot of places. Bishop Anderson and Rector Manning voiced strong opposition to the locale: the use of a backwater New England mill town was unsuitable. It also may be that Manning was anxious because he did not trust Gardiner to exercise discretion. Gardiner says that Manning wrote him "a long letter full of anxiety lest Mott and I should have no discretion." Manning "contended that people world-wide would be dubious of an international movement with such an address." It was a point well taken: "If I received a mailing of an international movement headquartered in Dime Box, Texas," suggests one historian, "I would not be impressed." To Robert Gardiner, however, "Bishop Anderson's [and Manning's] objection to the address is trifling."[3] So strong was the secretary's sense of place that Gardiner, Maine, was to him not a farmer's cowshed but an enterprising citizen's public rostrum. So Oaklands and Gardiner it would be. There he maintained his primary home and office, and there he would live and work after 1900.

2. Danny D. Smith to the author, October 16, 1999; Floyd Tomkins, "Talk with Mrs. Shepley, Oct. 1, 1964," Floyd Tomkins Papers, Archives of the Episcopal Church, Austin, TX; Elizabeth Gardiner, *Golden Memories,* 19; Harry W. Rowe to Frank E. Sugeno, May 16, 1963, Sugeno folder, Robert H. Gardiner Collection, Archives of the Episcopal Church, Austin, TX.

3. Gardiner to Brent, August 13, 1914, Gardiner Correspondence; Frank E. Sugeno to the author, July 10, 1997, Sugeno folder, Gardiner Collection; Gardiner to Manning, May 9, 1911, Gardiner Correspondence.

In the meantime by 1914, what had the Episcopalian purveyors of church unity accomplished? Despite the grind and wear of their often strained relationships, the answer was much. From October to December 1910 Anderson, Manning, Gardiner, and others had organized themselves and obtained funds. By April 1911 they had written to all Episcopal bishops, conferred with Congregationalists, Presbyterians, Disciples of Christ, and Methodist bishops, and declared that the ultimate aim of the Faith and Order Movement was to prepare the way for the *outward* and visible reunion of all who confessed Jesus Christ as God and Savior. (Their wording was an obvious repudiation of the federal ideal of churches cooperating in benevolence and works of mercy as the ultimate goal.) The immediate purpose of the Plan and Scope Committee was to induce all churches to appoint commissions and to plan for a conference in which differences and agreements about a world conference could be discussed. By July 1911, fifteen American denominations were on board with official commissions similar to that of the Episcopalians.[4] Interviews had been conducted with the Roman Catholic leader Cardinal James Gibbons and with Orthodox archbishop Platon of Sverdlovsk. Letters had been authorized to all Anglican bishops, archbishops, and metropolitans worldwide. Committees had been appointed to communicate with the Roman Catholic Church, Orthodox churches, Old Catholics, and Protestant churches abroad. Not the least, all racial designations of denominations were by vote of the Joint Commission to be deleted and never used again.

By the end of their first year in operation, the Episcopal Joint Commission had sent out one hundred thousand copies of the *Report of the Committee on Plan and Scope* to all Episcopal bishops and their clergy, to all Anglican bishops worldwide, to the delegates to the denomination's General Convention, to the leaders of the fast-growing Laymen's Missionary Movement, to the council of the Brotherhood of St. Andrew, and, as Gardiner proposed next, to all the cardinals and bishops of the Roman Catholic Church in the world and to all Roman Catholic clergy in the United States. It was an imposing start. Taken alone, the outward facts of what was developing out of this American effort to build a

4. They were as follows: the Episcopal Church; the Methodist Episcopal Church, South; the Southern Baptist Convention; the Northern Province of the Moravian Church in America; the Reformed Church in the United States; the Presbyterian Church in the U.S.A.; the Methodist Episcopal Church; the Evangelical Lutheran Church in the U.S.A.; the Presbyterian Church, U.S.; the United Presbyterian Church of North America; the Reformed Presbyterian Church of North America; the Northern Baptist Convention; the Conference of Free Baptists; the Reformed Church in America; and the Reformed Presbyterian Church in North America.

communicating network of people give the impression of certain, even smooth, progress. By October 1911 the secretary was receiving about one hundred letters a day. Many were simple requests for information or for reports or contained words of praise for the movement and other workaday communications. These could be quickly handled; others were from church leaders offering pointed comments and demanding not merely the attention of one of the three secretaries but of Ralph Brown or of Gardiner himself.

There were other accomplishments: Bishop A. C. A. Hall's already approved bibliography of major publications on church unity had been issued as a means of focusing attention and raising the movement's visibility. On December 14, the all-important Committee on Literature was appointed to show the world, as Gardiner later remarked to Bishop Hall, that "we have a momentary glimpse of something larger than ourselves." He added that they needed to get the materials out there without all the time worrying "as to whether an adverb shall or shall not—I forget which—be invariably placed at the end of a sentence."[5]

In early 1912 the ever-cautious Randall Davidson, archbishop of Canterbury, had been cajoled into joining the effort. Davidson, however, appointed a "co-operating," but not official, commission of Anglican bishops to meet the American deputation soon to arrive in Great Britain. Eastern Orthodox clergy had proved more amenable and quick to respond. They had drawn up an address for Archbishop Platon to blue-pencil, one that would go out not just to a committee of bishops but also to all the Orthodox faithful.

To keep momentum going while waiting for the results of the invitations sent to churches outside the United States, Newman Smyth and George Wharton Pepper made plans in late February 1913 for an informal American conference of church leaders. In March the denominational commissions' chairs and secretaries met in Washington, D.C., to prepare an agenda. Two months later, conferees assembled at the Hotel Astor in New York City where a committee of five prominent American Protestants was chosen as a deputation to the free churches of Great Britain. In late July the Episcopal Commission convened at Oaklands. There Gardiner gained the authority to send out all communications on its behalf, thereby relieving Bishop Anderson of the burden of letter writing and the commission of the burden of Anderson's inattention. By the late fall of 1913 the Old Catholics had appointed a commission, as had the Church of Ireland. In April 1914 the exuberant secretary wrote to Brent that "prospects

5. Gardiner to Hall, January 2, 20, 1913, Gardiner Correspondence.

are steadily growing brighter. We have practically the cooperation of [all] North America, of the Anglican Communion throughout the world, and of Protestants in most of the English speaking countries ... [together with] a good deal of interest in Europe and some of the Greeks are beginning to understand about it. The Russian Archbishop ... assured us of the cooperation of Russia." On June 5, 1914, Gardiner was able to write the French Protestant Paul Sabatier that at the end of the summer a deputation would go to all the European communions, "first to Holland, Denmark, Sweden, Norway, Finland, and Russia, thence to Berlin, Prague, and Vienna, Budapest, Bucharest, and other places en route to Constantinople, Athens, Jerusalem, and Alexandria."[6] It was to arrive in Europe on the first of September. It never did. The war changed everything. By early October the visit was officially canceled.

And then there was the Church of England. In the immediate prewar years American Episcopalians recognized that the support of the mother church was crucial. Before sailing home at the conclusion of the Edinburgh Conference in 1910, Brent made his move. He wrote Gardiner of an earnest appeal to Archbishop Davidson to put his weight behind the World Conference on Faith and Order. "His reply," Brent confided, "was full of sympathy[,] but there was a note of pain and perplexity in it." Brent saw that "if we can succeed in getting the co-operation of the Church of England, it will tend to influence both the Roman and the Orthodox Greek Churches." Gardiner agreed. They both felt that the movement must not be seen as a matter of bolstering American Episcopalian visibility. "Again, not only on our own account but for the sake of the World wide movement," Gardiner wrote Newman Smyth, "it is essential that we should have the cordial interest and support of the Church of England."[7]

Relations were not easy, however. On the one hand, there was English suspicion of colonial upstarts, on the other little awareness on the part of the Americans of the necessarily slower pace of a church established by law and beholden to the government. Closely related to its legal position was the Church of England's cultural tradition. Whether people actually *went* to church was less important than the fact that the church was *there,* a presence in each village and town, the steady toller of the bell of communal seasons, and the useful and

6. Committee of Five to Gardiner and William T. Manning, May 9, 1913, Gardiner Correspondence; Gardiner to Brent, April 29, 1914, Charles Henry Brent Papers, Library of Congress, Washington, DC; to Paul Sabatier, June 5, 1914, Gardiner Correspondence.
7. Brent to Gardiner, January 9, 1911, Brent Papers. For Davidson's continuing cold feet, see Gardiner to Tatlow, November 4, 1914; to Smyth, December 28, 1912, Gardiner Correspondence.

perennial butt of an amused literati. That the Church of England ever survived the combined force of Jane Austen's *Pride and Prejudice,* George Eliot's *Middlemarch,* Anthony Trollope's *Barchester Towers,* and Samuel Butler's *Way of All Flesh* is one of the more persuasive miracles of the nineteenth century. It was a venerable institution, nearly four hundred years old; from the English point of view the American Episcopal Church was a parvenu, "an upstart crow decked in our feathers." Americans wanted action; the English sought consultation, first among themselves but ultimately with the national government. The role of the latter in church affairs was strange to American ways. As Gardiner confessed to Brent early in 1911, "I never quite understand the working of the English [ecclesiastical] mind." Brent replied that he was more worried about the Church of England than about the Church of Rome: "That wretched State entanglement will be a great barrier to freedom of speech and action on the part of Anglicans." There was, Brent judged, more independence in the small Episcopal Church of Scotland than in either the English establishment or in its Scottish Presbyterian counterpart. For his part, Gardiner found the leaders of the Church of England "much oppressed" and, curiously, isolated, their position in the state tending to keep them from "terms of intimacy with their Protestant brethren." In the United States, where all lined up equally at the starting post and raced on the same turf, awareness of competitors was not merely essential but a given factor. Finally, Gardiner thought it inexpedient for the various branches of the Anglican church, as he wrote Lord Hugh Cecil, "to depend so entirely on Canterbury." American bishops, he admitted, enjoyed the connection to Great Britain's church with all its trappings just a little too much; it gives them "a feeling of exclusiveness and superiority to other Churches [in America] . . . on account of the Establishment and social reasons . . . [which do not] exist in this country."[8] Bishops who had daydreams that such exclusivity could somehow get packed in episcopal trunks for the return trip to America were like Kipling's village that voted that the earth was flat.

8. See, for instance, Tatlow to Gardiner, November 26, 1914: "If anything important is to be done we have got to be prepared to move rather slowly . . . your last visit left the impression that you had greatly underestimated . . . the possibilities of the pace at which we could work." For the English, publicity was to be avoided: an "immense amount of spade work [had to be] done behind the scenes by the leaders." This was the opposite of Gardiner's call for local conferences and lay participation. Gardiner to Brent, January 9, 1911, Brent Papers; Brent to Gardiner, August 31, 1911; Gardiner to Smyth, December 28, 1912; to Cecil, December 26, 1922, Gardiner Correspondence.

More generally, the two peoples were still distrustful of each other. America had after all fought two wars against Great Britain, and anti-British feeling persisted in the New World throughout the nineteenth century. Within Gardiner's living memory there had been the two Venezuelan affairs, in 1895 and 1902, the more dangerous one settled by secret diplomacy, the other by German-inspired arbitration at the Hague Tribunal. The trouble was that Americans were determined not to be a "negligible quantity," even to swagger a bit, and it did not help then or later. In the movement's early days Gardiner himself had bluntly declared to Congregationalist Newman Smyth that too many in the Emerald Isle "have the Englishman's rooted distrust of any new movement, of any American undertaking, and of anything which looks big." To make matters worse, he concluded that the English made little attempt to understand Americans. As he wrote to Herbert Kelly at the end of 1914: "The Englishman who comes over here and remains wholly English loses half his value and is very often distinctly detrimental." That the same might be said of American visitors to Great Britain did not at first occur to him. Gardiner judged that his fellow countrymen were not "nearly so self-complacent as the English are and, though I would not dare to say so out loud, I am quite sure that when the war is over, if England is to continue to be of value, there must be a new world there." The old "insularity" had to go, he remarked to the bishop of Winchester; England could "no longer stand aloof." It must, he told Brent, "come out into the world and take an interest in other peoples' movements, even if they do not appeal to her very much." The problem with English church people was that they "are still looking upon Christian Reunion simply as a negative, a mere cessation of ecclesiastical hostilities." When the secretary complained that the Church of England seemed to expect the free churches to come to it rather than actively extending to them the right hand of fellowship, Canon Tissington Tatlow readily, and graciously, concurred, bringing the two sides together would not be easy.[9]

In January 1914 came the first flash point between the English and American sister churches: Archbishop Davidson's Cooperating Committee voted not

9. Gardiner to Smyth, December 28, 1912; to Kelly, November 30, 1914; to Edward S. Talbot, February 5, 1918; to Henry Hodgkin, November 21, 1916, Gardiner Correspondence; to Brent, February 6, May 11, 1918, Brent Papers; to Tatlow, July 9, 1913; Tatlow to Gardiner, December 24, 1913, Gardiner Correspondence. Not until April 1924 did Great Britain have an inclusive body similar to the Federal Council of Churches in the United States in which different communions could get to know one another and embark on common enterprises. In that year the Conference on Christian Politics, Economics, and Citizenship was formed.

to appoint a representative to the Faith and Order's new interdenominational Advisory Council. The move seemed hostile to the Americans. Gardiner tried to calm down Episcopalian leadership in his own country. "I told them . . . I was quite sure no hostility was intended, but I did not succeed altogether in satisfying them, or even myself." To make matters worse, when news of the negative vote should reach other Anglican churches throughout the world that had already accepted the Americans' invitations to appoint commissions, "it will tend to make them repent of their action and withdraw the support." Gardiner guessed at English fears of seeming to be committing themselves officially by a positive vote. To the American Episcopalians, however, it looked like a ploy to isolate them from the rest of the Anglican Communion. "There seems to be a sort of implication in the vote," Gardiner complained, "that the Church of England and its branches is [sic] something distinct from the Protestant Episcopal Church in the United States." Hurt and angry, he concluded, "We claim to be just as much a part of the Anglican Communion as the Church of England in England is[,] and we don't like the appearance in the vote of being fenced off."[10]

Tatlow, whose experience as the general secretary of the Student Christian Movement in Great Britain and Ireland closely paralleled Gardiner's own,[11] was a member of Davidson's "committee" for the world conference and its secretary. Committed to its goals, he was quick to reassure his American counterpart that they had not meant to be hostile and that news of the resolution had not gone out to other Anglican churches. "Personally, I think they have been rather stupid," the Englishman let fall, "and I have persuaded the Committee to hold another meeting and reconsider their Resolution." He added, "Please treat this letter as confidential. I must not say, in my official capacity that my Committee is stupid, seeing that it is composed of illustrious persons." A month or so later the proficient Tatlow informed his American correspondent that the offensive rejection had been rescinded. Then in a second and private letter sent the same day, Tatlow blurted out that "the conservatism of this country is terrific." In addition, there was no cohesion among the free churches themselves; they "have got

10. Gardiner to Tatlow, January 14, 1914, Gardiner Correspondence.

11. For a description of the international scope and character of the SCM, together with many of the names that appear in this study, see Ruth Rouse, "Voluntary Movements and the Changing Ecumenical Climate," in *A History of the Ecumenical Movement, 1517–1948,* edited by Ruth Rouse and Stephen Charles Neill (Philadelphia: Westminster Press, 1967), 341. For opposition by the *Church Times* to this younger generation, see Tatlow to Gardiner, December 16, 1914, Gardiner Correspondence.

to be layed [*sic*] siege to and secured one by one." Confidentially, Tatlow reminded his friend, "I have got the reputation so far of being fairly wise, but I can only retain it by being prepared to move very slowly and cautiously. All is well, but it is going to take a long time to get the British Isles ready for a World Conference." All was not well, and time was running out. Though personally liked, officially Gardiner was told he had not made a particularly good impression on the English during the summer of 1914. At the end of the year Tatlow bluntly told his American counterpart that Gardiner's visit that past summer "left the impression, somewhat wide-spread, that you had greatly underestimated the difficulty of the whole situation in Europe . . . It would not be fair for me not to tell you this."[12]

In 1922 a more reflective Gardiner confessed to Alfred Garvie that in the early days of the movement, "our friends in England were inclined to think that Americans were a young and hasty people, altogether too apt to try to do things in a hurry." The secretary admitted the truth of the allegation. As far back as 1911 Gardiner had recognized this fact and had written to Cosmo Lang, bishop of Oxford, that the fear that the Americans were "intending to advance too rapidly" was shared by many. "One of the chief charms of Dr. Newman Smyth," he wrote to Tatlow some years later, "and one of the elements in his success in proclaiming the need of unity is his entire inability to see any difficulties, and he cannot imagine why there needs to be any delay." By the 1920s Smyth's enthusiasm had waned: "He never sticks to anything more than a little while," Gardiner wrote Frederick Lynch. "He was at first quite keen about the World Conference movement, but our intention of proceeding slowly and thoroughly was too much for him." On the other hand, as a result of Smyth's deputation the Congregational Union had appointed a commission, Primitive Methodists had named their committee, and at least one major Presbyterian had commended them cordially, as had the Free Church Conference of Norwich. He reluctantly acknowledged that Smyth wrote too many letters and actively pursued putting delicate business into the press. The English response was: "You will certainly have to hold Dr Newman Smyth in!" The Maine attorney promised to do his best. But the suspicion remains that Canterbury was miffed because the Americans and not the English established church had breached the walls of isolation between religious bodies in the United Kingdom.

12. Tatlow to Gardiner, February 10, March 30, November 26, 1914, Gardiner Correspondence.

Whatever the case, by the end of the year Gardiner was putting it diplomat-
ically to Tatlow, "I think you are probably wiser that we are, in that you are
doing more really valuable spade work behind the scenes than we are." It was a
timely admission, notwithstanding in the same breath he pushed his agenda, at
the heart of which was the reveille that "the whole body of Christendom must
be aroused." "Self-opinion, self-complacency, our sectarianism and our insularity
must all be abandoned if Christianity is to continue." Gardiner kept begging for
greater exposure in the British press. Not wanting to have their efforts seen as
an "American movement," Tatlow resisted. "If we are to interest religious people
in this country on a wider scale," he wrote Gardiner, "they must be taught to
think of it as a movement which is not being forced on their attention from
without, but which has its roots well established in our own borders."[13] It was
a point well taken.

But Gardiner was learning. He made friends in the United Kingdom. By
1917 he was keeping Archbishop Davidson informed of relations both with the
Russian and with the Roman churches. For his part, far from being reluctant
about publishing material in the British press, a more trusting Davidson looked
"forward with great pleasure to seeing you when you come to this side of the
Atlantic. . . . [In the meantime] I quite approve of the circulation in England of
your papers on Faith and Order." Six years later he had earned Davidson's fullest
confidence; the archbishop wrote that the secretary had a "unique experience as
recipient of the comments and outpourings of all sorts and conditions of men."
Despite occasional flare-ups, Tatlow and Gardiner also learned to solve their
difficulties and came to trust each other. For his part, Tatlow made it clear that
securing "the men of weight in this country" had top priority. He wanted the
leading figures to have a sense of responsibility for the movement and coun-
seled calm diplomacy. It was good advice. "I am hard at work in a quiet way
trying to get the leaders to move," he wrote. "The real danger is that the movement may fall into the hands of secretaries and not into the hands of the men
who have real weight."[14] Fear arose for both men that the ecumenical enter-

13. Gardiner to Garvie, December 28, 1922; to Lang, September 15, 1911; to Tatlow, April
18, 1914; see also for reactions to Newman Smyth, Gardiner to Kelly, April 6, 1915, April 15,
1918; Gardiner to Lynch, July 10, 1923; Tatlow to Gardiner, April 22, 1914; Gardiner to Tatlow,
May 1, December 11, 14, 1914; Tatlow to Gardiner, June 21, 1916, Gardiner Correspondence.
14. Davidson to Gardiner, September 19, 1917; to Gardiner, March 17, 1924; see also
Davidson to Ralph Brown, January 27, 1925; Tatlow to Gardiner, March 30, 1914, Gardiner
Correspondence.

prise in England would be frustrated by its opponents. "The recurring shock and disappointment amongst students and other young people at Christian conferences to find there was difficulty in the way of receiving communion with their friends belonging to other churches" led to anger and dismay. Nowhere had this been more searingly evident than in a violent controversy caused at Kikuyu in the highland area of south-central Kenya (Africa) in 1913 when two Anglican bishops extended an invitation to other churches to join them in the Eucharist.[15] Anglo-Catholics in both Britain and America went into orbit; the action appeared to lead the church into a purely Protestant position. "Some of us still remember the furor caused in Episcopal circles," Congregationalist Herbert P. Woodin later wrote Gardiner, "over that pitiful little gathering for a united Communion service in the heart of Africa some years ago." In the objection of the missionary bishop of Zanzibar, the young people of whatever stripe had been ambushed by a bias that denied intercommunion in what were entirely permissible "exceptional circumstances."[16]

Then too, as Tatlow frankly observed, there was the *Church Times:* "unprogressive and not friendly to such movements as the Faith and Order movement, or to any movements which are influenced by younger men and women who have come through the ranks of the Student Movement." To offset the *Times*'s preponderance, younger clergy and laity founded the *Challenge,* a newspaper edited by the highly visible William Temple with Tatlow himself as chairman of the board. The challengers appealed to America for funds: "It is an open secret," wrote Tatlow, "that important persons in the Church of England are watching with great sympathy and hope that the paper may be established."[17] It was.

Simultaneously, the war came. As in every other phase of European life, so in this, the results were devastating among the ranks of the youthful to whom the *Challenge* was directed. Looking back, Tatlow explained forlornly, "Our subscribers were practically all of military age, our Movement being supported

15. Ruth Rouse, "Voluntary Movements," in *History of the Ecumenical Movement,* edited by Rouse and Neill, 337; Alexander C. Zabriskie, *Arthur Seldon Lloyd: Missionary Statesman and Pastro* (New York: Morehouse, Gorham, 1917), 189.

16. Woodin to Gardiner, May 28, 1923, Gardiner Correspondence; Smyth, *A Story of Church Unity* (New Haven, CT: Yale University Press, 1923), 58. See also Stephen Charles Neill, "Appendix II: Intercommunion," in *History of the Ecumenical Movement,* edited by Rouse and Neill, 742.

17. Tatlow to Gardiner, December 16, 1914, December 1, 1915. Gardiner replied that he "knew of no more competent men in England . . . than you and Temple" (December 25, 1915). Gardiner's continuing support for Temple is seen in Gardiner to Tatlow, March 5, 1920; and Tatlow to Gardiner, December 16, 1914, Gardiner Correspondence.

largely by older members. Most of them have either been killed or ruined financially by the war." The "jolt which the war caused to religion in this country was very considerable," he lamented, "and it is impossible to predict what the ultimate results . . . are going to be." A similarly sad note was struck again by A. C. Headlam, bishop of Gloucester, when he noted that "the incomes of church people . . . had gone down. . . . The bishops, who are supposed to be well paid, find it quite impossible to live in their own [official] houses, and many of the clergy are in a state of real poverty." If they could stave off another war or a revolution, the bishop continued forlornly, things might get better. Tatlow reminded Gardiner that America's losses in the war were insignificant compared to Europe's: "You can imagine what it is like in a country where some of the best leaders among the younger men have been lost and where everything has been impoverished."[18] It was not the will, he declared, but the power to help that was lacking.

At first, Gardiner too was stunned by events. Upon his return to the United States in September 1914 he turned to his companions in the law. He wrote George Zabriskie shortly after he landed in New York: "Your gloomy statement of the condition of business is by no means too dark . . . [and] I entirely agree with you that [the war] is a life and death struggle between liberty and true democracy and military despotism, which would not only grind the life out of Western Europe but which would surely try to gobble North and South America as soon as opportunity occurred. . . . Of course the war will suspend our proceedings in Europe." The same day he also confided his alarm to Francis Lynde Stetson. Before the month was out he had noted to Thomas Hodgson in England that American papers were full of war news, and that everything else was on hold, and, he added a little wistfully, "on the day on which war broke out I received the last batch of letters needed to assure me the cordial reception for the Deputation in every place of importance in Europe." In early 1915 he despaired of the bitterness between the Allies and the Central Powers; it "so firmly determines each that the other shall be crushed that the situation is

18. Tatlow to Gardiner, January 20, 1920, February 11, 1924; Headlam to Gardiner, April 4, 1921; see also Tatlow to Gardiner, June 21, October 9, 1916, May 21, 1918, Gardiner Correspondence. When Gardiner complained to Cosmo Lang, the bishop of Oxford, that Tatlow was not paying sufficient attention to the World Conference movement, the overburdened Englishman erupted in justifiable anger (Tatlow to Gardiner, October 14, 1918). For his part, Gardiner begged forgiveness (Gardiner to Tatlow, October 31, 1918). Tatlow replied, "My wrath was not very great and it had entirely evaporated long before your letter arrived" (Tatlow to Gardiner, December 4, 1918, Gardiner Correspondence).

hopeless." As the months dragged on and British losses increased, Tatlow wrote that the war was draining the nation and the church: "I am afraid you will have to be patient with us until the war is over"; he judged that the whole unity movement would have to be started again after the war.[19]

But Gardiner refused to give up. He felt that the war would temporarily "throw us back on ourselves," as he wrote Peter Ainslie, "and compel us to greater effort." He suggested to Reginald Weller that the interval be spent "in getting really close together in the United States" so that when hostilities are over our churches "can effectively proclaim the gospel of the Prince of Peace." A month later, he added, "The cataclysm of the European war, which is involving almost the whole world, gives us the opportunity to make a new world united in the one Christ." To that end for the four years following he kept up a "very extensive correspondence with every country which could be reached by mail and with notable results." When the Joint Commission thought it best to sit tight on church unity until hostilities were over, he protested to Philip Rhinelander "that if the do-nothing policy... is continued, we might as well abandon the enterprise." He threatened to resign as secretary: "I don't see why I should continue in a position where I should be merely eating my heart out in disappointment over the failure to prosecute a promising effort." The following October (1915) he tried to impress on a reluctant Manning that the delay caused by the war gave them "a providential opportunity to instill into ourselves and into our [American] brethren something of the conference spirit." Brent agreed.[20]

Then came the Panama Congress of February 1916. There the conference spirit very nearly evaporated. Panama City was the gathering place for 304 Protestant missionary leaders from the United States (159), from the Caribbean, and Central and South Americas (145), all areas that had been omitted from the considerations of the World Missionary Conference in Edinburgh, in 1910. The Panama Congress sought to rectify that omission, and in this sense it was a continuation, via meetings in New York (March 1913) and Cincinnati (late

19. Gardiner to Zabriskie, September 9, 1914; to Thomas Hodgson, September 16, 1914; to Archbishop Nathan Soderblom, February 13, 1915. Gardiner found the Swedish primate "very sympathetic" toward the movement. See Gardiner to J. Howard Swinstead, October 30, 1915; Tatlow to Gardiner, June 21, October 9, 1916, Gardiner Correspondence.

20. Gardiner to Ainslie, September 1, 1914; to Weller, September 26, October 26, 1914; to Norman B. Nash, July 31, 1918; to Rhinelander, December 9, 1914; to Manning, October 25, 1915; to Bishop Gilbert White of South Australia and Tasmania, February 13, 1917; Brent to Gardiner, October 6, 1915, February 3, 1916, Gardiner Correspondence.

June–July 1914), of the previous world conference. At Edinburgh conferees declared that Latin American and Asian countries were both traditional and legitimate missionary areas for both Americans and Canadians. "Large masses in nominally Christian lands" (read Roman Catholic) were fair game. Anyone who did not believe the spiritual destitution of those "nominal" Christians could come and see for themselves. Subsequent meetings in New York and Cincinnati beefed up the Panama agenda with a heavy emphasis on cooperation and unity of purpose in publications, education, including theological, and an unfortunately termed "Territorial Occupation."[21] In light of President Woodrow Wilson's quixotic and moralistic policy toward Mexico's small-time Strong Man, Victoriano Huerta, it must have given pause.[22]

William Manning would have none of it. Both he and an even more vehement *Living Church* opposed any participation in the congress.[23] To join would be as much as to declare, so they thought, that the Episcopal Church was Protestant rather than Catholic. In February 1915 the Episcopalian Board of Missions voted to table the invitation to go to Panama. As the ever-cantankerous Paul de Schweinitz later reminded Gardiner, "You will recall how Dr. Manning, now Bishop Manning, did his best to prevent the Episcopal Church from participating in the Panama Latin-American Congress, but fortunately did not succeed." De Schweinitz concluded acidly that the Episcopal Church should put some "sincerity into its fine phrases." In the meantime, in March and April 1915 George Wharton Pepper and the Reverend Arthur Seldon Lloyd went to work. They argued that the motion to table should be reconsidered. It was. Gardiner followed up with a letter to Manning in September suggesting that here was an opportunity to bring in the Latin American Roman Catholics: he was sure that if the New York rector "took the matter up resolutely and promptly and with your usual tact and good address you could . . . persuade the authorities of the Roman Church in the United States to urge their brethren in South

21. The Panama Congress represented seventeen countries, twenty denominations, together with seventy visitors. See Charles McFarland, *The Church and International Relations* (New York: Federal Council of Churches, 1917), 5:287; and William Adams Brown, *Toward a United Church: Three Decades of Ecumenical Christianity* (New York: Charles Scribner's Sons, 1946), 57, 61–62 (Brown corrects McFarland's number of official delegates from 305 to 235, save one visitor who appears to have dropped through the cracks!), 287–89.

22. See, for instance, Howard F. Cline, *The United States and Mexico* (Cambridge, MA: Harvard University Press, 1953), 136–59. Parallels between Wilson and Huerta on the one hand and George W. Bush and Saddam Hussein on the other are as startling as they are depressing.

23. Zabriskie, *Arthur Seldon Lloyd,* 191–92.

America to attend officially or unofficially." Would not the Roman Catholic Church's position in South America be weakened if they stayed away? On the other hand, if they decided to go to the congress, might they not "possibly gain a good deal of help?" Manning paid no heed. Instead, in October he sought to have the Board of Missions reverse itself again. He was defeated. And what of the reaction of the Roman Catholic Church in Central America? Before the conference opened, Protestant leaders established cordial relations with the local Roman bishop of Panama. At the meeting itself they effectively quashed anti–Roman Catholic resolutions and sought to foster goodwill.[24]

And the significance of the Panama Congress? Gardiner unwittingly supplied the answer. When it appeared that there would be no Episcopalian participation, that is, before Pepper and Lloyd had done their work, Gardiner wrote to the Reverend George Craig Stewart (as if Episcopalians would not be attending): "Panama gave the Church in the United States an opportunity for leadership which does not often occur." If only the Episcopal Church had displayed "statesmanship, another word for Christian humility and love," we might have "secured the cooperation, or at any rate the interest of Rome." As it was, he guessed wrongly, the church missed a "great opportunity to make [by its very presence] a Protestant Conference truly Catholic in spirit."[25] Instead, in their rejection, the *Living Church* and its allies have given the Roman Catholics "an excuse to remain outside." And, he added, we have irritated Protestants and led them to despise us as insincere. Episcopal churchmen went to Panama, but the damage had been done.

Notwithstanding, there were lessons to be learned. In his long letter of September 1915 to Stewart, the secretary went further, theorizing that all those who stand aloof and claim that they alone can be the one, true church, "occupy the distinctly ultramontane position of Rome, which is likewise, in real essence, substantially that of many Baptists . . . as well as of the bulk of the Eastern Churches." He wrote without equivocation: "So long as the Holy Spirit . . .

24. Schweinitz to Gardiner, November 21, 1921, Gardiner Correspondence. See John Seabrook, "William Thomas Manning: A Study of Christian Unity," *Historical Magazine of the Protestant Episcopal Church* 34:2 (June 1965): 158–61. Gardiner to Manning, September 7, 1915, Gardiner Correspondence; Zabriskie, *Arthur Seldon Lloyd,* 192. Manning's *Constructive Quarterly* article, asserting Anglican demands prior to any reunion discussions, appeared. Both damaged the World Conference cause (Zabriskie, *Arthur Seldon Lloyd,* 193).

25. Gardiner to Stewart, September 10, 1915; also to Rhinelander, September 17, 1915, Gardiner Correspondence.

speaks through human mouths, His message will be limited or even strained almost to distortion." Should one love the heretic and hate the heresy? It was an extremely dangerous maxim. "Who am I," asked Gardiner, "that I should presume to pronounce anything heresy?" It was almost impossible for human beings, he judged, "to avoid personifying the heresy in the heretic." Rather, he sought to inculcate love toward the "heretic" that should "drive me to the utmost effort to understand and sympathize with him. . . . Possibly I might find that he was not as darkened as I thought and even that my light is not as clear as I have been supposing." Let those who object to the FCC, to Kikuyu, and to the Panama Congress learn to look for "the essential value [in others], even though it may be no larger than a grain of sand." As before, the bottom line for him remained the "promotion of Christian love and sympathy and the absolute surrender of self-will and self-opinion, and earnest prayer for grace to seek and follow God's Will."[26] Either he was dissembling or he meant it; there was no middle ground.

In the meantime, ever since the Hotel Astor meeting in 1913, planning for a comprehensive North American conference had picked up. By it organizers meant to provide a model. The onset of the war the following summer only hastened their efforts. "Inevitably Faith and Order work in Europe and other parts of the world came almost completely to an end," wrote Tatlow. "It was only in North America that further progress was possible." Once again, Pepper was at the heart of it. Early in 1915 he chaired the Committee of Seven, appointed by the increasingly influential Advisory Council that was made up of representatives of all the participating bodies. From January 4 to January 6, 1916, sixteen churches, including Moravians, the Alliance of Reformed Churches, the Society of Friends, and one Canadian Anglican representative, met in Garden City, Long Island. There delegates launched the most direct effort to date to plan for the World Conference: the North American Preparatory Committee (NAPC). Their purpose was to collect materials for the World Conference and, as Gardiner wrote the English scholar Walter H. Frere, "to educate North American Christians in the art of conference as distinguished from that of controversy." The committee itself was enormous, 170 members from different denominational commissions and representing all the churches of the United States and Canada, including two Roman Catholics, Wynne and Pace, "two Armenians, . . . [and] two Russian priests." There was an executive committee whose secretary was, of course, Robert Gardiner. As he subsequently wrote revealingly to his

---

26. Gardiner to Stewart, September 10, 1915, Gardiner Correspondence.

English Quaker friend, the renowned Henry T. Hodgkin, "The matter [of the NAPC] has been left so largely in my hands that it seems to me I should devote my winter to establishing that Committee." But he needed help and sought it at the end of hostilities in the able young American army chaplain and later bishop of Massachusetts, Norman Nash. The true purpose of the NAPC, he told Nash, "is the body in charge of the immediate preparation for the World Conference."[27] Would not the young chaplain join him? "You and I would be more or less in a free position." Nash declined and went into schoolwork. Gardiner soldiered on.

In the meantime, between 1916 and 1919, the secretary went ahead with plans to incorporate into the world conference movement the two great blocks of Christians, Orthodox and Roman Catholic. Success varied. On the one hand, Eastern Orthodoxy was seen at first, particularly by Americans, as strange, exotic, foreign; the very word, the *Easterns,* which Gardiner and others employed, said as much. This sense of outlandishness was particularly true with respect to the Russian Orthodox Church whose world seemed barbaric to many Americans. The West, notes one historian, "considered Russian to lie on the edge of the civilized world." Americans loathed the Russian autocracy;[28] their religion was one of smoke and icons. The Orthodox returned the compliment: the very word *Protestant* raised in Constantinople and in St. Petersburg visions of a dry, assertive, and graceless aberration. To make matters worse, the Easterns were considered by American Evangelicals as fair game for conversion. When in 1914 Gardiner had informed the British Bible Society's Thomas Hodgson that a deputation was on its way to Constantinople and sought a conference with the

27. Tatlow, "The World Conference on Faith and Order," in *History of the Ecumenical Movement,* edited by Rouse and Neill, 414; see Gardiner, "Report by the Secretary of the Progress Made in the World Conference Movement," in *North American Conference, Garden City, Long Island, N.Y., January 4–6, 1916,* pamphlet 30, esp. 11, 17, 19–21. Specific items reported on have already been covered in this study. Gardiner to Frere, February 16, 1917; to Hodgkin, November 21, 1916; also to A. C. A. Hall, January 3, 1917; to Nash, December 26, 1918, Gardiner Correspondence. Nash went on to become bishop of Massachusetts and was considered by John E. Hines to be the most skillful debater in the Episcopal House of Bishops and "the one I would least like to cross swords with" (as told to the author, May 1954).

28. Richard Pipes, *The Russian Revolution* (New York: Vintage Books, 1991), xxi; George F. Kennan, *Russia Leaves the War: Society and American Relations, 1917–1920,* 1 vol. (Princeton, NJ: Princeton University Press, 1956), 28. Kennan draws attention to Woodrow Wilson's antipathy. However, when Russia became democratic (March to October 1917), Wilson's attitude changed (C. Howard Hopkins, *John R. Mott, 1865–1955* [Grand Rapids, MI: William B. Eerdman's, 1979], 476).

Orthodox, he was waved off with a clear warning. Those, like Hodgson, who were on the ground there, were in a "very delicate" position; they were in fact "condemned as a 'Protestant' Society in league with every attempt to win over converts from the Orthodox folk." Calls for a conference would be treated with the greatest suspicion by Orthodoxy's many uneducated clergy. Despite earlier contact with Eastern and Russian leaders, particularly by the Church of England but also by Anglo-Catholics at New York's General Theological Seminary, it was clear that the many troubled, chaotic, and isolated Orthodox churches (from each other as well as from the West) demanded careful and sympathetic advances.[29] Otherwise, the organizers of the World Conference would never get a hearing.

Brent was particularly worried by the "great danger" posed by Methodists who "already have a foothold in Russia & Baptists, but for their blundering mode of approach . . . would also be busy with a propaganda. . . . Russia ought to be protected somehow," he pleaded, "from the introduction of American schismatic Christianity." Gardiner was very much aware of the problem. He had already convinced his influential friend in Athens, Hamilcar Alivisatos, that the conference's promoters only purpose was "to lift up before the world the Historic Christ, the Incarnate Son of God, crucified, risen, and ascended." Through Alivisatos he aimed at the Orthodox bishops, who in their turn would take care of their priests' suspicions. The aim was good. Alivisatos did not disappoint. By 1919 the two of them had won the confidence and the commitment of the patriarchs of Constantinople, Alexandria, Jerusalem, and Antioch; of the bishops and archbishops of the churches in Greece, Cyprus, Serbia, Bulgaria, Armenia, and Romania; as well as the cooperation of the Coptic Church of Egypt. That Protestants and Orthodox succeeded in overcoming mutual suspicions as well as they did marks one of the brighter pages of twentieth-century church history.[30]

29. Hodgson to Gardiner, July 14, 1914, Gardiner Correspondence; Nicholas Zernov, "The Eastern Churches and the Ecumenical Movement in the Twentieth Century," in *History of the Ecumenical Movement,* edited by Rouse and Neill, 645–74, esp. 651.

30. Brent to Gardiner, July 13, 1917, Brent Papers; Joint Commissions Report, *Journal of the General Convention of 1919,* 590. All of these had appointed cooperating commissions or reported favorably or both; see Ecumenical Patriarch Meletios of Constantinople to Charles Anderson, April 11, 1919: "We are convinced that the purpose of the Conference is indeed holy, in accordance with the prayer of our Lord"; and Metropolitan Stephen Gheorghieff, archbishop of Sofia, to Gardiner, August 3, 1921: "We believe with childish sincerity in the idea which gathered us in Geneva" (Gardiner Correspondence). See also the Orthodox statement, *Church Quarterly Review,* July 23, 1923; and Brent to Gardiner, October 12, 1923, Gardiner Correspondence.

Anglicans, such as A. C. Headlam, H. J Fynes-Clinton, F. W. Puller, Frere, and above all the American Methodist John Mott, served as significant bridges.

The war itself helped. In a long, impassioned letter written in the summer of 1921, Stephan Gheorghieff, the Bulgarian Orthodox archbishop of Sofia, revealed how the recent, shocking carnage had made all Europeans aware of the "great affair of universal union . . . now to be performed under hard and painful conditions." The terrible war, the archbishop wrote, produced torrents of blood spilled, thousands of lives broken off, families ruined, and "poisonous tares of spite . . . have taken root in human hearts . . . nations and churches afflicted with misfortune." The first victims, he went on, were children and old persons. Russians suffered particularly from illness and hunger. "Is there a possibility for the Christian nations," the Bulgarian asked, "for the whole Christian universe to look at such things quietly and indifferently and to explain the non-intervention into the Russian tragedy by any reasons of international politics?"[31] Christians, he concluded, know only the politics of love toward neighbors. Or ought to. The letter itself, a cry for help, poignantly manifested the desire for unanimity and conciliation.

By November 1916 Gardiner reported to the Joint Commission that contact with the East outside of the war zone was increasing in volume and importance. He had corresponded with Archbishop Antonius of Kharkov and with Dean Turkevich of the Russian cathedral in New York; his friend Palmieri had published an article in *Bessarione,* titled "The Efforts for Doctrinal Agreement between the Russian Church and the American Episcopal Church."[32] That July the impressive and fiery Nicolai Velimirovic, of the Serbian legation in London, urged the Joint Commission to send simultaneous deputations to Rome and to Petrograd.[33] Velimirovic urged the New World to consult the Old. Brent, like Metropolitan Gheorghieff, saw difficult times as opportunities. After all, "When God began His great work of order, He began on chaos." Brent rejoiced that

31. Gheorghieff to Gardiner, August 9, 1921, Gardiner Correspondence. His question was answered by the extraordinary efforts of an American Quaker named Herbert Hoover; see David Burner, *Herbert Hoover: A Public Life* (New York: Alfred A. Knopf, 1971), chaps. 6–7; and Bertrand M. Patenaude, *The Big Show in Bololand: The American Relief Expedition to Soviet Russia in the Famine of 1921* (Stanford, CA: Stanford University Press, 2002).

32. Report of the Secretary to the Executive Committee, November 9, 1916, in *Report of the Joint Commission, 1916,* 99–100.

33. Velimirovic, who later became bishop of Ochrida, preached and celebrated the Eucharist in English churches during the war (Zernov, "Eastern Churches," in *History of the Ecumenical Movement,* edited by Rouse and Neill, 651).

the unfortunate "props and stays" of czarist government had gone and that the Russian Orthodox were "now thrown on their own resources and the Divine Spirit." Russian churchmen were fumbling about, trying to get their bearings in the new, unfamiliar, and fragile democracy. Now was the moment, Brent thought, to put "a big vision of a united Church . . . before them." He suggested a deputation to Russia be "resident . . . for some time." He had heard "Father Nicolai" (Velimirovic) give an address: the Serbian ecclesiastic "spoke of the need for the various national churches to GET OFF THEIR ISLANDS," a pungent euphemism deserving, Brent thought, block letters. The same day that the Philippine bishop wrote Gardiner from France, June 14, 1917, the Joint Commission approved the secretary's plan to send a letter to all Russian and Greek bishops and, further, "that a deputation to Rome, and also one to Petrograd, with power to confer also with the Communions . . . be appointed, to proceed with all convenient speed." It was not to be. Fearing the Russians would think it a pacifist deputation, President Woodrow Wilson vetoed it personally.[34]

In the end the veto did not much matter: Mott had already made astonishing progress. "I think Mott's visit to Russia and his influence with Protestants in this country," Gardiner wrote the worried Brent, "will avert any danger of influx of Protestants to Russia." His—Mott's—experiences in that country "were simply wonderful and he displayed his usual statesmanship and truly Catholic spirit . . . and urged loyalty to past traditions of the Russian Church." Mott addressed the Russian Sobor made up of the archbishops and metropolitans of the church. They listened with "the greatest intensity and with unmistakable sympathy." At a service at Kazan Cathedral, Mott and Wilsonian Democrat Charles R. Cane were singled out along with three other Americans, taken in behind the altar, given communion in both kinds, and presented with gifts of "very rare and priceless icons." Mott then had a number of long conversations with the government's overprocurator, V. N. Lvov. Later, Brent replied that "a mission of humility from our Church should go to Russia and sit at the feet of Archbishops Platon and Tikhon." But the Episcopal Church, Brent concluded that October, "is so hide-bound that it has but little vision and lacks shamefully in the spirit of adventure." In the meantime the persistent Mott

34. Brent to Gardiner, June 14, 1917, Brent Papers; Report of the Joint Commission, *Journal of the General Convention of 1917*, 162; Gardiner to Herbert Kelly, September 19, 1917; to Zabriskie, June 27, 1917; Zabriskie to Gardiner, July 5, 1917; Gardiner to Zabriskie, July 6, July 11, 1917; Zabriskie to Gardiner, July 14, 1917; Gardiner to Zabriskie, July 16, 1917; to Mott, July 23, 1917; to Fosbroke, August 1, 1917, Gardiner Correspondence.

assured Gardiner that there would be a follow-up to the friendships he had made in Russia. In the end even Stalin's dark persecution failed to stamp out the Russian church with which Mott and others had achieved such a good beginning. For his part, Gardiner took heart from signals he had received that the Easterns were tending toward closer unity with each other and with Anglicans as well.[35]

The Church of Rome was a different matter. If the Russian Orthodox were remote and preternatural, Rome was very much at hand, oppressive, they thought, and all too familiar. Protestant mistrust of making any contacts with the papacy surfaced almost immediately. Newman Smyth was "nervous about the Vatican," Gardiner wrote Peter Ainslie. "I don't think he quite realizes how preposterous it would be to talk about a World Conference without inviting Rome." Far from being a "fruitless flirtation," Gardiner pointed out that they could hardly speak of "world-wide Christian unity unless we are including the Communion which organically and numerically is the strongest in the world." If Methodists and Baptists objected to the inclusion, "we ought to suspend proceedings until we have convinced them that that is not the proper conference spirit." There were others, such as Professor Francis J. Hall, who agreed that going to Rome should be a first, not a last, step. Between them they carried the Joint Commission. It was the "unanimous judgment of our Commission," he wrote Tatlow in the spring of 1914, that "the Catholic world must be definitely and formally notified . . . [lest they] feel that they have not been shown due consideration." For his part, Tatlow thought it inadvisable to make any approach to Rome at such an early stage: "A formal approach would only mean a formal snub."[36]

Gardiner pressed on, however, telling his English friend that he had dispatched Manning to see the ecumenically knowledgeable John Murphy Cardinal Farley

35. Gardiner to Brent, August 14, 1917, Brent Papers. George F. Kennan, in his discussion of the Root Mission, claims that it "is difficult to discover any instance in which these missions had any appreciable[,] favorable effect on the course of events in Russia" (*Russian Leaves the War,* 21). Mott also got carried away when he addressed three hundred officers of the All-Russian Cossack Congress and told them, in effect, to go after the Germans on the eastern front; needless to say, reverberations in both the German-American press in the United States and reactions among Christians in Germany were anything but positive. See Hopkins, *Mott,* 498–501; Mott to the High Procurator of the Holy Synod, July 5, 1917, Gardiner Correspondence; Brent to Gardiner, October 4, 1917, Brent Papers; Mott to Gardiner, June 26, 1919; Gardiner to Mott, February 16, 1920, Gardiner Correspondence.

36. Gardiner to Ainslie, April 6, 1914; to Smyth, March 30, 1914; to Ainslie, April 6, 1914; Hall to Gardiner, December 12, 1914; Gardiner to Tatlow, May 21, 1914; Tatlow to Gardiner, April 22, 1914, Gardiner Correspondence.

of New York and Rhinelander to see Gibbons in Baltimore. The initially unreceptive Farley apparently "went very much further than either he or either of the other two Cardinals in this country had ever ventured before."[37] What the "further" occasioned he did not say. In 1911 the secretary began to seek out Roman Catholic leaders.[38] "The matter of our relations with Cardinal Gibbons," Gardiner wrote Zabriskie, "seem to me of very great importance." He was sure that Gibbons wanted to be in close touch. Artfully, Gardiner suggested that their "ambassador to [Gibbons] ought to be a lay man who will have no personal dignity which he is bound to worry about, and who is accustomed to negotiations, and recognizes the value of a close but informal personal relation." Did Zabriskie himself fulfill these requirements? he asked. Yes, indeed. But Zabriskie was already on the Joint Commission's Roman Catholic Committee. Were he to be appointed, Gardiner suggested rather slyly, others on that committee might be jealous. What to do? "Although it seems a little presumptuous, I am inclined to suggest that . . . you or Stetson should move that the Secretary be instructed to keep the Cardinal informed of our progress."[39] And so it was.

At the same time, he moved swiftly to establish wider contacts. He sent to Zabriskie a list of Roman Catholic laymen in New York from which that attorney was to make choices. He enlisted his friend John J. Wynne, S.J., who put him in touch with New York attorney Andrew J. Shipman, a Catholic Social Gospeler among Eastern European immigrants who was "an expert in liturgical matters." It was through Wynne and Edward A. Pace that Gardiner gained entrées to cardinals: to Farley; to the formidable William Henry O'Connell of Boston; to Désiré Joseph Mercier, cardinal archbishop of Malines, who became a friend and correspondent of ten years; and to Buenaventura Ceretti, with whom he organized a week of universal prayer for unity. At the Vatican he was also in touch with Cardinals Gasparri, with whom he corresponded in Latin, and Marini. The former was papal secretary of state; the latter was chairman of the cardinals'

---

37. Gardiner to Tatlow, May 1, 1914, Gardiner Correspondence.
38. A precedent existed in the cordial support for the Edinburgh Conference of 1910 by Bishop Geremia Bonomelli of Cremona, a personal friend of sometime *Churchman* editor Silas McBee. Oliver S. Tomkins, "The Roman Catholic Church and the Ecumenical Movement," in *History of the Ecumenical Movement,* edited by Rouse and Neill, 680; see also Joan Delaney, M.M., *From Cremona to Edinburgh: Bishop Bonomelli and the World Missionary Conference of 1910* (West Haven, CT: n.p., 1999).
39. Gardiner to Zabriskie, October 6, 1911, Gardiner Correspondence.

Commission on Christian Reunion. Marini had devoted time to bringing the Roman and Orthodox churches together and, Gardiner remarked, "has been of late very cordial about the World Conference movement."[40] He thought Marini's promotion to the cardinalate and to the chair of the Christian Reunion Committee signs that Benedict XV himself had cooperation at heart. Gasparri also had given him hope for the future, for this papal secretary of state was a famed canon lawyer who had once looked favorably on the validity of Anglican orders.

Through Edward L. Parsons in Berkeley, Gardiner gained an ally in Archbishop Edward J. Hanna, a widely respected American Catholic spokesman, scholar of broad learning, and friend of Walter Rauschenbusch. At the same time, he cultivated the Swiss-born Benedictine bishop Vincent Wehrle of Bismark, North Dakota, who invited the world conference leaders to his home, and the former Anglican Atonement father Paul Francis of Graymoor. Abroad, as we have seen, he was in constant touch with the learned Palmieri. There were others: the internationally known patristic scholar Monsignor Pierre Battifol who knew Gardiner and wrote publicly of "the interest which Pope Benedict XV has taken in the plans of American Episcopalians for union"; Abbe Lugan of the liberal French *Le Mouvement;* the archbishop of Paris; then to round out the picture there was Jules de Narfon, editor of *La Revue Hebdomadaire* (Weekly Review) and the editor of *Figaro* who were reporting on the World Conference movement. Gardiner was aided by a brace of knowledgeable Italians: Dr. Alesandro Favero, influential Catholic lawyer and friend of Italian Protestant Hugo Janni; Salvatore Cortesi; and Father Luigi Bietti, all of whom kept him abreast of Italian Catholic news. So the lawyer from Down East was optimistic. To Bishop Eduard Herzog of the Old Catholic Church in Switzerland, he wrote of the "steadily increasing interest and sympathy on the part of eminent individuals in the Roman Church throughout the world"; when the war is over, he felt, the chances of the pope accepting a direct invitation were good. To Wesleyan Methodist Sir Robert Perks, he explained that he had been

40. Gardiner to Zabriskie, December 9, 1912; to F. J. Hall, December 7, 1914; to Mercier, July 21, 1914, November 8, 1922, September 7, 1923, April 1, 1924 (Gardiner visited Mercier in August 1923); to Ceretti, July 27, 1917; to Gasparri, November 2, 1914; Gasparri to Gardiner, December 18, 1914, April 7, 1915; Gardiner to Brent, March 2, 1917, for positive comment on Marini; to White, February 13, 1917; to the bishop of London, A. F. Winnington-Ingram, March 10, 1917, Gardiner Correspondence. The week of universal prayer for unity was January 18–25, 1918.

in touch with an important Catholic layman and also with a priest who had separately declared "that Rome should abandon its attitude of isolation."[41]

That this was in fact occurring is beyond doubt. In early 1918 in *La Ciencia Tomista* (Thomistic Science), an article appeared, really an open letter to the Joint Commission, titled "The World Conference of All Christian Confessions." It was written and translated into English in Madrid by the editors of that publication and signed by Father Luis Getino. It was clearly an important document that drew attention to concessions made to the Orthodox at the Second Council of Lyons in 1274. The editors believed that "in behalf of unity... [those concessions] may serve for the measure of what she [the Roman Church] is ready to do in behalf of union with Protestants." The authors declared that in 1274 "rites, language and a whole class of rules of discipline... local religious autonomy... save as regards dogmas... everything was offered and conceded... the election of prelates, the marriage of priests, communion in two kinds, the use of unleavened bread, the liturgy in the vernacular." Nor was there to be interference in Orthodox affairs. Then came a most important admission: the church's "practice is to adopt only such initiatives as are serious enough to deserve [attention], and obviously this initiative (the World Conference) offers claims of special character." They went further: "We Catholic editors should take up this question in order that the masses may be imbued with the desire of *rapprochement*." They wanted Spanish Catholics to read the Episcopal statement of faith "accepted at Convention of Fond du Lac a few years ago at the beginning of the present century." They then reproduced the Episcopalian statement in Spanish. It included belief that

> the church was a divinely founded society with three orders of ministry in apostolic succession, that bishops alone should ordain, that Holy Scripture was the Word of God, that the church was the guardian of Holy Writ, that the decisions of the ancient ecumenical councils were normative, that liturgical worship should be in the language of the people, that there should be feasts and fasts, prayers for the departed, and the Christian year observed.

41. Gardiner to Wehrle, January 4, 1921; also to John Pointz Tyler, Episcopal bishop of North Dakota, January 4, 1921; to Wehrle, January 4, 1921, Gardiner Correspondence; Pierre Battifol, "The Russian Orthodox and the Roman Catholic Churches," *Churchman* (Milwaukee), July 7, 1917, translated by Robert H. Gardiner from *La Croix* (March 24, 1917); Gardiner to Brent, March 29, 1917, Brent Papers; to the Honorable William Phillips, assistant secretary of state, June 27, 1917; to Cortesi, October 11, 1919; to Palmer, September 22, 1920; to Herzog, March 20, 1916; to Perks, April 18, 1918, Gardiner Correspondence.

At the end of the essay came this promise: "Once the Roman Pontiff decides to submit to public oral and daily discussion all the doctrines . . . the most difficult step concerning participation of Catholics may be said to have been taken." Moreover, the "letter addressed to you by his Eminence Cardinal Gasparri, in the name of his Holiness, certainly augurs an understanding on that point."[42] It is little wonder that Gardiner was emboldened.[43]

Further encouragement came early the next year from Archbishop Hanna in San Francisco. He, Parsons, and Episcopal bishop Nichols held an extraordinary conversation over a leisurely dinner at Nichols's house. The ever-vigilant Parsons told Gardiner that "the Archbishop is pretty well determined to bring up the matter [of Roman participation in the World Conference] in some form before the meeting of the archbishops in the spring." They agreed on the scope and method of the conference, the necessity of small groups meeting beforehand, and of emphasizing what people had in common. "There is no doubt that Archbishop Hanna is very deeply interested. . . . He is essentially a large minded citizen in his views of the world and religion." Although Hanna thought studious people would accept the Roman point of view and that Protestantism was "down and out," he nevertheless wanted "to bring Christians together and help forward the movement."[44]

The omens from Belgium, France, Italy, Spain, and America were auspicious. For his part, from the very beginning Gardiner meant to accommodate Rome. He thought that the world conference should be held at the Vatican and at the invitation of the pope himself. Not only was Rome the proper place to meet, but "ordinary courtesy would suggest that the Pope or his representative should preside at the Conference." He wrote challengingly to Bishop A. C. A. Hall:

> I still think we might find some way of stating our readiness to recognize some kind of primacy in the See of Rome, provided it was subject to the democratic principles which seem to me to be a part of the Constitution of the Church, so as to safeguard the idea that the Pope might be the mouthpiece,

42. Luis Alonso Getino, *The World Conference of All Christian Confessions* (Madrid, 1918), 8, 9, 10, 11, 12, 21–22.

43. At the same time Gardiner had a long conversation with Cardinal O'Connor who thought the movement too Anglo-Saxon (in itself a positive reaction) but thought well of the deputations going to "Rome and the East and the rest of Europe"; he also wanted to help get them proper interpreters in Rome as well as letters of introduction. See Gardiner to Talbot Rogers, December 18, 1918, Gardiner Correspondence.

44. Parsons to Gardiner, January 10, 1919, Gardiner Correspondence.

without submitting our selves to the Roman position that he is not only the mouthpiece but practically the mind.

When necessary he defended the Roman Church. Noting to one suspicious Protestant correspondent that Gardiner himself was a vice president of the American Bible Society, he argued that "Rome claims the highest reverence for the Bible." He confided to Edward Pace that the foremost difficulty in making Protestants accept the inclusion of "the great Church of Rome is that they think that Rome will have nothing to do with them." The presence of Pace and Wynne in the movement "would go far toward convincing them that the Roman Church is really interested in the question of unity."[45]

But objections would not down. After reading Gardiner's correspondence with Cardinal Gasparri, Bishop J. E. C. Welldon of the Church of England had a point when he reminded the secretary that "the Church of the Petrine Claims, of the Index, the Inquisition, the Syllabus of the Vatican Council . . . is herself the principal bar to the reunion of Christendom." In 1916 Sir Robert Perks growled to Gardiner that nonconformist churches in Britain would have nothing to do with the Roman Catholic Church. A "powerful political propagandist association," it stood against the House of Commons, against civil and religious liberty, against the Allies in the war, and in favor of the Central Powers. As a result the Allies would not allow any influence by the pope in peace negotiations. "No one here cares one little bit whether the Church of Rome joins the movement [for the World Conference] or not." Even Gardiner's close associate Bishop Edwin Palmer of Bombay drew attention to "those elements of paganism in the Roman Church, which we cannot but observe with the deepest sorrow." To these and other objections the secretary responded that the prejudices of both sides were equally baneful: "We ourselves have been accused of occupying practically the same attitude as Rome [on papal infallibility] in insisting on the historic Episcopate." He did not think papal intransigence "is different to [sic] that of any other Communion." He found that "the attitude of our Baptist friends seems to be substantially that of Rome, except that the individual Baptists if driven into a corner would claim infallibility for themselves."[46]

45. Gardiner to Rogers, December 10, 1918; to Charles Anderson, January 4, 1919; to Cortesi, October 11, 1919; to Hall, January 11, 1918; to William Haven, June 18, 1918; to Pace, January 18, 1917, Gardiner Correspondence.
46. Welldon to Gardiner, August 3, 1915; Perks to Gardiner, March 24, 1916; Palmer to Gardiner, June 11, 1923 (what those elements were the bishop did not say); Gardiner to Welldon, August 19, 1915, Gardiner Correspondence.

What Gardiner failed to understand was that Baptists and Catholics, not to mention others in both camps, were like ships passing in the night: infallibility for the Baptists meant going back to the purity of New Testament times, to the apostolic and subapostolic churches, to ridding Christendom of the whole Constantinian baggage, and walking and talking with Jesus and his disciples alone. Standing close to the one who imparted grace through faith reassured the sinner not only that she was justified but that she was in the process of sanctification itself. By no means unheard of in Catholic circles, or in Anglican ones for that matter, such restitutionism remained below decks in the post-tridentine Roman church, at least until the advent of the Catholic charismatics in the late twentieth century.

To Roman Catholics, on the other hand, papal infallibility was the inevitable result of the guidance of the Holy Spirit in the development of dogmas already inherent in the church of the Apostles. To add was to enrich, to realize what was already implicit, and to grow in that grace that infused minds, language, bodies, sacraments, priestly orders, traditions, and material objects. Thus, the impulse to purify clashed with the need to enhance religious meaning, simplification with elaboration, reformation with cultivation. Gardiner was overly confident that "our points of difference are neither so numerous nor so insuperable as we had supposed . . . that often they are merely different points of view or different degrees of emphasis on a particular truth." Still, he clung to his "new spirit of loving sympathy."[47] He had a point. In addition, he knew, as we have seen, that it sounded too simple and that oversight and organization were paramount to success.

Then there was his cultivation of Archbishop Ceretti. In February 1919 he met the papal secretary for extraordinary ecclesiastical affairs, talked with him, then wrote him (in Italian), and delivered the letter by hand at dock side in New York as the archbishop was embarking for Rome. During Ceretti's stay in the United States, Gardiner's relations with him as well as with the American cardinals in general had been "so cordial" as to offer fresh hope that the Church of Rome might join the conference.[48] News that the pope had turned down similar participation in a "Pan-Christian Congress" must have referred, Gardiner thought, to the Life and Work conference of the Scandinavian bishops. He

47. Gardiner to Reginald Weller, May 21, 1914, Gardiner Correspondence.

48. Gardiner in fact had been in correspondence with Ceretti about the week of the special season of "Prayer for Unity" on the part of all Christians; see Gardiner to Ceretti, July 27, 1917, Gardiner Correspondence.

hoped so. "I can hardly believe that the Pope would have declined our invitation," he wrote Gilbert White, "before it was officially presented to him." Then in early May, as Gardiner was seeing off the American deputation, Ceretti and his entourage came up the gangplank of the *Aquitania*. Gardiner, who already knew both groups were sailing on the same ship, lost no time in introducing them all around, all, that is, except Bishop Anderson who unaccountably took to his cabin, preferring to meet the cardinal only after they were on the open sea. Ever the believer in proper attire, Gardiner was more chagrined, however, by the fact that Ceretti was "followed by an impressing [*sic*] array of Bishops, priests, and laymen—all in shining silk hats and their best coats. I told our Deputation they must buy silk hats as soon as they got to London."[49]

What of the letter itself to Ceretti? It contained all that we have read before from the pen of the secretary: the centrality of the Incarnation, the removal of barriers of prejudice, the desire to understand others' points of view, the exchange of views about the creeds of the various churches, discussion of the general question of order and polity, concluding with a brief review of churches that had already signed on. "Then I pointed out," Gardiner wrote Manning, "that the Conference would offer a great opportunity to the Church of Rome to display its affection for the whole of Christendom." Finally, he hoped the papacy would appoint delegates actually to prepare the plan and program of the conference. Ominously, Ceretti assured him that the Holy Father, "the rock upon which our Blessed Lord himself established His visible Church . . . opens wide his arms to receive all those . . ." The sentence trailed off, and the veil of ceremony and of dissimulation fell away. On May 27, 1919, the pope turned them down flat. He would appoint no delegates.[50]

There were three reactions in the ranks of the Episcopalian leadership. First, outright indignation: As the American deputation left the Vatican, a hitherto silent Bishop Reginald Weller "raised his fist to heaven and expressed his judg-

49. Gardiner to White, April 30, 1919. This is precisely what the pope did; Gardiner knew earlier Ceretti was to sail at the same time. See Gardiner to Archbishop Ceretti, February 20, 1919; and Ceretti to Gardiner, February 22, 1919. Gardiner felt it incumbent upon him to remain in the United States and maintain worldwide communications in the central office of the Faith and Order Movement. Gardiner to Zabriskie, March 18, 1919, Gardiner Correspondence.

50. Gardiner to Manning, May 2, 1919; to Anderson, May 2, 1919; Ceretti to Gardiner, May 6, 1919, April 4, 1919, Gardiner Correspondence. The papal statement is reproduced in Tatlow, "World Conference," 416.

ment on the Bishop of Rome in terms more forceful than complimentary." Anderson wrote Gardiner, "It was very soon apparent after we reached Rome that a negative decision had been reached. . . . We had very little opportunity of presenting the case in any round table manner." When they finally met Cardinal Gasparri, he "lifted his hands to heaven and exclaimed how he yearned for unity in one fold under one shepherd." The pope received them with enthusiasm: "Nothing could exceed the kindness and courtesy and consideration of us, and nothing could be more pointed than the positiveness of his declination to appoint delegates to the Conference." As they were escorted out of the papal presence, they were handed a typewritten statement of what the pope had just said. "It had all been written beforehand. So there you are, and there we all are."[51] They had gotten the runaround.

The second reaction on the part of the Episcopal leadership was resignation: What turned out increasingly to be the consensus was summed up by Brent: "For my part, it is quite a secondary matter as to whether Rome accepts or does not accept" any new invitation. Just because they chose to be "bad mannered and unchristian," he indicted, "does not for that reason excuse us from being good mannered and Christian." Fosbroke spoke up confidently for "the opportunity that lies before us with the rest of the world participating." The pope's "nicely-rounded conception of unity," he disparaged, "is an obstacle to participation in the conference no matter whether we urge on him another conception . . . or leave him in peaceful possession of his own idea."[52]

Third, rationalization: Gardiner himself landed here. He tried, no doubt for political reasons, to put a good face on a bad situation. He wrote George LaPiana, the Italian Catholic modernist then just starting his brilliant career in medieval history at Harvard, "We want to make it clear that we understand that from the Roman point of view the refusal of the Pope is entirely justifiable. . . . [W]e have not taken into account sufficiently in most of our correspondence the position Rome takes, and in consistence with her other doctrines is obliged to take, that the Church of Rome is the only Church, possessing present unity, and that it cannot assent to any equality, except by surrendering its position." While Gardiner's disappointment in the papacy's decision was great, he continued to

51. Brown, *Toward a United Church,* 60; Anderson to Gardiner, May 27, 1919, Gardiner Correspondence.

52. Brent to Gardiner, March 16, 1922; Fosbroke to Gardiner, November 26, 1919; Fosbroke to Ralph W. Brown, November 26, 1919, Gardiner Correspondence.

hope that the Vatican would change its mind. Throughout his remaining years he kept the door open by regular correspondence with Mercier, LaPiana, Father Luigi Bietti, Wynne, and Palmieri.[53]

Did Gardiner go too far in defending Rome? Dean Fosbroke thought so. After they were turned down by the pope, Fosbroke wrote that Gardiner had given the impression of apologizing for Rome's defection. Gardiner confided to Brent that they had perhaps given too much publicity to Roman inclusion. Of those Protestants "who are violently opposed" to any Catholic presence, he agreed "that they must be converted, but I don't think we shall have so good a chance to convert them if we begin by stamping on their pet corns." At times the secretary's toughness surfaced. To Professor Edward Rohde at the University of Uppsala, he wrote that henceforth Catholics were ordered to take no part in the conference and that as a result the pope's decision "definitely aligns Rome against all the rest of Christendom."[54]

Though his indignation was reluctant, he was not deficient in political discernment. To Eduard Herzog he asserted that the pope's decision "was a great disappointment to a good many eminent Catholics in Europe and America . . . [but his] refusal may be an advantage, for it will remove . . . the question of infallibility which is one of the deep divisions between Rome and the rest of Christendom." A month later Gardiner was suspicious that the Catholic Church for its part was in "a more or less active campaign against us. . . . I am told that they hope to detach the Eastern Orthodox Churches from the Conference, on the plea that the result of the Conference will be to weaken the Christian Faith."[55] Increasingly, he went on, Rome seeks to make papal infallibility the only basis of reunion. And he sought out knowledgeable people for advice and counsel.

In August 1919 LaPiani warned Gardiner that the papacy was fearful of Protestant influence. The YMCA had been giving out unauthorized (by the

53. George H. Williams, "Professor George LaPiani (1878–1971): Catholic Modernist at Harvard (1915–1947)," *Harvard Library Bulletin* 21:2 (April 1973). LaPiani believed and often remarked that the church "was at its best when it had a powerful laity to oppose clericalism" (135). Gardiner to LaPiana, September 25, 1919; to Mercier, December 30, 1919, November 9, 1922, September 7, October 25, 1923, February 23, April 1, May 9, 1924; to LaPiani, September 25, 1919; to Boyd Vincent, December 26, 1919; for Wynne, see Gardiner to Fosbroke, November 1, 1922; other references are in Gardiner to Brent, March 27, April 1, 9, 1924, Gardiner Correspondence.

54. Fosbroke to Ralph W. Brown, November 26, 1919, Gardiner Correspondence; Gardiner to Brent, March 6, 1922, Brent Papers; to Edward Rohde, August 13, 1919, Gardiner Correspondence.

55. Gardiner to Herzog, July 10, September 3, 1919, Gardiner Correspondence.

Vatican) versions of the Bible during the war. The pope meant to "suffocate from the beginning the possibility of a Protestant revival in Italy and France." To make the "Catholic masses understand that the work of the World Conference was merely a Protestant device to entice Catholics, nothing could do better than a decree like the one issued by the Pope." The next step, LaPiani suggested, "is to stir up the feelings of the Orthodox against the *Protestant menace*." Lurking in the background, the professor went on, was Italian resentment of the short shrift the Allies had given Italy at the Versailles Conference. That in turn fed Italian—and papal—fears of Anglo-American predominance, the shabby, secret purpose, they suspected, of the World Conference movement itself. But LaPiani only reinforced views that the secretary already entertained. As early as 1917 he suspected that the Roman Catholic Church might try to torpedo the world conference movement by appealing directly both to Protestants and to the Russian Orthodox Church. "I have reason to suspect," Gardiner wrote Fosbroke, "that possibly the Pope is contemplating some move, perhaps in the nature of stealing our thunder." He added, "I think it would be most unfortunate, for he could hardly reach Protestants, as we have done, and unless the Revolution [in Russia] has put the conservative Russians hopelessly in the background, I doubt if Russia would respond to his appeal." Toward the end of his life, Gardiner grew more pessimistic about the Roman Catholic Church: "I doubt whether the cooperation of the Pope so long as the Papacy is in the hands of the Italian Curia is desirable," he wrote Palmer in the summer of 1923. "The differences between Romans and Anglicans are far deeper than orders or the advantage of a single executive."[56]

This postwar history shows one large matter very clearly: the center of the world conference movement was shifting from the United States to Europe. And there it would remain for the next thirty years under the leadership of a younger generation of Europeans.[57] No longer would the conferences with their plans and exhortations be in New York, Panama, or Garden City, but in

56. LaPiani to Gardiner, August 12, 1919; Gardiner to Fosbroke, August 1, 1917; to Palmer, August 11, 1923, Gardiner Correspondence.

57. Some of those already noted are Hamilcar Alivisatos, Nathan Soderblom, Tissington Tatlow, William Temple, G. K. A. Bell, H. N. Bate, and the archbishop of Athens and later patriarch of Alexandria, Meletios Mataxakis. Others were Ruth Rouse of the SCM, Bishop Stephen Charles Neill, W. A. Visser't Hooft of the Netherlands, Sergius Bulgakov (dean of the Orthodox Theological Institute in Paris), Professor Donald M. Baillie of St. Andrew's, Bishop Yngve Brilioth of Vaxjo, Sarah Chakko of the Syrian Church of India, Bishop V. S. Azariah of Dornekal, and the French scholar Suzanne de Dietrich, to name a few.

Canterbury, Geneva, Stockholm, Lausanne, and, on the other side of the globe, in Adelaide. There talks on reunion had taken a positive turn, so that Gardiner wrote Methodist bishop George Hall, "I am constantly watching negotiations for union in Australia with constant interest ... and trust you will keep me constantly informed."[58] However immediately successful or unsuccessful, both Mott's trip to Russia and Anderson's and Weller's to Rome and the Near East were indications of where the action would be.

After the misery and desolation of the Great War, Christians in Europe picked up on the cause of reunion. It gave a measure of hope to a shattered generation. As a result of it the Church of England emerged from its insularity. At the Lambeth Conference of 1920 amid scenes of fervent aspiration delegates rallied to the "Appeal to All Christian People." Under the leadership of the archbishop of York, Cosmo Gordon Lang, the church's isolation of which Gardiner had complained so often, was cast aside. Henceforth churchmen would no longer go it alone. The words of the appeal reflected the careful attention given by the 252 Anglican bishops to the "grave deliberations to which after solemn prayer and Eucharist, we have for five weeks devoted ourselves day by day." Delegates were bound together by a single, simple idea that motivated them all: world fellowship. "Men never prized the universal fellowship of mankind as they did when the Great War had for the time destroyed it." The four terrible years, the penitent bishops declared, had shown them the value of what they had heretofore ignored. People of "different classes and most various traditions" had been thrown together. In the midst of danger and death they had discovered the power of comradeship. Specifically singling out how "trade unions and other societies had changed the face of industrial life ... [binding] together workers in science, education, and social reform," they claimed on behalf of all "a fuller, freer life." That life was to be found in the Great Commandment to love both God and neighbor. They noted that in the midst of despair arose occasions for "the most conspicuous triumphs of love." The one that offered itself to the delegates at Lambeth, in 1920, was the realization that they "must take into account every fellowship that exists among men." For the church to act as a model it must "consider how the bands of its own fellowship are loosened and broken."[59]

The times demanded a new approach to the reunion of divided Christen-

---

58. Gardiner to Hall, August 9, 1920, see also March 12, 1920, Gardiner Correspondence.
59. "Lambeth Conference Encyclical Letter," *Churchman,* September 4, 1920, 14–16 and variously.

dom, one based not on the claims and positions of two or more uniting communions but "by their correspondence to the common ideal of the Church as God would have it to be." Sharing in "common faith, common sacraments, and a common ministry... toward this ideal of a united and truly Catholic Church ... we must set our minds."[60] And episcopacy? The bishops certainly saw a place for the historic episcopate in a united church. They went on to claim, not unreasonably as they hoped, that bishops themselves were the one means of providing this historic episcopate. "If the authorities of other Communions should so desire, we are persuaded that ... our Communion would willingly accept from these [same] authorities a form of commission ... which would commend our ministry to their congregations." It is not the place of this study to get into the complicated history of negotiations regarding the ministry, including ordination and episcopacy, and how the Lambeth appeal worked itself out in practice. For our purposes, there are just four points to be made. First, the Anglican bishops, led by the Church of England, opened a new era in church relations. Second, the appeal itself became a touchstone for the future debates that its promulgation set off. Third, and by no means least, it made recognition of other ministries and other churches a paramount conviction within the ranks of Anglicans themselves. Fourth, the fact that the appeal moved directly to the subject of the episcopate made the task of the world conference people more difficult. They did not want that issue raised until after people had had a chance to discuss both the nature of the church and that of the Christian ministry as a whole. "We must make clear," wrote Edwin Palmer, "that the World Conference is quite a different firm from the Lambeth Conference and that our work is not going to be stopped even if there is trouble about the Lambeth Appeal."[61] On the other hand, even while many, such as Vermont's A. C. A. Hall, would strongly disagree with the appeal, the die had been cast—irrevocably: the Church of England meant business when it spoke of a wider fellowship.

At first Gardiner was not altogether convinced of the appeal's place in the slower-moving process of convening a world conference. As we have seen, he wanted discussions of larger subjects before there was any recommendation about episcopacy. Canterbury and York, he wrote Brent, "went ahead altogether too fast." Brent disagreed. Was Gardiner a little put out that an English archbishop had become the prime mover? Then too the appeal opened up the possibility of

---

60. Ibid., 15.
61. Palmer to Gardiner, May 3, 1921, Gardiner Correspondence.

endless objections to the supposed weakening of episcopal authority in the con-
servative church press. Still, Gardiner meant to get as much mileage out of the
Lambeth declaration as he could. He wrote Cosmo Lang that interest in the
Faith and Order Movement "seems to have slackened in the United States, and
so far as I have learned only a half a dozen of our Bishops are taking particular steps toward enforcing the Lambeth Appeal." Would Lang write for the
*Churchman* of the "importance of the Appeal and of the necessity that the
Anglican Communion should support it actively and promptly?" Clergy had
failed to notice that "fellowship in Christ is the fundamental note of the Lambeth Appeal, and the only hope of the solution of the problems . . . which harass
the world." A year later Gardiner was glad to see press reports from England
about the positive reception of the appeal. He wanted "to urge it on the attention of the Church in conjunction with the World Conference on Faith and
Order."[62]

The second and more permanent sign that control of matters was moving
across the Atlantic from west to east were the twin Geneva conferences both of
August 1920, the one for Life and Work, the other for Faith and Order. At
Geneva, Soderblom and Gardiner, respectively, played the leading roles. In the
spring of 1919 in order to devote full time to the international scene, Gardiner
resigned as secretary of the Episcopalians' Joint Commission.[63] On November
20, 1919, in New York City, Episcopalians, Baptists, Congregationalists, Disciples of Christ, Friends, Moravians, Presbyterians and Reformed in both the
United States and Canada, United Lutherans, along with the Orthodox Armenians, Greeks, and Bulgarians instructed Secretary Gardiner, now of the international Continuation Committee, upon the completion of the Life and Work
conference, to call a preliminary meeting of the Faith and Order assembly. The
meeting would enlist worldwide representation. It would determine where and
when the World Conference on Faith and Order itself would be held, decide
the bases of representation by the participating denominational commissions,
and conclude what subjects would be dealt with. Everywhere the secretary was

62. Gardiner to Brent, August 14, 1922; Brent to Gardiner, August 16, 1922; Brent Papers;
Gardiner to Lang, September 24, 1921; to Charles MacFarland, January 5, 1921; to Palmer,
August 25, 1921; see also to Samuel Mather, May 31, 1921, Gardiner Correspondence; Gardiner
to Brent, August 10, 1922, Brent Papers.
63. See Gardiner to Talbot Rogers, April 11, May 19, 1919, Gardiner Correspondence.
Rogers was made secretary of the commission; Gardiner remained secretary of the North American Preparation Committee.

involved: in disseminating information about the preliminary meeting, communicating with the various commissions, arranging for speakers to make the preliminary effort at the better-known denominational assemblies, and issuing invitations to churches the world over. The planning was formidable.

At the very beginning of the process it became evident that Germany and Central Europe presented the biggest problem. Although the proximity of Geneva made it possible for impoverished representatives of Central European churches to attend, resentment at what seemed a gathering of the victors in the Great War surfaced immediately. With foresight Gardiner had enlisted neutrals in the task of approaching the German-speaking churches: Soderblom in Sweden, Herzog in Switzerland, Adolf Keller of the Swiss Federation of Churches, and Ernst Staehelin of the University of Basel. The procedure was beset with troubles. Staehelin refused to help. The Basel professor spoke bitterly of the crime of "the blockade [that] continued after the armistice." Certainly, Gardiner knew the statistics, Staehelin judged, "and if not I can send you some." An unnecessary torment had been inflicted on the living and on the unborn. Those who had personal experience of the lack of food "must be horrified ... and cannot find any right [on the part of the victors] to stretch out the hand of reconciliation before this barbarism is openly regretted."[64]

The second crime, Staehelin complained, was the peace treaty itself. Germans had trusted Woodrow Wilson and his Fourteen Points, "but he was too weak against the evil." The conditions of peace were a "terrible delusion to those who put their trust in him." True communion between former enemies was impossible "as long as this disloyalty is not confessed and repented." The treaty of peace had not only broken the power and wealth of Germany but also "done manifold damage to the kingdom of Christ." August Lang, professor of the theological faculty at the University of Halle, warned Gardiner, "Your movement will not enter in the hearts of German Christian people if fair words do not become deeds." Gardiner and his associates were "responsible for every destruction of the kingdom of Christ through your politicians and their hatred against Germany and German people." Gardiner thereupon sent him money to go to the Geneva Conference.[65]

64. See Gardiner to Soderblom, November 21, 1919; to Keller, August 14, 1919; Keller to Gardiner, September 24, 1919; and Staehelin to Gardiner, November 13, 1919, Gardiner Correspondence.

65. Staehelin to Gardiner, November 13, 1919; August Lang to Gardiner, December 4, 1919, June 22, 1920, Gardiner Correspondence.

The American's response was firm: the rights and wrongs of the war and the conduct of the Allies are, "of course, outside the scope of our Commission, whose only duty is to invite all the churches throughout the world ... to unite in preparing the World Conference." He deplored the suffering that "so many millions have endured in Europe since the Armistice" and trusted that the causes of that suffering would be removed. But there were two sides to the dispute: Germany, he argued, still had a large army ready for action at any moment. If that being so, harshness was justified. He ended with a challenge: "I believe the existing divisions among Christians are fundamentally responsible for the deplorable conditions of the world." In the meantime he cultivated more leaders in Germany: D. W. Freiherr von Pechmann, president of the Bavarian General Synod; Lutheran general superintendent Dietrich Kaftan of Baden-Baden; Pastor H. G. W. Mosel of the Old Prussian Union of the Evangelical Church; and the Roman Catholic Prince Alois Lowenstein.[66]

With these and with Friedrich Siegmund-Schultze at the University of Berlin he fared better, at least personally. Did Siegmund-Schultze remember him? Would he help with names and addresses for the Geneva meeting? He hoped "that the friendship which I trust we established at Constance may be deepened and strengthened." Siegmund-Schultze did indeed remember Gardiner. The Berlin professor declared that the "Constance Conference ... made it easier for me and many others to hold fast to our inner community with the Christians of other nations during the entire war." Now that peace had come everyone had a deeper obligation than that "of accusing and strafing one another." He was glad that in Germany "the recognition of guilt for the war is deepening, and thereby an example is given to others of how estrangement can be cleared away only by means peculiar to Christianity." Still at the present moment, he added three months later, "the enormous amount of falsity and calumny with which our Fatherland and our Church have been persecuted ... would mean for Evangelical Germany at present a downright lie to treat of questions of Christendom in common with the representatives" of churches in enemy countries. German and German-Swiss missionaries had been prevented in areas occupied by the Allied powers, a "very grievous prejudice of the missionary command of

---

66. Gardiner to Staehelin, December 9, 1919; for another discouraging letter regarding German Christians, see Gardiner to Tatlow, May 5, 1920; also to Palmer, June 21, 1921; to Mosel, January 5, 1923; and to Lowenstein, October 25, November 16, 1921, Gardiner Correspondence.

Jesus Christ." The Deutscher Evangelischer Kirchenausschuss therefore "finds itself not in a position to accept the invitation."[67]

Gardiner kept chipping away at the hard stone of animosity. In the end Siegmund-Schultze not only went to Geneva but took August Lang with him. They then reported back to the churches of Germany with positive effect.[68] The next year German commitment to church unity was greatly enhanced by a major address before the Association of Reformed Churches in Germany encouraging German participation in the World Conference movement by Lutheran A. W. Schreiber, who had himself been at Geneva.[69] By January 1921, August Lang had received from Gardiner no less than five letters in four months. Lang apologized for his "long silence. . . . I have spoken to crowded meetings on the days of Geneva not only here in Halle . . . but also at a meeting of the Saxon Provincial Synod. . . . I have [also] begun to write a series of articles upon the questions of the reunion of the churches." German minds were still distressed, Lang continued, and averse to anything that comes from the Anglo-Saxon world, so "we must first be content, if we prepare slowly the spirit of our country to a deeper inclination for the great Faith and Order thoughts."[70] It was a clear victory.

With Germany safely aboard Gardiner began to reach across the globe and to refine his and others' thinking about plans and purpose. He wrote one Indian churchman that "the meeting at Geneva . . . was attended by delegates from forty countries, representing eighty churches, including several from India . . . Dr. S.K. Datta [and] the Bishop of Bombay." Both Gardiner and Tatlow were keen on having native clergy representing their own countries. He was careful to explain the purposes of the Geneva meeting. All were to be free to express the idea and aims of the movement with respect to their standards of faith and order. The preliminary assembly needed to tackle a series of questions: What larger groups should be represented? How far can these churches that hold certain

67. Siegmund-Schultze to Gardiner, December 19, 1919, March 12, 1920, Gardiner Correspondence.
68. See Siegmund-Schultze to Gardiner, March 26, 1920; Gardiner to Siegmund-Schultze, April 24, 1920; and Siegmund-Schultze to Gardiner, October 9, 1920, Gardiner Correspondence.
69. Edward L. Parsons, "The Apostles' Creed, Church Unity and Internationalism: A German View," typescript, October 17, 1921, Gardiner Collection. In itself unusual for a Lutheran to speak before a Calvinist convention, Schreiber's address was full of references to the Apostles' Creed as the "common flag" of Christian faith, thus emphasizing the unity not only between Lutherans and Reformed but with Anglicans as well.
70. Lang to Gardiner, January 6, 1921, Gardiner Correspondence.

beliefs in common act in common? How will the actual world conference be composed so as to include adequate representation of communions? What preparation will be required? What will be the date and place of the ultimate conference? Most important, as he asked Tatlow, where will the organizing power reside? In a large, representative committee? Or in "a very small Executive Committee with a central office?"—at Gardiner, Maine, or Golders Green, London? "Shall there be one or more Executive Secretaries in either case?" Finally, there were besides the Continuation Committee two others set up at Geneva: the Subjects Committee and the Finance Committee. He asked Tatlow to "criticize and improve these rough notes." He wanted William Temple in Geneva. He acknowledged delightedly that England "is [now] as impatient as it used to fear America was." He looked forward to arriving in London in July, not only for the run-up to the Geneva conference but in order to have talks with S. K. Ratcliffe, editor of the *Sociological Review,* and with his young friend Lord Robert Cecil, then poised for a distinguished career in politics. The two would discuss, Gardiner hoped, the League of Free Nation's Association, of which he—Gardiner—was treasurer and on whose executive committee he sat.[71]

On August 23 he wrote William Manning: "The Conference is over, and we all feel that it was a great event in the progress toward reunion." The claim was modest enough. The days of persuasion alone were over. To carry the movement forward, new machinery was in place. Geneva in fact set the stage for future relations among the churches. No longer would they be a haphazard jumble. The intervening years down to the actual world conference itself at Lausanne in 1927 were to be the last of American oversight.[72] The many were to take over what the few had begun. But not just yet. The makeup of the all-important Continuation Committee, he told Manning, was still Episcopalian: "Brent is Chairman, Zabriskie is Treasurer and I am Secretary" and Manning himself a member of the committee. There were forty others, "representing all the important churches and most of the important countries." Unlike the general American political withdrawal from Europe and the rest of the world in the 1920s, churchmen and -women in the United States greatly strengthened their international ties.

71. Gardiner to Yohan Masih, September 7, 1920; to Tatlow, April 23, February 18, March 30, May 5, June 22, 1920, Gardiner Correspondence. The League of Free Nations Association was the American equivalent of the British League of Nations Union.

72. Gardiner to Manning, August 23, 1920, Gardiner Correspondence. Brent suggested 1925 in Washington, D.C., as the time and place for the first official meeting of the World Conference on Faith and Order. It was not to be. See Brent to Gardiner, March 5, 1922, Brent Papers.

During 1921 and into February and March 1922 Brent and Gardiner went
to work on topics to be considered prior to the world conference and on preliminary organization. The original drafting of the work sheets appears to have
been Brent's, the ordering of the notes Gardiner's. Whatever the case, between
them they came up with a clear plan. On the subjects to be discussed locally
and denominationally they adhered to the no-ultimatum principle. Broad and
basic matters were to be dealt at the beginning carefully and deliberately. Clergy
and laity were encouraged to discuss the origin, history, meaning, and value of
church, creeds, and confessional statements. "Fundamentals . . . should be dealt
with before proceeding to discuss" other matters. Those other matters were the
nature of the dominical sacraments and "other sacramental rites and obser-
vances"; the origin and history of the Christian ministry, the transmission of
orders and their historic variations, the origin and history of liturgical forms "as
expressions and guides of Christian experience," together with the place of
extempore prayer.

Gardiner created a working paper on organization from Brent's notes.[73] It
contained exact suggestions to local churches, presbyteries, bishops and dioceses,
commissions, and interchurch agencies about procedure and preparation. Brent
wanted "one programme for all Commissions in every Church." Between them
they meant to use existing orders: Episcopal dioceses, they tendered, were good
units to employ. They suggested that three or four groups be selected to go
around any given diocese, district, or presbytery. They urged interchurch conferences made up of both clergy and laity as well as small intercommission
conferences to discuss carefully worked out agendas. "What should be done
here [in the United States] is already being done in England and Scotland, and
done seriously."[74] It could be carried out, they added, in most countries. Insis-
tently, they asked that the program for the world conference "be sketched out
now and placed in the hands of all Commissions." With help from Fosbroke
they added for good measure another list of subjects: the "meaning of unity as
touching matters of faith; the place of creeds in a united church, the function
of confessional statements; the Bible in relation to the church, to the creeds;
church membership, its qualifications and meaning, and what constitutes an

73. ["Drafted by Bishop Brent"], "Topics for Consideration Preliminary to the Meeting of
the World Conference on Faith and Order in Washington, U.S.A. in the year 1925" (typed copy
by Gardiner, n.d. but probably February 1922), Brent Papers.

74. Gardiner and Brent, "World Conference on Faith and Order," typed copy, February 27,
1922, Brent Papers, 4.

authoritative ministry." Wisely, Fosbroke pressed them not to suggest books to be read, especially those on the nature of the church itself, lest they seem to push a particular point of view.[75]

Then on April 20, 1922, Gardiner was taken seriously ill. Overwork and discouragement with the American religious scene no doubt contributed. He was worn out. Pepper's resignation from the Joint Commission was a blow. The Philadelphia attorney and shortly to become United States senator had lost heart: "Neither clergy nor laity of anyone of the churches," he wrote to Gardiner, "really *want* unity... and they can't be made to want it." The secretary wrote Boyd Vincent that the principal difficulty was that "most of us in America, and especially our own Commission have tired of the game." Americans, he imagined, were very apt to take up a new idea "as a new plaything, but after a little while it grows wearisome, and then we drop it." He confessed to Anderson in January 1922 that the conference movement "seems to have come to a standstill in the United States, although very active all over the rest of the world." In a long letter to Manning, Gardiner protested that he was "almost ready to throw up the sponge about this World Conference movement." There had, he believed, "been a great increase in sectarianism [in the United States] since the war." The desire for unity had "disappeared almost entirely from the United States." To the ever-faithful Edwin Palmer of Bombay he confided, "The past six months have been ... the most trying and difficult of the twelve years since the World Conference movement was begun ... [W]e found it impossible to get any real interest in the United States ... as long as the ... [date] for the meeting was left in the vague and distant future." Since the appointment in August 1920 of the Continuation Committee, Bishop Anderson, he complained, seemed to think that denominational commissions were unimportant. "The Continuation Committee is helpless," he avowed, "without the aid of all the various [other] commissions." Later, he assured Anderson himself that while he had resigned from the Episcopal Church's Joint Commission for the World Conference on Faith and Order, he intended to "hang on as Secretary of the Continuation Committee as long as they can endure me."[76]

75. See in particular Gardiner to Brent, March 15, 16, 1922, Brent Papers.
76. I have been unable to ascertain the nature of the illness. That it was exacerbated by overwork appears certain. The Philadelphia attorney continued to be pessimistic about church unity (Pepper to Gardiner, September 7, 1921). Gardiner pleaded in vain with his friend to change his mind; see Gardiner to Pepper, September 9, 1921. Pepper to Gardiner, September 7, 1921; Gardiner to Vincent, August 11, 1921; to Anderson, January 12, 1922; to Manning, January 23,

Still, he could not believe that they would fail to revive interest: "The movement has been so signally blest." But he and Brent were having their troubles selling even the Episcopal dioceses on their plans for miniconferences. He wrote to Palmer that they had to spend too much time teaching the conference method and then how to apply it, "first to the discussion of the questions considered at Geneva and then of those proposed by the Subjects Committee." If the results of their first inquiries were disappointing, "we must keep on trying." Palmer replied in kindly fashion, "Buck up! Don't be discouraged. . . . I don't think we need be depressed about the [Geneva] Conference." The next year Brent also tried to cheer the secretary with the reminder that a person "is more untrammeled when he is dependent only on God & what he is, than when he is trying to be God. Anyhow that was Christ's way & ought to be good enough for the rest of us."[77]

It was clear, however, that the decline in interest in and support for the world conference was linked with the general disengagement by the people of the United States from the issues and politics of the larger world: the Senate's rejection of the Versailles Treaty, the nation's failure to join the League of Nations, the rejection of Wilsonian idealism, the "Red Scare," the resurgence of radical racism as evidenced by the revival of the Ku Klux Klan, and the intensification of nativist sentiments that led to congressional limits on the size and type of immigration into the country. The banners of reform were being furled.

For Robert Gardiner, there was the additional problem of money. He had always thought right along that they should be raising funds for the world conference. The Joint Commission did not think it necessary. In his lengthy epistle to Manning he avouched that "for eleven years the movement has cost me personally so much money that I am now the largest contributor next to the two Morgans." He was unwilling to advance more to "a sleeping movement." They were, he emphasized, in a "desperate condition." In November 1922 he reported to the Continuation Committee that he was owed $7,800 that he had spent from his own pocket, a sum that would increase by the end of the year to $12,074.24. He wrote F. M. Kirby of the F. W. Woolworth Company that as America had most of the wealth of the world, little financial help could be expected from

1922; to Mott, August 14, 1922; to Fosbroke, March 1, 1923; to Palmer, August 22, 1922; to Anderson, May 1, 1922, Gardiner Correspondence.

77. Gardiner to Palmer, February 16, 1921; Palmer to Gardiner, April 11, 1921, Gardiner Correspondence; Brent to Gardiner, September 25, 1922, Brent Papers.

Europe and elsewhere. Still, small amounts of money were coming in: "fifty dollars from Mexico from the Chinese Church . . . thirty dollars from an Old Catholic Bishop in the Netherlands . . . [and] a money order from Nyasaland for 3s 6d." The sum of $50,000 a year was needed to run the Continuation Committee. When he had asked American friends to help him raise money, he told Kirby, they "regretfully but with one accord declined for various reasons and the burden of the work falls upon me." With a final acid comment he laid down to Brent, "As far as I can make out from the . . . Church papers of the last meeting of the [Executive] Council, the smart Alecks on the Finance Committee made no appropriation for the World Conference for 1923, 1924 and 1925."[78] And so it went.

Added to the hornetlike problems of Episcopalian participation and money were gnats such as that provided by the persistently negative A. C. A. Hall. When Hall objected to the Lambeth appeal, Gardiner wrote Manning that it was probably better to let Hall "make a commotion" now than later. Then there was the uninterrupted opposition to church unity of the *Churchman* and the *Living Church*. Both continued to argue against Episcopalian membership in the FCC, which in light of the Geneva Conference made Gardiner and Brent's task all the more difficult. The letters from Frederick C. Morehouse of the *Living Church* were, Gardiner complained, nasty and disagreeable. Morehouse thought Brent "exaggerates the immediate necessity for unity." Brent's "unity at any price" struck him as the equivalent in national terms of "peace at any price." Morehouse concluded that Brent's "exaggerated idea" did not help toward the goal, "it only helps toward hysteria." In a letter dripping with mock horror, Gardiner wrote Brent in January 1923:

> I am getting a little distressed about you and it may be my painful duty to
> report you to the Editor of the Living Church whose policy with regard to

78. Gardiner to Manning, January 23, 1922, Gardiner Correspondence; see also January 11, 1922. "Report to the Continuation Committee," typescript, November 23, 1922, Library of Congress, Washington, D.C.; the current equivalent of twelve thousand dollars in 1922 would be approximately three hundred thousand dollars today; Gardiner to Kirby, February 23, 1922, Gardiner Correspondence; to Brent, January 2, 1923, Brent Papers. Money matters are dealt with in the following: Zabriskie to Gardiner, May 9, 1914, calling for "a common fund" to which all churches contribute; Gardiner to Zabriskie, December 27, 1920; to Ainslie, March 17, August 9, 1921; to Anderson, April 28, 1921; to Vincent, July 5, 1921; to White, December 6, 1921, June 4, 1923; to J. P. Morgan Jr., January 11, 1923; to Manning, March 8, 1921, January 11, March 8, 1922; to Fred Luke Wiseman, March 27, 1923; Ralph Brown to Vincent, December 1, 1922, Gardiner Correspondence.

Christian unity seems to be to make himself as offensive as possible to his Protestant brethren and would, therefore, be deeply grieved by your recent actions. I find you have been consorting with Congregationalists as if you really believed them to be Christians, and moreover on your list of appointments I find you are consorting with Baptists and other heretics.[79]

Humor helped both of them.

On Gardiner's flank were American Presbyterians disgruntled about the Geneva Conference. In a series of letters to Gardiner, J. Ross Stevenson, influential president of the Princeton Theological Seminary, complained that the Continuation Committee's choice of fellow-Presbyterian Arthur Judson Brown was not sufficient representation for the Presbyterian Church. Brown was not a member of their committee on unity. Stevenson did not like super committees anyway; they lost contact with constituents: "The Geneva Conference has already made a mistake in assuming that . . . [it] was better qualified . . . to indicate the kind of representation we should have." Cold-pausing, Stevenson warned, "We claim to know better than any outside committee or commission who is most competent to represent the Presbyterian Church." Despite Gardiner's explanation that the Continuation Committee would have been unwieldy had it attempted across-the-board denominational deputies and delegations, Stevenson was unmoved. "We are not at all in agreement regarding the wisdom of the course that was pursued at the Geneva Conference." The turgid correspondence marched on into 1922.[80]

However much he tended to nurse old wounds, Stevenson was not without justification. The House of Bishops of the Episcopal Church in 1919 had slammed the door on three simultaneous invitations to join the FCC, the Presbyterian-inspired Inter Church Movement, and the Presbyterian Organization on Organic Union. Gardiner was livid at the House of Bishops. By what

79. Gardiner to Manning, March 28, 1922; see also to Anderson, August 22, 1922, on Hall's refusal to sign the Lambeth appeal, Gardiner Correspondence; Gardiner to Brent, January 30, February 27, 1923; Brent to Gardiner, March 14, April 24, 1923, Brent Papers. For the Morehouse-Gardiner correspondence, see Gardiner to Morehouse, June 1, 1918; and Morehouse to Gardiner, June 4, 1918, Gardiner Correspondence. See editorial, "What Do We Propose to Do about Unity?" *Living Church* (January 20, 1923): 9; Morehouse to Gardiner, May 27, 1918; Gardiner to Morehouse, June 1, 1918, Gardiner Correspondence; and Gardiner to Brent, January 9, 1923, Brent Papers.

80. Stevenson to Gardiner, October 20, November 4, November 19, 1920; Gardiner to Stevenson, March 23, 1922; Stevenson to Gardiner, March 28, 1922, Gardiner Correspondence.

right, he asked Presiding Bishop Ethelbert Talbot, did they act on invitations directed to the whole church? "If we take the Roman attitude of *non posse,* we lose our position of advantage as the Church of the Reconciliation and alienate our Protestant brethren." Which is precisely what happened—on both counts. "To kill a matter in one House is not the action of the whole Convention," he rightly stated, "and, therefore, cannot be treated as an official act of the Church."[81] From start to finish the road was bumpy.

Then one day in April 1923, little more than a year before his death, the secretary's ever-voluminous mail contained a substantial package that greatly raised his spirits. "Just before Easter [he wrote Anderson] I received 187 typewritten folio pages of reports of group conferences...by members of the following communions: Anglican, Baptist, Congregational, Churches of Christ, Disciples of Christ, Eastern Orthodox, Lutheran, Mar Thoma Syrian, Methodist, Old Catholics, Polish Marianite, Presbyterian, Roman Catholic, Society of Friends, South India United, and the Y.M.C.A." The reports had come from around the world. "This has, of course, filled me with new courage.... The prospects in the United States have vastly improved of late, especially due to the splendid work which Bishop [James D.] Perry and [the Reverend] Floyd Tomkins are doing." Money had begun to come in. The pace of local conferences was picking up. News from Australia the previous year continued to hearten him. Less than a month before his death he wrote his friend Edwin Palmer, "My Roman Catholic friend [Palmieri] in Rome tells me they are beginning to take seriously the relations between Anglicans and Romans." In March 1924 he wrote his old friend Palmer, "Difficulties are a joy, for they give one the chance to put out his full strength in the effort to try to overcome them, and as long as the Lord gives me health and strength I am going to stick to my job."[82] But that full strength was not to last.

There had been premonitions: In April 1922 Bishop Charles Henry Brent reported to a meeting of the Joint Commission on the World Conference on Faith and Order that "Mr. Gardiner was very ill." Two years later at Oaklands

81. Gardiner to Talbot, November 26, December 2, 1919, Gardiner Correspondence.

82. Gardiner to Anderson, April 11, 1923; to Palmer, May 29, March 26, 1924, Gardiner Correspondence. See also Gardiner to Palmer, April 6, June 16, 1923, March 26, 1924; to Bell, July 13, 1923; to Bate, February 2, 1924, Gardiner Correspondence; and [George Hall], *A Conference Held in Adelaide, Australia, on May 30, 1922* (New South Wales: Angus and Robertson, 1922).

he died, on June 15, 1924, "after one week's illness with pneumonia."[83] He accomplished even that last act in the same unpretentious, dignified manner that he had maintained throughout his life. The scene was moving. A few weeks or so after his death, Alice Bangs Gardiner wrote to Bishop Brent: "I feel that you will like to know how gently and mercifully the Angel of Death came to him." She was sure her husband did not know he was dying. "I like to think of that long quiet night when I sat beside him holding his hand. He knew I was there and he talked—as if in a dream—about letters he had to write, etc." In the early morning she called in some of their children. "At last I said to the young doctor who sat at his feet, 'Is that all?' He bowed his head and said, 'Absolutely all.'" She continued: "Then I held his hand a little longer and when I laid it down it was still soft and warm, and I looked once more at the dear body I had shared for forty-three years and left it. It seemed to me it was no more to him and to me than a cloak laid aside. . . . But you must not grieve for me."[84]

83. Minutes, *Joint Commission on Faith and Order, April 20, 1922,* 286; [Floyd Tomkins], "Mr. Ralph W. Brown . . . ," ca. 1960s, Tomkins Papers.

84. Alice Gardiner to Brent, July 9, 1924, container 18, Brent Papers.

# SEVEN

※ ✝ ※

## Conclusion

Robert Hallowell Gardiner was an aristocrat, a leader, sure of his abilities, a man with vision, fortunate to live at a time when optimistic views of future possibilities were both encouraged and prevalent. The cause he championed with firm, delicate sagacity was possible because his denomination was in ascendancy, not in decline. The Episcopal Church was convinced that it carried influence, optimistic about its future, eager to lead. Its bearing throughout the period of the Progressive Era was commanding. At times it treated others, particularly evangelical Protestants, as if they were so radioactive as to contaminate its solemn rites. For their part, Episcopal rectors and bishops were expected to speak out on issues of the day, consort with and provide the conscience for financial and political lions, join the best clubs, head the nation's elite private academies, maintain theological schools of high standing, be men of prayer, and at the same time fulfill the charitable demands of the Gospel. Across the boards of all the major denominations, leaders behaved like chief executive officers of the old school: they were addressed respectfully by their titles, only in exceptional cases by their first—or last—names; they liked formality, wore dignified clothes, and stood forth publicly as people of integrity as well as energy. Many came from distinguished American families, North and South.

Almost but not quite: the status of clergy, no less than that of other professionals, was flexible; ladders upon which to rise in the social scale were provided; and democratic methods and the recognition of abilities counted. This was true equally for Episcopalians as for other denominations. Not all came from aristocratic backgrounds. William Manning, like Methodist John Mott, was a farmer's son. Edwin Palmer, Gilbert White, and Charles Henry Brent, like Peter Ainslie of the Disciples of Christ, were the sons of ministers. These Church of England and Episcopalian leaders, if they did not have it already by virtue of common birth, learned the common touch in their fathers' rectories.

Though he was already of the New England aristocracy, Gardiner too communicated with all sorts and conditions of men and women. But he had to learn to do so and did not come by it naturally. In the final analysis, unlike many of his class, he was not a snob; he had both seen and experienced hardship, even penury. Wealth, when it came, did not spoil him or make him less generous. He was also uninterested in the imponderables of class distinction within his own circle. He shunned braggadocio as well as the subtler forms of showing superiority, and he exhibited a simplicity of manners by which he came naturally. At the same time, he multiplied the number of those in whose fidelity he could repose unreserved confidence no matter who they were.

His personal achievement lay in his ability to see beyond and to move out of the context of the environment in which he was born and grew up and to knit up the raveled fabric of the larger world he saw around and beyond him. His public achievement was to force his denomination to face its peculiar self-satisfaction and self-righteousness. He did the same to other denominations. He took risks to achieve larger goals. He did not indulge in fresh mythmaking about the Anglican tradition but sought to go beyond it, to build a new international community to which it might contribute its talent, however modest. Above all, he sought to get back to first principles. Sadly, he remarked to Edwin Palmer, "It seems more important to some of us to have a new tesselated pavement in the chancel or to have a good choir than to reach out to the unchurched or to strive for that visible unity which will manifest Christ to the world."[1] He acted deliberately and perseveringly, often against daunting odds; especially was this evident toward the end of his life, when both his nation and his church were pulling away from involvement abroad. He was more than willing that others in foreign lands and in other churches than his should become the leaders. Thus, he practiced what he preached.

But what did he actually achieve? Through cajolery and occasional japery, through tough talk, threats of resignation, and appeals to Christian doctrines and to the magnanimity that was supposed to flow from them, he single-handedly

---

1. Gardiner to Palmer, March 26, 1924, Robert H. Gardiner Correspondence, 1910–1924, World Council of Churches, Geneva, Switzerland.

brought together people who had no intention of conversing with each other, who were perfectly satisfied that they alone either possessed the truth or were superior culturally to others or both. As I have shown, throughout it was a struggle to accomplish these ends. Ultimately, he created a movement that kept on following by and large the path he had set. And he did these things as a layman without theological education and without the ecclesiastical advantage of ordination and position. His achievement must surely be placed beside that of other lay reformers of the churches then and now: Dwight L. Moody, Frances E. Willard, Mary Baker Eddy, Jane Addams, John R. Mott, Verna Dozier, and William Stringfellow, to name some of the more prominent.

What did he fail to do? Certainly, the "small churches" toward which he momentarily gave attention, the Pentecostals, faded from his line of vision. The same might be said about the Fundamentalist Evangelicals. Whether he could have held these growing communities within the ecumenical orbit he created is something we will never know. Had his theology been less sacramentally and more biblically oriented he might have partially succeeded. Had he been less Johannine and more Pauline, less concerned with the "mystic sense" to sanctify life and more with the power of the preached word to forgive and to inspire to holiness, he might have had broader appeal. But such reflections are pure speculation. On balance, it seems unlikely that he could have prevailed universally.

For complex theological, social, and economic reasons, forces had been ineluctably set in motion in those two genuinely native American movements, Pentecostalism and Fundamentalism, that could not be contained. As it was, however, some very important worldwide groups of Christians began to communicate reflectively with each other for the first time; they concerned themselves about such large and significant issues as the nature of the church, and of its sacraments and ministry. Theologians from one or more traditions began to be read with appreciation by those from other traditions. There was a remarkable cross-fertilization of ideas and theologies as a result of the writings of such people as Karl Barth, William Temple, H. Richard Niebuhr, Reinhold Niebuhr, Paul Tillich, Dietrich Bonhoeffer, Carl Braaten, Karl Rahner, and Hans Frei, to name a few. Increasingly, what was taught in one theological seminary, be it Catholic, Orthodox, Anglican, or Protestant, might well be replicated in another, however much some chose to deny it. Baptists, for instance, like Robert T. Handy of Union Theological Seminary in New York, could lecture with sensitivity and authority about what it was like to be Anglican. Laity too in parish churches found new reasons to cooperate, to exchange ideas—and sometimes denominations. Only with the advent of the cultural wars over such matters as sexual lifestyle, contraception, abortion, military rearmament, the environment, war, and international law did the lines of communication and fellowship begin to fail and indeed to atrophy. Only in our time, when churches have become divided not only from one another but within, has the very idea of Christian unity been largely forgotten. Certainly, it no longer brings those in the stands to their feet. It is a pity that Robert Gardiner's vision has been so eclipsed.

Forgotten? Not quite. The glass of ecumenism is not half empty but half full. I have already alluded to Pentecostalism and Fundamentalism: in fact, they and other movements in the past fifty years have brought together many Christians in transdenominational unities cutting across denominational lines and uniting people in loyalties that often seem more binding than the older denominational ones. We have only to think of neo-Orthodoxy, the civil rights movement, the many peace movements, the neo-Evangelicals of the 1970s, the charismatics of the 1980s, and the feminist movements of the past 150 years to make the point. Still, with respect to Gardiner, *quod dixit dixit* about the command of Jesus Christ that his followers must be one, as He is one with the Father. That will be no less true in 2010 than it was in 1910.

# Appendix

## Chronology of Robert Gardiner's Life

This chronology is a reference guide to the episodes mentioned in the main text. Throughout, I refer to Robert H. Gardiner III as RHG.

| | |
|---|---|
| 1855 | September 9: RHG born at Fort Tejon, California. |
| 1859–1859 | Family returns to Gardiner, Maine. |
| 1866–1869 | RHG attends the Roxbury Latin School. |
| 1869–1870 | Family moves to Canada; RHG graduates from Montreal high school, age fifteen. |
| 1871–1872 | RHG given extra year at the Roxbury Latin School from which he also graduates. |
| 1872–1876 | Attends Harvard College. |
| 1876–1877 | Teaches at DeVeaux College (school) at Niagara, New York. |
| 1877–1878 | Teaches at the Roxbury Latin School. |
| 1878–1880 | Attends Harvard Law School. |
| 1879 | RHG's father dies; RHG assumes family leadership. |
| 1880 | Admitted to the Suffolk, Massachusetts, bar. |
| 1880–1900 | Practices law in Boston. Director of many businesses and trusts; chairman of executive committee of the Republican Club of Massachusetts; vice president of the Massachusetts branch of the National Consumers' League (founded 1899); president of the Brotherhood Council of Boston; member of the Standing Committee, Diocese of Massachusetts; treasurer of the Episcopal City Mission; treasurer of the Diocesan Board of Missions; |

treasurer of the Church Social Union; associated with Charles Henry Brent at St. Stephen's Church.

1881    June 23: Marries Alice Outran Bangs at Trinity Church, Boston.

1883    Brotherhood of St. Andrew founded in Chicago by James Houghteling.

1885    RHG founds the Church of the Redeemer, Chestnut Hill, Massachusetts; building is consecrated in 1891.

1886    Chicago Quadrilateral accepted by General Convention as the basis of Episcopalian unity with other denominations; 1888 accepted at the Lambeth Conference.

1888    Student Volunteer Movement founded by John R. Mott.

1892    Portland Deliverance: Watershed statement by the General Assembly of the Presbyterian Church (USA) of conservative biblical inspiration and authority.

1893    World's Parliament of Religions addressed by Philip Schaff on the subject of Christian reunion.

1894    Open and Institutional Church League (Elias B. Sanford).

1895    World Student Christian Federation founded.

1900    RHG moves his legal residence to Maine; thereafter, he is elected seven times a lay deputy to the Episcopal Church's triennial General Convention; from 1901 to 1924 he serves as either junior warden or senior warden of Christ Church, Gardiner, Maine.

        Ecumenical Missionary Conference, New York City.

1901    Beginning of Pentecostalism by Charles Parham in Topeka, Kansas: Spirit baptism, speaking in tongues.

1904    RHG elected president of the Brotherhood of St. Andrew; he begins to broaden its social concern, devotional life, and commitment to ecumenism.

1905    Interchurch Conference on Federation, Carnegie Hall, New York, leads to the founding of the Federal Council of Churches (1908) (hereafter FCC); RHG member of the executive committee of FCC.

1906    Racially mixed Pentecostal revival under the African American Holiness preacher William J. Seymour, Azusa Street, Los Angeles.

1909    RHG is taken ill; resigns as president of the Brotherhood of St. Andrew.

1910     RHG, William T. Manning, and others meet at Trinity Church, New York City (January), to plan for the reunion of the churches; World Missionary Conference convened at Edinburgh, Scotland (June), John R. Mott, chairman; Charles Henry Brent addresses twelve hundred delegates; Christian Unity Foundation founded at St. Thomas's Church, New York City (July); William T. Manning proposes to the Episcopal Church's General Convention that a Joint Commission to call a World Conference on Faith and Order be formed (hereafter WCFO) (October); Committee on Plan and Scope (which becomes the Executive Committee, April 1911, hereafter EC) organized at Trinity Church, New York, RHG secretary; J. P. Morgan gives one hundred thousand dollars to the Joint Commission; National Council of the Congregational Church responds positively and appoints a commission to respond to the Episcopalians; Bishop A. C. A. Hall and Gardiner to make a list of communions within the scope of the world conference.

1911     April 20, EC reports: Letter sent to all Episcopal bishops to support world conference; prayers for unity drafted; Disciples of Christ appoint a commission; General Assembly of the Presbyterian Church, USA, contacted; F. J. Hall completes bibliography on Christian unity; Methodists and Alliance of Reformed Churches throughout the world respond positively. Purpose stated: ultimate aim of WCFO *outward* and visible reunion of all who confess Jesus Christ as God and Savior (an obvious repudiation of the federal ideal). Interviews with James Cardinal Gibbons and Archbishop Platon, metropolitan of Odessa.

July 25: The following have appointed commissions: Methodist Episcopal Church, South; Southern Baptist Convention; Northern Province of the Moravian Church in America; Reformed Church in the U.S.; Presbyterian Church, USA; Methodist Episcopal Church; Evangelical Lutheran Church USA; Presbyterian Church U.S. (Southern); United Presbyterian Church of North America; Reformed Presbyterian Church of North America; Conference of Free Baptists; Reformed Church in America; Reformed Presbyterian Church in N. America.

Archbishops and metropolitans of the Anglican Communion to be asked for advice and to appoint commissions; committees appointed to contact Roman Catholic Church, the Orthodox, Old Catholics, and Protestants abroad. Special committee appointed for churches for whom no provision has yet been made (presumably African American churches and Holiness and Pentecostal churches). Racial designation of denominations deleted; EC votes to send deputation to England; letters sent to Anglican bishops worldwide.

October 25: RHG reports to EC that one hundred thousand copies of the Plan and Scope Committee's report sent to all members of similar denominational commissions, to all bishops and clergy of the Episcopal Church, all Anglican bishops worldwide, to all delegates to Episcopalian General Convention, to Laymen's Missionary Movement in Canada and the United States, and to the Brotherhood of St. Andrew's Council. He plans to send the report to all cardinals and bishops of the Roman Catholic Church worldwide and to all Catholic clergy in the United States. Is receiving heavy mail, about one hundred letters a day.

December 14: EC appoints Committee on Literature, A. C. A. Hall, chair.

1912    Deputation from United States to the Church of England to enlist cooperation; Archbishop of Canterbury Randall Davidson appoints a "cooperating committee" but fails to create a commission with full powers and requests no press coverage in Great Britain of WCFO movement; Eastern Orthodox Committee will meet with Archbishop Platon to plan communication with the Orthodox churches; EC awaits results of initial communication to various churches.

1913    February 20: Newman Smyth and George Wharton Pepper plan informal conference of the commissions of American churches.

March 4: Meeting of commission chairs in Washington, D.C., to prepare agenda and mechanics of an American conference.

May 8: American conference convenes at the Hotel Astor in New York City; Committee of Five, including RHG, appointed to represent American Conference of Commissions. Church of England representative, Tissington Tatlow, suggests a deputation from the United States to the free churches of Britain. Conference considers what should be the discussed at WCFO: (1) similarities, differences, and values of distinctive beliefs; (2) no forcing particular schemes of unity on anyone; and (3) questions to be formulated in advance of WCFO. Russian Orthodox present at Hotel Astor.

July 25–28: EC meets in Gardiner, Maine. Bishop Hoder of the Polish National Catholic Church to invite participation of similar bodies meeting at the Old Catholic Congress, September 4.

November 19: Old Catholics appoint a commission. Episcopal Church of Scotland and Anglican Church of Ireland appoint commissions; Moravian Bishop Leibert to contact Moravian Church in Europe; Archbishop of Canterbury delivers invitation to Presbyterians in Britain; RHG wants the Church of England to help in contacting Eastern, Roman, and Protestant churches in Europe; RHG authorized to send out letters on behalf of the commission, thereby bypassing Bishop Charles Anderson (president of the Episcopal Joint Commission).

Bishops A. C. A. Hall, Phillip Rhinelander, and George Wharton Pepper to get other churches' commissions to begin to formulate questions for discussion at the WCFO; Kikuyu controversy: intercommunion in Africa and the reaction; Ralph W. Brown now RHG's assistant; Roman Catholic interest increases.

1914    January 13: South African Anglicans appoint a commission.

March 13: Deputation from U.S. churches to Protestant churches in Britain returns; Peter Ainslie of Disciples gives RHG a list of eight hundred names in Britain to be placed on the mailing list; Bishops Brent, Rhinelander, and Anderson appointed to deputation to churches of Europe and the East.

April 14: John R. Mott added to deputation.

June: RHG in England as representative of Federal Council of Churches; he does double duty as delegate to Federal Council peace conference, financed by Andrew Carnegie, and as representative of the Episcopal commission of WCFO.

August 3: Arrives in Lake Constance for peace conference; war declared.

August 4: Conferees leave Germany. Visit of deputation to European churches cancelled.

September 8: RHG arrives back in New York.

December 3: Commission treasurer, George Zabriskie, presents a budget for first time; commission finally getting cost-conscious; RHG had urged fund-raising from the start but, due to Morgan's gift, was ignored.

1915    January 14: RHG pushes for decision to keep moving forward and not let the war interrupt plans; discussion of feasibility of approaching the pope and also churches in neutral lands; RHG proposes that each bishop in the Episcopal Church have diocesan conferences devoted to church unity "to consider whether the present World crisis is not a call to Christian people to do whatever may be required in order that Christianity may speak with the power of a united voice."

Professor Wilfred Monod requests invitation for L'Union Nationale des Églises Reformées Évangéliques de France. Spanish Dominicans react positively in *La Ciencia Tomista* to proposal for WCFO.

March 11: RHG seeks an advisory council made up of members of denominational commissions in the United States for the purpose of organizing WCFO; each commission to appoint a single delegate with an extra delegate for each half million communicants up to fifty; council is to appoint officers, adopt rules, and formulate questions for discussion at WCFO; each communion is to formulate faith and order statements of its own, stating what it holds in common with other churches and what it holds uniquely and the ground on which it stands apart from other communions; the Advisory Council will issue the invitations to the WCFO; it is also to have a board of advisers representing different traditions to formulate further questions for discussion; in the case of a state church, the head of state may send two personal representatives in addition to those sent by the ecclesiastical authorities.

October 14: Preparations for a North American Preparatory Conference; Pepper appointed chair of Committee of Seven by the Advisory Council to plan the conference, select questions for discussion, and plan the agenda; RHG proposes addition of women to the Episcopal commission in order to ensure women's interest and cooperation.

1916        January 4–6: North American Preparatory Conference at Garden City: sixteen churches, including the Alliance of Reformed Churches, the Church of England in Canada, Moravians, and Society of Friends (Quakers), sixty-three church leaders.

February 3: Panama Congress on Christian Work in Latin America, the largest gathering of Protestant bodies since Edinburgh 1910; it raises the issue of evangelical work in Roman Catholic lands and the nature of the Episcopal Church itself causing strains in the movement toward WCFO.

1917        May 3: Episcopal Commission resolves to send invitations to European and Eastern churches by deputations; Dutch Reformed and Congregational churches of South Africa invited; deputation to the Russian Orthodox Church postponed on advice of President Woodrow Wilson and John R. Mott; RHG asks Cardinal Marini about a good time for a deputation to Rome.

Archbishop Davidson withdraws his prohibition of newspaper publicity in Britain.

May–June: Root Mission to Russia: John R. Mott.

1918    Swedish archbishop Nathan Söderblom and other Scandinavian bishops propose calling a peace conference and inviting Rome and the Orthodox.

September 13: RHG unable to arouse North American Preparatory Committee to recognize its obligation for WCFO.

December 5: EC: deputation to Europe and to Rome to go as soon as possible.

1919    January 23: Northern Baptists decline invitation to WCFO; they will maintain fraternal relations with all evangelical churches but do not believe organic union with others is possible; report of European deputation, pamphlet 32 of commission.

April 24: Samuel Mather and J. P. Morgan Jr. agree to pay expenses of American delegation to upcoming preliminary conference to plan WCFO; it meets in Geneva in the summer of 1920; Morgan gives fifty thousand dollars.

May 27: Pope rejects Roman Catholic participation in WCFO.

RHG works to overcome German reluctance to participate in planning WCFO; Brent appointed to EC; Pepper resigns from Joint Commission; Chauncey Brewster appointed in his place; there are 3,195 appeals for prayer for unity sent out from RHG's office.

November 20: Representatives of American church's Commissions meet at Synod Hall, New York: Episcopal, Baptist, Congregational, Society of Friends, Methodist, Moravians, Presbyterian and Reformed in United States and Canada, Orthodox (Armenian, Greek, Bulgarian), United Lutheran; voted that Episcopal Joint Commission call an international preliminary conference in Geneva in August 1920 to determine when and where WCFO is to be held, what subjects discussed, and basis of representation of participating commissions; Episcopal Church to bear cost of accommodations, printing, salaries of clerks and interpreters; RHG reports on movement of South India United Church, St. Thomas Syrian Church, and Anglicans toward organic union; RHG and EC to send information about Geneva Conference to religious press, to get ministers to preach about the movement; RHG to communicate with commissions of other churches to offer services of every member of Episcopal EC and other speakers to make WCFO known at official assemblies of churches.

1920    January 15: Report of European deputation published in Italian and French; official invitations to Geneva Conference sent to L'Union des Église Reformées Évangéliques de France, Mar Thoma Syrian Church,

Reformierter Bund für Deutschland, African Methodist Episcopal Church, African Methodist Episcopal Zion Church (few of the latter two bothered to answer); negative reply from archbishop of Finland.

March 18: RHG reports to EC that press releases on unity being ignored in the United States, more interest in England; RHG increasingly responsible for getting bishops to speak on WCFO, arranging meeting places in Geneva, sending out invitations to European and American churches.

May 11: RHG reports more invitations sent out: Christian Reformed Church in Holland, Reformed Church of the Netherlands, Swiss churches, Czech Catholic Church (a breakaway from Rome); German Evangelical churches show bitterness due to the war; Orthodox publications show readiness of those churches to draw closer with Anglicans; 184 American theological schools contacted; American church interest waning, European interest increasing.

July: Lambeth Conference's "Appeal to All Christian People."

August 12: Geneva Conference on WCFO; creation of new international Continuation Committee; RHG secretary of Geneva Conference on Life and Work.

October 21: Episcopal Church pledges ten thousand dollars for the Continuation Committee of Geneva.

December 2: Brent proposes 1925 for world conference, sixteen hundredth anniversary of the Council of Nicea.

1921    January 20: Zabriskie reports that commission's cash is low, five thousand dollars.

March 31: RHG sees a problem in keeping interest in WCFO in America alive; he proposes a North American gathering of denominational commissions.

October 20: Continuation Committee out of funds; RHG has loaned six thousand dollars of his own money; Episcopal Commission asks presiding bishop for five thousand dollars toward a fifteen thousand dollar budget.

December 1: Bishop Charles Anderson tenders his resignation as president of the Episcopal Commission; RHG tenders his resignation as secretary: he is busy with Continuation Committee after Geneva.

1922    Presiding bishop appropriates one thousand dollars for the Continuation Committee (Geneva).

April 20: RHG very ill; Brent urges that he be relieved of his duties as secretary of EC, but he continues pro tem; EC is empowered to organize a women's auxiliary to raise money.

December 7: Bishop James D. Perry (Rhode Island) elected chair of EC; Bishop William T. Manning elected president of Episcopal Commission for WCFO; RHG sends pamphlets to Chautauqua lecturers asking them to publicize WCFO in their letters and speeches.

1923    January 19: Floyd Tomkins accepts post as secretary of Episcopal Commission; he is elected April 4; RHG goes to diocesan conventions to push WCFO; he works on men's groups and women's auxiliaries to support WCFO.

1924    February 21: Some dioceses have formed WCFO committees.

April 24: RHG reports that he is preparing a conspectus of the requirements for ordination in all churches for the Subjects Committee of the Continuation Committee; both Roman Catholic and Eastern Orthodox discussions of reunion are placed on WCFO agenda by the Continuation Committee; Cardinal Marini is asked to secure participation of Rome; EC of Episcopal Commission reports that twenty bishops have resolved to support WCFO; they have appointed committees to set up local conferences; some have met to discuss the creeds; fifteen church summer schools have provided opportunities to the commission to offer courses called "Church Unity and the Method of Conference"; the executive secretary, Ralph W. Brown, has been invited to speak at five theological seminaries.

June 15: RHG dies.

1925    October 15: General Convention of the Episcopal Church appropriates ten thousand dollars a year for the Episcopal Commission on WCFO; they had asked for twenty-five thousand dollars.

November 19: Continuation Committee (Geneva) hears report of the Stockholm Conference on Life and Work; Continuation Committee adopts a subject agenda for WCFO; Lausanne, Switzerland, 1927, agreed upon for place and date of world conference.

1926    January 14: Tomkins becomes secretary of Continuation Committee.

December 2: Continuation Committee meets in Berne: needs to raise two hundred thousand dollars for Lausanne Conference.

1927    August 3–20: First World Conference on Faith and Order held at Lausanne, Switzerland; 385 men and 9 women from 108 churches representing Anglican, Lutheran, Reformed, Orthodox, Old Catholic, Methodist, Congregationalist, Baptist, and Disciples of Christ;

Africa, the United States, and Europe are well represented; only two nationals from Asia together with Western missionaries; most delegates had been members of the World's Student Christian Federation; some had been leaders in their university days. Brent elected chairman of the conference. Before conference ends a Continuation Committee of 92 men and 3 women appointed, Brown executive secretary, Zabriskie treasurer.

1928     March 21: Continuation Committee of WCFO meets in Prague, elects Archbishop Strenopoulos Germanos (Greek Orthodox), Adolf Deissman (Lutheran, German), Charles Merle d'Aubigne (Reformed, French), and Archbishop Nathan Söderblom (Lutheran, Swedish) as vice chairmen.

1929     March 27: Brent dies.

         Archbishop of York, William Temple, elected chair of WCFO; American leadership passes to Europe.

1930     April: Anderson and Hall die; Zabriskie seriously ill; a generation passes.

# Selected Bibliography

Brent, Charles Henry. Papers. Library of Congress, Washington, DC.

Gardiner, Robert H. Collection. Archives of the Episcopal Church, Austin, TX.

Gardiner, Robert H. Correspondence, 1910–1924. World Council of Churches, Geneva, Switzerland.

Gardiner Family Papers. Oaklands, Gardiner, ME.

Hays Family Papers. Cumberland County Historical Society, Carlisle, PA.

Huntington, William Reed. Papers. Episcopal Divinity School, Cambridge, MA.

Manross, William T. Papers. St. Mark's Library, General Theological Seminary, New York, NY.

Records of Harvard Graduates. Harvard College Archives, Pusey Library, Cambridge, MA.

Tomkins, Floyd. Papers. Archives of the Episcopal Church, Austin, TX.

# Index

Johnson-Reed Act of 1924 (Quota Act), 97–98

Joint Commission Appointed to Arrange for a World Conference: Committee on Literature, 133, 168, 186, 200; Continuation Committee and, 118–19, 141n65; criticisms of, 137, 148; deputation to Britain, 150, 200; deputation to Europe, 151–52, 201; deputations to Russia and Rome, 151–52, 216, 221n43, 224–25, 228; disagreements on, 123–25, 132, 161, 199; division of labor in, 122, 132–33; dogma of, 176, 183–84; formation of, 115–19; funding for, 127, 199, 237; Gardiner as secretary of, 121–26, 230, 236; goals of, 116, 119, 132, 181; increasing contact with the East, 214–15; invitations by, 118–20, 143–44, 146, 172, 199–200; makeup of, 116–17, 136–37; Plan and Scope Committee of, 117, 199; process of, 118–19, 121–22, 129–31; progress by, 150, 199–200; relations with Catholics, 119, 124–26, 147–48, 217–20; structure of, 117, 121, 124, 199; during WWI, 209, 215–16. *See also* Correspondence

Joint Commission on Sunday School Instruction, 37

Jones, George, 6

Justice, 67n56, 69, 104

Kaftan, Dietrich, 232

Keller, Adolf, 231

Kelly, Herbert, 134, 181–82, 187

Kennan, George F., 217n35

Kenyon College, 40

King, Joseph H., 145

Kingdom of God, 50, 65n51, 92, 179, 182–83

Kingsley, Charles, 94

Kip, William Ingraham, 23

Labor, 69, 71, 90

Laity: Brotherhood of St. Andrew and, 87, 91–92; clergy and, 108–9, 145, 182; clergy vs., 43, 60, 124–25, 136; cooperation among, 104, 244–45; Episcopal, 140; Gardiner as, 124–25, 244; leaders of, 2–3, 8–9; preaching by, 24–25; role in unity movement, 125, 135; support for Gardiner among, 134–35; women's role in, 60, 135–36

Lake Constance peace conference, 155–58, 232

Lambeth Appeal, 238

Lambeth Conference of 1888, 83, 103, 181

Lambeth Conference of 1920, 228–30

Lang, August, 231, 233

Lang, Cosmo Gordon, 208n18, 228

Language: Gardiner's talent for, 28, 30, 32–34; of Joint Commission's correspondence, 32–33, 141, 146, 218; of Joint Commission's pamphlets, 150

LaPiani, George, 226–27

Lausanne. *See* World Conference on Faith and Order (Lausanne, 1927)

Law, Christian, 64, 66

Law practice, Gardiner's, 10, 33–35, 45, 121

Lawrence, William, 32

"A Lawyer's View of the Function of the Church" (Gardiner), 61–70

Laymen's Forward Movement, 93

Laymen's Missionary Movement, 5n8

*Leader in Religious Education* (journal), 40–41

League of Free Nation's Association, 234

League of Nations, 102, 237

League of Nations Association (Foreign Policy Association), 102, 158

Lee, Henry, 97

Lee, Joseph, 98

Legislation, social, 69–70, 72

Lewis, William H., 10

Liberals, 6–7, 101–2

Liberal theologians, vs. higher-life, 48–49

Liberty. *See* Freedom

Life and Work Conference (1920, Geneva), 230, 232–34, 239

Life and Work Movement, 73–74, 223

La Ligue Internationale des Catholiques pur la Paix, 155

Literacy tests, as means of exclusion, 97, 101

Lloyd, Arthur Seldon, 210–11

Lloyd, Edward, 20

Lodge, Henry Cabot, 97–98

Loisy, Alfred, 165

Love: as answer to social problems, 71–72; as Gardiner's theological basis, 61, 90, 174, 212

Lovett, Robert Morse, 78–79

Low, Seth, 116

Lowell, A. Lawrence, 98

Lowell, Francis Cabot, 31

Lowell, John, 44

Lowell, Katharine Bigelow, 44